Ex Libris
Pace College

41 PARK ROW, NEW YORK

D1116942

My Dearest Polly

Courtesy of The John Marshall House

"MY DEAREST POLLY"

Copy by an unknown artist of a sketch done by her son, Thomas, when she was about forty years old. The only authentic portrait.

My dearest Polly

LETTERS OF

Chief Justice John Marshall

to His Wife, with Their Background,

Political and Domestic

1779-1831

By

FRANCES NORTON MASON

GARRETT & MASSIE, Incorporated

RICHMOND, VIRGINIA

1961

COPYRIGHT © 1961 BY
FRANCES BEMISS MASON
RICHMOND, VIRGINIA

LIBRARY OF CONGRESS CATALOG NUMBER 61-15099

MANUFACTURED IN THE UNITED STATES OF AMERICA

E
302.6.
M4M3

THIS BOOK

IS

DEDICATED TO

THESE WORTHY DESCENDANTS OF

THE GREAT CHIEF JUSTICE

AND

HIS WIFE

WHO, TOO, ARE

"POSSESSED OF ALL THE AMIABLE AND

ATTRACTIVE VIRTUES OF THE HEART":

CYANE MASON CABELL

JOHN KERCHEVAL MASON, II

LOCKERT BEMISS MASON, M.D.

HATLEY NORTON MASON, JR.

AND

FRANCES MASON WALLER

ACKNOWLEDGEMENTS

To those courteous and knowledgeable members of the American society, professional librarians, this study owes its finest values, especially to James A. Servies, Librarian of the College of William and Mary, for his constant interest, advice and the contribution of many rare documentary items which enrich these pages; to William G. Harkins, one-time Librarian of William and Mary, now of the University of Florida, for the initial vision of such a commentary; and to John Melville Jennings, Director of the Virginia Historical Society, whose judgement in a final reading gave the work definite shape.

We are grateful to Dr. William F. Swindler, Professor of Legal History at the College of William and Mary for drawing our meandering enthusiasm into a straight channel, and to Librarians of many institutions across the country for discovering our desires and so promptly supplying them.

Louise Cadot Catterall, archivist for the Valentine Museum shared her precise knowledge and judgement in selecting and procuring illustrations for this book. Susanne K. Sherman, authority on the early stage in the southern United States, stepped aside from a busy career to kindly correct traditions concerning the Richmond theatres, and to add color and interest to this account of them. Alexander H. Sands, historian and lawyer, has generously lent his great knowledge and memories to strengthen this story. Joyce K. Cooper, Assistant to Administrator, Pennsylvania Hospital, procured for us the medical history of the Chief Justice's surgical operation in Philadelphia in 1831. Frederic W. Franck, Instructor in the Department of Romance Languages, West Virginia University, contributed the delightful engraving of the Fauquier White Sulphur Springs identifying the Marshall and Monroe cottages, sending with this several old press items describing the Chief Justice at the Springs. Parke Rouse, Director of the Jamestown Foundation, historian and journalist, kindly encouraged us in this study and patiently read the manuscript, adroitly correcting a cherished attitude. Mary Wingfield Scott, authority on Richmond society and building, has been most patient in answering a multitude of questions, always giving the information or telling where to find it. To Randolph Nelson Waller is due whatever is clever and correct in this spelling which suffers from association with Early Republic orthography. To all of these we gladly acknowledge our gratitude.

FRANCES NORTON MASON

May 30, 1960   Richmond, Virginia

CONTENTS

Page

Acknowledgements vii

Foreword xii

I Polly 1

II A New World 13

III The Marshalls on Fairfax Lands 23

IV The Amblers 35

V The Constitution 41

VI The First Letter 57

VII General Marshall 63

VIII The Second Letter 75

IX Letters from an Adams Man 87

X Letters from an Envoy Extraordinary 107

XI The "Un" Lucky Letter 117

XII Congressman 131

XIII J Marshall, Chief Justice 147

XIV A Newspaper 157

XV The Court on Trial 165

XVI The Burr Trial 175

XVII A Most Attractive Household 195

XVIII The New Church 209

XIX "Old Cushing is Dead!" 215

XX The Era of Good Feeling 233

XXI The Colonization Society 249

XXII The Steamboat Case 261

XXIII Master of the Human Heart 273

XXIV "My Old Wife" 285

XXV A New Day 303

XXVI Eighteen-Thirty 317

XXVII "Farewell, My dearest Polly!" 327

Five Cousins 347

Amblers 348

Marshalls 349

Fifteen Children of Col. Thomas and
Mary Keith Marshall 350

Basic Sources 353

Notes by Chapters 355

Index 369

ILLUSTRATIONS

My Dearest Polly .... Frontispiece

Facing page

Page from J. Marshall's Law Notes 20

Richmond in 1810 52

Polly's Mansion 84

Letter from J. Marshall to Polly 116

Thomas Marshall 148

Chief Justice Marshall 180

Fauquier White Sulphur Springs 212

Oak Hill in Fauquier County 244

"Mammy" 276

"The Last Meeting of the Giants" 308

Chief Justice Marshall 340

FOREWORD

Much has been written about the life, character and judicial opinions of John Marshall, Chief Justice of the United States from January of 1801 to July of 1835. He has been greatly praised by many, strongly challenged by many, and among his contemporaries greatly beloved, except by two gentlemen, his cousin—Thomas Jefferson, and his fellow jurist, Spencer Roane. So well known was Marshall during his lifetime that a visitor to the United States remarked, "His name has become a household word with the American people, implying greatness, purity, honesty and all Christian virtues." This is often quoted record.

But of his wife of forty-nine years, Mary Willis Ambler, called "Polly," historians have been content to leave off with the comment that she was a burdensome invalid. It is therefore the purpose of this commentary to set forth his letters to her in their background, domestic and political, thus to show her as her family and fellow citizens knew her. This study does not pretend to be history of a period; it is history only as John Marshall's resounding passage through public affairs vibrated on Polly's sensitive nature.

There exists only one side of this correspondence, for while Polly saved his letters to her, he left to the prying eyes of historians not one word written by her to him. We know that he called her "My dearest Polly." What she called him we can only guess, probably in the custom of her day, "Captain Marshall" at first, and then "General." Richmond came to speak of him as "Judge," while servants called him, "Hizzonner."

Out of this background there emerges not only a picture of Polly, but also the joyful, strong and tender personality of John Marshall, Chief Justice of the United States, during over thirty-four years of crucial national development.

Though transcription of recorded incidents and memories falls into story form, this book is not fiction. It is a deeply studied interpretation of facts discovered in a sentence here and there in old letters, from family notebooks, from documented attitudes and personality impressions cherished in communities where Marshalls have lived, from jokes old people loved to tell, from names tenderly given infants, from an affectionate honor which hung like sunshine over the minds of Richmond citizens not long ago, and from records of the Supreme Court of the United States that trace the transition of American justice from royal colony through a Confederation of States for Permanent Union to States, United, but ever keeping a foot in the door of secession.

CHAPTER I

Polly

THE FIRST letters signed "Your affectionate J Marshall" that Polly Ambler ever saw were not addressed to her. They were written to J Marshall's father, Colonel Thomas Marshall, in command of the Virginia State Artillery stationed at York Town in Virginia during that bitterly cold Winter of 1779 and '80. They had been written in army camps, or in darkened bivouacs beside ravaged battlefields; for young Captain John Marshall was a member of those companies of light infantry which, made up of men especially picked from all ranks and services, became known as the elite of General Washington's Continental Army. Some of the letters had been scribbled in the muffled glow of a lantern where young officers, awaiting a midnight order for desperate assault, were writing last messages to be taken from their bodies next day and sent to next of kin, or to heart's desire. In spite of issuing from stark military surroundings, the letters were blithe, spiced with amusing anecdotes, full of affection for fourteen younger brothers and sisters, and full withal of devotion for a hard pressed Commander-in-Chief.

Colonel Marshall could never resist temptation to read these letters to all and sundry who would lend an ear. Seated around a glowing hearth in a long all-purpose room next door to the officers' quarters, the Ambler family gladly listened. That family was Councillor of State Jacquelin Ambler, his coy and beautiful wife, Rebecca Burwell, and his four daughters, stalwart Eliza, sensitive little Polly, dainty Ann and baby Lucy. While they listened, icy blasts of wind rattled shrubbery against the windows, and blew the smoke back down the chimney. In Tidewater Virginia this was the coldest Winter within the memory of man.

Unhindered winds whipped the Town, for on high bluffs above the York River where it opens into Chesapeake Bay, a king had ordered a city to be set like a crown upon his affluent commerce. Sheltering forests had been rolled back to make room for fields of tobacco yielding a royal revenue.

1

Church, customs house and courthouse, built by royal decree, were strung on a street shaded by a king's mulberry trees. Behind them stood handsome dwellings, with gardens laid out in English patterns. The houses were of pinkish Virginia bricks or native timber painted white. Paint and window glass, nails and hardware had been purchased and taxed in England, and stood on the books of British merchants as unpaid accounts. Then out from those mansions came English gentlemen pledging their lives, their fortunes and their sacred honor to rid Virginia of royalty.

Jacquelin Ambler's fortune had been one of the first to go. By the year 1777, his mansion in York was rented out, his servants either sold or leased to less patriotic Virginians, his horses and carriages sold, and his family divided among the homes of hospitable relatives. Eliza, an eager thirteen, and Mary, called Polly, a sober twelve year old, were bundled off to cousins who were adventuring in the frontier town of Winchester, a rough and perilous spot fraught with romance.

Eliza was a fluent correspondent, and she kept a letter book in the custom of that day. During this visit in Winchester her quill borrowed the soaring spirit of the bird from which it was plucked. Exuberantly she told of encountering numerous young officers and gentlemen adventurers, all eligible in her eyes. Her relatives being young themselves, she wrote, "we were left entirely to our own wayward humors . . . I could tell you many pretty stories of sighing swains, tender billets, love inspiring sonnets, etc. . . . blended with so many childish absurdities . . . but for the remarkable discretion of my Sister, who was only twelve years of age, my cousin and myself would have been perpetually involved in difficulties."

Such airs did the young females acquire in a town to which everyone had come to better their fortunes, that, stopping at Fredericksburg on their way home, they professed great embarrassment when young officers discovered them travelling in a hired conveyance. They were telling these eligible gallants that they had but temporarily left their coach broken down, and would be overtaken by it shortly, when up rode Mr. Ambler in the public stage and let the truth out of the bag. Eliza adds a note in her letter book that she eventually married one of these officers.

In the Fall of 1779 Mr. Ambler gathered his family together again in York, not in their former mansion, but in a "small retired tenement," rendered desirable by a situation next door to the billet of officers commanded by Colonel Thomas Marshall. Eliza notes that most of these officers were Colonel Marshall's relatives, and one or another of them were daily posted to guard the Ambler family.

When the Ambler girls stepped out of the rented doorway, Eliza's cheeks flew a rosy flag of welcome to the army, but little Polly was "timid and retiring." Her teeth chattered, and her mittens froze to the iron rail while she waited for Eliza to turn from the smiling soldier. Then Eliza would pull Polly's hood closer to her pale cheeks, binding the ribands from chin to topknot to keep the little mouth from making so chilly a noise.

Icy puddles along the narrow brick sidewalk were cold to slippered feet. But the Ambler girls could not run to keep warm; for in this Winter they had become ladies, aged fourteen and fifteen. With only an occasional skip they must walk to that high shelf of land beyond the churchyard wall, where for awhile they could watch an exciting reach of river, opening so widely blue into the Chesapeake Bay. There along the line of horizon British frigates moved menacingly.

Below the high meadow the girls could see the town's curving beach where deserted stores and warehouses lay like forgotten toys. Here and there empty lighters clung on frozen ropes to wharves that wore petticoats of brackish ice at ebb tide. Out in the channel rode the tobacco fleet, with gulls wheeling between the masts raucously crying the foolishness of idle ships.

All the Town knew that idle ships and closed warehouses were packed with tobacco owed these two years to British merchants. Though the customs house was now an empty threat, there was still devious trade with London merchants who let not their right hands know how their left hands were increasing old American debts. Goods trans-shipped in the West Indies were slipping in at such inflationary prices that in Williamsburg a price-fixing commission was kept busy.

Nothing was safe. Nothing was sure. An American agent in France warned his correspondents in York that their bills of exchange were not getting through to him. Letter boxes, captured by British privateers, were being broken open, paid up bills of exchange stolen and others thrown overboard. All correspondence was going in two, three, or sometimes seven different copies on as many different ships. For on the high seas all shipping was prey to English, Dutch or Spanish privateers.

Sometimes, watching that blue reach to the Bay, the girls would see a schooner slip past the belching cannon of British frigates and enter the river. Then they did run, with capes outspread like the wings of Virginia redbirds, and crying, "A ship is in! A ship is in!" Out from handsome doorways, out from tavern and courthouse would come the people, young and old, huddled in any old wrap against the wind that was speeding news of families and enterprises shrouded in lowering distance.

All the Town hurried down the hill to the wharf to watch sails beat up the river, or to loose small boats and row with cold-bitten hands to catch the news as it sped. Like the flight of the gulls above them, Polly's heart would soar and droop. The beat of their wings was the "What? What? What?" of the crowd around her. When the answers came ashore she smiled to hear, "Thank God." But at a whispered, "God help us," her heart lay at the feet of friends who turned to trudge up the hill, not by the jostled road, but by quiet paths to back doors.

Though the Town was suffering a barbed anxiety, a shortage of money, a strangulation of trade and a confusion of government, it lost none of its sociability. Windows still twinkled with firelight. From outbuildings still drifted fragrance of baking breads and spitted meats. Hearty welcome was still a-tiptoe at every door, and around warm hearths the issues of revolution were inseparable from family affairs.

Colonel Thomas Marshall sat often in the Ambler tenement, lacing the needs of the army into the sentiment of the Council of State. Behind his chair the Ambler girls would be occupied in household tasks; for the Councillor now had but one servant, Old Sam, a Negro slave whose duties included wearing the threadbare family livery, fetching firelogs and catching fish for the family table. Household fashion was maintained by family ladies. Thus Polly, as she polished ancient silver spoons first heard of starving soldiers at Valley Forge, of their frozen horses, their short pay and the negligence of Congress. She heard of the gay hearted young Captain who was called "Silver Heels" because his mother knit his blue socks with white heels. Polly heard how those heels became a symbol of blithe courage when Captain Marshall led soldiers to play while horror walked naked in bloody footsteps. In their bleakest dispair he made men laugh and sing. Laugh and sing! Silently Polly would lay her spoons aside and turn to watch flames singing their way out of logs behind the black andirons while Colonel Marshall pulled a sheaf of worn letters out of his pocket and began to read what the Amblers already had heard once or twice.

Every reading amused and encouraged the family, but to Polly the letters brought something new. She was always straightened with awe in the presence of her father. Here was the wonder of a father and son who laughed together and merrily told their affection for each other. Suddenly Polly saw that flickers of firelight on the walls were chasing shadows away.

What a swivet York girls were in when they heard that Captain Marshall was coming to town! They jeered, in a genteel manner of course, at little Polly when primly she gave them permission to flirt with him temporarily, explaining that though she had never seen him, in her own good time she intended to marry him.

Eliza Ambler wrote in her letter book that J Marshall came to York shortly after Christmas of 1779, and announced that he intended to enroll in the College of William and Mary in Williamsburg, twelve miles from the Ambler tenement. Expired enlistments and desertions had caused his regiment to dwindle away, and he had been ordered to Virginia to train recruits. But except when the tyrant's foot was at the door these free Virginians would not enlist in an army. J Marshall wrote in the Autobiography: "I availed myself of this inactive interval for attending a course of law lectures given by Mr. Wythe, and of lectures of Natural Philosophy given by Mr. Madison then President of William and Mary College."

J Marshall's cousin, Thomas Jefferson, had been on the Board of Visitors for the College one year, long enough for his propensity for revolution to reorganize the curriculum. The Chair of Divinity, being subject to the Established Church of England, was replaced with a Chair of Law and Police, an innovation in America. Also new in the College was the students' freedom of choice in subjects, limited only by the cost, any two being offered for one thousand pounds of tobacco per annum. Out of school, Captain Marshall holding his commission in reserve, would be available for any service such as sudden invasion by the enemy or attending ladies at social affairs.

Eliza's book says that he was not the maiden's idea of a dashing young officer. He was just a tall, gawky countryman with fine eyes and a delightful smile. She decided to be a sister to him, saving her coquettish wiles for the more mannerful French officers stationed in the Town. Nowhere does Polly tell how, in her shy way, she peeped between other girls' shoulders for a sight of this countryman, and listened day and night for his laugh. J Marshall says that he did not see her until the week before her fourteenth birthday, which was March eighteenth, 1780.

War-ridden and poverty-stricken Virginians still assembled for balls. Eliza says these affairs were "simple and frugal as to viands, but brilliant as to company," with music supplied by a Negro slave with a French horn. When such an invitation was distributed about the middle of March, Polly announced that though she had not yet been to dancing school she intended to go to this ball. So from durable London finery, a generation old, a dancing dress was contrived for the slight figure, with ribands and laces to set off her flower-like face, with ancient silver flowers to crown her brown curls. Then J Marshall saw her. Her bulging blue silk dress was so much wider than she was that he laughed softly, which made her eyes shine, and her answering laugh set the silver flowers a-shimmer with candlelight. Marshall remembered that he "would have climbed Alleghanies of skulls and swum Atlantics of blood to have her."

Whether Polly was proficient at dancing or not, henceforth the young Captain singled her out among York girls, and since Mrs. Ambler was ever alert for eligible gentlemen, he became a happy and well-liked guest at the Ambler hearthside. All the rest of his life the epitome of joy for J Marshall was a hearth where Polly lingered.

To his college dormitory he carried a fat leather-bound notebook. The pages may have been as clean as a new sail, or they may have already held a scheme of law notes gathered before his army years. Whatever the state of the book before Polly's fourteenth birthday, it was never again to be only law and arithmetic; for on the fly-leaf, and across Marshall's heart Polly wrote her name. On the book she wrote, "Miss Maria Ambler," Maria being more modish and romantic than Mary. But from his heart Marshall copied the name, "Polly," above several columns of legal learning.

J Marshall's name was scribbled too at this time, but not on a book. A century ago workmen found it inscribed on the plaster of the College hall along with the names of several of his classmates, a rather boyish prank for a twenty-four-year-old Captain of the army. But then most of his fellow students were still in their boyish teens. They were beginning the study of law while he had already steeped his mind in two editions of Blackstone's Commentary on the laws of England which were in his father's library by the time J Marshall was seventeen years old. Also before entering the army he had read law in the office of an attorney in Warrenton, walking eighteen miles there and back each day. It is said that on that long walk he often carried a large tome of legal learning, borrowed from the lawyer to read at night by the light of pine knots when his legal cogitation exhausted his allotment of candles.

He must have been a good borrower of books, for when his youthful classmates came too often unprepared to moot court, he seems to have borrowed a volume from that "gift of

Kings and gentlemen," the College library, and set off walking or riding to visit the Ambler girls in York. There by the
glowing hearth he read to them, poetry of course, and it may
be *The Vicar of Wakefield,* which was a favorite with Amblers. Though Eliza calls him awkward and unpolished, she
says she learned the beauties of good literature from these
readings.

"Girls at this time," wrote the Chief Justice, "appeared in
company earlier than they do now." And to appear in company in Virginia meant to hear the tramp of history just beyond the parlour windows. It meant to lay aside the book
and listen to news the post brought of the Continental Army
in defeat to the northward and to the southward. Captain
Marshall told the reason. "New raised armies, unused to danger, and from which undeserving officers have not been expelled; their conduct was not uniform. Some regiments, especially those who had served the preceding campaign, maintained their ground with firmness and intrepidity of veterans,
while others gave way as soon as they were pressed." Also, he
says that "the soldiers of the line carried muskets scarcely fit
for service . . . and of unequal calibre so that cartridges could
not be well fitted . . . and therefore their aim could not
match the fire of the enemy."

To appear in company meant that the girls would hear
that in their own State young General Marquis Lafayette
was giving no aspect of lion-in-the-path to the enemy, for
plantations lay devastated in the wake of the British. It
meant that they would be angered at hearing of slaves carried
off by red coated soldiers, and appalled that Virginia's regiments were falling apart from desertions.

Gravely, kindly Captain Marshall told why these things
were happening. No supplies or pay could be counted on
from the Continental Congress, which in turn could compel
no revenue from the states. Half paid, half fed, half clothed
men, too often retreating, too often routed, could not be held
by brave words. "Don't Tread on Me" brought to mind more
of the snake than the eagle.

That was no eagle's feather with which Captain Marshall
had been thrusting forth his argument. It was a Dutch quill,

now grasped in its flight by a soft little hand, once more to write "Maria" above the law notes.

Freedom in Polly's life was like the waves forever biting away the town's lovely cliffs, forever removing familiar things. All persons who considered themselves British subjects were ordered by the Council of State to leave Virginia. Friends who had played with the Ambler girls in the gardens or on the beach were, by edict, put at odds with their playmates, and departed in a cloud darkly. Several York mansions were closed.

Even the pillars of faith were crumbling under the tide of change. It was noised abroad that Thomas Jefferson had forwarded a bill in the General Assembly to set religion at liberty. This was promptly branded by Established Churchmen as tolerating the propagation of atheism. Polly's religion lost the warmth of assurance as the name of Thomas Jefferson cast its first cold shadow across her life.

Then winter melted. Spring speared the patterned gardens with green and shook out her basket of gold over the meadows. Roadsides between York and Williamsburg wore a grassy fringe. Woods were lit with dogwood bloom and in low places circles of purple iris lay like spots of discarded royalty.

In April, because of the sorry state of the armies, Congress proclaimed a Day of Fasting, Humilation and Prayer. York's Church bell rang summons as peremptory as ever in the days of the Queen who had given the bell. The Amblers repaired to their family pew to acknowledge that only a nation whose God is the Lord can stand against principalities which would despoil it. "Despoil it, despoil it," echoed in Polly's mind.

Dinner tables in York lay bare all afternoon. Eliza must fast. Would nervous little Polly be denied a small supper? Children, Tories and servants were excused from fasting. Polly, who always slipped back into childhood when night crept into the house, may have been allowed a glass of milk, else in the long, hungry dark, the sound of waves folding on the beach would seem the noise of creeping danger, and a sinister IF rise up in her heart not to be dispelled except by

the joyous laugh of a young law student, if he should happen
to ride into town next day.

In this April, Governor Thomas Jefferson moved the State
capital from Williamsburg to a place called Richmond
Town. More of York's mansions were vacated. More town
houses in Williamsburg were closed and shuttered. More
friends of the Ambler girls became the far end of a most
unreliable postal service. Eliza's letter book filled up.

Shortly the *Virginia Gazette,* whose printing house had
long been the guardian of the Williamsburg postoffice, also
moved to Richmond. Somewhere along the way it lost its
Jeffersonian motto proclaiming, "The freedom of the Press is
one of the Bulwarks of Liberty, and can never be restrained
but by despotic Government."

On a blue and gold afternoon in May, when J Marshall
found the Ambler girls, skirts and ribands a-flutter, walking
on the high field beyond the church, playfully, boastfully,
he asked them to behold him, a newly made Phi Beta Kappa.
And what might that be? Eliza would ask. Something military? It could be that without glancing at Eliza, Marshall
caught one of Polly's ribands, and laughing, explained that
it was very full of talk and without danger. He was too en-
tranced by girls at the moment to take it seriously. The minutes of the society record that he was assigned to argue the
question of "whether any form of government is more favorable to our new virtue than the Commonwealth," and that
he was answered by "gentlemen not immediately interested."
The new virtue was being called "liberty," and the Commonwealth was the old colony of Virginia, now calling itself a State.

Late in June Captain Marshall departed from the halls of
formal learning. Councillor Ambler found that he must move
his family to the new State capital. On their way to Richmond they visited in Williamsburg for two days and nights,
long enough for a group of young gentlemen to organize a
ball in the Palace in honor of the Misses Ambler. Eliza says
that her heart fluttered when she received the invitation.
Polly says nothing of her emotions. She plucked a red geranium blossom, and rubbed her pale cheeks with it.

Eliza admitted that she accepted the invitation from one of her current suitors, whom she professed to scorn, only that she might show him her "consequence" and "play off a thousand airs." Marshall, Eliza says, was "more successful" devoting himself to little Polly even though female competition "consisted of more Beauty and Elegance" than these girls had ever had to contend with.

After the ball he walked home with Polly along the starlit street under fragrant mulberry trees. How did they part at the door? Polly half smug with conquest, half wistful at ending such an evening? John, with sudden resolve to leave college and ride on to Richmond Town with the Amblers?

Certain it is that the Amblers drove on to Richmond next day. On the evening of the second day they reached "that Metropolis," as it seemed to Eliza, and dismounted before a small rented cottage "on the Hill," which a Scotch factor had built to conserve life without embellishing it. It was so small that Eliza had doubts that all the family could enter at one time. Marshall seems to have been around, "acting Pa" for two weeks, helping the Amblers squeeze their cherished possessions and themselves into a new life. On the corner of a page of his note-book he wrote, "Polly Ambler, Richmond."

CHAPTER II

A New World

RICHMOND TOWN in 1780 was for business only, just two hills and a valley striped with the overgrown lanes of a "town plan." A squat frame church crowned the top of the eastern hill. On the western height lay a rumpled pasture accommodating pigs and cows, but handsomely called The Capitol Square. Between them roads dropped jaggedly across the "plan" to the green valley floor where a rope factory and tobacco warehouses stood beside sparkling Shockoe Creek. The whole valley tilted toward a landing on James River. Sparsely scattered over the sloping plots stood about three hundred Scotch cottages, some of stone, but more of timber with wooden chimneys. They looked, Marshall observed, "as if the poor Caledonians had brought them over on their backs, the weakest of whom were glad to stop at the bottom of the hill, others a little stronger proceeded higher, while a few of the stoutest and boldest reached the summit." These in 1780 were over crowded with the sudden arrival of State government families.

Eliza says, "It is indeed a lovely situation and may at some future period be a great city, but at present it will scarcely afford one comfort in life." At first the Ambler girls found Richmond "an absolutely New World," very dull, and very warm. All Summer, dust rose lazily from broad wheels of covered wagons as they creaked past the crowded cottages, trailing an odor of barns, of redundant fields, and forest coverts. For the wagons had come from the "upper country" with farm produce, tobacco, skins and wood and coal to be sold in the open field beside Shockoe Creek.

The voice of a new world is thump of hammer and groan of saw. In Richmond Town there was rhythm to the noise, for the laborers were Africans who had learned in slavery to sing and prance with loads on their heads. So contagious was this rhythm that behind the hedge of the rented garden the Ambler girls could not have refrained from an unladylike caper, or resisted humming a few bars of Negro melody.

13

Indeed they found themselves swaying in time with the builders as they watched a market shed going up down by the Creek, or roofs being hammered on flimsy cabins intended to serve for executives offices at the foot of Capitol Square. An unimpressive shelter called Common Hall already clung to the western slope of the valley, and down by the river stood a town gaol. On court days the whole town plan was enveloped in dust from the feet of horses bringing plantation owners and small farmers to do business in the capital.

On August twenty-eighth, 1780, out of that dust cloud rode Captain Marshall to tie his horse to the rack in front of the Governor's office. That day Governor Thomas Jefferson signed the license which admitted his cousin, John Marshall, to practice law at the Virginia Bar, signing thereby much future annoyance to himself.

A few months only were the Ambler girls bored by this New World. For in the fall it was rumored that General Lord Cornwallis, though eminently victorious in the Carolinas, had concluded that the war against the Americans could most quickly be won with the capture of the Virginia government, and therefore had ordered the renegade Arnold to the State to harry the countryside, to disrupt the seat of government, and to capture the Governor and Executive Council of which Mr. Ambler was a member. "Outrageous barbarians," the British soldiers were called in the presence of the girls. At bedtime Eliza and Polly snuggled against each other, horrifying themselves with whispered gossip of British evildoing, pausing now and then to make sure they heard their father safely snoring in the next room.

Polly and Eliza had hardly finished their girlish magic for New Year's Day when Captain Marshall, in uniform again, bent his head beneath the low Scotch lintel to bid them a soldier's farewell. He was to be off with two hundred militiamen to harass a possible landing of the enemy at Westover on the James River, so few miles from Richmond, so few Americans against so many British. He had come to bid all the Amblers goodbye. But his black eyes, half proud, half pleading, were all for Polly who for a moment hung back, peeping over Eliza's shoulder. As he mounted his horse Polly suddenly pushed her sister aside, and brazenly stepped forward so that she might be the last Ambler Captain Marshall would see as he rode away.

A week or two later the cold silence of a January night was shattered by the town bell. Bong! Bong! it tolled until children in the crowded cottages were crying, and dogs in the frosty lanes were barking, and men, half dressed, went inquiring at each other's doors. It was the signal that the British had not been repulsed by the small troop of militia with J Marshall in the line.

Ladies in the cottages began packing treasures in carriage trunks while they quieted babies, ordered gentlemen about, and laid out an abundance of warm garments. By daylight the British were seen at the outskirts of the town.

In the midst of this confusion Eliza did not forget to grab up a letter she was writing to a girl friend, and stuff it in her pocket. Then, as stiff as so many barrels, encased in cloaks as they were, Mrs. Ambler and the four girls crowded into a hired coach with the Councillor. With Old Sam on the box, they fled as fast as two horses could bump the vehicle over frozen roads until they came to The Cottage in Hanover County.

Edward Ambler, older and more affluent brother of the Councillor, had built this elegant small dwelling when York was no longer safe for conspicuous patriots. Then he had died leaving a landed fortune scattered across Virginia. In The Cottage the Widow Ambler settled, nervously muffling her only surviving son, John, in apron strings, though he was twenty years old, handsome and one of the richest youths in the Colony. When the Councillor's coach clattered to the door on this Winter night, mother and son eagerly welcomed cousins into the warm parlour. This sudden influx of young females to his fireside gave John a chance to vaunt his restless manhood by reciting robust tales of British atrocities. Soon he had Polly clinging tearfully to her mother. But Eliza could not contain her excitement. She pulled out her unfinished letter, and thrills poured from her quill.

"What a panic for us all," she wrote. "Such terror and confusion you have no idea of. Governor, Council, everybody

scampering . . . Here will we stay with our friends but my
father will return to reconoitre." There the letter suffered
another interruption. Mr. Ambler could have reconnoitred no
further than the highway when he caught frantic news
that the British were moving into Hanover County.

Four days later Eliza continues her letter from another
Edward Ambler plantation, this one in Louisa County. "We
had only time," she wrote, "to learn that they were on the
road from Richmond when we were in the carriage and in a
few hours reached this place . . . We endeavor to make ourselves as comfortable as we can in the Overseers tiny dwelling which scarcely holds us all."

Even here there was no security for the Councillor. Every
night when the family was settled within the cabin, Mr.
Ambler would return to the coach. Old Sam would tuck
blankets around him, and then mount the box with the reins
under his feet, ready for sudden departure should the enemy
approach. In perfect confidence the master slept. In perfect
patience the slave watched.

On a pallet beside the hearth little Polly turned and
turned against Eliza's comforting back, wishing the Virginia
militia would be quick about running away from the ruthless
British. In fact she wished the enemy would chase them
right on up to Louisa County, which made her stifle a giggle against Eliza's shoulder.

The girls did not know that in this night John Ambler
cast off apron strings. As the Councillor's coach rolled away
from The Cottage John turned toward his mother with such
an air of defiance that she hastily fetched a rifle from a closet,
and handing it to him, said that though he was her last and
only child she would now send him forth to defend his property and his liberty. Catching up with the nearest body of
militia he began that night a military career that was in a
few years to take him to the rank of Colonel.

He may have saved the Ambler girls. For Eliza says that
on the fifth night in Louisa County, "while eating a frugal
supper of Bonny Clabber & honey etc a terrible clatter of
horses at the door sent us all scampering—! the British, nothing but the word British did we hear . . . a party of miser-

able militia . . . had called to give notice that the enemy were actually proceeding through the County, but not one of them could tell which way they had taken . . . So on we travelled through byways and brambles," until it was discovered that the British had somehow gotten ahead of the Ambler coach, and were well on the way toward Charlottesville. So the Amblers turned back to the overseer's cabin, a spot which Eliza defied the enemy or even the devil himself to find, and certainly not a country bumpkin Captain of the Continental Line.

The Amblers spent a few more weeks in frightening flight, and then as Spring seemed about to convert roads into flowing streams they returned to their tenement on Richmond's hill, where the air was still heavy with the odor of smouldering tobacco warehouses. As a result of these frenzied weeks, Eliza had adventures to recount all the rest of her life, but Polly could never again endure confusion.

On February twelfth, 1781, due to terminating enlistments and the lack of recruits, Captain Marshall's regiment was permanently disbanded. He resigned his commission and began to look around for a law practice, never doubting that Virginia courts would open again. But Polly was growing up too slowly for an impatient lover, and the law tapped too seldom at his office door in Fauquier County. Therefore, restlessly, suddenly, vigorously, J Marshall set out afoot for Philadelphia.

Thirty miles a day his long legs travelled. Upon arrival in that Mecca of medical science, he had himself vaccinated against smallpox which so frequently showed a scarred face in Virginia where State law made vaccination so difficult that it was almost prohibited. When he returned to Virginia his handsome face became familiar in political circles. His sparkling eyes, wrote one who remembered, "were full of good humor and benevolence, and his smile was like sunshine."

In April, 1782, he stood for a seat in Virginia House of Delegates representing Fauquier County, and won it. In this Spring the Virginia courts were opened in the old pattern of county courts under Thomas Jefferson's design of a

High Court of Chancery with a Court of Appeals. In this
Spring Councillor Ambler became Treasurer of Virginia, and
in November J Marshall was elected by the House of Delegates to a seat on the Council of State, whose function was
as advisor to the Governor.

Marshall was twenty-seven years old at this time, a veteran
of the Continental Army and of its Judge Advocate bench.
But Judge Edmund Pendleton, President of the Virginia
Court of Appeals, was moved to complain in a letter to
James Madison: "Young Marshall is elected a Councillor . . .
He is clever but I think too young for that department,
which he should rather have earned as a retirement and reward, by ten or twelve years in the Assembly." Did someone
point out to Judge Pendleton that Councillor James Monroe was three years younger than Marshall? But then Monroe always had a more solemn aspect than Marshall.

Judge Pendleton was to see a thing or two when young
Marshall, upon the opening of the Legislature, was immediately appointed to several weighty committees, one of them
for Courts of Justice. This committee made some changes in
Jefferson's design for a State judicial system; for example,
juries in the Chancery Court were abolished in the interest
of more expeditious procedure. In this, his freshman session
of the Assembly, the gentlemen with whom he held his own
and occasionally led, were his own father, Colonel Thomas
Marshall from the District of Kentucky, Patrick Henry,
Thomas Jefferson, Richard Henry Lee, Benjamin Harrison,
William Cabell, and others of like stature.

Busy days, indeed, these were for the young statesman, and
busy evenings! Courting Polly was uphill, downhill, and up
again. At the Ambler tenement Marshall found himself to
be one of a company of suitors, "one in the parlour, and two
on the doorstep." When he was demoted to the doorstep, he
could ride on down the hill to one of the new taverns on
Main Street, and there listen to liberated men talk of a nebu-
lous democracy. Or he could join his friend, Councillor
Monroe in a solemn walk to view the James River from
Richmond's eastern hill top.

Suddenly Marshall's suit in the Ambler parlour ended in

success. Persistent family tradition holds that finally he laid his question before the lady in unequivocal terms. She refused him. He bade her farewell, and rode off in the direction of Fauquier County. She watched him as far as the turn in the muddy street, and promptly went into hysterics. Nothing could stop her. She was near to strangling with holding her breath. The Treasurer of the State of Virginia could only call for his horse and ride off after the young lawyer to assure him that when Polly said "No" she meant "Yes."

Thus it happened that on January third next, being the year 1783, Mary Willis Ambler and Captain John Marshall were married with all the appurtenances of a wedding of Virginia aristocrats, robed minister, white clad bride, flowery maids, mirthful groomsmen, guests, toasts and music. With fifteen Marshall brothers and sisters and Ambler kin as numerous as the sands of York shores the affair was much too large for the Scotch tenement. Treasurer Ambler therefore borrowed hospitality from that familiar refuge, The Cottage in Hanover County. There, Episcopal Churches being in ruins, the parlour, decorated with Christmas greens, served for chapel.

As Winter dusk crept across the windows and candles were being lighted, guests in festive attire began to arrive. At eight o'clock Treasurer and Mrs. Ambler stood at the top of the stairs. The company at once made way for a procession of the parents, then the bride and groom followed by six maids and six groomsmen. In the parlour Parson Buchanan with Prayer Book open stood smiling at the pretty bride as she approached, for he lived with the Amblers as one of the family. An English lady says that at this point in Virginia weddings the parson calls all to attention with serious tone then performs a ceremony which is

"little more
Than you take John and John take thee,
I give my blessing heartily."

When the company had wished the couple health and joy, supper was served in the dining room where groomsmen and maids waited on the bride and groom with much gaiety. After the repast there was dancing and singing until Winter dawn shed enough light on the roads for the guests to return to their homes. Then Marshall, with a solitary guinea in his pocket, an Account Book full of expectations, and a wedding present from his father of three horses and a Negro named Robin, took his little bride, seventeen years old, to a two-room dwelling in the yard of the Ambler tenement on Richmond Hill. Thenceforth Polly hung on J Marshall's life like a delicately wrought lantern in which his presence lit the flame.

Slowly Richmond Town grew around the young couple. Gradually Marshall acquired a law practice and urban responsibilities. He joined companies and clubs as they sprang up in the taverns. He joined the Sons of the Cincinnati, a seriously purposed association of the officers of the disbanded Continental Line of the Revolution army. Jefferson and Spencer Roane scorned the Cincinnati as tending too much toward aristocracy. Marshall joined the "St. Taminy" Society, as it is spelled in his Account Book, which was a merrier company of politicians, who chose a purebred American for patron saint, Chief Tammany, and celebrated his day dressed as Indians, whooping and dancing as they supposed Indians did. Dues were good fellowship and whiskey.

Marshall turned his book of law notes upside down and began to keep lively expense and receipt accounts on the reversed pages. The first extant entry is, "given Polly 6 dollars & £ 4.0.2." Further down the same column are the cozy items of housekeeping such as "coffee pot," "sugar Boxes," "candlesticks," "two pieces of bobbin," "ink stand" and "thimble." Marshall had bought £4 worth of candles for his brother James Markham Marshall and as many more for himself. He had purchased oats, land warrants and butter.

He paid a tailor for a coat that he might appear well dressed when he stepped out with his bride. For Polly was one of Richmond society's leading young matrons, pretty, sprightly, he says, gracious, and according to the Account Book, fashionably dressed when she attended dinners at the Governor's house, such as one celebrating General Washington's birthday, or when she stood with friends in the starry

Assumpsit   Polly Amber

The P[laintif]f must set forth every thing essential to the
Gist of the action with such certainty that it may
appear there was cause of action, but the law
requires no greater certainty than the nature of the
thing requires

The Def[endan]t must shew there was no contract, or that the
contract was void & without consideration or that
he has performed it

March   An entire promise cannot be apportioned.
Co. La. 483   The Def[endan]t cannot plead that he has revoked the promise.

Polly Amber

Polly

Courtesy of the College of William and Mary

PAGE FROM J MARSHALL'S LAW NOTES (reduced) showing Polly's
name scribbled above and below the law that a promise cannot be
partly kept.

night to watch fireworks from Richmond Hill. She danced with her joyful husband at balls in the Common Hall. Everywhere she was the center of a crowd, for her husband was the spark that kindled laughter for young and old. From his presence radiated such friendliness that strangers drew near and friends sought him out. Of her, Marshall says that to her "very attractive person" she added "uncommonly pleasing manners," and that "though serious as well as gentle, she possessed a good deal of chaste and delicate wit."

CHAPTER III

The Marshalls on Fairfax Lands

F OR HIS MARRIAGE, Marshall says, his plan was to spend Winters in Richmond and Summers in Fauquier County. At Oak Hill, the Marshall home on the slopes of the Blue Ridge Mountains, Polly learned that to marry a Marshall meant to marry the long contentions of Fairfax land titles.

J Marshall's father had been born in Westmoreland County and had grown up there among the pretentious families whose land holdings, in many titles, predated the proprietorship of Lord Culpeper.

Virginians had never condoned that vast grant of lands by Charles II in 1659 to nobles whom he deemed loyal to him in exile, for they too had been loyal, refusing to reject Charles as their monarch, even when the presence off shore of Cromwell's gunboats had subdued Jamestown, and the Puritan party had grasped ascendency in the Virginia Assembly. Virginia's loyalty, Charles rewarded by a freehanded appropriation of the Colony's powers and benefits. In "the Usual policy and custom of all Nations but in more especiall Manner of the state of England" for military service, he lavished upon seven gentlemen exiled with him in Holland the proprietary rights to over five million acres of Virginia, giving them power to grant, sell and lease lands upon which more than five hundred and seventy grants already stood in the King's name. At once protests sprang up in the Virginia Assembly and in London through the Colony's commercial agents.

Upon his restoration to the throne of England, Charles was forced again and again to adjust and compromise these favors, but never to retract them. Powers to grant became an irksome confusion. By 1673 the proprietorship of that rich wilderness known as the Northern Neck of Virginia had settled upon two of the original grantees, Thomas, Lord Culpeper, and Lord Henry, Earl of Arlington. In 1683 Lord Culpeper's son was Governor of Virginia. He purchased Arlington's grant for a sum which was to be paid one half on "the feast of S. Michael the Arch Angel" and one half on the "Annunciation of the Blessed Mary."

Then was Lord Culpeper sole owner and proprietor of that area of Virginia which spread from the Chesapeake Bay at the mouth of the Potomac River westward to its source in the heights of the Alleghany Mountains, then southeastward diagonally across the rich Shenandoah Valley to the peaks of the Blue Ridge Mountains to a system of mountain springs which, flowing eastward, became the Rappahannock River and carried the boundary line back to the Chesapeake Bay, a vague designation of vast privilege.

Lord Culpeper appointed Receivers General in each county to collect two shillings per hundred acres quit-rent every year on the "feast of St. John Baptist," which is England's Midsummer Day. The fifteen-year tenures terminated if the rent became in arrears, or if three out of every fifty acres had not been improved in three years. To further complicate deeds, the terms of the grant held that if in seven years there was found "any over plus" of lands in any deed, Lord Culpeper and his heirs and assigns forever were to be paid twenty-five pounds per annum per hundred acres.

Then Lord Culpeper began to sell manorial grants for various prices with varying conditions, the first of these sales being to a shipwrecked traveller by the name of John Washington, who chose a handsome area washed by the Potomac River.

Fate put the King's bounty into the hands of the King's implacable enemy. When Lord Culpeper's sole heiress, his daughter, married William, Lord Fairfax, Baron of Cameron, General of Cromwell's army, even the name of Culpeper was usurped in the proprietorship. Henceforth the royal gift was known as "Fairfax lands."

In 1731 Joist Hite and Robert McKay, who had long been on the land without deeds, petitioned the Virginia Assembly for a grant of 100,000 acres in the valley of the Shenandoah for settlement of one hundred Pennsylvania families, and secured an order for this acreage to be taken up within three years. They could lure only fifty-four families onto the land.

The Assembly allowed him to file survey for fifty-four thousand acres of the western part of the Northern Neck. Lord William Fairfax protested this encroachment on his wife's possessions by the Virginia government and petitioned the Crown for a judicial ascertainment of the boundaries. Two years later his son Thomas, Lord Fairfax, eighth Baron of Cameron, came to the Colony to press the claims he had inherited.

On September twenty-third, 1736, the Virginia Assembly passed an Act "confirming titles to lands in the Northern Neck, held under the Right Honorable Thomas, Lord Fairfax, Baron of Cameron in that part of Great Britain called Scotland." This Act assured titles in dispute, giving ownership under "rents and services by grants reserved," and ratified the old Culpeper title.

In the year 1748 certain grants from the Crown were made while the boundaries of Fairfax land were still uncertain. Again in that year an Act of Assembly, consented to by Lord Fairfax, confirmed title to the grantees in leases to be held by Lord Fairfax, all rents, services and emoluments to be paid him.

It was to stake off these claims that young George Washington of Westmoreland County went into this wilderness, taking with him his friend, young Thomas Marshall. On the springing floor of that forest Thomas Marshall's feet felt at home. In the glades of virgin forest he found freedom of thought. In the patience of ancient growth he touched the mystery of peace. Marshalls were never again so much at home anywhere as in the upper country of Fairfax lands.

Four years later Thomas Marshall inherited from his father a plantation in affluent Westmoreland County, called The Forest, but which was, in fact, scrub fields worn down from years of profit-taking tobacco planting. He lost no time in deserting this open land. With his widowed mother, Elizabeth Markham Marshall, his younger brother and sisters, at least eighteen Negro slaves and several horses, he moved westward to the forests of Prince William County, settling near Germantown as agent for Lord Fairfax.

There in a small Glebe of the Church of England,

Thomas Marshall found much to his liking Mary Randolph Keith, daughter of the Reverend Mr. James Keith, minister of surrounding Hamilton Parish, and married her in 1754. For her housekeeping he rented the ironworker's cottage where their first son was born on September twenty-fourth, 1755, and named John Marshall.

When this son was ten years old, and there were four other children, Thomas Marshall pushed on deeper into the westward mountains. In a high valley watered by Goose Creek he leased three hundred and fifty acres from the Lee estates for the lifetime of himself, his wife or his oldest son, whichever should live longest. Choosing a place near lonely Goose Creek Church, he built the finest house in the far-flung neighborhood, three rooms down and one upstairs. It was constructed of squared logs and plaster sheathed in hand-hewn oak and pine. The Marshalls called it The Hollow. Here six more Marshall children were born.

As the family increased, so did Thomas Marshall's importance in the countryside. When in 1759 Fauquier County was cut from Prince William County, he held the highest offices of county and vestry, and represented Fauquier in the House of Burgesses. As a trained soldier he was an officer in the Colony militia. As an active surveyor the tangled titles of land patents turned him toward the law. He was so sound a businessman that by 1773 he had accumulated two thousand acres of Fairfax lands. Then he sold the Lee lease, and built Oak Hill at the western foot of Cobbler's Mountain. This house too had more elegance than any within a day's journey, boasting four rooms below and three above stairs, with that rare luxury, window glass. There were eleven children when the Marshalls moved into Oak Hill. Four more were born there. Thus all fifteen children of Thomas Marshall learned to walk on Fairfax lands.

Six years after the Marshalls moved into Oak Hill, in that sorry year of 1779 when the State seemed exhausted by futile warfare, the Virginia Assembly passed confiscatory laws declaring that all leases and privileges in patents under the British crown were null and void, all lands thereby granted were to be in freehold, to the end that "the proprietors of land within the commonwealth may no longer be subject to any servile, feudal or precarious tenure, and to prevent the danger to a free state from perpetual revenue."

Lord Fairfax had held office in county and church under the Commonwealth of Virginia, had fought her Indian wars and since 1748 had conducted his manorial business, collecting quit-rents and conveyancing his lands as a citizen of Virginia at his home, Greenway Court in Frederick County. Here, at the age of ninety-three, he was told of the surrender of Lord Cornwallis at York Town. Saying, "Take me to bed, Joe, it is time for me to die," he lay down, turned his face to the wall, and within a few days had left his troublesome earthly estate to his brother in England. But Robert, Lord Fairfax, also was finding the New World too much for him, and soon passed on without issue. The Cameron title fell upon one nephew. The Fairfax lands in Virginia went to another who assumed the name and arms of the estate.

An Act of Virginia Assembly in 1782 sequestered all quit-rents due the Fairfax estate in the hands of lessees, until the right of descent should be known, and the General Assembly could restore to the legal representative of the proprietor the quit-rents due at his death. It was then determined that the right of descent lay with an English clergyman, the Reverend Denny Martin, who by Act of Parliament had added the name of Fairfax to his own. Then Denny Martin Fairfax retained Captain John Marshall to collect the rents due him.

In his childhood Marshall had loved Fairfax lands with the earth possessing majesty of a barefoot boy. Tramping this wilderness he had learned to be quick and sure-footed on demand, to have sharp vision and sensitive ears, and had won faith in ever-renewing creation. No matter who held the deed, the beds of those streams and the floors of those forests were as the soles of his feet, while the Reverend Mr. Fairfax evinced no sentiment for wilderness manors. Therefore, brash as a young oak confident of expanding seasons, Marshall offered the Fairfax heir twenty thousand pounds for his uncounted acres. The Englishman seems to have ignored this offer.

But then J Marshall won Polly, and the first Summer of

their marriage was spent at Oak Hill on Fairfax lands. To travellers along the road between Fredericksburg and Winchester, Oak Hill was known as "the big house." When Polly first saw it, it must have seemed too small for all the Marshalls who burst from doorways, tumbled out of windows and ran around corners of the house to greet their older brother. She probably clung tightly to the sleeve of her husband's sack coat until Elizabeth, the oldest daughter, took her by the hand and big-sistered her.

Crowding Polly and Elizabeth were Mary and Judith, twenty-four and seventeen years old. Then came fifteen-year-old Lucy and three little girls under eight. Beyond them were five of the brothers. Squeaking and roaring his welcome came blithe Alexander, until Lewis, dour even at ten, nudged him aside so that he might have space to make a proper bow. The twins, Charles and William, lanky sixteen, beat Marshall's shoulders with rough affection. Lieutenant James Markham Marshall, aged nineteen, met his brother as soldier to soldier and presumed to kiss his sister-in-law. Under Colonel Alexander Hamilton, James had stormed the last held bastion of the British at York Town a year and a half ago, and showed a disposition to choose Hamilton as his leader in civil affairs.

Gently dominating the welcome moved the mother of the crowd with two-year-old Nancy clinging to her apron. Hanging on the wall of Polly's Richmond house today is a portrait of Mary Randolph Keith Marshall in old age. Even then she was beautiful, with an expression of tenderness and strength. The last brother to greet Polly was Thomas junior, twenty-two-year-old Captain from the Revolutionary army. From far fields he had seen the arrival, and turned his half-broken horse toward the house. In this year he had taken over management of the farm.

The charm and beauty of Oak Hill must have touched Polly's delicate taste. A simple white house stood in a park of forest oak and poplar trees. Close behind it lay the square domestic area, marked off with white outbuildings, kitchen, wash house, weaving room, smokehouse, canopied well and cabins for the house servants. Further off could be seen barns and quarters for field hands. "My people," the Marshalls called them. Rolling meadows were alive with flocks of sheep and herds of cattle and horses, while chickens and turkeys strutted in and out of the barn doors.

In the Summer days that followed, Polly watched Elizabeth conducting school for younger brothers and sisters, and reaching always to lift her mother's daily burden. It must have been in that mother's serenity that Polly renewed her own poise.

For when Polly detoured the noisy routine of the household to rest in the cool parlour, Mrs. Marshall would pause there on her way from one duty to another. J Marshall too may have looked in on his pretty wife. Then as he turned and smiled at his mother, and she returned that greeting, it must have seemed to Polly that an arch of honour and confidence hung between mother and son. Bright though it was, it never drew them closer than two ends of a rainbow, for the eldest of so many children in so hardy a life had small share of his mother's intimate moments, only those at bedtime when with her arms around his head, she taught him to pray "Thy kingdom come" and "Now I lay me down to sleep."

Marshall says that his father was the "only intelligent companion" of his early youth. But in this Summer Colonel Marshall was not at Oak Hill. He was out in the District of Kentucky prospecting for a new homestead for his family and for a firmer foothold for the Virginia government on a burgeoning frontier where Spaniard, Frenchman and Englishman were conniving with Indians for a stake in the rich valleys of the Ohio and Mississippi Rivers.

What a tumult the first Sabbath Day at Oak Hill must have been for Polly. Since the Amblers fled York there had been little church going for that pious family. St. John's on Richmond Hill was seldom open for worship. But a few miles from Oak Hill, Cooling Spring Meeting House was regularly served by J Marshall's old tutor, James Thompson; and it was the rule of the household that all who could walk or ride the short distance must there attend worship every Sunday. There for two hours Polly sat on a backless bench,

between restless Marshalls who continually stretched or
folded their long legs in the narrow space allotted them,
while the Word of God with a Scotch burr was hammered
into their souls. When Mr. Thompson called for the singing
of a Psalm, sober cadence was shattered by Marshall voices
raised in any pitch and any time to praise God from Whom
their hardy blessing flowed. Polly could not cover her ears
against the noise of newly-gotten inlaws.

Weary though she might be at the end of the service, in
the valley churchyard Polly must again be the center of a
crowd while worshipers mixed politics with business and
society. She must be introduced to innumerable new relatives. She must let her nervous fingers be shaken by the hard-
ened hands of backwoodsmen who had been her husband's
constituency, and might again be asked to send him to the
State Legislature. For Fauquier was still his county.

It may be that Polly was glad to return in September to
the two-room cottage behind her mother's tenement. Standing in that yard where apple and apricot trees bowed with
fruit, she could look over the sloping town plan, marked
now by ditches filled with purple and yellow bloom. Up
from the valley warehouses drifted the opulent aroma of
stored tobacco. The morning sun hung gold on swirls of dust
that followed members of the Virginia Assembly riding into
town. There was a lilt of wings in the breeze. It seemed to
Polly that the New World was about to keep an exciting
promise, and all the joy of all creation rode on her husband's
laugh.

Happy was the Winter of 1783 and '84 in the two-room
house full of young society before a hearth so glowing that
embroidered shields were set to protect fair faces during sessions of chocolate and gossip, or taffeta-clad shoulders when
the company turned to card tables. Among Richmond ladies
card playing was so fashionable and so extravagant that almost every issue of the press carried letters of masculine protest. J Marshall does not record Polly's gaming accounts. His
own are plainly written in the Account Book. Sometimes he
won and sometimes lost at whist, backgammon and horse
races.

When the ladies occupied the card table, J Marshall sat aside with his desk opened on a table near a window. He listened to the chatter a moment, then merrily wrote to James Monroe that Tabby Eppes had "grown quite fat and buxom" and that "her charms are renovated," so much so that within the last six weeks "Carrington, Young, Seldon, Wright (a merchant) & Foster Webb have alternately bow'd before her and been discarded." He tells of another Tabby being "in high spirits over the success of her antique sister" and is speaking of "Matrimony as of a good which she yet means to experience." "The excessive cold weather," Marshall explains, "has operated like magic on our youth. They feel the necessity of artificial heat & quite wearied of lying alone, are all treading the broad road to Matrimony." In fact two weddings among their acquaintance would take place within a week.

Merry the letters of J Marshall to James Monroe were, but they were also seriously concerned. Together these two young lawyers were working out a settlement of the financial accounts between the State of Virginia and the Congress of these United States. Also Marshall was endeavoring to sell Monroe's military warrants, and enjoying real estate business. "I have been maneuvering amazingly," he wrote, "to turn your warrants into cash if I succeed I shall think myself a first rate speculator." A few weeks later Marshall wrote Monroe, "I am no longer a member of the Executive, the opinion of the Judges with respect to a Councillor's standing at the bar determined me to retire from the Council board." To that board there was shortly elected a younger politician, a protégé of Judge Pendleton, one Spencer Roane.

Monroe at this time was a member of the Fourth Congress meeting in Annapolis, where he shared lodging and a French cook with Thomas Jefferson. Shy Monroe was increasingly intrigued with sonorous theories about liberated people, while Marshall who loved people was beginning to discover a conviction that, in so extended a nation, the people would have peace and prosperity only if they endowed a common government with strength and equity.

Not only with Monroe was Marshall busied with debts

and collections. In January 1784, Congress ratified a treaty
of peace with Great Britain. Among other things this treaty
called for payment of the debts of the Colonists to British
merchants. It has been estimated that in Virginia alone these
debts amounted to between two and three million pounds
sterling. A prospect of having to pay them raised the dander
of State legislatures. Constituencies were asking, "If we have
to pay our debts what did we fight for?" State legislatures
hastened to make State laws abrogating this term of the national treaty. But they shilly-shallied. One session would
annul the debts and the next reinstate them, finally
conditioning payment upon reparation for slaves stolen by
the British soldiers, and release of fur trading posts still held
by the enemy.

This confusion piled high the desks of lawyers. Much of
the business fell on the table near a window in the two-room
rented cottage. Thomas Jefferson retained his cousin, Captain Marshall, to pin down the law that covered British merchant debts in the estate of his father-in-law, John Wayles.
Jefferson had sold land inherited by his wife to pay these
debts, but the British merchant was refusing to accept the
notes in which Jefferson had been paid, ready money being
almost nonexistent in Virginia. Marshall wrote to Patrick
Henry that Jefferson, whom at this time he called "one of the
ablest men and soundest lawyers in America," maintained
that lands devised by will were still liable to British debts.

Another term of the treaty threw a tangle of claims and
rights into the patched-up Courts of the Commonwealth. In
that small parlour, over Tavern tables and in county court-
yards, John Marshall began the long, long business of clearing Fairfax land titles. Less and less of his deliberations were
done in the parlour, for it would have been beyond his powers of restraint not to turn from his papers to listen proudly
to the cry of an infant.

For on July twenty-first, a son was born to John and Mary
Willis Marshall, to be named Thomas. He was not rocked in
a hooded cradle low on the floor like a frontiersman. The
cradles of Tidewater Amblers hung high, with netted cano-
pies and linen curtains. Here in the two-room cottage he

slept like a prince, this little Tom who was to stretch his stride to fit his father's footsteps on Fairfax lands, and to bring affection like flowers to decorate his mother's life.

Chapter IV

Amblers

THE BABY was christened when his grandfather, Colonel Thomas Marshall, suddenly appeared in Virginia from Kentucky. The rite was performed by Parson Buchanan in the small parlour, and celebrated afterwards with cakes and the best Madeira wine. Toasts were poignant rather than merry, and cakes were divided between sisters in solemn childish ritual. For Colonel Marshall was preparing to move half of the family by flat boat down westward-flowing rivers to Kentucky. That the intrepid traveller, Daniel Boone, would be their companion through the Indian country, was more suggestive of danger than of protection. Polly's spirit was shaking like leaves whipped by arrows until Mary Keith Marshall took the baby into her arms and, kissing the wet Cross on his forehead, whispered, "It is also a Crown, you know." Like a hymn was Polly's whispered response, "Oh, how beautiful!"

Then the family separated. Colonel Marshall, taking his wife and younger children to Kentucky, left Elizabeth to keep house for his son Thomas at Oak Hill, who would raise fine Virginia horses for the Kentucky plantations. Lucy and Alexander were left with the young couple in Richmond. So Marshall rented a larger house over on Shockoe Hill. Thereafter he seems never to have had enough beds. "Bed," "bedstead," "blankets," "sheeting" are ever-recurring items in his Account Book. Members of his family were always visiting him.

Near the Marshall's new residence Jacquelin Ambler, financially assisted by his well-to-do Aunt Martha Jacquelin, was building a white painted mansion. From its upper windows the Treasurer could look across the pasture called Capitol Square and see an unpainted frame house of four rooms which was the official residence of Virginia's Governors. Around that drab structure so many lawyers were building handsome dwellings within spacious grounds that the neighbourhood was acquiring the name of "Court End of Town,"

Carringtons, Nicholases and Randolphs, Harvies, Calls and Washingtons were laying paths through their gardens toward each other's gates.

Unto her hills Richmond was gradually drawing the important life of the State. More and more people came to town on public and private business. And they came mostly on horseback. Before Main Street's taverns and shops, horse racks were more conspicuous than sidewalks. The town acquired schools, a French dancing master (M. Rouselle, says Marshall's Account Book), a fire company, a marine insurance company, a dentist, doctors and surgeons, and a bank. Shops were offering the trimmings of life, musical instruments, books, frills and furbelows, and Dutch quills with finest post paper, wafers and sealing wax.

A large and clever troupe of actors, the American Company, came to town to perform for months at a time in a commodious shed built for their use down in the valley near the market and tobacco warehouses. Though the roadway along Main Street was long and muddy, Eliza Ambler says she often attended the plays, and that at one of them she again found one of those eligible officers who had intrigued the Ambler cousins in Winchester. He could not keep his eyes on the stage, and she could not repress the smile that went in his direction.

The Ambler mansion still smelled of fresh paint and wet plaster on the twenty-first of March, 1785, when in the new parlour, Parson Buchanan pronounced Eliza Ambler and Captain William Brent man and wife. Dandelions spread a golden carpet for her new shoes when she ran across the yard to her husband's carriage. But they were sere weeds when, too soon, she returned to the new house. By the middle of June Captain Brent was dead. While taking his bride on a tour of family visits, he became stricken at his mother's house in Fairfax County with what must have been acute appendicitis, and died within a few days.

Eliza says her father sent "darling brother Marshall" to fetch her home, and that no one else could so tenderly have strengthened her spirits. The road home led through Hanover County. There torrential rains forced them to take shelter in The Cottage where John Ambler kept a housekeeper ready to welcome members of the family on stop-overs. For two days the storm kept them there. Eliza did not waste the time in futile tears. She found a tall cupboard stuffed to the top with Ambler family documents, deeds, indentures, wills and genealogies. So she drew the past like a curtain across the sadness of her future.

With a quill she took notes for a family history, and new-made democrat that she was, was not concerned with her forebears beyond the first American among them, who, she found, was Edward Jacqueline. He was the heir of a wealthy and high born French Huguenot family who had been circumspect enough to convert their estate into gold and silver before taking refuge in England at the time of the St. Bartholomew's Day Massacre. From there in 1697 Edward Jacqueline came to Virginia and built a good house on Jamestown's Back Street, with the straggling village before it and the Pitch and Tarr Swamp a mile behind it. Having an unimpeachable character and sharp but honest business acumen, he soon was made Burgess for James City County.

Not far from the Jacqueline house stood a handsome small church, patterned after English village churches, with a belfry, Gothic windows and graves under the aisle. Like the English churches it seemed too large for the hamlet around it, but it served a numerous parish in outlying plantations. In this church Edward was married to a widow who soon succumbed to the miasmic climate of the island, and was buried in the walled churchyard. As she was no one's ancestor her name was of no interest to Eliza. Not long after she died, Edward Jacqueline was married again in the same church, this time to Martha Cary, daughter of Colonel Miles Cary of Warwick County. They lived an expansive life, travelling in England, having family portraits painted by the best artists, making gifts to the church and prospering withal. Deeds in the cupboard showed that as the pomp of colonial government moved to higher ground at Middle Plantation, Edward bought up the shell of a town and then the swamp-rich lands around it. No son carried on the name of Jacque-

line. Of their six children only three daughters lived past
early youth, Elizabeth, Mary and Martha.

A spinster at fifty, Martha gave herself the title of "Mrs."
Mary married John Smith of Shooters Hill of Gloucester
County. Elizabeth was the grandmother whose name Eliza
bore. It was this daughter who inherited the Jacqueline island property. She married Richard Ambler.

Eliza's quill spluttered a bit as she wrote that Richard
Ambler "was an honest Yorkshireman" who settled at York
Town in Virginia in 1716, and became "a respectable merchant." Then she wrote, "Our grandfather at the age of 43
discreetly married our grandmother the inheritor of Jamestown." In his pleasant brick mansion on York bluffs, Richard Ambler conducted the honorable office of Collector of the
King's Revenue for the Port of York during many turbulent
years. The Cottage papers revealed that he had added to his
wife's inheritance until the Amblers owned all of the island
of Jamestown with its crumbling village and watchtower
church.

Of the children of Richard and Elizabeth Ambler only
three sons grew up. Of these sons John died unmarried in
Barbadoes, where he had gone for his health. Edward mar-
ried Mary Cary, daughter of Edward Cary of "Celeys" in
Elizabeth City County, and built for her a mansion in York.
At his father's death he became Collector of the Port of
York, purchased several plantations and, in time, built The
Cottage.

Eliza glanced around the handsome room, remembering
this and that of Aunt Ambler. She had died only a few weeks
after releasing John Ambler to his rightful place in the Revolutionary forces. On her death bed she sent for him, and
with her last words admonished him to bury her beside her
husband in the churchyard at Jamestown. This of course had
been impossible with the British army in possession of the
island. So she had lain in a grave under the myrtles in the
garden behind The Cottage until after the surrender at
York Town. Between her two funerals gossip which had
been only whispered before her death, came out into the
open. It was said that Mary Cary had been General Wash-

ington's earliest sweetheart, but that Mr. Cary had dispatched the young Colonel with harsh words to the effect that such a marriage would be beneath his daughter's opportunities. Later Eliza was to discover that Aunt Ambler did resemble Lady Washington. When Edward and John Ambler were chosen for a traditional English education and sent to Leeds Academy in England, Jacquelin was consigned to learn trade and commerce in the house of a successful merchant of Philadelphia.

Eliza's quill spluttered on beyond the documents. Jacquelin Ambler had returned to York where he was captivated by the piety of a young girl living in the gayest, most fashionable mansion in the Town. When her mother had been buried in the graveyard of the Burwell estate in Gloucester County, nine-year-old Rebecca Burwell was sent to her father's sister Elizabeth, wife of the Honorable William Nelson of York. Rebecca told her children that when there were worldly dancing crowds in the Nelson parlours she retired to a chapel which she had arranged under the eaves of the attic. But her devotions must have picked up the lilt of the fiddles below stairs, and her knees given place to light fantastic toes. For Eliza recalled that along with a reputation for piety, her mother was known as beautiful charmer, unexcelled on the dance floor. There Jacquelin Ambler, solemnly stepping the sets beside Rebecca, discovered that her piety matched his, and they were married in 1764.

Eliza looked up listening to the last of the rain dripping from eaves. Was that the sound of tears for the dead? Or was it mystery tapping at the door of the future? Briskly she gathered up her papers and made ready to continue the journey to Richmond.

In October of this year, 1785, Eliza walked across the open field to Polly's house where there was to be another wedding. Elizabeth Marshall was to be married to Rawleigh Colston of Frederick County. Bravely Eliza smiled while Parson Buchanan read for Elizabeth the service he had read for Eliza so brief a time ago. Elizabeth needed smiles since her mother was not present at her wedding. Mary Keith Mar-

shall never returned to Virginia after that dangerous trek to
Kentucky, and the daughter who had shared her mother's
burdens never crossed the mountains that separated them.

CHAPTER V

The Constitution

J MARSHALL'S NAME first appears on the record of cases before the Virginia Court of Appeals in the Spring of 1786. The successors of Joist Hite were suing Denny Fairfax for fulfillment of promises made by Lord Fairfax. Marshall assisted Attorney Baker for the defense. Opposing them, Edmund Randolph and John Taylor pressed the claims of the Hites. In the 1736 compromise of Crown, Assembly and proprietor, Lord Fairfax had agreed to make certain conveyances to Hite in fee simple if his settlers should remain on the land for a number of years. But in 1749, Lord Fairfax reported to the Assembly that Hite had claimed all the rich lowland, and by his settlements had isolated the highlands. He therefore refused to issue further grants until the survey should be reformed. Twice thereafter the General Court of the Colony entitled Hite's descendants to the land, once in 1769 and again in 1771. So Baker and Marshall lost the decision, but in his argument before the Court, Marshall grasped the opportunity to prove that the basic Fairfax title was incorruptible.

A few weeks after the close of this court, Captain and Mrs. Marshall's second child and first daughter was born, bidding, he later said, as fair for life as ever was seen. More slowly than after the first baby, Drs. McClurg and Foushee brought Polly back to a measure of health. She was a listless invalid during months when Marshall's citizenship was growing in scope and power. Thus to the giant in his character was added a great tenderness.

He bought a house for her across a field from her mother's. It stood a little withdrawn under forest trees in a spacious park-like lot. One of the outbuildings was a frame office. No longer must business caucus rumble under Polly's nursery floor. He bought servants to wait on her. He provided a horse and fine saddle for her exercise, and purchased a carriage for her to go a-visiting her mother, her sisters, Great-aunt Martha or any of a dozen cousins, or just to be seen as

41

pretty Mrs. Marshall riding out in the Court End of Town.

The Account Book became full of "Polly" "to Polly," in more and more generous amounts, pounds and shillings changing to dollars and cents. For Polly's satisfaction, too, were the good clothes he bought for himself, though he always forgot to wear them.

One January day of the first Winter in this house, Polly went from window to window watching flames shoot up from Richmond's new business district down Main Street hill. All day snatches of news were brought in to her. Two stores are ashes. Now Anderson's Tavern is burning. Now Byrd's warehouse! Smell the scorching tobacco! The warehouse is full of packed hogsheads, and of baskets of cured hands of leaf, the wealth of many a plantation. Marshall was down in that inferno with other gentlemen of the town, endeavoring to save important papers in the Treasury and in other public buildings. The financial loss to private business was so great that on the morning after the fire a subscription was taken to relieve the distress. Marshall's Account Book records twenty pounds as his contribution.

Soon Marshall's law practice became one of the most notable in the State. Edmund Randolph, appointed Governor of the Commonwealth in 1786, put his practice in Marshall's hands. In the first ten years of his marriage Marshall sat as Delegate in seven sessions of the Assembly, first from Fauquier County, then from Henrico County and finally from the City of Richmond. In all of these he served on weighty committees, but was most cogently concerned with the Committee for Courts of Justice of which he was chairman. In spite of some alteration the courts were still an awkward remnant of the Colonial system of justice, complicated by local politics.

For a while he was City Recorder, which gave him an opportunity of being instrumental in organizing a lottery for a Masonic Hall. He was interested in everything. He contributed to the living of both the Episcopal and the Presbyterian minister, there being no clergy salaries at the time. He was a member in high degree of the Grand Lodge of Ancient York Masons, and enthusiastic member of the Jockey Club, of the social assemblies and the circulating library. What with campaigning for elections, attending races at the Broad Rock track, meetings of Formicola's Tavern Club, dinners and cards and barbecues, J Marshall in his slow-going way went everywhere that gentlemen foregathered.

Though he moved so deliberately that he was often accused of indolence, the pace of his life was too much for Polly. When her spirit was shaken by it, he sent her to that fountain of his own equanimity, Fairfax lands at the foot of the Blue Ridge Mountains. His Account Book notes that even in chilly November she was in Fredericksburg on her way to Oak Hill.

Frail though she had become, Polly was never separated from her husband's strenuous patriotism. Marshall says she shared his every thought, and that her judgment was "so sound and safe" that he often sought it in "situations of perplexity," and though he "never regretted the adoption of her opinion" he "sometimes regretted its rejection."

Freely to her hearthside he brought the foremost gentlemen of Virginia, those militant guardians of burgeoning freedoms. When it became known that Colonel Thomas Marshall and Daniel Boone had come the long and dangerous way from the District of Kentucky to Richmond as Delegates to the General Assembly, and were guests in the Marshall home, more than ever Polly's small parlour was crowded with gentlemen. Some came in fashionable broadcloth coats turned back to show ruffled shirts, and some wore the fringed leather jackets of the frontier buttoned up to their weather-beaten throats. Some were elderly, like Judge Pendleton with a shock of white hair and walking on crutches. Some were young and handsome, stepping blithely, assured of their opinions, like Francis Corbin of Middlesex County and Light Horse Harry Lee; or like Colonel James Monroe, now thirty years old, Mr. Madison, four years older, middle-aged like her husband, Polly thought, was often present. Here, too, was his cousin Governor Edmund Randolph. Most of these were veterans of the war which made them the young aristocrats of a new world. All through the room Patrick Henry's rich voice could be heard as he argued with elegant

George Mason. These two believed in the same liberties; but Henry talked like hot toddy, while Mason poured out his wisdom like cool cream. Such a mixture, thought Polly, was given to curdling rather than to improving a new drink.

The gentlemen would have arrived in a mellow mood, for at the close of each session of the Assembly, Senators and Delegates passed through the Governor's dining room, where a large bowl of punch made up for the meagre majesty of the executive residence, then went on their friendly way to air their maxims in the relaxation of someone's parlour.

Polly moved about the room, shyly doing her manners. Marshall says that she was a delightful conversationalist, telling her stories with grace and pretty mimicry. She must have paused a moment beside the Chippendale bench where her husband sat, leaning forward, sharp elbows on his sharp knees, his dark eyes eager and bright as he talked with his father, who seemed a very rock of positive political wisdom. Colonel Thomas Marshall and his son, John, were compounding an Act by which the Virginia Assembly would give statehood to the District of Kentucky in 1791. Turning from them she heard gentlemen gossiping about General Washington's anger with the States for whom he had so hardly wrought a victory, and who now nullified Congressional taxation to pay for the war. Others were speaking of the scarcity of money and the confusion of the Confederation's finance and commerce. Though there was a general system of specie, each State printed paper money which fluctuated in value as it crossed State lines. Banking hovered under a shell of local jealousies, and States engaged in trade wars with other States throwing up tariff barriers in reprisal. Each State had its separate judiciary structure, each county its court, with a bench which was in practice self-perpetuating and monopolistic, independent of that arbitral tribunal which Congress selected from representatives of the States each time there was a boundary dispute.

Marshall says that "differences in State legislatures proved that everything was afloat." Gentlemen were quoting General Washington as saying that the Confederation was "a half starved, limping government . . . tottering at every step."

For the Confederation was in truth just the old colonies calling themselves States, separate and independent, drawn together for rebellion and protection, governed by those citizens who by fortune and character, not by popular election, became their leaders. The Articles of Confederation and Permanent Union were signed on July 9, 1778, by delegates appointed by State Legislatures, not chosen by the people. And the delegates had not seen fit to make the Articles provide for a central executive. The States retained complete sovereignty, independence and sole jurisdiction. Only a State legislature could levy taxes. The Congress established by the Articles could request but could not command a revenue. The Congress could take no action of any kind unless nine States agreed to it; and rarely did representatives of that many States appear at a session.

Thus the States would give the Congress no means for force or honor. Brazenly England was carrying on the commercial war interrupted by the battle of York Town. Spain was master of the Confederation's southern boundaries, and France of the west. American shipping was a helpless waif on the high seas. Alarm did kindle some indignation, but violent language was the smoke of a dying fire. There was no more strength in the Confederation than in a warm ember at Polly's feet. Somehow power and honor must be given the American nation.

Marshall says, "The question of a continuance of the union or a separation of the states was sometimes discussed; and each side of the question was supported without reproach." "Mr. Madison," he says, "was the enlightened advocate of union and of an efficient federal government." Of his own stand, Marshall says, "The tendency of state politics convinced me . . . no safe or permanent remedy could be found but in a more efficient and better organized general government."

These were the matters that Polly heard spoken of as she moved about among her husband's guests. Suddenly she found that most of the gentlemen had fallen silent. Even Mr. Henry stopped swinging his coattails, and stood quietly before the fire, listening to James Monroe's pleasant voice.

Monroe was repeating the report which he had made to Congress the previous year, concerning a meeting in Annapolis of delegates from Maryland and Virginia. They had gathered there to form a compact for peaceable trade on common waterways, and had eventually agreed upon a reciprocal system of tariff for these two States. They also had agreed to maintain jointly a naval force in the Chesapeake Bay to protect the trade of Maryland and Virginia. This was a pattern that might be followed by the whole Confederation. Indeed Colonel Monroe would go further. "To put the commercial economy of every state entirely under the hands of the union . . . will give the union an authority upon the states respectively which will last with it & hold it together in its present form longer than any principle it now contains will effect."

More and more often the gentlemen met to talk of Colonel Monroe's commercial federation, until, Marshall says, "Measures were taken in Virginia which . . . terminated in a proposition for a general convention to revise the state of the union . . . In the Virginia Assembly, Mr. Madison was the parent of a resolution for appointing members to a general convention to be held at Philadelphia for the purpose of revising the confederation."

"Will you be appointed?" Polly must have asked a little breathlessly. Marshall would have softened his hearty laugh as he told her that only the mightiest in the State would be chosen by the Virginia Assembly, and those would undoubtedly be General Washington, Mr. Madison, Governor Randolph and Mr. Mason of Gunston Hall.

Though Polly may have indulged in a ladylike "Pooh!" she was at heart glad that he would not be away from home when the little daughter was learning to walk. In that portentous month of May, 1787, together Polly and J Marshall watched their children romping in the buttercup-gilded field between their house and the Amblers', while in Philadelphia, delegates from all of the States except Rhode Island, fifty-five in all, met to form a more perfect Union of the American Nation; and thus, in secret wrangling, the

Articles of Confederation were supplanted by a Constitution of United States.

What a storm gathered when the delegates returned home and their document was made public! An uproar came from the people, who seemed obsessed that a strong central government would destroy personal freedom.

When Thomas Jefferson in far away Paris heard of the riots and disorders stirred up by the common people in America who opposed the New Plan of government, he wrote to his friend, Mrs. Abigail Adams, wife of John Adams, United States minister in London, "The spirit of resistance to government is so valuable on certain occasions that I wish it always to be kept alive. It will often be exercised when wrong, but better so than not to be exercised at all. I like a little rebellion now & then. It is like a storm in the atmosphere." That particular storm, however, left the atmosphere thunderous for all of Jefferson's subsequent career. For, "impiously irritating the avenging hand of Heaven," the constitutionalists became the Federalist Party.

A rumble of that thunder came from Pennsylvania, New York and Massachusetts in massive resistance to "consolidated government." Plain people every where were against the Constitution whether they could read it or not. "They believed," said Rufus King, "that some injury is plotted against them—that the system is the production of the rich and ambitious."

Many a man was saying that the New Plan secretly led to the establishment of an aristocracy, even to a king or an emperor. It certainly took the sovereign power from the States, they said. Men were horrified at the idea of a standing army. "Had I an arm like Jove," cried a New Englander, "I would hurl from the globe those villains who would dare to establish in our country a standing army." And a farmer from the same rocky hillside, said, "I cannot see why we need, for the sake of a little meat swallow a great bone, which if it happen to stick in our throats can never be got out."

New York's Governor George Clinton composed a new petition for the Episcopal Litany. "From the insolence of

great men, from the tyranny of the rich, from the unfeeling
rapacity of the excise men and taxgatherers, from the misery
of despotism, from the expense of supporting standing armies, navies placement, sinecures, federal cities, senators,
presidents, and a long train of etceteras, Good Lord, deliver us."

But James Madison had said, "The national government
should be armed with positive and compleat authority in all
cases which require uniformity, such as the regulation of
trade, including the right of taxing both exports & imports,
fixing the terms and forms of naturalization, Etc., Etc."

A man's hand became the size of a great cloud when Jefferson wrote, "Make the States one as to everything connected
with foreign nations, & several as to everything purely domestic."

In September Marshall brought his family home from
Oak Hill just in time for the opening of the General Assembly in which he was the Delegate from Henrico County. At
once he entered the conflict beside those who were urging
ratification of the new Constitution. Opposition was heated
and persistent. The most that the constitutionalists could
achieve in this session was a House resolution to call a State
convention to "freely and amply discuss" the New Plan.

Polly could smile when her husband showed her a clipping from a northern paper describing the Constitution as
"government for the rich, the wise and the good." It did
seem to her that gentlemen were expecting gentlemen to
be elected to office. To her way of thinking the rich, the wise
and the good had been Amblers for a long time. And when
on December third, her second son was born, she touched
his forehead with a protestant finger, once for each of those
virtues, and gave him the name of Jacquelin Ambler, re-
minding Marshall that without an aristocracy the people
perish.

On New Year's Day began the calmly calculated but
deeply emotional contest to elect delegates to the Convention
to discuss the Constitution. Marshall was a candidate. Polly's
lantern never burned more brightly. Proudly she moved
among the pros and cons in her parlour, showing off the

infant she had marked for an aristocrat. As Winter passed, and the hearth was allowed to cool, and windows were opened to garden-sweet air, Polly bloomed so sweetly that her husband made her a present of a mirror.

There was a new hive of bees in the Marshall garden, not quite organized when Polly found it. Feverish droning told that avid business was afoot within the cramped dome. Well, thought Polly, Richmond too was an overcrowded hive this Spring. Now there were nearly a thousand houses strung up and down the hills, with several taverns and hostels. However, tourists and drifters drawn to this small capital of the State were so numerous as to be beyond the capacity of these. There were so many homeless on the streets that gentlemen formed an Amicable Society "with the benevolent object of relieving strangers and wayfarers in distress for whom the law made no provision." The Society was exclusive in membership limiting enrollment to sixty. Marshall was admitted at the second meeting. When private subscription did not meet the cost of this charity he persuaded the Virginia Assembly to authorize a lottery to support the Society.

Arriving with the tourists and drifters in this Spring were also gentlemen of high financial standing in the North. They came to Richmond to make sure that the "right" delegates were elected to the Convention. So important to these capitalists did Virginia's action on the Constitution seem that special postriders were engaged to carry reports and advice between New York and Richmond. "God grant that Virginia may accede," wrote Alexander Hamilton to James Madison. "The example will have a vast influence." For, in that year, Virginia's population was one fifth of the whole Confederation; and her soldiers and statesmen were still the voice of the nation.

Since Christmas the mighty pens of Hamilton and Madison had been at work on the minds of Americans in a series of pamphlets called *The Federalist*. So well did they argue for ratification that by March first six States had more or

less grudgingly ratified the United States Constitution, and
two more were unhappily on the carpet.

Then on a day in May, oak trees sifted yellow pollen
across the shoulders of Marshall's comfortable old coat as
he walked up from the polls in the court yard to inform
waiting Polly that Governor Randolph and himself had been
elected to represent Henrico County in the Convention. She
smiled, thinking that this mightily resembled a vote for the
wise, the good and the someday rich. Otherwise it was a
strange choice; for Henrico County was averse to resigning
its powers to a central government, and Randolph's stand
was doubtful, while Marshall was in outspoken disagree-
ment with his constituency.

Of all the visitors to Richmond this Spring, Polly found
the Morris family of Philadelphia most to her liking. They
were a religious family, with children ranging in age from
seven to nineteen, two of them girls as beautiful and gay as
Polly's younger sisters. James Markham Marshall, busied in
Richmond under Alexander Hamilton's tutelage, looked
more than once at lovely Hester Morris. Robert Morris was
the second richest man in these not-so-very-United States,
and a conservative aristocrat. His wife came from an equally
aristocratic family, the well-to-do Whites from New Jersey.
Robert Morris had been a member of that colonial Congress
to which the Declaration of Independence had been first
read. On that sweltering June day he had voted against
independence again and again. When he found that Congress was determined to accept the document, he signed it,
and thereafter gave himself and his fortune unstintingly to
the revolutionary efforts. He was a wholehearted advocate
of General Washington's policies, and believed that Alexander Hamilton had the cure for the nation's financial confusion.

Robert Morris had a twofold purpose in Richmond. He
had unhesitatingly signed the new Constitution in that
closed meeting in Philadelphia last September, while two
high prerogative Virginians had refused to do so. George
Mason and Edmund Randolph must politely be made to

change their minds. While Morris was bringing these gentlemen to think in line with Washington, he was also engaged on business matters of his own. Young Captain Marshall was his attorney in Virginia. Morris was purchasing literally millions of American acres to sell in Europe. Many of them were in the Virginia District of Kentucky, so numerously inhabited by Marshalls, of whom several were now guests in Polly's house. So positive was Mr. Morris of the virtues of the New Plan that she wondered why the gentlemen bothered to gather in formal meeting. Here was an Episcopalian who could settle the matter.

But on June first as planned the Convention opened in the New Academy building on the side of Shockoe Hill. It was the season of the Jockey Races. Overcrowded homes and taverns were taut with contest, races and government vying for attention. When Patrick Henry spoke, the Convention hall was jammed with spectators. When Pendleton or Monroe spoke, the race track drew a milling crowd. What was seen, heard or wagered was all jumbled together in conversation around the dinner tables of Richmond homes. Marshall's account for Madeira this month was the largest ever recorded so far in his housekeeping. There was a mellow June in Richmond this year of 1788.

The Academy hall was warm and heavy-aired with the scent of fading honeysuckle blossoms, heavy-aired with the depth of feeling that divided the almost equal parties gathered there. For three hot weeks they argued. The antis, who now began to call themselves Republicans, had a hundred things to say, all of them picturesque, romantic, full of human nature. The pros hammered away at practical strength, at orderly commerce. The antis expressed horror that a Constitution should require all States to abide by the terms of a national treaty, or should enforce contracts, or impose taxes to maintain a standing army and a federal city. With stately logic James Madison answered the antis, but his well bred voice was so low that David Robertson, the first shorthand reporter ever to cover a public meeting in America, saved only a garbled account of his words.

The delegates talked and talked, threatening tyranny,

raising ghosts of mythology, or delivering absentee opinions, as Patrick Henry did when he warned the company that Thomas Jefferson counselled Virginians to reject this Constitution.

In a warm and dreary session Marshall seems to have diverted himself with writing poetry of a sort. The scribble is preserved in the library of the College of William and Mary.

> The State's determined Resolution
> Was to discuss the Constitution
> For this the members came together
> Melting with zeal and sultry weather.
> And here to their eternal excuse
> To find its history spared three days.
> The next three days they nobly roam
> Through every region far from home
> Call in the German, Swiss, Italian,
> The Roman robber, Dutch Rapscallion,
> Fellows who Freedom never knew
> To tell us what we ought to do.
> The next three days they kindli dip yea
> Deep in the river Mississippi—

There is a note on the scribble that the poem was presented to Gouverneur Morris who was one of the northern gentlemen present to insure proper action by Virginia. It must have put him in a state of confusion, for he wrote to Alexander Hamilton: "My religion steps in where my understanding falters, and I feel Faith as I lose Confidence. Things will go right but when and how I dare not predict."

It is too bad that the people were at the races when the president of the Convention, the venerable Judge Pendleton, answered those who were afraid to trust a central government. "There is no quarrel," he said, "between government and liberty; the former is the shield and protector of the latter. Who but the people can delegate powers, or have a right to form a government? . . . Government to be effective must have complete powers, a legislature, a judiciary, and executive. No gentleman present would agree to vest these three powers in one body. The proposed government is not a consolidated government. It is on the whole

Courtesy of The Valentine Museum

RICHMOND IN 1810. Engraving by Peter Maverick for William Wirt's Letters of a British Spy.

complexion of it, a government of laws, not men."

There were too few people at the races on the day that Governor Randolph inadvertently spoke of The People as "the herd." He never lived down that slip. Randolph had been won over to support the constitutionalists, if not actually approving the instrument, by June first. Standing for ratification, often huddled together with their backs to a sunny window, were Judge Pendleton, Chancellor Wythe, Captain Marshall, General Light Horse Harry Lee, Governor Edmund Randolph and James Madison. Aligned against them were the noble and popular Patrick Henry, powerful George Mason and beloved Colonel Monroe, who suddenly saw his union of commercial economy in another light.

There was a clause in the New Plan, some said composed by James Madison, which lay upon Congress the duty to establish a national judiciary system, with a Supreme Court at its peak which should have appelate jurisdiction over such inferior courts as Congress from time to time might decree. The executive would appoint the Justices of the high court with the consent of the Senate. These Justices were to hold office during good behavior, and be forever independent of Congress. This court was to preserve the sovereignty of the several States in local rule, police, education and land titles. It was to uphold the central government in interstate and international affairs. It was to sit without a jury.

To Marshall fell the lot of subduing explosive opposition to this clause. After explaining that the present arrangement of State and County courts was so cumbersome that many cases could not be brought before a tribunal before those persons concerned were dead and gone, he argued that the people need have no fear of being oppressed by a national judiciary. "If a law be exercised tyrannically," he asked, "to whom can you trust? Your judiciary. What security have you for justice? Their independence." Then he asked whence the power of all government would be derived, and answered, from the people through their representatives in Congress.

Patrick Henry demanded to know by what right the framers of the Constitution had substituted the words, "We the

people," for, "We the States." He cried, "The ropes and
chains of consolidation . . . are about to convert this country into a powerful and mighty empire." The New Plan,
he said, "is not a Virginian government but an American
government." He foresaw an American chief "who would
come at the head of his army to carry everything before
him." He avowed that this chief would "do what the Chief
Justice would order him to do." After spellbinding hours,
Mr. Henry announced huskily that he had not "spoken
one thousandth part" of what he had on his mind. There
was the matter of slavery on his mind, and the Fairfax land
titles. The word *treaty* always brought before Virginians
that old nobleman who had known when it was time for
him to die.

When Marshall stood up in that hall to commend this
instrument of democratic government for which he was to
give the rest of his life, he was younger than any existing
portrait of him. But we are told that he was tall and ungain-
ly. His abundant black hair was tied losely at the back of
his neck. His complexion was ruddy. His mouth was wide
and always ready to smile. His eyes were beautifully shaped
and very dark and alert. His manner was eager rather than
poised, and his voice was dry and thin as if he had spoken
for years against a wind. When he spoke that June day to
Virginians he laid the premise of his whole career before the
American people. "It is the people that give power and can
take it back," he said. "The virtues and talents of the members of the general government will tend to the security
instead of the destruction of our liberty . . . United we are
strong . . . Divided we fall . . . It requires a superintending
power . . . to call forth the resources of all to protect all . . .
On this government depending on ourselves for its existence I will rest my safety."

When Patrick Henry saw defeat rolling in upon the
antis, he rose in that humid room, and mournfully cried that
he saw "an awful immensity of danger" in the Constitution.
"I see it!" he groaned, "I feel it! I see beings of a higher
order anxious concerning our decision!" And thereupon
was Henry confirmed as a political wizard. For the room

darkened. Thunder rumbled. Lightening like the wrath of Heaven struck the hillside beyond the open windows of the New Academy.

A few hundred yards up the hill in the Marshall dwelling Polly gathered her children under a feather quilt, and wondered whether government would always be a storm. She wished her husband would come along home.

The storm passed. Two days later the Convention voted to ratify the Federal Constitution by a bare majority of ten out of one hundred and sixty ballots, but recommended twenty amendments, reiterating that Virginia retained her sovereignty.

"The parties," wrote Marshall, "had not yet become so bitter as to extinguish the private affections." So when the voting was over everyone shook hands with his opponents and invited pros and cons home to dinner. However this friendliness did not mean acceptance of the New Plan. That very night there was a meeting of the disgruntled ones to plan measures of resistance to a national government. To this meeting Patrick Henry made his last heart-touching speech. He had fought the Constitution, he said, "in the proper place." Now that the contest was settled he would not disturb the peace. He advised the gathering that "as true and faithful republicans, they had all better go home."

Next morning at ten o'clock the Virginia Assembly met for the first time in that classic edifice for which Thomas Jefferson had sent a model from France. Imposing the columned building was, but the Square around it was still the pasture for the town's cows, still streaked by short-cut paths, still the rendezvous of swine escaping from market carts.

On March fourth, 1789, the Constitution ratified by eleven States was declared by Congress assembled in New York to be in effect. General Washington was unanimously chosen by sixty-nine electors to be President of these United States. The States of North Carolina and Rhode Island were not represented as they had not yet ratified the Constitution, and New York had refused to appoint electors. John

Adams of Massachusetts was elected Vice President. When the President set about selecting his cabinet, Thomas Jefferson was made Secretary of State, Alexander Hamilton of Treasury, and General Henry Knox of War. For Attorney General of these United States, Washington chose Colonel Edmund Randolph of Virginia.

The Fourth District Court opened in Fredericksburg in April. At once, fourteen gentlemen who may have dined together the afternoon before, presented themselves as applicants for license to practice as attorneys under the Constitution. These were John Marshall, James Monroe and Bushrod Washington. With them were William Waller Henning who was building a house near the Amblers in the Court End of Town, but nearer the Randolphs. Here too were Richard Brent from Aquia Parish, and his neighbour John Taylor, destined to be among the most charming of Marshall's enemies. Here were John Brooke and Robert Brooke, Andrew Buchanan, Oliver Towles, John Mercer, and John Minor, Charles Simms and John James Moand, makers of history all, but so recently free from old tyranny that they refused to pay the customary license fee of fifteen pounds, a goodly sum in that day.

When the Federal District Court convened in the State Capitol on December seventeenth, 1789, these gentlemen had no cases ready to lay before it, so the court adjourned to meet in Williamsburg in March. On that first District bench sat Judge Spencer Roane, twenty-two years old.

For the post of Attorney General of the State of Virginia Washington selected Marshall, who declined the appointment pleading the pressure of his business. He might have truthfully pleaded the pleasure of a growing law practice and the satisfaction of his situation at home and in society. In all of these he stood in the first rank in the State.

CHAPTER VI

The First Letter

IN THE YEAR 1789 Marshall had purchased the lot in front of his house, and built a white-painted law office, with a chimney opposite the door that opened on the street, and windows over a new garden he was laying out for Polly. On the Ninth Street corner of the lot he began building a brick mansion for Polly as much as possible in the fashion of York dwellings.

While Marshall was again preoccupied with politics as a member of the House of Delegates, another son was born living too brief a time to leave a name. Polly grew more frail, needing more constant attention. Noise "shook her frame." In spite of this Marshall says that in all the relations of life, mother, homemaker and wife she was a model of pleasure and comfort.

Though all day men came and went on the path to Marshall's office, she knew that when the crowded hours were over he would cross the garden to her door. "She was the companion of my retired hours," he says. Softly into her love she would fold the turbulence of his day, so exhilarating to him, so fatiguing to her. Life brought her so few gifts, only her family; while for him there was daily excitment in dawn and sunset, in earth's resurgent seasons, in untrod forest tented in limitless sky, and in the joyful brotherhood of man. Often at the latter edge of night he would slip out of bed and out of doors to watch the black sky turn to silver while clumps of darkness became trees and peaked roofs over friendly dwellings. When in broad daylight Polly would awaken to find him gone, was she indignant? Did she sometimes smile to see a topknot of curls and two tiny hands at the edge of her mattress? And did she reach to pull the little one into his place?

In 1790 the Marshalls moved into their new house. It had the Marshall character, sturdily, honestly, simply designed on the weather side, elegant and charming in its warm and sociable heart. The dining room was of generous

57

dimensions to accommodate Marshall's lawyer dinners which
were becoming the foremost social event for Richmond gentlemen. As life expanded the table was set cater-cornered in
the room to seat thirty-two jocund guests.

These were expensive repasts, cooked in an outside kitchen by a woman bought in Gloucester County, assisted by
a free Negress calling herself Mrs. Bird, who hired herself
out for such affairs. She concocted pastries and blanc mange
in fashionable shapes, such as doves on nests or nested eggs.
As the guests arrived, a bowl of toddy, old Cognac with a
dash of Madeira, was set upon the parlour table. At three
o'clock in the afternoon dinner was announced. The dining
room table, covered with a white damask cloth, held dishes
of mutton with caper sauce, of sora, roast turkey and potato
pudding, with many side dishes and no decoration. When
this main course had been removed and the blanc manges
were eaten, then black Peter and Robin would lift the white
cloth revealing one of red damask ready for bowls of raisins, nuts and oranges while much wine was poured into
stem glasses. As daylight withdrew against tall windows,
candles were lit until the room was aglow with spits of flame
that wagged solemnly in the gusts of laughter.

At one of these dinners Marshall told the story of the
removal of his brother Captain Thomas Marshall, to Kentucky in the usual flat boat trip down the Ohio River. In
three boats a hundred feet apart going fast with the current
the party were using oars vigorously, for they were in hostile Indian country. Suddenly they saw that they were nearly overtaken by savages in canoes. Captain Marshall ordered
the men from the last boat into the next in line and loosed
the last craft as a decoy. He, himself, with a red bandanna
around his head, stood up in the stern of the second boat
manning the rudder. But the Indians were following that
red bandanna, and Captain Thomas Marshall expeditiously
drew the first boat alongside and piled all persons aboard,
letting the second boat loose in the path of the enemy.
This satisfied the Indian and the white travellers escaped.
Do you know why? In the second craft were fat cows and

the fine Oak Hill horses. There will be some very good horses bred in the wilds of Ohio.

During these dinners for gentlemen only, Polly retired to her mother's house. When the guests had departed, or all but two or three gone, Marshall would fetch her home, closely guiding her through the night-covered garden.

The Account Book in the Spring of 1791 tells of a new carpet for the house, and of a trousseau for Lucy Marshall. On May twenty-first down the lovely stairway, with her mittened hand on the turned cherry rail, came the first bride in the Marshall mansion. White roses decorated the drawing room for the wedding of Lucy Marshall and John Ambler of Jamestown and The Cottage. The Reverend Mr. Buchanan performed the ceremony. If there was music afterwards in the garden it was made by a free Negro violinist, Si Gilbert, onetime servant of Lord Botetourt, who performed in a brown wig with side curls, and a costume of such elegance that it was suspected of being one of fifty suits named in the nobleman's will.

This was John Ambler's second marriage. His first wife, Frances Armistead, had been mistress of the ancient Ambler mansion on Jamestown island only a short time when she died leaving him two small children. To this same swamp-ringed estate he took Lucy Marshall, and in that humid atmosphere a year later her son was born and named Thomas.

All of this time growing ever stronger in Marshall's mind was the vision of a national government of integrity, equitable justice and peace. Growing ever stronger against him was the Republican party, espousing the supreme power of State legislatures, opposing big business, national funding of State debts and National Banks, opposing freehold suffrage and neutrality, scorning things English and glorifying things French from fashions to policies.

Richmond society was becoming increasingly Republican and slightly French. The young Marshalls had many friends of both persuasions. Though Marshall enjoyed French associates and literature, he was innately British, and Polly was the foil every good wife should be. If he warned the company that, "Our independence [is] brought into real

danger by the overgrown inordinate influence of France,"
she would have piously corrected him. Had not France
been our ally, and was not Britain still our enemy, arrogant-
ly, brutally seizing American vessels trading with France,
lifting their cargoes and impressing their crews to man
British warships? Had a single slave stolen by the British
army been paid for? Was not England now threatening
arbitrarily to draw a new boundary line between the States
and Canada without our agreement?

Marshall could smile at her "soft and gentle temper" and
"real firmness" which he says few females possessed in equal
measure. But he could gently explain that the Americans
also were not too careful of the terms of the treaty.

He might smile as he left her, but when he opened the
door of his office his smile would fade, for he must practice
law amid public anger that boiled up everywhere against
the terms of the Treaty of Peace, against anything that hung
inherited liabilities upon new-won freedoms. Legal action
must cut fresh roads haunted by liberty, a wraith of ever-
changing shape. It seemed to young lawyer Marshall that
there was an "organized system" at work to destroy the only
courts the Nation possessed.

Above the warmth and grace of life in the new mansion
hung clouds of dangerous dissension. New England was
crying for secession from a central government. Southern
States were boldly talking of the right of State legislatures
to amend the "repugnant" clauses of the untried Constitution. Peace seemed a myth and justice a pliant word easily
molded to fit a man's purpose.

In February of 1792 a fourth son was born to the Marshalls. In the following summer, that crucial season for infant health, Marshall wrote the first letter to "My Dearest
Polly," a letter which has never been seen since she read it.
It was preserved in part for us when Marshall wrote to his
beloved Joseph Story many years later.

"You ask," he wrote, "if Mrs. Marshall and myself have
ever lost a child. We have lost four, three of them bidding
fairer for life and health than any who have survived them.
One, a daughter about six or seven . . . was one of the most

fascinating children I ever saw. She was followed within a fortnight by a brother whose death was attended by a circumstance we can never forget.

"When the child was supposed to be dying I tore the distracted mother from the bedside. We soon afterwards heard a voice in the room which we considered as indicating the death of the infant. We believed him to be dead. I went into the room and found him still breathing. I returned and as the pang of his death had been felt by his mother and I was confident he must die, I concealed his being alive and prevailed on her to take refuge with her mother who lived next door across an open square from her.

"The child lived two days during which I was agonized with its condition and with the occasional hope, though the case was desperate, that I might enrapture his mother with the intelligence of his restoration to us. After the event had taken place his mother could not bear to return to the house she had left and remained with her mother a fortnight.

"Then I addressed to her a letter in verse in which our mutual loss was deplored, our lost children spoken of with the parental feeling which belonged to the occasion, her affection for those who survived appealed to, and her religious confidence in the wisdom and goodness of Providence excited. The letter closed with a pressing invitation to return to me and her children."

Did Marshall send this letter by his favorite servant, Robin, and then from Polly's window watch across the open field until the side door of the Ambler mansion was opened to Robin's knock? Did he see the slight figure of Dearest Polly on the threshold reading the letter, and then without a backward glance at her mother, run down the steps and across the field, crumpling a piece of paper as she ran to the only comfort of her life? She could not have seen that his his head was bowed and his heart lifted in mute "Thank God."

A postscript to the letter to Joseph Story says, "This letter has been delayed for the purpose of sending you a copy of what I wrote. But 'tis lost." The Account Book includes under the date of August 1792, "Coffins for my son & daughter, 9.2."

CHAPTER VII

General Marshall

THE SEASON of tears passed, and the time for fires on new hearths returned a glow to life in the Marshall mansion. The family were living handsomely now, except for his manner of dress which often caused Polly to look upon her husband with chilling disfavor. It was said that his knee buckles, though made of silver, had a way of coming loose, a mishap that he never noticed until Polly reprimanded him. And then the mud on his shoes! He was too preoccupied with the faces of men to notice how the streets clung to his feet. Eventually he formed a habit of leaving the offending shoes on the porch of the handsome house.

But that was not only Richmond mud on the steps behind him. Some of it came from Fairfax lands. Around the fireplace in the white-painted office where Robin kept logs blazing in the Winter of 1793, four eager Americans were organizing a syndicate to purchase a large part of that ancient manorial grant that covered Virginia between the Potomac and Rappahannock Rivers. John Marshall, his brother James Markham Marshall, their brother-in-law, Rawleigh Colston, and Governor Henry Lee, were composing a contract of purchase to offer the Reverend Denny Martin Fairfax in May, when the Fairfax wilderness would be adrift in dogwood bloom. They offered fourteen thousand pounds sterling. James Markham Marshall was well on his way to wealth as European commercial agent for the cities of Charleston, New York and Boston. Rawleigh Colston, who had used his inherited estate to raise and equip a regiment for the Revolutionary Army had recouped a fortune in the West Indies during the war. John Marshall had financial courage and a lucrative law practice. To contribute to the corporate enterprise Light Horse Harry had a store of expansive dreams.

It would take, however, more than money and dreams to acquire a deed to Fairfax lands. It would take a strict adherence to the terms of the Treaty of Peace between Britain and

America. In the year 1789 the State of Virginia, acting under her separate sequestration laws, had granted to a wealthy Shenandoah Valley farmer, David Hunter, seven hundred and eighty-eight acres of Fairfax land, which had already been purchased, or otherwise acquired, by settlers from Denny Fairfax. In a case entitled Timothy Trititle vs Lessee of David Hunter these settlers brought suit in ejectment against Hunter. In April of 1791 the Superior Court of Shenandoah held at Winchester upheld Trititle on the grounds of the terms of the Treaty of Peace. But general sentiment in Piedmont Virginia for extinguishing entirely the Fairfax title encouraged Hunter's lessees to carry the suit to the Virginia Court of Appeals, where it was pending while the Marshall syndicate was organizing. Now these gentlemen must move expeditiously, promptness being the arrow of success when laws were like birds on the wing breaking out of clouds of "no precedent."

When they had talked enough of business the syndicate would repair to Polly's parlour where glasses of Madeira, a-sparkle with firelight, awaited them. Other brothers would be there, for Marshalls had an affinity for each other's company, and the presence of traveller James would be the magnet for a family conclave. Charles, practicing law in Warrenton, would have come over frozen roads that traversed the Fairfax forest. His twin, William, who had recently completed a fine house on Church Hill for his first wife, would have ridden down into the frost-riven Valley and up the lane that crossed Capitol Square, to hear what James had to tell of the foreign world.

James would tell them of his recent round of visits to the courts of Europe on a mission for President Washington, pleading for the release of Marquis de Lafayette from some secret prison where he had been thrown for defending the French king against the furious passions of liberty, equality and fraternity. The mission was not successful. Only royal France had been America's friend.

Lafayette was not the only prisoner of the French of whom the Marshalls spoke. Lewis, seventh of the Marshall brothers, lay in a Paris gaol. From medical school in Edinburgh, Lewis Marshall had gone to France with a group of students to bask in the excitement of a people engaged in overthrowing an ancient monarchy. The students had been tempted to throw a few stones during the storming of the Bastille, and had stood by at the murder of the Swiss Guard. Unprotesting they had watched many atrocities committed. In the first turn about of mob passion they were thrown into prison and condemned to death. The duplicity—here James tossed imaginary gold—of a gaoler had saved Lewis' life, but had not affected his release.

James' account of blood-drenched free Paris made Polly leave the room to walk through her mansion, touching its beauties with a trembling hand. As she wandered about, she could still hear those dry Marshall voices discussing the war which seemed to engulf all Europe, and to endanger America's embryo trade. England, they were saying, had sent abroad an order to her cruisers "to stop all vessels loaded wholly or in part with corn, flour, or meal, bound to any port in France." And France had retaliated with an order to her ships of war and privateers to "stop and bring into the ports of the republic, such neutral vessels as are loaded . . . with provisions belonging to neutrals and destined for enemy ports." Both countries were seizing American merchantmen and impressing into their own navies such seamen as they chose to take, often leaving not enough crew to bring the captured vessel into port.

The brothers talked of wishing for peace and fearing war when the Union was not ready for war. They said that some of the people seemed convinced that Great Britain was the natural enemy of America, while they loved France more than she deserved. They said that Secretary of State Jefferson and President Washington, two gentlemen by nature autocratic, were pulling further and further apart in foreign and internal policies. They said that the Secretary had proffered his resignation, but upon the President's request he would defer his departure from the Government until the last of the year. Lastly as she mounted the stairs Polly heard the brothers laughing at her husband for serving Spanish instead of French wine at the dinner he had recently given in

honor of the Duke de la Rochefoucauld. There were several
of their French friends present at this affair. They did not
seem to Polly such stuff as pirates are made of. At the turn
of the stair she paused to glance back at those tall, slow-spo-
ken men whose minds, it seemed to her, were the Atlas
upon whose shoulders rested the New World. It made her
weary to think of such a burden.

The Secretary of State who followed Jefferson in office
in January of 1794 was the charming Edmund Randolph.
But no social graces could quiet the restlessness of the people under the President's efforts to maintain an even-handed
peace, when England seemed bent on war and France
seemed bent on piracy.

In April, 1794 so many vexations and spoilations had been
committed on American merchantmen by British ships, and
so many terms of the Treaty were being ignored, that President Washington, noting "a serious aspect of our affairs with
Great Britain," announced that he thought it proper, "in an
effort to pursue peace with unremitted zeal," to send John
Jay, Chief Justice of the Supreme Court of the United States,
as envoy extraordinary to his Britannic majesty "to vindicate
our rights with firmness and to cultivate peace with sincer-
ity."

From people and press went up a great protest against
this mission. To deal with Britain was "a pusillanimous surrender" of American honor, and an "insidious injury to
France." One Virginia Democratic Society cried, "Let us
unite with France and stand or fall together." England was
pictured as a destroyer of freedom wherever her flag flew,
and France as a liberty-capped head rising above the wreck-
age of tyranny.

Together the press and the Summer waxed hot. Under
old trees at Oak Hill Polly was more content to wave the papers at insects that ventured near than to read. For Marshall
says, "The artillery of the press was played with increasing
fury" on supporters of neutrality. "Language," he says, "will
scarcely afford terms of greater outrage than were employed
against those who sought to stem the torrent of public opinion, and to moderate the rage of the moment." And Mar-

shall was one of those. Every hesitant peep into newspapers stung Polly with opposition to her husband's ideas. How could they? Or should she advise him to change his mind? Uncertainty, too, shook her frame.

The press abuse that disturbed Polly was, however, for Marshall a small item in an ample life. His law practice was now foremost in the Virginia Bar. "He was," wrote one who remembered, "what is called a common law lawyer in the best and noblest acceptation of that term." But in the many cases he argued before the Richmond Chancery Court and the Virginia Court of Appeals, he lost almost as often as he won the verdict. And so, until each case was decided, ambition pricked Polly's nerves anxiously. She found more satisfaction in his Masonic activities, secret though they were. As Grand Master of Masons in Virginia, in solemn and colorful rites he laid cornerstones while high prerogative gentlemen looked on. All of the best citizens of Virginia, she smugly observed, were Masons. Several of them wore the beautiful Past Commander's Jewel. She would certainly make her husband wear his best coat when he had the Jewel to hang around his neck. Or could she?

She was pleased when Captain Marshall became Brigadier General, elected to that office by the Virginia Militia. The blue and buff uniform was becoming to him, if he just would brush his hair more carefully. Very handsome dark hair.

In July of 1793, Marshall donned that uniform and set out at the head of a force of infantry, artillery and cavalry to enforce that neutrality for which he stood with the President. A French vessel, berthed at Smithfield, was fitting out as a privateer to harass British shipping and that of other nations who would trade with Britain. The County's commanding officers, says Marshall, "seemed not to have become sufficiently impressed with the Sovereignty of the law." The County militia were obstructing the United States marshal in the performance of his duty to hold the French vessel. Governor Lee's order to the new Brigadier General to march and prevent this nullification of Federal decree gave the General latitude in strategy and tactics.

"The executive know," Lee had written, "that in your hands
the dignity and rights of the Commonwealth will ever be
safe, and they are also sure that prudence, affection to our
deluded citizens, and a marked obedience to the law . . .
will equally characterize every step of your proceedure." In
"frequent conversations with individuals," Marshall says,
he won that war. The Virginia Militia had a pleasant outing
down the river, and were ordered home before ever they
saw the battlefield, well impressed with their General's
power of persuasion. No "Dearest Polly" letter was written
from Smithfield, for Marshall's horse would have outdis-
tanced the mail in arriving at Polly's door.

In February across stormy seas to a stormy welcome
came Justice Jay from England with a so-called Treaty of
Amity, Commerce and Navigation between Great Britain
and the United States. But the amity was one-sided. The
terms gave England all that Americans had fought for, except separation and that basic ingredient of progress, peace.
It reaffirmed that term of the earlier treaty which established Britishers' titles to American lands.

Then "that great party which denominated itself The
People," as Marshall calls them, rose in garrulous indignation which became increasingly directed toward President
Washington personally and his friends. A "malignant and
furious spirit . . . infused itself into the publications of the
day," says Marshall.

An Englishman who observed this situation wrote, "It is
the spirit of dissatisfaction which forms a leading trait in
the character of the Americans as a people, which produces
this malevolence; if their public affairs were regulated by a
person sent from Heaven, I firmly believe his acts, instead
of meeting with universal approbation, would by many be
considered as deceitful and flagitious."

"No consideration," says Marshall, "appears to have had
more influence than the apprehension that the amicable arrangements made with Great Britain, would seriously affect
the future relations of the United States with France."

"The predetermined hostility," Marshall continues, "to
the Treaty increased in activity as the period for deciding its

fate approached," not against particular merits or demerits of its terms "because they were unknown, but on the general question of reconciliation with England." Those dissidents declared that "the friends of the administration were an aristocratic and corrupt faction, who, from a desire to introduce monarchy, were hostile to France and under the influence of Britain," and so they "rushed impetuously" to condemn the Treaty "without weighing the reasons which induced it and in many instances without reading it."

The wrath of the people boiled over in public meetings loud in condemnation of the President. From Kentucky came a resolution branding the Treaty as "shameful to the American name." And in Virginia a toast was drunk which wished "a speedy death to General Washington." It was there in Kentucky that James Markham Marshall and James Brown, afterwards minister to France, had hot words about the President which caused these gentlemen to meet at dawn with pistols.

Conversations in Richmond produced the hottest words of all. The President wrote to that mutual friend of his and the Marshalls, Alexander Hamilton, that the citizens of Richmond "have out done all that has gone before them. They have cried against the Treaty as a mad dog." But, says Marshall, "many intelligent men stood aloof, while the most intemperate assume, as usual, the name of the people."

For a time Marshall stood aloof. All of these tumultuous weeks Polly watched him suffering strange spells of silence. If she asked him what he might be thinking he looked up and smiled, then got up from his chair by the fire and went out to sit alone on a bench in her garden, even though the air was cold and raw. There he sat pondering some problem, until passers-by paused to repeat Polly's question, What might be the thoughts that needed to be kept chilled? That always brought a quick smile from the General and a merry answer. Afterwards the sunshine seemed cozier and the shadows moved more contentedly across the sidewalk.

In Marshall's mind the conviction was growing that Jus-

tice Jay had procured the best terms Britain would make
with a nation which could show no strength. John Quincy
Adams had written from London, "War with Great Britain must be total destruction to the commerce of our country; for there is no power on earth that can contend with
the existing naval British force." Also Adams wrote, "The
maritime law of nations recognized in Great Britain is all
comprised in one line of a popular song, 'Rule, Britannia!
Britannia, rule the waves.' "

Weaving the state of the nation into a pattern with the
state of her adversaries, Marshall came to the conclusion
that it was in the best interests of the States to accept the
Treaty. "Its chief merit . . . ," he says, "consisted in its
tendency to produce future amicable dispositions and friendly intercourse." He saw that war with any nation now
would wreck the magnificent financial system so strenuously
achieved for the federal government by Alexander Hamilton.

In March the President laid the Treaty before the Senate, and by a majority of only ten votes he was "advised" to
ratify it. Because on this occasion the Senate sat behind
closed doors, the very words that had fired the Revolution
were flung across the country, "'Tis most unconstitution-
ably done!" And Polly heard an echo of tides against York's
cliffs.

In Philadelphia, Robert Morris had only one ear to lend
to the voice of the people. The other was full of wedding
plans and demands. For in a fine affair on April ninth, his
daughter Hester became the bride of James Markham Marshall.

When Summer lay like a moist blanket over Virginia,
Thomas Jefferson sat on his mountain top writing to a fascinating Anglo-Italian lady whom he had known in Paris:
"While my countrymen are making a great buzz over the
Jay Treaty . . . I am eating the peaches, grapes & figs of
my own garden." A little later from the same cool spot he
wrote that Virginians were "never more unanimous" than
in their opposition to the administration and the Treaty.
Only "4 or 5 individuals of Richmond, distinguished by

their talents as by their devotion to the sacred acts of the government, & the town of Alexandria," would Jefferson admit were supporters of the President. Of those "4 or 5," he called Marshall the leader.

For Polly in this Summer there were no mountain top breezes. Another baby was on the way, and she was afraid to be away from Drs. Foushee and McClurg, though both of them were outspoken political enemies of her husband.

"In the afternoon of the 11th of August," Marshall says, "the President arrived in Philadelphia; and on the next day, the question respecting the immediate ratification of the treaty was brought before the cabinet." Only Secretary of State Randolph voted against it, and confirmation of the treaty was secured. Though ratification was a matter for Cabinet and Senate, implementation was a matter for the people's pocketbook, of which the strings were held by Congress.

On the thirty-first of August Marshall sat on the porch beside Polly, and with a chuckle that made her think he had won high stakes, laid a letter in her lap. She smiled when she saw that it was from the President. She read a pleasant and friendly message to her husband that offered him the post of Attorney General of the United States, suggesting that with the office there was the prospect of a lucrative law practice in the city of Philadelphia. Silently for a minute she gazed at the message, then laughed, for she had seen her husband's smile. Like dolls in the peep show, they shook their heads, and laughed again. The Richmond mansion surrounded by family and friends was the stick for their candle.

Before the long twilight was pierced by candlelight Marshall had replied to his good friend at Mt. Vernon. "I had the honor of receiving a few minutes past your letter . . . The business I have undertaken to complete in Richmond, forbids me to change my situation tho for one infinitely more eligible." He tells General Washington that the offer gave him "real pride & gratification . . . at the favorable opinion it indicates." And he promises to tell no one that he declined such an offer.

On September seventeenth another daughter was born
to the Marshalls and promptly named Mary. While the infant was still a bundle of rosy wonder the first bride in
Polly's house, Lucy Marshall Ambler, died in that Jamestown mansion surrounded with cypress swamps, and was
buried in the graveyard with only the ruins of a church to
stand watch.

J Marshall wrote this heartrending information to his
father in far away Kentucky. Colonel Marshall replied,
"The death of our Lucy is a heavy affliction. . . . But why
am I describing my affliction to you who must have felt the
same more than once in all of its bitterness."

Rarely could Marshall ease that bitterness in the hope-
fulness of his nursery. For unexpectedly, in spite of his un-
popular loyalties, he was again elected to represent Richmond in the House of Delegates, and in the Fall term of
the Court of Appeals he had at least eleven cases to argue.

When a case was lost Polly wondered if the judge might
have been inattentive that day, or had her husband failed to
follow her advice? But lose or win, some neighbour would
drop by and tell her that Marshall had made a mighty
good statement of law. In fact, one of those losing days she
was told how, after court adjourned to the shade of trees in
the Capitol Square, the judge had laughingly declared that
Marshall's lucid exposition of the law involved had won the
case for his opponent. Polly did not find this an amusing
story.

When the Virginia Assembly convened in the Fall the
House of Delegates proceeded at once to a resolution commending the Senators from Virginia for voting against the
Treaty, which action was in effect a censure of the President by the legislature of his own State.

All the night following that resolution, Polly watched
shadows of gentlemen moving across the candlelight in the
office window. Next morning at breakfast Marshall's black
eyes were less merry, but she could see that he was nonetheless determined to brighten the State's affection for its greatest son. At dinner time she must have heard that those
gentlemen who had visited late in the office were prompt

upon the floor of the House of Delegates to add to yesterday's Resolution an assurance of the State's confidence in the President for his "great abilities, wisdom and integrity." At once there was bitter wrangling over the word "wisdom." Not until that term had been removed did the House agree to the Resolution. The confidence expressed was so dispirited that it was barely a tip of the hat to the soldier-statesman who had carried the infant States across the first raging torrent of their common history.

Infant States and infant Marshalls! How mixed up Polly's life was! The trouble was that she could not pour all of her mind at once into one department and then another as she poured tallow into candle molds. Standing by the kitchen table measuring tallow and wax to exactly the proper proportions half of her mind was on that Christian gentleman, Colonel Edmund Randolph, for a while Secretary of State.

In this country where freedom of opinion had but recently been set rampant, and love of liberty had not yet become love of America, loyalty was as fluid as the warm liquid she was pouring. It happened occasionally that gentlemen in high places under-measured the ingredients of patriotism. Thus Secretary of State Randolph may have poured too much national gratitude and not enough discretion into a chat with the French agent Fauchet, who twisted the Secretary's words, and made sure the American government would have a French version of Mr. Randolph's pleasantries. The Secretary was relieved of his post by the President. There were those who said that President Washington had acted too hastily, as Polly did at this moment, spilling wax on her apron.

Marshall says that as mistress of a household, Polly was a model. Three hours a day she spent supervising her servants, with skirts pinned up to escape the dust of labor, moving from nursery to laundry to kitchen. The ladies of Richmond were modernizing their kitchens with stoves called "rangers" built into the old open hearths. It required much patient instruction by Polly to persuade the cook bought in Gloucester to use the contraption.

The duty of filling the larder, however, did not fall to

Polly. In Richmond marketing was considered a manly art, and the valleyed market stalls no place for a lady. Daily the gentlemen of the town, basket on arm, gathered among the farmers by Shockoe Creek, and then in the storehouses down Main Street, bringing home the best of country produce, imported delicacies and gossip.

Of yet another duty were the ladies of Virginia relieved. They had no more voice in government than the slaves in their household or the free Negro on the streets.

CHAPTER VIII

The Second Letter

IN 1796 no one travelled in Winter except on urgent business. The post stage however, plodded on over mud holes and frozen ruts three times a week between Richmond and the seat of government in Philadelphia, taking, if the passengers were lucky, five days and five nights each way, but more often a precarious week. For though it was the postmaster's order that the mails go forward day and night, the roads were such that sometimes not four miles an hour could be made. There were strange split detours around huge trees, the coachman taking whichever side seemed less likely to spill his passengers. Often male passengers were ordered out to chop down saplings to widen the road where a mud hole had usurped the right of way, or to right the coach that had gone over on its side when the driver defied the laws of gravity.

The mail bag was tucked somewhere among the baggage on the coach, but the coachman gave his passengers preference when it came to a matter of time or protection from weather. When the order was given to lighten load as frequently happened at an ominous stretch, the mail bag, having no one personally interested, was often left under a bush beside the way. For travellers the journey was unspeakably comfortless. For those whose eager humanity could transcend these exigencies there was always the pleasure of fellow travellers, as Marshall found when he took the stage for Philadelphia on urgent business just past the middle of January. His first letter home got safely through to Polly.

It was addressed to "Mrs. Mary W. Marshall," in the manner of that day which attached a wife's first and middle names to her husband's obediently forsaking her father's. Polly had to send to the postoffice for the letter and pay the postage. It cost her twenty cents which must be in specie, the postoffice being skittish of State currency. Thus J Marshall writes:

Philadelphia Feby 3^d 96

My Dearest Polly

After a journey which wou'd have been beyond measure tedious but for the agreeable company with which I came I am at length safe at this place. My business wou'd be speedily determined if Mr. Campbell wou'd come on. We wait only for him to enter on the cases concerning British debts. My own cause I greatly fear will not be taken up & I shall be under the very disagreeable necessity of returning without any decision. It is a cruel thing on me to be kept here extremely against my inclination because Mr. Campbell will not come on.

I have not yet heard from my beloved wife & children. You ought not to keep me in any suspense about you. I was at the play last night & very much admir'd Mrs. Marshall who is the favorite of the town but with all her good qualities she does not equal our Mrs. Bignal.

No information has yet been receiv'd of the arrival of the vessel which carried my brother & his wife. We expect every day to receive intelligence from them.

Kiss our children & especially our sweet little Poll for me & tell Tom I expect him to attend to his brother & to write to me. I count on Jaquelin's great improvement before my return

I am my dearest Polly your affectionate

J Marshall

Polly could hardly have found this a love letter. Line for line he had written more about "our children" than any other person or subject. He would have her kiss them for him, but never does he bribe them. "I count on him," he writes, and "I expect of him." Tom was twelve years old, Jaquelin nine, and little Poll still in a cradle rocked by coloured Mammy Venus.

She could notice too that Marshall had time to attend the theatre of which he could be considered a connoisseur; for Richmond was used to the best of that art. Well could he judge between "our Mrs. Bignal" and Philadelphia's pride. Ann West Bignal was young, pretty and a sweet singer. Her parents, Mr. and Mrs. John Wade West, with her husband, John Bignal, managed a clever company of over thirty actors which had the reputation of being superior in the American theatrical business, travelling by water between the cities of the eastern seaboard with a full complement of scenery, scene designer, dancers and musicians. Sometimes

Mrs. West's brother, Mathew Sully was featured as a "high tumbler." They played Sheridan and Shakespeare besides much trivial tragedy and merriment. At this time Mrs. West owned the New Academy building in Richmond. Her troupe spent the greater part of their time in Virginia, finding these audiences so compatible that they eventually named themselves the Virginia Company.

No wonder that Marshall was in high spirits in Philadelphia, for he was here to make his first appearance before the Supreme Court of the United States in this capital which was staunchly Federalist in sentiment and society. Marshall says that he was delighted with the gentlemen from New England who moved in that society and in Congress this session. He says that he was particularly intimate with Fisher Ames from Massachusetts, and that he was also received with a degree of kindness which he had not anticipated by George Cabot, Samuel Dexter and Theodore Sedgewick of the same State, and by Peleg Wadsworth of Connecticut and Rufus King of New York. While Marshall was not misled into thinking these Congressmen sought him for his personal charm rather than for his influence in the Southern States, he enjoyed them greatly, being in accord with their affection and honor for President Washington.

Here when Washington's coach-and-four rolled through the streets with outriders in handsome uniforms, the people stood hat in hand as he passed. And when the President attended the theatre, the chief actor stepped down from the stage to meet him at the entrance and escort him to a box decorated with the presidential shield which was actually the Washington Coat of Arms.

And that Philadelphia theatre building! The President's love of the stage had overbalanced the ubiquitous Quaker conscience so far that a beautiful New Chesnut Street Theatre had been constructed to house a stage of thirty feet and an audience of two thousand. Everything was the best, largest and handsomest, for it had been financed in the American spirit by the four richest gentlemen in the country, Robert Morris, William Bingham, Charles Biddle and

John Vaughn. The best scenery artist in England had been imported for backdrops. Circles of candles hung from the ceiling to light The People on backless benches in the pit, and to illuminate high society ensconced in three tiers of luxurious boxes.

This theatre had been ready for performers in 1793, but due to an epidemic of yellow fever was not opened until a year later. The Quakers explained this as God's punishment on the city for importing "children of iniquity," meaning distinguished players brought from England by Messrs. Wignal & Reinagle of Philadelphia.

"My brother and his wife" mentioned in Marshall's letter to Polly were James Markham Marshall and his wife, Hester Morris. Robert Morris had commissioned his son-in-law to negotiate with Dutch bankers for a loan on the vast Morris holdings in America so that he might advance monies to the Marshall syndicate for a down payment on Fairfax lands. This couple were so often abroad that two of their children were born on warships anchored in the Thames River.

Polly knew Mr. Campbell. He was one of that company of lawyers who dined and wined in her house. She knew him for a slightly conceited polished gentleman, a conventional lawyer, but a political radical to her way of thinking. The case that he and Marshall must argue before the Supreme Court was Ware *vs* Hylton, involving large sums due British merchants by former colonists. Associated with Patrick Henry and James Innis, Marshall and Campbell had defended the former colonists in the Federal District Court in Richmond, Justices Jay and Iredell, and Judge Griffen on the bench. John Wickham and John Baker of Richmond represented the British merchant. The case hung on the question: Can a national treaty of peace abrogate a State law?

Arguing before the court in Richmond, Marshall used a phrase which was to rise like a squawking crow above some of his weightiest opinions later on. He rebuked "those who wished to impair the sovereignty of Virginia." He and his associates won the verdict in this court with arguments so brilliant that Justice Iredell said they banished fatigue, warmed the heart and instructed the understanding. In appealing to the Supreme Court the Americans retained only Marshall and Campbell, and this Court reversed the Virginia Court, Justice Iredell, this time concurring.

Polly, sitting before her fire, could read her letter and smile, thinking of these before the elegance of the High Court, Mr. Campbell neatly dressed, suave, confident, often sarcastic; her husband, unfashionable, slow to speak, alert to humanity, leading the mind from question to certainty, offering the answer as cooperation rather than fiat.

Young William Wirt, a Richmond lawyer visiting Philadelphia, was a spectator in the Supreme Court. He arrived home before Marshall, and may have stopped by to tell Polly about it, for he was a favorite of the Marshalls, he says. He says that Alexander Campbell was one "whose voice had all the softness and melody of a harp, whose mind was an orchard and flower garden loaded with the best fruits and smiling in gay coloured bloom of spring, whose delivery, action and manner were perfectly Ciceronian," and that "his quiver was filled with polished arrows of finest points, and were launched with Apollonian skill and grace," and that before this court Campbell "played off his Apollonian airs, but they were lost. Marshall spoke as he always does to the judgement merely, and for the simple purpose of convincing. Marshall was justly pronounced one of the greatest men of the country. He was followed by crowds, looked upon and courted with every evidence of admiration and respect for the powers of his mind. Campbell was neglected and came home disgusted."

Campbell's departure may have been the cause of Marshall's "own case" being delayed. For this was the case of Hunter *vs* Fairfax's Devisee in which Campbell was counsel for Hunter and Marshall for Fairfax. In the Virginia Court of Appeals Attorney General Charles Lee had explained that the issue was "whether the defendent in error being an alien can take and hold land by devise. And it will be contended that his title is completely protected by the Treaty of Peace." The decision of the Virginia Court on April

twenty-fourth, 1794, upheld the Shenandoah Court, Judges
Spencer Roane, Fleming, Lyons and Carrington concurring.
Hunter appealed to the Supreme Court of the United States,
and asked Alexander Hamilton to act as his counsel there,
offering him four hundred dollars to be raised to one thous-
and if he should win a reversal. Hamilton declined, and
Hunter had to be content with Ciceronian Campbell.

Back at home in March, Marshall had a story to tell
Polly and their company around the dinner table. It seems
that James Monroe, now United States minister to France,
had given too "free scope to the genuine feelings of his
heart" which under the influence of Jefferson, the Marshalls
believed, had become definitely pro-French and anti-Wash-
ington. So "fervent were the sentiments expressed" by Monroe on a public occasion in Paris that the French government decreed that flags of the United States and France
should hang together in a place of honor. So Monroe had
presented the French government with an American flag,
again expressing the affection of the *people* of the United
States for the *people* of France. Thus he assumed the French
attitude, for each French minister to the United States
these days was addressing himself to the American people
behind the back of the executive. Monroe's compliment had
been returned. The new French minister, M. Adet, had
arrived in the United States with official letters addressed
not to the President or to the State Department, but to the
Congress. Also he brought a French flag to present to the
States. M. Adet landed in Charleston and travelled around
the country for some weeks, keeping both the flag and papers
until Congress should meet. Before that body in January,
with a mouthful of fine soft words behind which anyone
could hear the groans of American sailors in French pris-
ons, M. Adet presented the flag to the representatives of
the people, complimenting *them* on their victory over tyranny. Then President Washington, who had won that victory, rose from his throne in the hall of the House of Representatives, and in tones of such icy dignity that one looked
to see if a window had blown open, said, "*Born*, sir, in a land
of liberty . . . my best wishes are irresistibly attracted when-

ever, in any country I see an oppressed nation unfurl the banners of freedom." The President forthwith ordered the flag deposited in the archives of the country, and the papers delivered to the State Department.

Marshall says that Monroe was recalled from France by the President for failing to fulfill an obligation to the country which he represented, then gently explains that Monroe had "misconceived the views of the administration."

With lilacs in bud, and jonquils parading beside the garden paths, the Jay Treaty seemed to Polly as uninteresting as last Winter's overshoes. But gentlemen beginning to move their chairs out to Richmond's porches discussed the treaty as vehemently as ever. Word went around that a majority in Congress blocked every resolution to appropriate funds for its implementation. "The whole country," says Marshall, "was agitated; meetings were again held throughout the United States; and the strength of the parties was once more tried."

Male citizens could argue and vilify in hired halls, and then go home to dinner with each other. But the females who got the vilification second hand suffered palpitating, sleepless nights listening to the sounds of a small town after dark, a dog barking, a restless cow-bell, the cry of the night watchman, until roosters called back yesterday's sun.

A public meeting in Richmond was contrived by Marshall and Polly's brother-in-law, Colonel Edward Carrington. The vigilant press labeled it "Federalist," but in truth Marshall and Colonel Carrington had gone beyond the mere voters, inviting all the inhabitants of the countryside, whether freeholders or not, to attend and express their support of President Washington in a petition to Congress to appropriate funds for implementing the Jay Treaty. It was public opinion they wanted, not votes, which in that day were separate powers.

So strong was feeling against the treaty that Marshall was uncertain of having a crowd until the hour for the meeting arrived. Then on an April day, standing at the door of the hall he watched a crowd of over four hundred persons converge from up hill and down hill, riding or walking in companies of twos and threes, greeting each other, and

chatting as casually as if they were bent on a picnic, not on
forging a political weapon. He wondered if they could be
persuaded to give moral support to a treaty they had not
written with their own hands.

Every man told the story of the meeting as it pleased himself. Edmund Randolph, still irked with the President and
those who stood by him, attended this meeting, and then
wrote to James Madison that Alexander Campbell and Marshall "were the principal combatants." He said that Polly's
admired physician, Dr. Foushee, "was extremely active" in
opposition, and that "Campbell spoke elegantly and forcibly,
and threw ridicule and absurdity upon his antagonist with
success." However, Marshall seems to have parried the ridicule, for he got a resolution urging Congress to support the
Jay Treaty.

Polly fretted that night, waiting for him to come in
from the office, while the light in his window continued to
glow hour after hour. Fresh from steadying the ship of
state Marshall could not settle down in her soft affection.
Alexander Hamilton was the measure of his leaping triumph. He wrote him: "A meeting was called which was
more numerous than I have ever seen at this place; and
after a very ardent and zealous discussion which consumed
the day, a decided majority declared in favor of a resolution
that the welfare and honor of the nation required us to give
full effect to the treaty negotiated with Great Britain." Still
restless, Marshall drew another page of clean paper forward, and wrote to Rufus King in England. He told the
same story, then added that "the republicans of Virginia
are extremely irritated at the vote of today, and will spare
no efforts to obtain a majority in other countries."

So though Polly and the children sought tranquillity in
Fauquier County, even there they were in a briar patch of
political diatribe. On the very day of his arrival to join her,
Marshall had set her heart aquiver, wondering if he could
be tempted to take flight from all of it. For he told her that
the President had offered him the post of minister to France
in Monroe's place. France! Could his family accompany
him? He could laugh, and wave his hand at the Fairfax

forest sweeping up to the peaks of the Blue Ridge mountains. Leave that? On the very day the President's message
was delivered to him, he had replied to his aging General
that the "present crisis" of his personal affairs required that
he should not leave the country.

It was more than likely that it was the present crisis in
public affairs which prevented Marshall from paying a promised visit to his father in Kentucky at this time. For in a
meeting with Colonel Marshall, a personal crisis would have
been eased in the usual manner of Marshalls with each
other. In September the following letter was waiting in the
white-painted law office. It was addressed: "The honble
John Marshall—Richmond. honord by Judge Fleming."

Septr. 9th 1796. Buckpond

Dr. Son

I rec'd yours by Colo Fleming as also that by Mr. Dunlap. I am
happy to hear that you & your family are well but as all the pleasures
of this world [are] chequer'd with evil the same conveyance brings
me the news of Mr. Colstons loss & that of the postponment of yr intended visit to me. The thoughts of seeing you once more I really
believe is a principal mea[ns] of keeping me alive. And I will endeavor to live one year longer in hopes of that event. I am told Mr.
J. Ambler talks of coming out with you; Happy shall I be to see him
with you, and all my family & friends who may think it worth
while to ride out to this country to take leave of me b[efore] I close
my eyes for ever. The subject of [his?] letter, tho' not quite domestic enough, was very [plea]sing to me. Next to that of my own
family, which you know I am dotingly fond of, The good of my
country & our *worthy president* is nearest my heart. And the part
you take in the present Storm gives me much pleasure, indeed you
never seriously disobliged me in your life. I would ask that your
Sons, or as I can say truly from my Heart, my dear Sons Tom &
Jacquiline may accompany you out, but am affraid their tender age
would prevent their being able to support the fatigues of such a
journey, & the loss of one of them, if occasioned by the attempt,
would be more than I could support. If James & Lewis should be
return'd from Europe by the time you come out you may conceive
but not I describe how much it would add to my happiness. Charles
& Billey never write to me; surely knowning my age and infirmity
they can't expect me to write often to them yet I do sometimes.
When I write to you I think I write to them all. Tell Polley & all
my daughters in law—God bless them. When you come out I mean

to make a full division of what property God has bless'd me with.
The Land I have given Susan I have been since offer'd £ 3000 for. I
think what I [shall] give Lewis is worth 3 or 4000 £ but he will have
to wait till mine & his mothers death for it. Mrs. Colston nor my
poor daughter Ambler has yet had nothing. The former when you
come out shall be rememberd, & the latter or rather her son, God
bless him, shall not be forgotten indeed I wish to see you partly on
that acct as I would willing make all my children as nearly equal as
I possibly can. I have again paid the taxes on your military [lands]
but [torn] my grandson Tom in Fayette I have [torn] nothing
with. You neednot be affra[id] of distressing me by bringing out fr
[torn] with you; for of such as I have [torn] accustomed to I have
enough.

Colo Fleming will give you the news [of] this Country. I shall
therefore only obs[erve] that I think the political Horizon [torn] to
clear up. God Bless yo[u] [torn] once more prays. Yr. [torn] T.
Marshall

P.S. Tell Collo Carrington that I have sent Mr. Shorts accts and
other papers to Mr. Walcot. I am unable to write more or I would
write to him.

T.M.

It may be seen that this letter was not entrusted to the
postoffice, a precaution not observed by President Washington when he dispatched the appointment as minister to
France to Marshall. Enclosed in that communication was a
substitute appointment for General Charles Cotesworth
Pinckney of Charleston, South Carolina, to be forwarded to
him by post if Marshall should refuse the office. This letter
was lost in transit, a noticeable mishap since the General
had enclosed in it three one hundred dollar bills for the
sufferers from a Charleston holocaust.

Polly's first concern upon arriving at Richmond was to
see her mother. Before she entered her own house she
walked across the field through Michaelmas daisies as high
as her elbows. When she stepped through the Ambler gate
there were bees in the jeweled boughs of apricot trees. Was
that a bee in her bonnet? At Fredericksburg they had heard
the announcement of President Washington's irrevocable
resolve to retire from public life. Patrick Henry had firmly
stated his refusal to allow his name to be mentioned as the
second President of this commonwealth of States, saying

Courtesy of The Valentine Museum

POLLY'S MANSION. From a photograph taken in 1902. *Inset*: oldest known drawing of the house, published in "Homes of American Statesmen," 1854.

that if the people for whom General Washington had done so much could treat him so badly in his old age, what might they not do to a man "of the common stamp" such as himself. A question was truly buzzing about Polly's head! Would her husband be nominated by the Federalists for the presidency? Could she, Polly, follow in Lady Washington's steps? She snatched off her bonnet, threw it at the bees and ran to her mother's genteel, but by no means stately, parlour.

The first subject of conversation when society reconvened after the Summer separation was the death of mutual acquaintances. Old people died in March, said the servants, and children succumbed to heat and mosquitoes in August. It was neither chill wind nor insects that had taken off Alexander Campbell this Summer. By his own hand he had died, devising that, "No tombstone be raised over me, because it will merely hinder something from growing on that spot. If all men had tombstones erected over their graves, the earth in a few centuries, would be one entire pavement."

To the Marshalls this must have seemed a parsimonious attitude toward land. For in the Fall session the Legislature of the State of Virginia cleared the way for the syndicate to acquire title to over one hundred and sixty thousand acres of Fairfax lands. In response to a petition of two hundred settlers on the Northern Neck for a once-and-for-all settlement of their titles, the Virginia Legislature had passed a resolution proposing that the State would relinquish "all claim to all lands specifically appropriated by . . . Lord Fairfax to his own use either by deed or actual survey . . . if the devisees of Lord Fairfax, or those claiming under them, will relinquish all claim to lands . . . which were waste and unappropriated at the time of the death of Lord Fairfax."

Acting for the syndicate, Marshall accepted these terms on condition that an Act pass in the current session of the Legislature confirming the titles of those claiming under Denny Martin Fairfax the lands reserved by the late Thomas, Lord Fairfax, for his own use, agreeing to execute deeds extinguishing title to waste and unappropriated lands when conveyance should be made to the Marshalls. This was not all the area the syndicate had hoped to purchase at this time, but it will be seen that the Marshalls continued to acquire Fairfax lands for two generations.

The case of Hunter *vs* Fairfax was on the docket of the United States Supreme Court in the Fall term of 1796. Hunter requested a delay because of Campbell's death. Attorneys for Fairfax, now Charles Lee and Jared Ingersoll of Philadelphia, protested that delay would be worse for their client than an adverse decision. However, Judge Chase allowed the delay on the grounds that this was a case of great moment, affecting title to over three hundred thousand acres of land, and would influence such claims in other States.

In the next February, 1797, James Markham Marshall in Holland, assisted by a Dutch banker named Hottenguer, raised seven thousand pounds on Robert Morris's credit, which was at once applied as part payment to Denny Martin Fairfax. The deed signed by Denny Martin Fairfax and the syndicate in the next August, withheld the manor of Leeds until full payment should be made. Light Horse Harry Lee had withdrawn from the syndicate by this time.

In the year 1797 James Markham Marshall individually purchased from Denny Martin Fairfax some of the land around Winchester which was involved in the Hunter claim. But Marshall's "own case" was to rest for thirteen years.

CHAPTER IX

Letters From An Adams Man

Benjamin Latrobe, the architect, sojourning in Richmond in 1797, inscribed in his diary, "Where every man feels himself a political character, every man naturally becomes a politician. The Virginians of whom both inclination & habit have now made me one, are all politicians. I believe they are all honest republicans & true lovers of their country, but they understand by republicanism, & propose to advance the welfare of their country by, two very different lines of conduct. The nicknames of Aristocrat & Democrat are not yet worn out, & it were a pity they should be if they are to be succeeded by those of the British & French faction . . . In point of abilities of manly spirit, of free unprejudiced modes of thinking, I never saw so fine an assemblage of young men as are collected in this City, many of whom reside here as students of the law, under the different attorneys practicing here, and others are members of families settled here."

Especially did the tide of politics ride high in Virginia during the Fall months of 1796, when, for the first time, there was national contest to name a President of the United States. Virginia freeholders were choosing electors to go to Philadelphia and cast ballots in the House of Representatives for John Adams, the incumbent Vice President, who was the President's choice of successor, or for any one of a number of candidates. There is a tradition that Washington still believed Edmund Randolph to be of foremost influence among the political gentlemen of Virginia. It is said that Washington wrote a letter of many directions to Marshall, concerning the election of Adams, adding, "a little judicious flattery can accomplish a great deal with Edmund Randolph."

On December fifteenth, 1796, Marshall wrote to Judge James Iredell in North Carolina: "I have seen the votes of North Carolina, & you I presume have seen the votes of

87

Virginia. Mr. Adams would have received one more vote
had Mr. Eyre really been elected, but he was left out by
accident. There was supposed to be no opposition to him &
in consequence of that opinion the people in one county on
the eastern shore did not vote at all & in the other a very
few assembled. On the day of the election the people of
Princess Ann whose court day it happened to be assembled
in numbers & elected Mr Nimmo who voted for Mr. Jefferson. For that gentleman you will have heard there were
twenty votes, for Mr. Saml Adams 15, for W. Clinton 3,
for Burr 1, Genl Washington 1, Mr. Pinckney 1, Mr. John
Adams 1. I received a letter from Philadelphia stating that
five votes south of the Potowmack would be necessary to
secure the election of Mr. Adams. It is then certain that he
cannot be elected.

"Our assembly which you know is in session displays its
former hostility to federalism. They have once more denied
wisdom to the administration of the President & have gone
so far as to say in argument that we ought not by any
declaration to commit ourselves so as to be bound to support
his measures as they respect France. To what has America
fallen! Is it to be hoped that North Carolina will in this particular rather adopt such measures as have been pursued by
other states than tread the crooked path of Virginia?"

Marshall was wrong in his prediction. In spite of an ener-
getic press for Jefferson, and of open meddling on his behalf
by French agents in the United States, a majority of three
electoral votes made John Adams the last of the Federalist
Presidents, and Thomas Jefferson the headstone of a Republican Party.

Almost the first news from abroad after Adams' inauguration was that the French government had brusquely expelled
the American minister. General Charles Cotesworth Pinckney, having eventually received his appointment as minister
plenipotentiary to France, had reported in Paris in February,
1797, only to be met with "studiously marked indignities
toward the government of the United States." He was
threatened with the police and shortly ordered to quit the
territories of the French Republic, because the administra-

tion in Philadelphia refused to give up a stand of neutrality between Britain and France. M. Adet had been called home from the United States. French privateers had sunk three hundred and forty American vessels in the last eighteen months, torturing their captains, and imprisoning their sailors and American tourists.

President Adams lost no time in calling Congress to convene on May fifteenth in extra session to consider these indignities to the United States. In an opening speech, which, the Vice President criticized as too belligerent, the President announced that he intended to send a mission extraordinary to join Minister Pinckney, and negotiate with the French government for "an accomodation on terms compatible with the rights, duties, interest and honour" of the United States, to put an end to French piracy of American vessels, and "to preserve peace with all nations."

Jefferson was opposed to this measure, and greater still was his disapproval when he discovered that Adams had been able to persuade John Marshall of Virginia to accept a place on this mission.

Was this one of those regrettable occasions when Marshall failed to follow Polly's advice? For her the very suggestion of the expedition was like peering into the lion's mouth. Her husband to walk the blood-streaming streets of Paris? Her beloved on the raging deep whence so many ships never returned? And how, she would like to know, had Mr. Adams been able to prevail on her husband to accept this post when General Washington could not?

With the June morning sweet and fresh over the garden, with the sound of cheerful labor stirring in outbuildings of neighbouring estates, with sleepy friends creeping out earlier than usual to wave a foremost citizen off on a foreign mission extraordinary, Polly, marked by a sleepless night, could only stand by in dumb misery while her rooms, and her porches, and her yard filled with people.

Confusion shook her frame more than ever. Noisy assurances that there was no danger ahead of the traveller, only set her more aquiver. Her moment of farewell was all crowd and haste. As Marshall mounted his "stalking horse" he

must have looked back at a shattered Dearest Polly, surrounded with unavailing comforters. When he reached the
outskirts of the city the booming of cannon saluted him—
and sent Polly into complete despair.

On the second evening Marshall reached Mt. Vernon.
Sitting on the veranda there, with his venerable friend
watching June twilight fade over broad lawns and free-
flowing river, wishes for Polly's presence flickered like fire-
flies through the gloomy advice General Washington was
giving him for the business in France.

Marshall hurried on next day to the house of his mother's
brother, James Keith, in Alexandria. There he wrote the
following letter to Polly, sending it not by post, but by Dick,
the servant who would return with the horses that had
brought the minister extraordinary thus far on his journey.

Alexandria June 24th 97

My dearest Polly

I am thus far on my way to Philadephia & have come without any
inconvenience from a stalking horse. All your other fears will be
as foundationless as this & I shall soon see you again to be the
two happiest persons on earth. I came this morning from Mount
Vernon where I was pressed to pass the day & which is certainly one
of the most delightful places in our country. Had you been with me
I shou'd have been there as happy as I cou'd be any where. I shou'd
have been quite happy as it was cou'd I have been certain—quite
certain that your mind was perfectly at ease. Nothing distresses me
but that. Let me hear from you by the time I have been two days
at Philadelphia & do tell me & tell me truly that the bitterness of
parting is over & your mind at rest—that you think of me only to
contemplate the pleasure of our meeting & that you will permit
nothing to distress you while I am gone. I cannot help feeling a
pang when I reflect that every step I take carrys me further & further
from what is to [me] most valuable in this world but I will suppress
such sensations & will be at quiet if I can only be certain that you are
so. Even sending away Dick wounds me because it looks like parting with the last of the family—but I will not yield to these sensations—only let me know that you have conquer'd them & all is
well. I am now at my uncle Keiths where everybody treats me
with the utmost affection & friendship. They always have done so.
I dine here today with kind friends who make the time as agreeable
as possible—but this is not Richmond.

I shall write to you as soon as I get to Philadelphia & am thinking of you always. Farewell—I never was peremtory but I must now give you one positive order. It is be happy. Once more Farewell—

I am ever your affectionate truly affectionate
J Marshall

I brought away by mistake two letters. The [one to] Genl. Young send to Mr. Hopkins. That which is unsealed send to my brother.

Again I am your
JM

Marshall's great soul is darkened with anxiety. He cannot forget Polly's stricken face and clinging hands.

Those letters carried off by mistake! Marshall's misplaced papers were the bane of Polly's housekeeping. A contemporary speaks of the "instinctive neatness and precision" of Marshall's mind. It is to be wondered what Polly would have said about that. As she grew older the crisis of a lost letter did not blow her into flurry from one pile of papers to another that lay everywhere about her rooms, on her handsome mantels, heaped on tables intended for tea trays, stuck between volumes in her beautiful bookcase, even in the gilt frames of her mirrors—press clippings, pamphlets, letters! Dusting, of course, was interdicted. It is remembered that at intervals she patiently announced that there would have to be a change. Then she would put on her best bonnet and set out for a day of visiting her sisters, while Marshall and the servants, adding brooms and scrub buckets to the precision of his mind, wrought a miracle of order. But in this June of 1797 her hands fluttering through papers must have been feeling for his touch upon them.

Two hot weeks passed over Richmond. Garden paths became covered with blown rose petals. Sweet lavender hung a blue veil beside box hedges, and a fragrance of ripeness drifted on the sultry breeze. Tom's and Jaquelin's little legs itched in fashionable long pantaloons, and baby Mary was covered with prickly heat.

It was hot! Servants were prone to move more slowly, and to laugh more often. Only black Jacob had energy to come cart-wheeling from hands to feet along the path when called from the stable. He explained, "Thar warnt so many steps that way." The walk across the field from Polly's door to her father's house seemed oppressively long, and often when she arrived in his parlour she found him suffering from shortness of breath. Her mother enjoyed the delicate health that befits a lady. Now they placidly sat side by side, while a small colored maid with a large turkey feather fan stirred the air about them.

Sharing their breeze, Polly momentarily shared their peace. Only then could she calmly open the letter which had just been brought from the postoffice.

Philadelphia July 2d '97

My dearest Polly

I am here after a passage up the bay from Baltimore which would have been very unpleasant but for the company of a very agreeable family which greatly alleviated the vexatious calamity of a dead calm under an excessive hot sun. I din'd on saturday in private with the President whom I found a sensible plain candid good temper'd man & was consequently much pleased with him. I am not certain when I shall sail nor have I yet taken a vessel but I conjecture it will be early in the next week. Do you however my dearest life continue to write to me as your letters will follow me shou'd I be gone before their arrival & as my heart clings with real pleasure & delight only to what comes from you. I dined yesterday with Mr. Morris. That family receives me with precisely the same friendship & affection as formerly & seems to preserve in a great degree its vivacity but it must be discernible that a heavy gloom hangs around them which only their good sense restrains them from showing. They live what we shou'd style most elegantly nor is there in the house any apparent change except in the crowd of company which formerly frequented it. I wish most earnestly for their sakes that they may be able to retrieve their affairs nor am I without some hope of its being possible.

I was on friday evening at the Vauxhall of Philadelphia. It is indeed a most elegant place. I wou'd attempt to describe it to you but shou'd fail. The amusements were walking, sitting picnik ice cream &c Music & conversation. I rode out yesterday to see Mrs. Heyward but she was not at home. She lives in the neighborhood of Philadelphia on the bank of the Schuylkil at one of the most enchanting spots you ever saw.

Thus my dearest Polly do I when not engaged in the very serious business which employs a large portion of my time endeavor by amusements to preserve a mind at ease & prevent it from brooding too much over my much lov'd & absent wife. By all that is dear on earth I entreat you to do the same. Our seperation will not I trust be long & letters do everything to draw its sting.

I am my dearest life your affectionate
J Marshall

Everyone knew that President Adams was plain and candid, but that he was sensible and good tempered was indeed news. The Congress considered him stubborn and irascible. The press found his every move execrable, and said so. But at the excellent private dinner provided by Mrs. Adams, Marshall discovered congenial pleasure in good food and drink. He could smile at the domestic warmth with which Mrs. Adams kept the President's well-fed form in neat light drab suits with crisp ruffles in the sleeves, and white silk stockings nicely clean. His hair too was carefully powdered and tied behind in a "rose and bag" as General Washington's style was called.

This dinner with the President was served in a rented executive mansion for which Mr. Adams must pay one thousand pounds annually. Mrs. Adams complained that the Washingtons had paid only five hundred for the same property. This was the more irksome since she had seen the half-built dwelling which Philadelphia was hopefully erecting for an executive mansion, in spite of the well-announced Act of Congress to establish the national capital on a hill beside the Potomac River where foundations for a "palace" were already staked off. She knew that this Act had been a deal between Thomas Jefferson and Alexander Hamilton whereby Jefferson's support of the Act for national assumption of war debts of the States was traded for Hamilton's endorsement of a site for the capital city where Virginians could keep an eye upon it.

The Vauxhall of Philadelphia was one of those public gardens which, in London fashion, adorned the Quaker City with pavilions where refreshments were served at tables set in parterred courts, surrounded with music. Occasional genteel fireworks were enjoyed, but so sedately gay was this city that the feature entertainment was advertised as "decorous vaudeville."

Dinner with the Morris family also took place in a rented

dwelling, one that stood on fashionable Chestnut Street directly across from a colossal marble building without a roof. Their rent was in arrears and those marble walls seen from the windows were all that accrued to Robert Morris from a contract he made with the French architect, L'Enfant, for a sixty thousand dollar residence. Without conscience, the Frenchman had squandered the Morris funds, and when they gave out, deserted the contract, leaving Italian marble as uninhabitable as a pile of handsome gravestones. And gravestones they were for one of America's earliest large fortunes.

For Robert Morris, who with his own credit had financed the American Revolutionary Army, who had been Superintendent of finances for the Confederation, who still owned vast acres of America, was bankrupt for cash, and was besieged by "furious duns ravenous to madness." Among the multitude of creditors suing him were the three Banks he had so largely founded, The Bank of Pennsylvania, The Bank of North America and The Bank of the United States. And, he said, if he owned Paradise there would not now be found one man to credit him two hundred dollars, adding, "Who in God's Name has all the money? For everybody seems to want."

With the Morrises at dinner may have been Mrs. Morris's brother, Bishop White, for he and Marshall were congenial spirits. The Bishop was one of the last visitors at the bedside of the Chief Justice when, years later, he lay dying at Mrs. Crim's boarding house in this city.

A friend of Morris and of all Marshalls, Alexander Hamilton, came from New York to Philadelphia when he heard that General Marshall was there. He too had orders for the envoy extraordinary. For President Adams, Hamilton had a cold shoulder, as well as for Vice President Jefferson, who cold-shouldered him in return. It therefore took a congenital diplomat or a merry soul with a gift for inspiring laughter to attend to "very serious business" with this triangle.

Jefferson, however, had no smiles for his cousin's humor. He was so disgruntled at this moment that he wrote a friend, gone are the good old days when "gentlemen of different politics would then speak to each other, and separate the business of the Senate from that of society." The Friend of The People felt sad that "intimate friends cross the street to avoid meeting, and turn their heads another way, lest they should be obliged to touch their hats," and this, he found, was very "afflicting to peaceable minds." But Marshall was having a pleasant time.

Newspapers were proclaiming that the delay in departure by the mission was due to lessons in French for the envoy from Virginia. This also gave Marshall a smile, for he had many French friends with whom he conversed in a merry American version of the language. The reason for the delay was a matter of Adams' paying a political debt, or so Adams thought.

Elbridge Gerry of Massachusetts, being a neighbour, had voted for Adams for President, apologizing to Jefferson for doing so. Adams, not knowing of that apology, thought to reward Gerry with a place on this mission to France. The Cabinet was unanimously against this appointment. Only Vice President Jefferson was pleased. Gerry dallied, either being loath to leave his wife, seventeen years his junior, or waiting for Jefferson's advice.

Marshall fretted under the delay. As the days dragged out, neither the contentious council tables, nor the theatre, nor the ever-bubbling laughter of his nature could allay his anxiety about Polly when no letter arrived from her. Hastily he grabs a moment from urgent events, and writes:

Philadelphia July 5th '97

My dearest Polly

I have been extremely chagrin'd at not having yet receiv'd a letter from you. I hope you are well as I hear nothing indicating the contrary but you know not how solicitous how anxiously solicitous I am to hear it from yourself. Write me that you are well & in good spirits & I shall set out on my voyage with a lighten'd heart. I believe I shall sail in the course of the next week for Amsterdam where it is expected that I shall join Genl. Pinckney. I have not taken my passage but I think I shall go in the brig Grace Capt. Wills. However you will hear from me more than once before my departure. I din'd yesterday in a very large company of Senators & Members of the house of representatives who met to celebrate the 4th

of July. The company was really a most respectable one & I experienc'd
from them the most flattering attention. I have much reason to be
satisfied & pleas'd with the manner in which I am receiv'd here
but something is wanting to make me happy. Had I my dearest
wife with me I shou'd be delighted indeed. Not having that pleasure why do you not give me what is nearest to it. I am just called
off.

Farewell
your affectionate
J Marshall

Four days later he received the letter from Polly. She was
one of those writers for whom pen and paper simply meant
heart-breaking distance. For in spite of informing him that
her health was improved, she convinced him that her spirits
were low. He answered it in a rare mood of depression.

July 10th '97

My dearest Polly

I have had the pleasure of receiving by the last post your letter
of the 30th of June. I thank Heaven that your health is better. To
know that it is so, will take off one half from the unpleasantness of
a voyage over the Atlantic. In your next I promise myself the
delight of receiving assurance that your mind has become tranquil &
as spritely as usual. Good health will produce good spirits & I wou'd
not on any consideration relinquish the hope that you will possess
both. Remember that if your situation shou'd be as suspected melancholy may inflict punishment on an innocent for whose sake you
ought to preserve a serene & compos'd mind. Colo. Gamble a day or
two before I parted with you express'd the wish of Mrs. Gamble to
see you frequently & by her good & cheerful spirits to aid yours but
that she felt some difficulty on account of your not encouraging an
acquaintance. I mention the fact & leave it to yourself to decide what
you will do.

I have been delay'd extremely & very much to my mortification.
Every day which passes before I set out threatens to make it a day
longer before I return & is therefore most irksome to me. If my
journey was to be postpon'd for any considerable time I wou'd certainly visit Richmond & all that is dearest in the world & which
Richmond contains once more before my departure, but I expect to
sail in the course of the present week or at any rate in the com-
mencement of the next. This delay is so cruel as to retard my business without the consolation of seeing you. It is as yet out of my
power to speak positively concerning my return. Indeed it will not
be in my power until I reach Paris. The time depends so much on

the course of business there as to make it impossible to know here what its length will be. I still hope however to return as early as we contemplated. Of this I kn[ow it] will be certain, all my efforts will be [used to] shorten as much as possible an absence the full misery of which I did not calculate til I felt it. Remember me affectionately to your mother & to all our good friends & relations. Tell the boys I please myself with the hopes of their improvement during my absence & kiss little Mary for your ever affectionate

J Marshall

Colonel Robert Gamble, mentioned in this letter, was a well-to-do Richmond merchant, an importer of fine goods. This may have been a buying trip for him. Though the French Revolution had put the bottom rail on top in Paris, French clothing, furniture and objets d'art were the peak of fashion in the United States. In Richmond society a gentleman who imported dry goods and wines from Europe, rum, coffee and sugar from the West Indies, was a merchant. A storekeeper who ordered his wares from the North was just a peddler.

It would be interesting to know what Polly did about Mrs. Gamble's offer. Catherine Grattan Gamble was the daughter of an Irish family who settled in Rockingham County, Virginia. She was very handsome, noted for a "firm and decisive character." When the Burr trial came on in Richmond, though her family were all anti-Burr, and her son-in-law prosecuting attorney in the case, she vociferously condemned the court for gaoling the prisoner, and carried jellies to his cell. She seems to have found Polly cool to her advances when they met in Richmond parlours. This, however, did not deter her from including the Marshalls in invitations to her affairs. She recognized a "coming" citizen.

As sailing time became imminent, Marshall wrote every day to Polly. The address on the following letter says that it was by the "Hand of Mr. Marshall." It would be hard to say which of his brothers this was. But that it was one of them is probable. Such stilted use of formal reference to a gentleman when speaking to a lady was the custom in Richmond society.

My dearest Polly

Altho Mr. Marshall does not go directly to Richmond so that a letter by tomorrows post may perhaps reach you before this I cannot avoid writing to you because while doing so I seem to myself to be in some distant degree enjoying your company. I was late last night at the play & saw the celebrated Mrs. Merry in the character of Juliet. She performs that part to admiration indeed but I do not think our Mrs. West jr. is far her inferior in it. I saw Mrs. Heyward there. I have paid that lady one visit to one of the most delightful & romantic spots on the river Schuylkil. She express'd much pleasure to see me & has press'd me very much to repeat my visit. I hope I shall not have time to do so. Tis said she is about to be married to a very wealthy young Englishman nam'd Baring. This I think improbable as he is not more than four & twenty & being rich himself has no temptation to marry merely for money.

I know nothing more concerning myself than I did yesterday. I am beyond expression impatient to set out on the embassy. The life I lead here does not suit me. I am weary of it. I dine out every day & am now engaged longer I hope than I shall stay. This dissipated life does not long suit my temper. I like it very well for a day or two but I then begin to require a frugal repast with good cool water. I wou'd give a great deal to dine with you today on a piece of cold meat with our boys beside us & to see little Mary running backwards & forwards over the floor playing the sweet little tricks [she is so] full of. But I can have no [such pleasure.] I wish to Heaven the time which must intervene before I can repass these delightful scenes was now terminated & that we were looking back on our separation instead of seeing it before us. Farewell my dearest Polly. Make yourself happy & you will bless your ever affectionate

J Marshall

"Our Mrs. West jr" was none other than "our Mrs. Bignal" in 1796. John Bignal died that year. The bereft widow had married in haste, repenting a short time later with a "legal deed of separation" registered in the Norfolk court. Mrs. Anne Merry was one of those "children of iniquity" imported by Wignall & Reinagle from Bath, England, where she had swept the town off its feet. She married Wignall in 1803. After his death she married William Warren and went to Virginia to perform with him. But Polly never saw her, for Mrs. Warren died before the troupe left Alexandria, Virginia.

That wealthy young Englishman was Alexander Baring,

and he did not marry Mrs. Heyward after all. In August of the next year he married Anna Louise, daughter of the wealthy William Bingham.

Though Polly had a trembling spirit, Marshall seems always assured that she had a business head. He remembers some papers which he overlooked in the haste of departure— or in his despair that she was distraught when he needed her company to be delightful. He writes her about the papers:

Philadelphia July 12th 97

My dearest Polly

I must beg of you immediately to take the trouble to look in one of the outer drawers in the pine desk on the left hand as you go into the office for a parcel of deeds which are bound up together & which are conveyances of land in the upper country from Banks & sundry other persons to Hobe. This parcel of deeds I wish to be lodg'd immediately with the clerk of the Genl. court. If there is any difficulty in opening the drawer by putting your hand under to the end & pushing it the difficulty will be overcome. Altho I dine out every day & am treated with much attention I am sick to death of this place. I am impatient to get on board & I find considerable delays still in my way. I hope however to sail this week. The captain of the vessel speaks of going on thursday but those who are best acquainted with the usual course of things suppose we shall not sail til sunday. Every day seems lost & I cannot help regreting that I came so soon from Richmond. Perhaps I have expedited my departure by coming but yet I think I might have remain'd one week longer & have been in as much forwardness as I am. That week wou'd have been worth a year of feasting in Philadelphia. Our Virginians are all gone who fill'd the house except Mr. Brent & he goes tomorrow. Altho we never agreed in politics my spirits sink at parting with them. I reflect that without being sensible of the happiness they will pass through Richmond. I who wou'd prize it so highly [am] going in a different direction. But only let me hear often that you are well & I shall be happy. I will be so. Farewell my dearest Polly. My heart is incessantly offering prayers for you.
I am your affectionate
J Marshall

"Mr. Brent" was Congressman from Virginia Richard Brent, a devotee of Jefferson, a State Sovereignty man, anti-Hamilton, anti-National Banks and federal funding. He was later Senator from Virginia, 1809 to 1814 when he died in Washington, a fate that seemed so lugubrious to Randolph of Roanoke, that if he felt ill in that city, he mounted his horse and sped homeward.

August was a riot of clematis bloom over outbuildings in Richmond yards when the next letter reached Polly:

Philadelphia July 14th 97

My dearest Polly

Tomorrow the Grace in which I am to embark for Amsterdam will sail from this port. I shall go down to New Castle & go on board there on sunday. All concur that the vessel is a very fine & very safe one & that the season is most favorable for a good voyage. I hope therefore to reach Amsterdam by the latter end of August & from thence I will write to you as soon as possible. My letters however cannot be calculated on till some time in october. You must not therefore, after I sail count on hearing from me till october, unless there shou'd be extraordinary & unlooked for delay you will I think receive letters from me in that month. I shall then have it in my power to give you some more certain intelligence concerning my return. At present I can add nothing to what I have always said. My utmost endeavors will be us'd to get back by christmas. If that shou'd be practicable you will see me; if it shou'd be impracticable, you must not permit your fears in any situation to subdue you. If you will only give me this assurance I shall be happy. Mr. Brown came in the last stage & says he was too much hurried to give you information of his journey but I am satisfied all was well or he wou'd have heard it was not so. My son Tom wrote to me on the 6th of the month & I was pleased with his letter. I am happy to perceive from it that you retain your better health. I flatter myself you do because he does not mention your health. Thus will I continue to please myself concerning you & to believe that you are well & happy. This belief smooths the way before me & beguiles the melancholy of many an hour.

I din'd yesterday with Mr. Bingham at his celebrated country seat on the Schuylkill. The entertainment was elegant but not by any means so expensive as I had been led to expect. It is the practice here to place in the center of the table a large oval vase almost like the waiter of a tea table but of silver or gold & ornamented with Cupids on which are glasses with flowers. The table is then cover'd all round with small dishes, none being plac'd in the center. In consequence of this large dinners here are not so expensive as with us. Mrs. Bingham is a very elegant woman who dresses at the height of the fashion. I do not however like that fashion. The sleeve [does] not reach the elbow or the glove come quite to it. There is a vacancy of three or four inches & just [above] the naked elbow is a gold clasp.

Independent of relationship I like no body so well as the family of
Mr. Morris. There is among them throughout a warmth & cordiallity
which is extremely pleasing. But Virginia & my own dear connec-
tions are not only more belov'd but appear to me more to deserve
love than any body else. Farewell my much lov'd wife. Once more
before I go on board will you hear from your

J Marshall

It does seem that Mr. Brown going as Marshall's secretary to France might have stopped by the Marshall house to
take a message from Polly. But he was a precise man, probably afraid of feminine emotion. He was an indispensable
member of the mission, though the reports give him scant
mention. Six times he copied each long dispatch with a
quill. Six different ships brought the most important of
papers to the United States. Later John Brown became
widely known for the corps of court clerks he trained to
be distinguished for the "beauty and neatness" of the records they inscribed. A polished wire for hot words they
were when the Burr trial for conspiracy had to be committed
to paper.

William Bingham not only had a celebrated country seat,
he had an equally celebrated mansion in the city at Third
and Spruce Streets, patterned after, but larger than, the London residence of the Duke of Manchester, and lavishly furnished from France. At this time Bingham was Senator from
Pennsylvania. His wife, beautiful Anne Willing, was indeed a spectacular personality. She had been presented at
the court of Louis XVI, and frequented royal society in all
the European courts. On one occasion in Paris, so stately was
her beauty and so fabulous her attire that she was mistaken
for the Queen. Mrs. Adams, the American executive lady,
however, was quite critical of Mrs. Bingham's style of dress.
She found it too scanty below and too much around the
bosom. Marshall refrains from risking a bit of scandal to
Polly's chaste humor. Mrs. Bingham was introducing to Federal court society her daughter, Maria Matilda, who had
recently divorced a French husband whom she had secretly
married. Mrs. Adams was quite haughty when the girl was
presented to her.

And that not so expensive dinner! It is true that Mrs.
Bingham served a mound of flowers at her dinners, but she
also served "turtle and every other thing," sweetmeats of
twenty sorts, flummeries and jellies, raisins, pears, peaches
and Madiera in abundance.

When Marshall at last set out for the port he had packed
in his writing desk, or his trunk—it is to be hoped not in
his pocket—five hundred dollars in American specie, and
three thousands dollars in letters of credit on European
bankers and governments, which the treasury department
had given him for expenses. His instructions from Congress
and President were to join General Pinckney in Holland, and
proceed to Paris where they were to placate whatever government France might have at the time. In all things they were
to preserve the honor of the United States in friendly operations with all nations.

While Gerry dallied, Marshall sailed, writing to Polly
while the ship slowly tacked southward in the Bay of Delaware. She paid forty cents for this letter.

The bay of Delaware July 20th 97

My dearest Polly

The land is just escaping from my view the pilot is about to
leave us & I hasten from the deck into the cabin once more to give
myself the sweet indulgence of writing to you. On the 17th as I
mention'd in my last we left Philadelphia in order to join our vessel
at New Castle & on the 18th we came on board & weigh'd anchor at
about 10 o'clock. There has been so little wind that we are not yet
entirely out of the bay. It is so wide however that the land has
the appearance of a light blue cloud on the surface of the water &
we shall very soon lose it entirely. The wind is now fair & tolerably
fresh. I have been so long on board that I can form a very tolerable
estimate of the accommodations to be expected on the voyage. The
cabin is neat & clean my birth a commodious one in which I have my
own bed & sheets of which I have a plenty so that I lodge as conveniently as I wou'd do in any place whatever & I find that I sleep
very soundly altho on water. We have for the voyage the greatest
plenty of salt provisions, live stock & poultry & as we lay in our
own liquors I have taken care to provide myself with a plenty of
excellent porter wine & brandy. The Captain is one of the most
obliging men in the world & the vessel is said by everybody to be a
very fine one. In addition to Mr. Brown Mr. Gamble & myself two

dutch Gentlemen are passengers who appear to be intelligent men well disposed to make the voyage agreeable. I have then my dearest Polly every prospect before me of a passage such as I cou'd wish in every respect but one. At this season of the year there are such frequent calms as to create fear of a lengthy passage. We have met in the bay several vessels. One from Liverpool had been at sea nine weeks, & the others from other places had been out proportionably long. I hope we shall do better but in spite of me fears mingle with my hopes. I shall be extremely impatient to hear from you & our dear children. I have written a letter to Tom which I sent to Winchester in expectation that he might be there. If he is at Fauquier court house let him know it that he may endeavor to have it sent to him. Colo. Carrington or Mr. Hopkins will give your letters a conveyance to me. I think it better for the present that they shou'd some go by the way of London to the care of [torn] King esquire our minister there, some by the way of Amsterdam or the Hague to the care of William Vans Murray esquire our minister at the Hague & perhaps some directed to me as Envoy extraordinary of the United States to the French Republic at Paris. Do not I intreat you omit to write. Some of your letters may miscarry but some will reach me & my heart can feel till my return no pleasure comparable to what will be given it by a line from you telling me that all remains well. Farewell my dearest life. Your happiness will ever be the first prayer of your unceasingly affectionate

J Marshall

The envoy suggests two federal officials to whom Polly might trust letters. Mr. John Hopkins was United States Commissioner of Loans, and a neighbour in the Court End of Town. Colonel Edward Carrington, was friend of General Washington, and had married the young widow, Eliza Ambler Brent. He often took Eliza to visit at Mount Vernon. They happened to be there when suddenly it was evident that ceremonies were afoot for the birth of Madame Washington's great-grandchild. The Washingtons were not only royalty in the eyes of their countrymen, but surrounded household events with all the protocol of republicans remembering the pleasant side of monarchy. Eliza was dismayed when Colonel Carrington, who was seventeen years her senior, made their excuses and carried her off to Alexandria before the high moment. The arrival of anyone's baby was an exciting affair for Eliza, for she had no children of her own. Her husband had ten brothers and sisters, and as

"Aunt Carrington" she was an awesome legend down to the third generation.

Rufus King and William Vans Murray were also friends of the Mount Vernon household, good Federalists and appointees of President Washington. Rufus King had been joint author with Alexander Hamilton and James Madison of letters signed Camillus which had given implementation of the Jay Treaty such a lift over the stile. William Vans Murray was as a part of Marshall's own mind about the Constitution, and drank that document's wisdom comfortably before it became muddied with controversy. These names gave Polly no comfort. They magnified the rolling waves between the Court End of Town and Paris.

Out of sight of land! Polly longed for the white church on York's cliffs, where through high windows she had often watched gulls wheeling against the sky, knowing that beneath their wings a ship was on its way to rough waters and high tempest. "Safe into the haven guide," she would sing. And when the scanty congregation went on to another verse of the hymn, she repeated over and over, "Safe into the haven." That good Church of England minister, Mr. Davenport, would understand if he heard her. From his high pulpit he could see the winging fleets.

For Polly, in Richmond there was only a substitute church. Since the road across Shockoe Valley was too rough for the fashionable equipages of the Court End of Town, St. John's Church was opened only for funerals and for Communion three times a year. Episcopal Reverend Buchanan and Presbyterian Parson Blair conducted their respective forms of Morning Service on alternate Sundays in the hall of the House of Delegates in the Capitol, with the same congregation and the same choir. Though Mr. Patrick Gibson played his flute sweetly, and the most respectable citizens chanted cheerfully, the words they sang struck terror to Polly's heart:

> "When through the torn sail the wild tempest is streaming,
> When o'er the dark wave the red lightening is gleaming,
> Nor hope lends a ray the poor seaman to cherish,
> We fly to our Maker: 'Save Lord! or we perish.'"

To Polly, Richmond seemed more and more like tide-for-saken sands, though for business in general, life ran as full a current as ever.

Chapter X

Letters From an Envoy Extraordinary

MARSHALL HAD CALCULATED correctly that it would be October when Polly received his first letter from Europe. Forty-eight days he sailed, with everywhere evidence of British supremacy on the seas. Three times the *Grace* was overhauled by British men-of-war, and boarded by a Captain who, when he heard that there was an American diplomat on board, courteously sent the *Grace* on her way. This conduct, Marshall says, was designed to conciliate America by exhibiting a perfect contrast to that of France. The British navy could afford to be polite when it chose, for Marshall says it held "entire dominion," blockading the French fleet in Brest, the Spanish at Cadiz, and the Dutch in the Texel River.

Marshall reports to Secretary of State Pickering that on the morning of August twenty-ninth, the *Grace* arrived at the mouth of the Texel where thirty Dutch ships-of-the-line and frigates were bottled up, preparing to give battle on the first favorable wind. By leave of a British Captain the *Grace* was allowed to pass the blockade and proceed to the harbor. Was this the captain to whom the following letter was entrusted?

Thursday Aug. 3d 1797

My dearest Polly

A vessel is just in sight which appears to be sailing for America & with the hope that I may get it on board her I hasten to scribble a few lines to you. We are now 12 or 1300 miles from the capes of Delaware in the direct course for the channel & have had yet awhile a favorable voyage except that we have in the general too little wind. We have not made quite a third of our way to Amsterdam. We had for three days a strong breeze but all is calm again & we scarcely creep along. I shou'd disregard this if I did not so greatly fear that a long passage may too much delay my return. I have had scarcely any sea sickness & am now perfectly well. My only sollicitudes are for the success of my mission & for the much lov'd person I leave behind me in my own country. Sometimes I am melancholy & sink into fears concerning you but I shake them off as fast as possi-

ble & please myself with the delightful picture of our meeting on
my return. I fancy myself by your side with our children round
us & seem to myself to have such a hold on happiness that it cannot
slip from me. I have with me more books than I can read during the
passage & that circumstance tends very much to diminish the tedious-
ness of such a voyage. The Captain is remarkably obliging & we
have abundant stores of everything which can tend to make our
situation comfortable. Indeed if I cou'd know that you were perfectly well & happy I shou'd feel as much content & satisfaction as
can be felt with the prospect before me of so long a seperation from
you. I will indulge the sweet hope of hearing from [you] very soon
after my arrival in Europe & I will believe that your letters will all
aprise me that you are well & happy. Tis that belief alone which
can keep up my spirits.

Aug. 29th 97

The vessel by which I expected to have sent the above did not
give me an opportunity of putting it on board. I have this instant
arriv'd in Holland & seen a vessel whose Captain will sail for
America as soon as the wind permits. I seize the opportunity
to let you know that I am safe & perfectly well. I can add nothing
further as I have not yet reach'd a place where I can collect any
intelligence & as I detain the Captain while I add with what affection I am your

J Marshall

The postscript, added twenty-six days after the letter was
begun, is blotted and scrawled as if written in haste.

Marshall hurried on to The Hague where he met General
and Mrs. Pinckney and their young daughter who was ill
with recurring fever. In General Pinckney, he says, he found
a "sensible man, and one of high and even romantic honour." The personality of Charles Cotesworth Pinckney could
easily please Marshall. He was a gallant soldier, a devoted
family man and an aristocrat of that charm peculiar to
Charlestonians. It was said of Marshall when he died that
he left "no friendship broken, no confidence betrayed."
Such was the bond between these two gentlemen from that
day in Holland until the death of Pinckney in 1825.

Again Marshall catches a good wind for a letter to Polly.

The Hague September 9th 97

My dearest Polly

I have just heard that a vessel sails as soon as the wind will permit from Rotterdam for the United States & I seize the opportunity of writing to you.

I reach'd this place on the 3rd instant & immediately saw Genl. Pinckney with whom I am very much pleas'd. We had agreed to set out immediately for Paris for which place the minister of France is authoriz'd to give us passports. Genl. Pinckney however two days after my arrival receiv'd a letter from Mr. Gerry written at Boston informing of his intention to embark immediately & of his expectation to join us here the latter end of August. He has not yet come but we anxiously wait for him. We shall wait a week or ten days longer & shall then proceed on our journey. You cannot conceive (yes you can conceive) how these delays perplex & mortify me. I fear I cannot return until the spring & that fear excites very much uneasiness & even regret at my having ever consented to cross the Atlantic. I wish extremely to hear from you & to know your situation. My mind clings so much to Richmond that scarcely a night passes in which during the hour of sleep I have not some interesting conversation with you or concerning you.

This place was formerly the residence of the Prince & Princess of orange & being the court was also the residence of all the foreign ministers. It is still the latter. The former palace is bestow'd on the Minister from France. There are at the Hague a great many elegant walks which are very unusual in the midst of a city but the pride & boast of the place is a very extensive wood adjoining the city which extends to the sea. This is I believe the only natural wood in Holland. It is intersected with a variety of walks. It is indeed in the summer one of the most delightful situations in the world. The society at the Hague is probably very difficult; to an American it certainly is & I have no inclination to attempt to enter into it. While the differences with France subsist the political characters of this place are probably unwilling to be found frequently in company with our countrymen. It might give umbrage to France. Genl. Pinckney has with him a daughter who appears to be about 12 or 13 years of age. Mrs. Pinckney informs me that only one girl of her age has visited her since the residence of the family at the Hague. In fact we seem to have no communication but with Americans or those who are employ'd by America, or who have property in our country. Near my lodgings is a theatre in which a french company performs three times a week. I have been frequently to the play & tho I do not understand the language I am very much amus'd at it. The whole company is consider'd as having a great deal of merit but there is a Madame de Gazon who is consider'd as one of the first performers in Paris who bears the palm in the estimation of every person.

The Directory with aid of the Soldiery have just put in arrest the most able & leading members of the legislature who were consider'd

as moderate men & friends of peace. Some conjecture that this event
will so abridge our negotiations as probably to occasion my return to
America this fall. A speedy return is my most ardent wish but to
have my return expedited by the means I have spoken of is a circumstance so calamitous that I depreciate it as the greatest of evils.
Remember me affectionately to our friends & kiss for me our dear
little Mary. Tell the boys how much I expect from them & how
anxious I am to see them as well as their belov'd mother.

I am my dearest Polly unalterably your
J Marshall

The French Directory had been taken over by Napoleon
on September fourth, and strong conservative members of the
National Assembly had been imprisoned. Talleyrand was
now the French Minister for Foreign Affairs, the virtual
mouthpiece of the soldier who was mounting the steps of
Empire. The Netherlands, now the Batavian Republic, became a tool for Napoleon's hand.

Marshall and Pinckney waited a week for Gerry and then
went on toward Paris without him, travelling through a
country which preserved its wealth at the price of liberty.
Marshall wrote General Washington that the Dutch had
"relinquished national independence for individual safety,"
and adds, "What a lesson to those who wou'd admit foreign
influence into the United States!"

The laggard Gerry landed in Amsterdam a few hours after Marshall and Pinckney left The Hague. Shortly he over-
took them, so that the three envoys presented their creden-
tials together at the office of the Foreign Minister in a meeting that Talleyrand insisted was informal, but which the
Americans found lacking in good manners. The Americans
were given "cards of hospitality," which were merely police
passes. From there on they got no diplomatic courtesy they
would not pay for, since the United States merited no consideration, said Talleyrand.

Of this mission Marshall wrote: "History will scarcely
furnish the example of a nation, not absolutely degraded,
which has experienced from a foreign power such open con-
tumely and undisguised insult as were on this occasion suffered by the United States in the persons of their ministers."
They were constantly refused recognition as official envoys.

The Paris Marshall saw had not yet taken on the spacious beauty of the Empire city. It was still mostly a brownish huddle of medieval structures, with here and there an ecclesiastical jewel of carved stone and stained glass. All around, largely in dire poverty and partly in confiscated luxury, lived a lavish, wicked people who enshrined license above goodness, and held all human relations for sale. Here political parties, "ready to devour each other," were united only in an excessive hatred of England, and love of no country, not even their own.

France resounded with talk of invading England, mentioning always the "money worshippers" in America as the only source of means whereby a French army could be put on British soil.

Weeks dragged on, with only "unofficial" visits from agents of the French foreign office, setting the price of an official audience with Talleyrand at fifty thousand francs for private pockets. Moreover these agents gave the Americans to understand that such a conference would be to discuss a loan from the United States before the Directory would consider the matter of piracy of American commerce and other unpleasant French behavior. Through all, the Americans steadfastly refused to purchase an audience.

Gerry and Marshall at first lodged uncomfortably over a stable, until Talleyrand, who had known Marshall in Virginia, remembered that sociable spirit. He arranged that these envoys should find more pleasant rooms in the house of a Madame Villette, whose reputation was "La belle et la bonne," and very religious. To her he sent orders, which were to plant in the minds of the envoys a fear that he would use the pro-French parties in America to inflame the American people against their own government, and to ruin Marshall, Pinckney and Gerry. Madame Villette found Gerry already a good Frenchman, Pinckney a smooth and honorable diplomat, and Marshall an entertaining wall of integrity. To them her machinations were entirely apparent, but her house was comfortable and her repartee amusing. In her pleasant drawing room Marshall sat down to write to Polly:

Paris November 27th 1797

My dearest Polly

I have not since my departure from the United States receiv'd a single letter from you or from any one of my friends in America. Judge what anxiety I must feel concerning you. I do not permit myself for a moment to suspect that you are in any degree to blame for this. I am sure you have written often to me but unhappily for me your letters have not found me. I fear they will not. They have been thrown overboard or intercepted. Such is the fate of the greater number of the letters addressed by Americans to their friends in France, such I fear will be the fate of all addressed to me.

In my last letter I inform'd you that I counted on being at home in march. I then expected to have been able to leave this country by christmas at furthest & such is my impatience to see you & my dear children that I had determin'd to risk a winter passage. I now apprehend that it will not be in my power to reach America til april or may—but on this subject all is yet uncertain. I wish you wou'd present my compliments to Mr. Wickham & express to him my wish that the case of Randolph exrs. & Colo. Meade may lie til my return. I think nothing will prevent my being at the chancery term in may. Oh God how much time & how much happiness have I thrown away!

Paris presents one incessant round of amusement & dissipation but very little I believe even for its inhabitants of that society which interests the heart. Every day you may see something new magnificent & beautiful, every night you may see a spectacle which astonishes & inchants the imagination. The most lively fancy aided by the strongest description cannot equal the reality of the opera. All that you can conceive & a great deal more than you can conceive in the line of amusement is to be found in this gay metropolis but I suspect it wou'd not be easy to find a friend. I wou'd not live in Paris to be among the wealthiest of its citizens.

I have chang'd my lodgings much for the better. I liv'd till within a few days in a house where I kept my own apartments perfectly in the style of a miserable old batchelor without any mixture of female society. I now have rooms in the house of a very accomplished a very sensible & I believe a very amiable lady whose temper very contrary to the general character of her countrywomen, is domestic & who generally sits with us two or three hours in the afternoon. This renders my situation less unpleasant than it has been but nothing can make it eligible. Let me see you once more & [torn] venture to assert that no considera[tion] will [in]duce me ever again to consent to place the Atlantic between us. Adieu my dearest Polly. Preserve your health & be as happy as possible till the return of him who is ever yours.

I inclose this letter under cover to Colo. Carrington. Whenever that happens you will admit to paying the postage

[no signature]

This letter reached Polly in January when she was still "in the straw" after the birth of a son on the fifteenth of that month. That it was not signed may have weighed more on her mind than his mention of an accomplished, sensible and amiable lady who spent afternoons sitting with the envoys. People were speaking of the envoys as Shadrach, Meshach and Abednego, captives in a fiery furnace. Then on February tenth Polly's father died, and that simple Christian was buried with a panoply of gloom that rolled like the smoke of the Biblical furnace over Polly's spirits. She lost all interest in everything, even the tiny son named John.

Eliza says, "My much loved sister fell into a deep melancholy from which no one could relieve her . . . only her husband who might have by his usual tenderness (had he been here) dissipated this terrible gloom." Day and night Eliza travelled a triangular course from her own house to Polly's, and then to her mother's, who, she says, "as Polly's malady encreased herself went down under complicated sufferings."

Knowing nothing of the little son nor of Polly, Marshall sat with Mr. Brown composing reports to Secretary of State Pickering in Philadelphia. To Madame Villette's house came the agents of Talleyrand almost daily. They were for the most part bankers without a country. Hauteval was a Swiss, Hottenguer a Dutch banker, and Bellamy a discontented American. The American press gave them the algebraic nonentity of X, Y and Z. Marshall says they brought insinuations rather than messages from Talleyrand, all to the effect that "we should pay for the spoilation committed on our commerce . . . and make [the French government] a considerable loan [$250,000] . . . Besides this . . . there must be something [$50,000] for the pocket for the Directory Minister." No official audience with Talleyrand would be arranged until these demands were met.

The envoys answered positively that until the spoilation of American shipping was stopped other things could not be considered. "The capture of our vessels," said the report to

Pickering, "seems only to be limited by the ability to capture. That ability is increasing, as the government has let out to hardy adventurers the national frigates."

Marshall says that when the agents pressed further for monies, he answered that "to lend money to a belligerent power is to relinquish our neutrality." "But," parried the agents, "other states of Europe have been obliged to buy peace. Did not the Americans know that nothing is to be obtained without money?" Then an order from the Directory loosed the French sea wolves in wider range.

Staunchly Marshall and Pinckney held out against every suggestion of bribery and for open and aboveboard diplomatic negotiations. Talleyrand finally demanded that President Adams publicly retract his speech to Congress in which this mission was announced. The Frenchman fretfully complained that a *small* part of the American press had been unfriendly to France. In the matter of the President's speech the envoys could point to its veracity. As to the press, Marshall wrote Talleyrand, "Among those principles deemed sacred in America . . . there is none . . . more deeply impressed on the public mind, than the liberty of the press. That this liberty is often used to excess, that it has sometimes degenerated into licentiousness, is seen and lamented; but the remedy has not been discovered. Perhaps it is a shoot which cannot be stripped from the stalk, without wounding vitally the plant from which it is torn."

In spite of Mr. Brown's finest handwriting, the envoys had reason to believe that Talleyrand never read their communication. Restlessly they tarried, urging the proper reception of their mission, all except Gerry. Belonging to the pro-French party, and knowing that the young United States government had paid itself out of trouble before, he would have followed the example of Monroe in dealing with the French on their own terms. He held separate meetings with the French agents, and indeed, with Talleyrand himself. Stubbornly the French minister refused to receive Marshall and Pinckney, refused to acknowledge their status as diplomats, refused to abate the destruction of American shipping.

There is a tradition in the Tazewell family of Virginia

that about this time another Virginian unofficially joined the envoys. William Tazewell of Williamsburg, a medical student in the University of Edinburgh, being threatened with consumption, came to Paris on his way to the south of France for his health. Finding himself in financial straits there he appealed to the American ministers. Marshall asked him if he could speak French. "Like a native," replied William Tazewell. Thereupon the medical student was appointed interpreter for General Marshall, who, the story goes, had to say when occasion demanded, "Donney moi a fork."

Marshall may have been restless and worried about Polly, but he was not bored. He was forty-two years young and eager. The iniquity of the French government appalled him. The degradation of the people shocked him. But the flighty humanity of the drawing rooms amused him mightily. He made many new friends and discovered several old acquaintances. One of Talleyrand's agents, M. Hottenguer, was probably the banker who had raised the money in Holland with which James Markham Marshall had made a down payment on Fairfax lands for the syndicate. M. Beaumarchais who was brought briefly into the "unofficial" conferences was an old client of Marshall's. These men could turn business off and on like a spiggoted pipe. When the unpleasantness was disposed with, sights of Paris were enjoyed in complete neutrality.

Marshall sat to the sculptor Jean Antoine Houdon for a bust, which must have afforded artist and model sprightly hours of recollections of the Washingtons and Mount Vernon. He also sat for a miniature by an unidentified painter. In this picture Marshall's expression suggests that he had just told one of his famous amusing stories, and now wondered whether the Frenchman would repeat it without variation.

During daylight, when Talleyrand's agents were under cover, Marshall poked about among purloined treasures in dingy shops and bought presents for Polly: a lovely pair of heart shaped cameo earrings, a mahogany workbox with gilt trimmings, a clock which still holds up its hands in horror at what it had seen on palace floors. General Pinckney was depressed and worried. Negotiations were blocked and his child was more and more ill. Subtle threats of imprisonment for the envoys were in the air. Gerry however was so happy that Rufus King wrote to Marshall that "Gerry had mistaken the lamps of Paris for an illumination on his arrival."

More often, as months went by, the French agents came after dark to visit at Madame Villette's house, until one of them in a temper demanded to know *what* America would give for peace. Also in a temper, Pinckney shouted, "Not a sixpence!"

The envoys were convinced that negotiations on an honorable level were impossible, and asked for safe conduct out of the country. Talleyrand replied that they would have to ask for passports like any ordinary tourist. Marshall and Pinckney refused to leave except as ambassadors. Finally, angrily, the French government sent these two safe conduct papers, inviting Gerry to remain. Pinckney in proper ambassadorial form requested leave to stay in southern France until his child was able to travel safely. Gerry stayed on in Paris, expecting to hear of a wave of indignation engulfing Marshall when he returned alone to America.

When Marshall boarded the *Alexander Hamilton* at Bordeaux he sent gay messages back to his Paris friends, especially to Madame Villette. He regretted very much that his leave was so hastily taken that he could not procure a supply of French wines for his lawyer dinners in Richmond.

There was formerly a letter in the Marshall family from Marshall or James Markham Marshall which told that while in Paris these two brothers had bought Lewis Marshall out of a French prison. In the usual manner of Directoire business, the money probably passed privately to prison authorities, and Lewis promptly and quietly left France. He lived to a "bluff and dictatorial" great age, never allowing his French career to be mentioned. His experience must have been useful when he served two colleges as president: Washington in Lexington, Virginia, and Transylvania in Kentucky. But never again was his name spelled like a Virginian. Henceforth he was Louis Marshall.

Aug. 20

My dearest Polly

I have just returned from a visit to Mount Vernon where I pass'd an evening. Mrs. Washington asked me to bring you to see her when you shoud visit this city. She appears tolerably cheerful but not to possess the same sort of cheerfulness as formerly. You as a widow woud I hope show more firmness.

Tell Jaquelin I was much pleasd with his letter. If he will keep his word & get a lesson every day & while Mr. Bruce is absent & will afterward continue & get a few extra lines he will soon overtake the class he ought now to be in. Farewell my dearest Polly

I am your ever affectionate
J Marshall

Courtesy of the College of William and Mary

LETTER FROM J MARSHALL to Polly written in Washington when he was Secretary of State, 1800, admonishing Polly to show more fortitude as a widow than did Mrs. Washington.

Chapter XI

The "Un"Lucky Letter

Vice President Jefferson had not idly awaited results of President Adams' business with France. He used the Federalist crisis to increase membership in the Republican party. The press, "maliciously designed to ruin men of the other party," says Marshall, fell in behind Jefferson. When a Navy Department was established by the Federalist Congress the press accused Adams of ordering useless fleets. The Federalist Bench was vilified and good Federalist names smeared with slander.

All the while young Philadelphians were still parading for Adams, cheering for Marshall and exalting General Washington. Mrs. Adams took umbrage at the celebration made for Washington's birthday. She felt that Philadelphians were lacking in tact to cheer for a former President in the presence of the gentleman in office. General Washington had not won the war by himself.

The first report from the envoys preceded Marshall to America, where it was read to Congress in secret session. Republicans demanded that it be made public, and then looked aghast at what they had done to their own party. The people were "astonished and confounded at the perfidy of the French" whose theories of liberty they had been wont to admire. The foreign policy of impotent America had often stooped to buy peace. But here were agents of the United States emerging in a posture of defiance, demanding mature and honorable agreements. Americans suddenly felt self-respect revive. By the thousands they returned to the Federalist party. Bravely they demanded the nullification of all French treaties. Political clubs of young men began to sing a new song written by one of Philadelphia's leading lawyers, "Hail Columbia, Happy Land!"

Three Congressmen from Virginia deserted their posts and went home. One of them was John Clopton from Richmond whose seat in the House of Representatives would within a year become a stepping stone to the Supreme

117

Court. The others were John Nicholas and William Giles, such charming gentlemen that Polly never could understand why they could not agree with her husband.

On June eighteenth, after a voyage of fifty-two days, Marshall arrived unannounced in New York. Quietly he hurried off to Philadelphia to report to the President and the Secretary of State Pickering. Two days on the road brought him to Frankford. From there word of his approach ran ahead of him. Corps of uniformed cavalry followed by fleets of vehicles carrying Congressmen and foremost citizens met him six miles from Philadelphia. How delighted Marshall must have been to find himself in a triumphant march on the streets of the capital, surrounded by cheering crowds while church bells rang and cannon thundered! It was "an immense concourse of citizens," said the press, including Republicans, all applauding the mission which had returned a sense of honor to the American people.

Thus engulfed in welcome did Marshall arrive at O'Eller's Tavern. There he learned of Polly's collapse, and that she was in Winchester with the Colstons, that a son had been born to him and called by his name. Also he learned that President Washington was again General Washington on duty organizing a new army to meet the twofold threat of war with France and Britain, and that Robert Morris was in debtors' prison where his wife must pay his board month after month.

Early next morning with a sense of urgency, Marshall called on the President and Secretary of State. Then he hurried to his friend in debtors' prison. While he tarried there, he had a caller at the Tavern. Vice President Jefferson dropped in to pay his respects. When word came that Marshall was at Frankford, Jefferson was about to leave Philadelphia for his mountaintop mansion, but hearing that Marshall was on his way to the city, decided to wait and observe the fall of the mighty. He was shocked to see that Marshall's reception took place "with utmost éclat."

Twice the Vice President tried to find Marshall at the Tavern, then left the following note:

Thomas Jefferson presents his compliments to General Marshall.

He had the honor of calling at his lodgings twice this morning, but was so ᵘⁿlucky as to find him out on both occasions. He wished to have expressed in person his regret that a pre-engagement for today which could not be dispensed with would prevent him the satisfaction of dining in company with General Marshall, and therefore begs leave to place here the expression of that respect which in company with his fellow citizens he bears him.
June 23, 98

Marshall is said to have remarked that this was one of the few times Mr. Jefferson almost told the truth. Next day he wrote his reply:

J Marshall begs leave to accompany his respectful compliments to Mr. Jefferson with assurance of the regret he feels at being absent when Mr. Jefferson did him the honor to call on him.

J Marshall is extremely sensible to the obliging expressions contained in Mr. Jefferson's polite billet of yesterday. He sets out tomorrow for Winchester & would with pleasure charge himself with any commands of Mr. Jefferson to that part of Virginia.

This letter is preserved in the National Archives.

The dinner which Jefferson declined delayed Marshall one long day from speeding to Polly. In O'Eller's Tavern that afternoon one hundred and twenty of the foremost gentlemen of the country sat at round tables for a jubilant dinner in his honor. Members of Congress and Cabinet, justices of the Supreme Court, and the two bishops of the American Episcopal Church were there. Toasts with "unbounded plaudits" were drunk. Some guest, now forgotten, caught the spirit of General Pinckney's angry words in Paris, and with raised glass gave the assemblage—and the nation— "Millions for defense, but not one cent for tribute."

Then Marshall left for Winchester, travelling in a trail of triumph across Pennsylvania, into Maryland and to northern Virginia. Strapped around his waist were two thousand dollars, paid him on account by the State Department. It was like having Fairfax lands in his pocket.

When Elizabeth Marshall, oldest daughter of Colonel Thomas Marshall, married Rawleigh Colston in Polly's house, the bride, aged twenty-nine was rated an old maid. But Mr. Colston was not her first love. She had been affianced to a young officer who was killed in one of the early battles of the Revolution. This opened a window of Heaven on her life which so enlightened her heart that thereafter those who needed comforting sought her out. Thus to her home in Frederick County little Polly, with all her defenses down, was taken as soon as the roads were passable in the Spring of 1798.

Marshall could hardly have reached her before ripening wheat stalks were doing obeisance to Summer. Then his enthusiastic affection must have revived her spirit with the assurance that she was still young and beautiful. He spent four or five weeks with her, at the Colstons, or travelling the circuit of Virginia Mineral Springs, a very fashionable thing to do. Wherever they went he treated her with large doses of cheerful society, horseback riding, and whatever baths the particular Spring afforded.

Renewing their joy, so far were they from the noise of public opinion that it came as a surprise to Marshall, alone on his way to Richmond, to find citizens of Republican Fredericksburg turning their backs as he passed, and booing when a band played, "Hail Columbia." Slowly the hand of Jefferson was grasping Virginia.

But, nearing Richmond, Marshall's friendliness felt no scorch. Whatever his politics, he was bringing home good fellowship, wholesome hilarity, and to some minds, legislative sanity. Miles up the road he was met with a rejoicing welcome. First came a troop of horses, then the Richmond Light Infantry Blues escorting the Governor's carriage and Councillors of State. Old officers fell in with the Hanover Cavalry from which not a member was lacking. The *Gazette* says that all along the road farmers turned out to "behold the defender of their common rights." At the confines of the city Captain Dunscomb's artillery fired a salute.

"The joy of the day," says the *Gazette*, "was so infectious a nature that each patriotic bosom caught the generous contagion until the glow of enthusiasm became as general as it was laudable. It is thus that wisdom and virtue, patriotism and firmness will ever be rewarded by a free, enlightened and grateful people."

There is no wonder that Marshall was delayed in writing

to Polly. On the day after his arrival there was a public meeting at which Dr. John Adams, brother-in-law of Marshall's brother William, made an address of welcome on the part of citizens who had already themselves spoken much on that subject. Barely recovered from that affair, two days later the Mayor and Common Council gave a dinner in Marshall's honor on the Quoit Club grounds under the trees in Buchanan's Old Field. On this occasion Bushrod Washington, Associate Justice of the Supreme Court of the United States, made the address.

In the midst of all these affairs, Marshall was trying to renew his acquaintance with his three-year-old daughter Mary, while meeting for the first time the son who bore his name. He was also concerned with unpacking the things which he had purchased in Paris, that miniature and Houdon's bust for which he sat in Paris, also some glass and china, and the regal clock. Still he regretted that there was no French wine.

Finally on a steaming August afternoon he wrote to Polly:

Richmond Augt. 18th 98

My dearest Polly

I reach'd this place about a week past & have scarcely had time to look into any business yet there are so many persons calling every hour to see me. I have been a little indisposed by the hot & disagreeable ride but am now perfectly well & if I cou'd only learn that you were entirely restor'd I shou'd be happy. Your Mama & friends are in good health & your Mama is as cheerful as usual except when some particular conversation discomposes her. Your sweet little Mary is one of the most fascinating little creatures I ever beheld. She has improv'd very much since I saw her & I cannot help agreeing that she is a substitute for her lovely sisters. She talks in a way not easily to be understood tho she comprehends very well every thing that is said to her & is the most coquetish little prude & the most prudish little coquet I ever saw. I wish she was with you as I think she wou'd entertain you more than all the rest of your children put together. Poor little John is cutting teeth & of course is sick. He appeared to know me as soon as he saw me. He wou'd not come to me but he kept his eyes fix'd on me as on a person he had some imperfect recollection of. I expect he has been taught to look at the picture & had some confused idea of a likeness. He is small & weakly but by no means an ugly child. If as I hope we

have the happiness to raise him I trust he will do as well as the
rest. Poor little fellow, the present hot weather is hard on him
cutting teeth, but great care is taken of him & I hope he will do well.

I hear nothing from you my dearest Polly but I will cherish the
hope that you are getting better & will indulge myself with expecting
the happiness of seeing you in october quite yourself. Remember my
love to give me this pleasure you have only to take the cold bath,
to use a great deal of exercise to sleep tranquilly & to stay in
cheerful company. I am sure you will do everything which can
continue to give you back to yourself & me. This hot weather must
be very distressing to you—it is so to every body—but it will soon be
cooler. Let me know in time everything relative to your coming down.

Farewell my dearest Polly

I am your ever affectionate

J Marshall

Polly might smile that her husband supposed an infant
could recognize a likeness in a miniature, but could she take
comfort from this letter describing "the poor little fellow"?
"If" we raise him, he says. In tidewater Virginia at this time,
infant mortality was so usual a tragedy that the church
acknowledged that swift "if" by permitting a parent to bap-
tize a failing infant as long as he used the words, "Father,
Son and Holy Spirit," and said the Lord's Prayer.

Before Polly returned to Richmond in October, Marshall
was again involved in campaigning for public office. In the
past September President Adams had proffered him a seat
as associate Justice on the bench of the Supreme Court of
the United States. Still aglow from holiday with Polly, he
asked to be excused, pleading family affairs. But he was
called to order by that patriot who had never let family matters interfere with public duty.

From General Washington came a peremptory invitation
to visit Mount Vernon in company with the General's nephew, Justice Bushrod Washington. They were not even to
consider the weather in being prompt upon the door sill of
that mansion. Prompt they were indeed, and very wet. For
it is said, "They came on horseback, and, for convenience,
or some other purpose, had bestowed their wardrobe in the
same pair of saddle-bags, each one occupying his side. On
their arrival, wet to the skin by a shower of rain, they were
shown into a chamber to change their garments. One un-

locked his side of the bag, and the first thing he brought
forth was a black bottle of whiskey. He insisted that this
was his companion's repository; but on unlocking the other,
there was found a huge twist of tobacco, a few pieces of
corn-bread, and the complete equipment of a wagoner's
pack-saddle. They had exchanged saddle-bags with some
traveller on the way, and finally made their appearance in
borrowed clothes which fitted them most ludicrously."

It is said that in neither mirth nor sorrow was the General
ever seen unrestrained, but this time his laughter so heartily
joined that of the younger men that it could not be told
whose was the loudest. Although for those long conferences
on the veranda overlooking a wayward river, he faced victims
awkwardly clad in his own clothes, he lost no time in chit-
chat. Shortly and positively he informed Marshall that it
was his duty to run for a seat in Congress. It was, said the
General, "the sacred duty of every man who could contribute
to the success of sound opinion . . . to offer his services to the
public."

Marshall took his hand out of the pocket of the borrowed
broadcloth coat, and replied that he had "large pecuniary
engagements" dependent upon the income from his law
practice, which to neglect now might mean the loss of Fairfax lands. These were two stubborn men who argued thus
for four days on the veranda, and late into the firefly-pierced
nights. Finally they haughtily bade each other good night.
Before dawn Marshall crept down from his bedroom all
booted and spurred now clad in his wrinkled riding clothes,
ready to fetch his horse and ride off toward Richmond before
a friendship would be shattered by hardheadedness. But the
wily General who had captured Lord Cornwallis was not to
be circumvented by a subordinate. He was waiting on the
doorstep. When Marshall reached Richmond he declared
himself for Congress.

In October the State Department paid Marshall the balance due for his French mission, $14,463.17, which he ap-
plied largely to payments on Fairfax lands. And in October
he rode to Fredericksburg to meet Polly. He laughed with
her over the situation into which General Washington had

forced him. Marshall's opponent for a seat in Congress would be that John Clopton who had deserted Congress last June rather than be on hand to honor the Federalist envoy. Do you think you can win? My wise, pretty Oracle, you do the guessing!

Upon arriving in Richmond, Polly found the campaign taking on momentum, and for one recovering from a nervous breakdown it must have been a soul-shaking experience. For this was not to be an ordinary election. Marshall says the issues were deeper than a contest between a Federalist and a Republican candidate. This campaign was not for or against the Alien and Sedition Acts, nor yet for or against war with England or France. This was the gigantic struggle of the first American political machine to come into being, and Jefferson was its master mind. Next to Washington, Marshall was its strongest antithesis, and he was in the full vigor and charm of expanding influence.

Therefore by pen and press and rumor, Jefferson fought Marshall's election to Congress in a campaign that is historically characterized as "one of the most acrimonious." The stilted forms of the early American press could hardly contain the growing tempers. However, Jefferson wrote to Polly's brother-in-law, Colonel Carrington, that were it left to him "to decide whether we should have a government without newspapers or newspapers without a government, I should not hesitate a moment to prefer the latter. But I mean that every man should receive those papers and be capable of reading them."

So the campaign was prosecuted by gazette and pamphlet, but most effectively by private letters intended to be passed from hand to hand, and by gatherings in tavern taprooms, and around barbecue fires in open fields. In these gatherings Marshall's gifts were supreme. He could always raise a laugh from friend and foe. He told jokes aptly and without venom. He made quick verses that laughed at both factions. He danced the country dances as only Silver Heels could.

When the Jeffersonian press spoke scathingly of Marshall's hilarity at political meetings, Polly went out into the garden to air her indignation in the fragrance of early roses.

What do the people want? Joy? Or promises? She cupped a rose in her hands, and then leaned to investigate fresh shoots of garden pinks. Hastily she called Peter, for the promises—she meant pinks—were being ruined by insects.

With an open heart and determined mind, Marshall applied himself to the campaign, never too hopeful, but, he says, "I had reason to know that a politician even in times of violent party spirit maintains his respectability by showing his strength; and is most safe when he encounters prejudice most fearlessly."

Polly, who was sunk under opposition one day and encouraged by enthusiasm the next, could not sleep at night. Marshall read to her until she dozed off. Scott's novels, English poetry or the new American Book of Common Prayer could generally induce sleep for her. Sometimes she had to listen to a press effusion of Marshall's supporters, such as a questionnaire in the Alexandria paper contrived to exhibit Marshall's policies. Some friend of her husband signing himself "Freeholder" had written it to answer the Jeffersonians who demanded to know how Marshall stood on the Alien and Sedition Acts, that controversial product of the Federalist administration.

To that question Freeholder quoted Marshall as saying that he was not an advocate of the Alien and Sedition Bills. He would have opposed them if he had been in Congress when they were propelled through that body by Federalists. He thinks them fraught with all those mischiefs ascribed to them by Virginians generally. He believed them useless and unnecessarily irritating "at a time when our very existence as a nation may depend on our union." By their very terms these laws were about to expire, and if they should again come before Congress he would indisputably oppose them. His foreign policy, Marshall had told Freeholder, was, "Commercial intercourse with all, but political ties with none . . . never connect ourselves with any nation whatever."

Polly may have felt the atmosphere clearing for a moment. But then the New England papers copied the article. Those very Federalists who had treated Marshall with pleasant attentions upon his first appearance in the Supreme Court in

1796, now poured their ire into the press. Fisher Ames of Massachusetts said that Marshall's character was done for. Theodore Sedgewick of the same State and party declared that it was a "mysterious and unpardonable" electioneering trick for Marshall to come out against a bill of his own party. But George Cabot of Massachusetts had a gleam of hope. "Some allowance," he said, "should be made for the influence of the Atmosphere of Virginia which doubtless makes every one who breathes it visionary & upon the subject of free government incredibly credulous."

Marshall's friend, Secretary of State Pickering, wrote to Mr. Sedgewick that he had not met with one good Federalist who approved of Marshall's stand on the Alien and Sedition Acts, but that it could not be called an electioneering trick, for, he added, "General Marshall is incapable of doing a dishonorable act." When northern papers called him "aristocrat," "tory," "British agent," to which Jefferson added "hypocrit," the *Aurora* of Philadelphia had the grace to apologize for "attacking a man whose talents are splendid and whose private character is amiable."

In the midst of the campaign an armory was being erected at the foot of Capitol hill in Richmond. It was intended that it should be stocked with arms and ammunition in case the Federal government should encroach upon State prerogatives.

If in Polly's presence anyone should presume to differ with her husband's politics, she would politely imply that General Marshall had full knowledge of the affairs of government. Alone with him she would ask, "Are you sure you are right?" He could laugh and catch her ribband that smelled of geraniums. He was sure of just one thing—that she was the fairest treasure of his life. She did wish that sometimes he would be on the same side of the political fence with the Nicholases, Brockenboroughs and Tuckers, and other best families in the Court End of Town.

The impression that not Mr. Clopton, but Mr. Jefferson, was Marshall's enemy hung like a dark cloud in Polly's mind. Her mother eventually gave her sympathy. On sunny mornings Mrs. Ambler would ride with her daughter, Mrs.

General Marshall, or if the day was dull, sit with her in the parlour warming hands at glowing coals and hearts in a shared disgust.

Mrs. Ambler was that Rebecca Burwell, a love of Jefferson's youth, whom he spoke of as "Fair Belinda." His horse had beaten the same path between York and Williamsburg that Marshall took seventeen years later on the same kind of errand. For a while mingling among the principal families of York in Grace churchyard, Belinda had given the youth from Goochland County a comehither, then had turned a cold shoulder and married Jacquelin Ambler, while Marshall had been successful in courting Belinda's daughter.

Then mother and daughter were off to the good old days of rich plantations, of grand mansions for which British merchants had never yet been paid, of the concourse of fashion and aristocracy, of business and politics in the old churchyards, and of the desolation now of the old chapels. Mr. Jefferson was responsible for that too, with his loose talk of freedom of religion. Certainly Polly must have heard her husband say that unless we control our commerce others will do it for us. Well, the same is true of religion. Freedom, fiddlesticks! Look, my dear, at the state of religion under all this freedom. Only one church, that is, one Episcopal church, in Richmond, and that at the far end of town from most of the fashionable people. It may easily be understood how it is impossible for it to be opened except on Easter, Whitsunday and Christmas. And so cold then! It is terrible for funerals to be held there, but there is no other place for fashionable people to be buried. That long road twisting and turning to keep the carriages from dragging the horses backward into the creek!

But there now. There now. Talk of funerals always does make you cry. Poor kind, sweet Mr. Buchanan was so untidy at the last one. Bishop White now—he is a gentleman to grace the pulpit. Mrs. Morris's brother, you know. He says that in all the American empire, the devastated condition of the church is worse right here in Virginia, Mr. Jefferson's state. Of course, I know Mr. Jefferson is your husband's cousin. All great families had a few publicans and sinners.

As April began to brush the trees with green, Marshall walked across the garden to his office, and there wrote his brother, James Markham Marshall: "The fate of my election is extremely uncertain. The means to defeat it are despicable in the extreme and yet they succeed. Nothing I believe so debases or pollutes the human mind than factions." And Jefferson wrote to a friend, "The tide is evidently turning . . . from Marshall's romance." But the tide did not retreat according to expectation. Patrick Henry, hearing that he was being quoted as opposed to Marshall as an aristocrat, wrote one of those intended-to-be-shown letters, addressed to Archibald Blair, a neighbor of Polly's.

By the time it got to Polly's hand it was well worn. She read the fine sentences describing the difficulties of the French mission. She was glad Mr. Henry had said France would destroy our "virtue, morality and religion . . . the armour . . . which renders us invincible." She pursed her lips and, calling Belinda's attention, read aloud what Mr. Henry had to say about "infidelity under the name of philosophy." To herself she read again and again the paragraph in which Mr. Henry boldly stated that "General Marshall ever stood high in my esteem as a private citizen. His temper and disposition were always pleasant, his talents and integrity unquestioned. These things are sufficient to place that gentleman far above any competition in the District for Congress . . . it is really astonishing, that blindness itself should hesitate in the choice . . . Tell Marshall that I love him because he acted as a republican, as an American. I really should give him my vote for Congress, preferably to any citizen in the State at this juncture, except one only excepted."

It was generally held that the one exception was General Washington. But might it not have been Patrick Henry himself? For he was also campaigning at this time in Charlotte County for a seat as Representative in Congress. He was opposed by a young upstart in politics called "Jack Randle" by his neighbors, but signing himself Randolph of

Roanoke. Polly remembered seeing him once as he rode into Richmond on a fine horse, as dapper as a girl masquerading in gentlemen's riding clothes, and as beautiful. She always thought of silver when his name was mentioned. Silver spurs he wore on his boots and silver bells in his voice. He was twenty-seven-years-old this year, but his youth had no fire, only a silver sheen. Two black servants always rode with him, Jubal and John. Their low jungle voices were a basso to his silver tenor.

Though his own party jeered, "You have lost the affection and applause of the world," Marshall was elected by a moderate majority on the most pugnacious election day Richmond had ever seen.

It is to be wondered whether Polly, walking along the path from her mother's house, put out her hands to ward off collision with fifteen-year-old Tom, or twelve-year-old Jaquelin running to tell her what they had seen and heard in the courthouse yard. There under the trees long tables served as polls. At each end sat a candidate separated by election judges. All around in the yard constituents dispensed strong drink from handily placed kegs. Gleefully the boys reported knock-down, drag-out fights all over the place, in which everybody seemed to be involved except their father and Mr. Clopton, who were all the time hopping up to bow when a voter stepped up to the table and said, "I vote for Mr. Clopton" or "General Marshall." But if a man —I mean a gentleman, 'scuse me, ma'am—said Mr. Clopton, everybody'd beat him up, and if he said Pa he would get beat badder—worser, I mean. And you ought to have seen Mr. Rutherfoord, Mother; you know, all puffed up and respectable—like this, Mother, you know. He voted right, but Mr. Clopton's man—warn't anybody you know— he stepped up and—look, Mother, like this—he said he would smash Mr. Rutherfoord's mouth in on his teeth. I didn't say it, he did. And you know what, Mother, you know what? Everybody is fighting. You can hear the heads crack. And banged-up eyes! Everywhere! You oughter smell the whiskey. No'm, we didn't drink it. It's all gone now anyway. The men—I mean gentlemen—got to rolling, and the kegs got to rolling, and what warn't drunk up was all over the ground.

All day the boys must run back and forth between the courthouse and Polly's ear. Only sunset and reinforced police put an end to their excitement. Only the loud voice of an election judge put an end to disputes over the count of votes, and declared General Marshall to be the winner. It is doubtful that Marshall had time to read to Polly that night. She must be content with the tales the boys continued to tell after they had been ordered to bed, putting their heads through a crack in her door for one more, and one more.

In August Marshall rode out to Kentucky for that long-promised visit to his aging father, spending all of his time there, walking over the broad acres of "Buckpond" and "Liberty Hill," discussing farming, and family legacies with Colonel Thomas Marshall. They may have laughed over Marshall's tales of French foibles, masculine and feminine. They may have given each other news of old veterans of the war they had fought together. But on his return to Richmond, Marshall heard that it was being said that he had gone out to Kentucky to prevent Kentucky's Resolution to resist the Alien and Sedition Acts. He laughed when he read another of those to-be-passed-around letters of Mr. Jefferson which said, "The visit of the apostle Marshall to Kentucky excites anxiety." Mr. Jefferson was like an admiral sitting on a bluff sending out fleets of rumors.

CHAPTER XII

Congressman

WHEN THE Sixth Congress convened in Philadelphia on December second, 1799, Polly was with her husband in that capital city. Benjamin Franklin once remarked that to comtemplate a town where everything is as well arranged as it is in Philadelphia would make an atheist believe in God. Polly already believed in God, so it was a gratuitous foretaste of Heaven for her to be for a while where cleanliness and order were community habits. As she rode about town she was enchanted by clean wide streets where young trees etched a veil of wintry shadows across the faces of red brick mansions. The size of those mansions amazed her. Many of them were three times larger than hers in Richmond. They all had marble steps trimmed with iron railings, that led to handsome doorways flanked by gleaming white pilasters. They all had shining brass nameplates on polished mahogany doors. And Polly could hardly believe her eyes. White women servants down on their knees scrubbing the brick pavements in front of the mansions! When Robin Spurlock on the coachman's box saw those white servants he cocked his elbows more jauntily, and held his whip before his face as if it were the Mayor's mace.

Polly glanced indifferently at the Greek Temples housing the Bank of Pennsylvania and the First Bank of the United States, for Richmond had had a brief architectural spell of Greek Temples too. But Philadelphia's beautiful Gothic churches raised her spirits as if all seven branches of the golden candlestick had been lit at once. With shining eyes she looked back at the spires when Robin turned into a street of shops.

Philadelphia fashions were as exciting as Philadelphia cleanliness. When Polly first saw them worn by ladies in a drawing room she pursed her lips and looked away. For she had first appeared in society in a bulging gown of made-over London finery decades old. Here everything was new, and French. That meant no stays, skirts narrow and clinging,

131

arms bare above the elbow, and soft sashes worn close "under
the rich luxuriance of Natur's Charm," as Mrs. President
Adams put it, and with "no screening kerchief." And, dear
life! how the faces were painted! Bold red splotches on each
cheek that never could have been made with crushed geranium blossoms!

The modish muslin caps, frilled about the face and neck,
were, however, entirely to Polly's taste, and very becoming
to her. She puchased two or three at once. Probably also
she bought a top hat for her husband since she found that
it was the custom for Congressmen to wear them during the
sessions. It is to be hoped that she bought one of those new
red broadcloth cloaks trimmed in white fur for herself. She
was thirty-three years old, that age when a woman's loveli-
ness is most secure. There was a lilt to Polly's expression
then that belied the spells of gloom which often overcame
her. Marshall would have thought that she became the
cherry-colored wrap. He would have smiled proudly when
she called with him on President and Mrs. Adams.

The Marshalls also called on young Maria Jefferson who
was hostess for her father, the Vice President, in a pleasant
residence beside the Schuylkill River. The seven Negro
slaves and five spanking Virginia horses in the Jefferson
menage would not have caused Polly a lifted eyebrow, but
the French cook was a curiosity. And, of course, so was Mr.
Jefferson when he came striding in. To Polly he seemed as
brightly painted as the Philadelphia ladies. His face, his
waistcoat and small clothes were all brick red. His coat was
blue with shining buttons. His unruly hair was red, tied
into a stiff queue, which to Polly's way of thinking seemed
to be pointing the way backward to all comers. Mr Jefferson
was very polite, paying her the most proper compliments,
which she accepted absently, being busy thinking that she
preferred black hair.

The call, says the Norfolk *Gazette* and *Public Ledger,*
was not returned. Ten years later that paper published the
story under the heading, "A true Annecdote."

"Mr. Marshall was, as will be recollected, one of the federald

members from the state of Virginia in '99, when Mr. Jefferson was
vice-president. As was and is the etiquette, Mr. Marshall waited on
the vice-president soon after he reached Philadelphia. The canvass
was then commencing, which terminated in the vice-president's
elevation to his present station, and was the common topick of
conversation. In a mixed company where every gentlemen present
was expressing freely his opinion on the subject, Mr. Marshall
seemed to regard lightly many objections started in opposition to
Mr. Jefferson's election; adding that for his part, he should be comparatively at ease, in case of his success, was there no better ground
to apprehend national injury from such an event; but he believed the
vice-president had unfortunately imbibed an overweening partiallity
for France, which he dreaded as the fruitful source of woe to our
country, should he be advanced to the helm of state, in the then
convulsed situations of Europe.

"The incautious declaration . . . was quickly conveyed by one of
the gentlemen present to the vice-president . . .

"The vice-president took care to announce to Mr. Marshall his
knowledge of the conversation . . . by omitting him only in the return of the ceremonial visits he had received."

It made small difference to Polly! She was basking in the
"flattering attention" always paid her husband in the city of
Philadelphia. Not only with the officers of State were the
Marshalls invited to dine, but in many of the private mansions. At the Binghams' Polly was quite startled by high
fashion. When the handsome door was opened, a white
footman in elegant livery called loudly, "General and Mrs.
Marshall from Virginia!" She saw that at every door stood
an equally elegant white servant who took the call from the
footman and sent it on to the man at the next door, and
the next and the next, until they arrived at the parlour
where Mrs. Bingham waited to receive them. The General
laughed at Polly. On his last visit to this mansion, a companion legislator had so far misunderstood high society custom as to answer loudly, "I'm coming as fast as I can." Polly's
laugh always made Marshall happier than ever.

But Polly was shy, and when she found that Philadelphia
ladies scorned to play cards for amusement, rather priding
themselves that they could entertain each other with conversation, she stopped accepting invitations. She could not
chatter. She was generally at home in their rented rooms

when Marshall came in after the day's session of Congress. He would be eager with conflict and conquest. He was winning the New Englanders. Theodore Sedgewick, Speaker of the House, who once accused Marshall of political trickery, was now writing home, "I have been much in company with General Marshall . . . He possesses great powers and has much dexterity in the application of them . . . In short we can do nothing without him . . . His intentions are perfectly honorable, & yet I do believe he would have been a more decided man had his education been on the other side of the Delaware." And George Cabot of Massachusetts wrote, "In Congress you see General Marshall is a leader. He is I think a virtuous & certainly an able man. But you see in him the faults of a Virginian. He thinks too much of that State, & he expects the world to be governed according to the rules of Logic . . . He seems calculated to act a great part."

He brought a laugh home to Polly one day, about Randolph of Roanoke. "Jack Randle" was a freshman Congressman with Marshall. He strode into the House every day in riding clothes, even the silver spurs, and carrying a crop. He seemed to be racing to prevent any change in any old order. As soon as John Randolph found his sea legs on the Ship of State, he rose to advocate the reduction of armed forces, referring to regular troops as "mercenaries" and "raggamuffines." That night at the theatre Randolph was insulted by several young officers who resented the appellation. Now he was demanding Congressional action against the officers. The House became like a bug on its back trying to find which leg could turn it right side up. They argued all day as to whether this constituted breach of Congressional privilege. After four days of laughter with Polly about this crisis, Marshall could tell her that he had gotten up and given it as his opinion that "the incident did not call for intervention of this House." The business was settled accordingly.

The office of conciliator seems to have fallen to Marshall at the start of this Congress. More and more often he was assigned the task of drawing opposing opinions into line until they spoke to the same purpose. For while the American people were privately happy and prosperous, they were irritated by government and jealous of the powers of a chief executive.

The speech with which President Adams opened the Sixth Congress pleased no one. He felt that he was acting with courage and righteousness. Congress felt that he was stubborn and exceeded his authority. He announced that against the advice of his Cabinet, he was sending a second mission to France. Then he reported that setting aside a verdict of the Pennsylvania courts, he had pardoned Lieutenant Fries, who was under sentence of death for leading armed resistance against the federal tax collector, an act that needed executive explanation. This man had not levied war against the United States, only against a tax collector. He was a political criminal who threw himself undefended on the mercy of the court. Adams had looked down the vista of untried democracy, and hesitated to initiate the practice of hanging in such a case. For would such judgement have been constitutional? Or would it have been old time tyranny?

With the grumbling at its worst, Marshall was chosen to draft an answer to the President's speech, which Congress hoped would rebuke the President. But Marshall wrote a smooth and diplomatic address, directed to inspiring the people with confidence in the Constitution and the administration. Congressmen accepted it with glum dissatisfaction, and in a doleful procession the gentlemen in top hats carried the address through the streets of the City of Brotherly Love to the rented executive residence. The President being in a mood for compliments, not diplomacy, accepted it with equally glum discontent.

A few days later in Congress Hall Marshall was engaged in pouring his good humor into this situation, when he was touched on the shoulder, and informed that a passenger on the stage from the South had brought word of the death of General Washington. Stricken for a moment, Marshall then rose, asking for the attention of the House. The Congressional Record says that "in a voice that bespoke the anguish of his mind" and with "countenance that expressed the greatest regret," General Marshall gave the sad news, adding, "After receiving intelligence of a national calamity so heavy and afflicting, the House of Representatives can be but ill fitted for public service." He therefore moved an adjournment, and both houses retired until the next day.

Marshall must have gone out to find Polly, for, he says, "She was the solace of my life." Next morning he was appointed to make the formal announcement of the tragedy to Congress. Then that voice that was generally so sharp and dry was softened and deep as he said: "Our Washington is no more! The Hero, the Sage, and the Patriot of America—the man on whom in times of danger every eye was turned and all hopes were placed—lives now only in his own great actions and in the hearts of an affectionate and afflicted people."

Marshall was also appointed to read the Congressional Resolutions prepared during the night by Light Horse Harry Lee, who was too much affected to trust his own voice. In these Resolutions the term American Empire gave place to the term American Nation, and for the first time Washington was called, "First in war, first in peace and first in the hearts of his countrymen."

For a while those countrymen saw no more through politics darkly, but were face to face with loss. They spoke of Washington as the leader "who more than any other . . . had contributed to found this our widespread empire, and to give the Western World its independence." The press was as unrestrained in praise as it had been in condemnation. Mrs. Adams thought the praise too extravagant, as she was convinced that General Washington had not won the war by himself, and she thought too little was being said about the nation's good fortune in having so fine a successor in the office of President, a fact which she would have too much delicacy herself to advertise.

A pall of sincere grief spread over the land. Federal court entertainment continued, but now the ladies wore black sashes on white dresses. This however was all a distant cloud on the horizon for Polly, for she was enclosed in that bright affection she craved, and Marshall's grief was colored with contemplation of a great and good life, whose work begun must be continued by the Federalists.

The Congress returned at once to its business. Under the surface of immediate legislative action seethed a conflict in which the parties vied for leadership. President and Vice President were set against each other as candidates for election to the executive office. The consummate power of Thomas Jefferson to marshal public opinion was arrayed against John Adams' practical dedication to founding a government. So equally divided were the parties that disputed elections were a dangerous possibility. "Looking forward to the election," said the Speaker of the House, the Federalists offered a Bill for Deciding Disputed Elections of President and Vice President by a Committee with definitive power, of Representatives, Senators and Supreme Court. In cloak room conversation Marshall talked this bill to death, thereby saving the political career of his remorseless enemy, Thomas Jefferson; for Senate and Court were predominantly against the Jeffersonian party at this time.

A bill which Marshall did support was the Bankruptcy Law which some say was designed by friends of Robert Morris, and which when passed would release him from debtors prison by Easter. This passed by one vote. The Speaker of the House says Marshall's influence accomplished that. Of especial interest to Polly was a petition of free men of color asking the House to revive the fugitive from justice laws and the anti-slave laws deferred now by the Constitution until 1808. They also prayed Congress to take such measures as should in due course free all slaves. This petition piqued no partisanship. Upon a motion from Samuel Goode of Virginia that this was a subject from which the general government was precluded by the Constitution, the matter was dropped by a vote of every member of the House except one, a Congregational minister from Massachusetts.

Then in the Marshall rooms early on the morning of February thirteenth, was heard the infant voice of James Keith Marshall greeting the toddling republic which had learned to talk, but not yet to walk like independent man. In the Quaker city his cradle was rocked by a Negro slave,

Mammy Venus, who, if subjected to the Catechism question, "Can you tell me, child, who made you?" would have answered, "God." If asked, "Why did God make you?" would have answered, "To nurse Marshall children."

When James was three weeks old, Marshall unexpectedly took his first stride on that long climb to his place in history by fixing a Constitutional interpretation in the face of opposition. To Polly it simply meant that she must listen again to the distressing "Jonathan Robbins" story of mutiny and murder on board a British ship on the high seas, of the escape of the murderer to America, of his discovery in Charleston, South Carolina, of President Adams' request to the Federal District Court in South Carolina for the sailor to be turned over to the British authorities in accord with the Twenty-Seventh Article of the Jay Treaty, of the seaman's confession and execution by the British—all past now, but an available vehicle for moving public opinion. The Republicans would use it to stigmatize the Federalist President in a Resolution condemning him on the eve of elections. He was accused of interfering with the American courts when he refused to hold the sailor for trial in South Carolina.

It was all horrible enough to shake her frame, but Polly could not have resisted if Marshall asked her to join the audience of ladies in Congress Hall on the day he expected to rise on the floor and defend the President for protecting the national honor by adhering to the terms of a treaty. The Winter day was bright, and Robin Spurlock drove cautiously so that she relished release from her long weeks indoors. She would have enjoyed the flattering attention shown her by the audience who recognized her as the wife of General Marshall from Virginia. She felt that it was proper for her to look down at her muff while her husband meandered through his introductory remark that he felt impelled to rescue public opinion "from numerous prejudices which surround it." But she looked up quite excited when he began to hammer out the fiat that the Constitutional clause fixing trial by jury in American courts did not apply to alien fugitives whose crimes were not committed on American territory. The Constitution, he said, "is not designed to secure the rights of the people of Europe or Asia, or to direct and control proceedings against criminals throughout the universe." Thus the extradition was not a matter for the American courts to decide upon, but was "a National demand upon the Nation, and the President is the sole organ of the nation in its external relations."

The speech was long and weighted with example and illustration so that Polly's attention wandered to the audience. She was pleased that they were so much more attentive than she was to the words being uttered by her handsome, awkward, tall, intelligent husband. She watched Mr. Gallatin with brightened eyes, pacing like a fretted lion behind the gentlemen of Congress. When Marshall finally sat down, she saw friends of Mr. Jefferson pull Mr. Gallatin forward, urging him to answer Marshall. She smiled when she heard him reply, "Answer it yourself. I think it unanswerable."

She probably rode back to her lodgings before the balloting which defeated the resolution of censure by a resounding majority of both parties.

Often she must have marveled that the streets of so large a city could be so quiet. Was it the influence of Quakers who, though never conspicuous, were everywhere evident in quiet voices, in gentle language, in a sense of restraint? Or was it that she missed the sounds of laughing, singing Negro labor which filled the streets of Richmond like sunshine?

Robin caused quite a sensation in Philadelphia. He was so pompous, always adding weird color to the Marshall livery with scraps of feathers or purloined gold braid. He was provided with long black stockings, but when he appeared ready for duty the stockings had strangely become bright yellow. When he walked about the streets of this sedate city his comic costume and ridiculous airs drew such crowds of amused followers that once police were called to quell a near riot. Polly tucked her pretty chin into the white fur collar of her cherry red cloak to muffle a chuckle as she remembered how Robin, a wedding present from Colonel Marshall, had strutted into the small cottage behind her mother's house. From that day, sixteen years ago, Robin had

been king of the servants' quarters. As the number of servants increased, so his majestic manners burgeoned.

At the close of Congress, Speaker Sedgewick again writes
about Marshall. "His character stamped itself on the measures of the present sessions . . . He is a man of very affectionate disposition, of great simplicity of manners and honest and honorable in all his conduct. He is attached to pleasures, with convivial habits strongly fixed. He is indolent
therefore, and indisposed to take part in the common business of the House. He has a strong attachment to popularity but is indisposed to sacrifice to it his integrity. He is
disposed . . . to express great respect for the sovereign people & to quote their opinions as an evidence of the truth.
This gentleman when aroused, has strong reasoning powers;
they are almost unequalled."

Before the Sixth Congress had closed, President Adams
was in a temper with the leaders of his party, but most of all
with his Cabinet. Peremptorily he ordered the resignation of
his Secretary of War, James McHenry, and nominated
Marshall for the post. In his Autobiography Marshall says,
"I was really surprised . . . I did not believe myself to be
well qualified for this department, and was not yet willing
to abandon my hopes of reinstating my self at the bar. I
therefore addressed a letter to Mr. Adams making my ac-
knowledgment for his notice of me, and requesting that he
would withdraw my name from the Senate, as I was not
willing openly to decline a place in an administration which
I was disposed cordially to support . . . I proceeded immediately to Richmond . . . Mr. Adams did not withdraw my
name, & I believe the nomination was approved."

It was approved, but Polly and the children at home in
their own house and garden, surrounded by friends and
family, made the practice of law in his own office seem very
attractive. "I have always believed," he says, "that national
character as well as happiness depends on the female part
of society more than is generally imagined." Therefore in the
midst of casual joys Marshall was again surprised and perplexed when he was notified that Adams had dismissed his
Secretary of State and named him to this post also. Long and

long he pondered this. "I never felt more doubt," he says, "than on the question of accepting or declining this offer." Pickering was his well liked friend; and "a stubborness of temper" was piqueing Marshall to run again for Congress in the face of falsehood and irrational abuse by the press, still concerned to ruin him for the French mission. "I could not bring myself to yield to it," said Marshall.

"On the other hand," continues the Autobiography, "the office was precisely that which I wished, and for which I had vanity enough to think myself fitted. I should remain in it while the party remained in power; should a revolution take place it would at all events relieve me from the competition for Congress without yielding to my adversaries. . . . I determined to accept the office."

In July, all in a clamor of protest from Mrs. Adams, the seat of government was transferred from Philadelphia to Washington. This slight hill surrounded by swamps, Mrs. Adams thought, was a good place to contract the ague. When Summer's first warm breath waved the laundry stretched in the Palace parlour, Mrs. Adams ordered her husband home to their new house at Braintree, Massachusetts, where his admirers had shown their loyalty by dumping a mountain of seaweed which he would personally plough into his fields. The Vice President repaired to his mountain top where from a pillared portico he would direct an army of Negro slaves in scientific agriculture, and then sit down to a bowl full of quills and a world full of politics.

The Secretary of State found himself to be acting government, and had to forego his plans to tour the Virginia Mineral Springs with his family. Instead he must move into an improvised office in the improvised Capitol, where there was trouble aplenty for the State Department, trouble with Barbary pirates, trouble with France, with England, still with British merchants who had given credit to colonists.

There was trouble, too, with an unbridled and purchasable press. Noah Webster of Connecticut was writing, "No government can be durable . . . under the licentiousness of the press that now disgraces it." The British minister took official exception to some unflattering editorial comment, and demanded an apology from the State Department. Marshall replied that the British press had been equally guilty of international libel, adding that "newspaper charges and surmises . . . are always causes of infinite regret to a government" and would be prevented if the means of prevention existed.

Marshall seems to have expected Polly to join him in Washington. But she was moving about her lovely house, touching the uncluttered mantels upon which candlesticks were not at the moment acting as paper weights, and minueting figurines did not peep over stacks of old letters. Without a crowding fringe of clippings in the frame of her mirror Polly could see that her Philadelphia bonnet was very becoming. Home was vastly convenient after months of boarding.

When she wrote to Marshall on the fifth of August her letter must have told of the new baby's development, the affairs of the Chickahominy farm, messages from friends, and reached the bottom of the page before she thought to mention her health. He answers that letter promptly:

Aug. 8th 1800

My dearest Polly

I have this moment receiv'd yours of the 5th & cannot help regretting that it affords me no hope of seeing you soon or that you are perfectly well.

I am delighted with the account you give me of Mary's dinner with you & of John's good breeding. Tell him I say he is a fine boy for his attention to his sister & his love for his Mama. I approve of you sending the boys up the country. I receiv'd a letter from Tom inclosing the sermon I wrote for but he did not say a single word about you. This was a cruel disappointment to me because I cannot flatter myself with respect to you that silence is an evidence of good health.

I am my dearest Polly
your
J Marshall

Some time during the next four days the Secretary of State spent another long afternoon on the veranda at Mt. Vernon. Madame Washington was sad, and Marshall's tenderness for her suddenly made him homesick for Polly. As soon as he got back to his rooms he sat down and wrote her:

Aug. 20

My dearest Polly

I have just returned from a visit to Mount Vernon where I passed an evening. Mrs. Washington asked me to bring you to see her when you shou'd visit this city. She appears tolerably cheerful but not to possess the same sort of cheerfulness as formerly. You as a widow would I hope show more firmness.

Tell Jaquelin I was much pleased with his letter. If he will keep his word & get a lesson every day while Mr. Burns is absent & will afterwards continue to get a few extra lines he will soon overtake the class he ought now to be in.

Farewell my dearest Polly
I am your ever affectionate
J Marshall

Toward the end of August, shimmering heat in Richmond was broken by a southeast wind which began mildly enough in the night with a few banging shutters. In the morning Polly and the servants spoke gratefully of the cooler air. But all day the wind grew stronger, all night, and all the next day. Gusts whipped green leaves from the trees as if Autumn had come without waiting for Summer to die. Laughter and gloom in the servants' quarters became as sporadic as the sunshine which seemed to be blown in streaks and splotches.

Then the rain came in driven sheets against the Marshall windows. Dripping servants ran in from the kitchen, from the laundry, even Peter and Moses from the stables, and huddled together in the hall, all except Joseph who set about lighting candles. The children seemed to suddenly become twice their number, running about and shouting above the storm. The house was full of wet footprints and noise. Polly, who could not endure confusion, was clenching her teeth until they ached. Almost audibly she decried public affairs that kept her husband from her in this tumult.

Then through the storm the town bell began to toll—to clang urgently. The servants left their huddle and stood apart listening for some sound between the bell and the rain. When Polly dropped her hands from her face, there with his back against the door stood the butler, Joseph, arms outstretched as if he would shut out some danger. Mammy

Venus with the baby in her arms crouched at Polly's feet. A pulse hammered so hard at Polly's throat that she could not speak to little Mary who danced about gleefully crying, "The bell! The bell!"

Then the rain stopped as suddenly as it had begun. At last a knock could be heard at the door. But Joseph would not move. Fiercely he demanded to know, "Who dar?" Only when he recognized the voice of a neighbour would he open a crack. The neighbour pushed the door open, asked Polly if all was well, walked through the lower rooms and, stopping in front of each Negro man, scrutinized him silently, until all were whispering, "Nawsir, Nawsir, 'tain't none of ussen." Then, as mysteriously as he had come, he departed, before Polly could force voice from her throat. But the late sun breaking through great tumbling clouds proclaimed the foolishness of fear.

Next morning, the neighbour returned, and where neither children nor servant could overhear, explained to Polly that a dangerous situation had been met through the loyalty of a slave and the quick military action of Governor Monroe. It seemed that for the past year, under the leadership of Mr. Henry Prosser's slaves, Gabriel and Pharaoh, and Mr. Mosby Sheppard's Solomon, Negro blacksmiths on the plantations, from the limits of Chesterfield County westward to Albemarle, and north to Caroline, had been making crossbows and beating farm implements into jungle knives and spears. With these they had armed six hundred free Negroes and nearly a thousand slaves to rise against the white people of Virginia. A rendezvous was ordered by Gabriel at Ground Squirrel Bridge north of Richmond on the last night of August. In the night the Negroes were to march on the city, break into the treasury, kill the Governor and take over the Capitol. Every man, and woman and child was to be slain, except Quakers, Methodists, Frenchmen and white women who owned no slaves. As the insurgents were travelling toward Ground Squirrel Bridge about noon the storm broke, stopping many of them in their tracks. Envoys were dispatched to Gabriel pointing to the storm as the wrath of God on the uprising. Then Gabriel pulled out a Bible and declared that the Good Book said, "Delay breeds danger," and ordered the company to make ready to march. Solomon's wife had watched him slink off into the darkness just before day and then had wakened her master and mistress warning them of danger to the plantations, which were at once alerted. The city was alarmed by another of the Sheppard servants who had joined the rendezvous, but became so frightened at the storm that he swam the swollen creek, and escaped to the town office of the Sheppards, giving the information which had set the town bell to ringing.

Promptly the Governor mustered the militia in such force that all that was necessary to disband the Negroes was to send Mr. Sheppard's man back to tell Gabriel what he had seen. Slaves slunk quietly back to work on the plantations. Free insurgents were suddenly lost behind inscrutable countenances of the town's day laborers, horse shoers, draymen, carpenters, tobacco hands, coal peddlers, all now subservient and polite, but less songful. Only a burst of unrestrained laughter when two or three passed close to one another told that somber action had been checked. Shortly the three leaders and several lieutenants were lodged in the penitentiary.

For several nights at the doors of Richmond mansions coloured servants sat in one-eyed sleep, guarding their owners. Not since Israel sojourned in Egypt has an alien people been so trusted and so direfully feared as these transplanted Africans. For a few days gentlemen were required to carry arms as they went about business. Then a night guard was set, and a wandering watchman to alarm the sleeping citizens every hour crying, "Oyez! Oyez! All's well!", setting up a cacaphony of barking dogs.

In the Fall the Virginia House of Delegates asked Governor Monroe to consult with President Adams about purchasing lands beyond the limits of the State to be used for colonizing free persons of colour. But Adams, disgusted with The People, was on the doorstep, going out of office. He left the matter to the incoming President. On June fifteenth, 1801, Monroe wrote to President Jefferson: "I inclose you a resolution of the General Assembly of this Commonwealth,

of the last session, by which it is made my duty to corres-
pond with you on the subject of obtaining by purchase lands
without the limits of this State, to which persons obnoxious
to the laws or dangerous to the peace of society may be removed. This resolution was produced by the conspiracy of
the slaves which took place in this city and neighbourhood
last year, and is applicable to that description of persons only.
The idea of such an acquisition was suggested by motives
of humanity . . . to provide an alternate mode of punishment
for those . . . doomed to suffer death."

Rufus King was requested by the United States State Department to investigate the possibility of purchasing land
from a private company of Englishmen who were developing
a settlement at Sierra Leone in the west coast of Africa. But
that company was going out of business, and Jefferson
dropped the matter. However, the Virginia Legislature was
engaged for years in discussion of a means of removing the
free coloured population. Because of the delicacy of the
question the discussions were held in secret.

Chapter XIII

J Marshall, Chief Justice

A s heat waves rose along the banks of the Potomac River, so too the heat of a presidential campaign rose with gathering intensity from julep-drinking groups on the porches of Richmond's gracious homes and from farmers loitering around piles of late corn and apples in Shockoe Valley. For, every white male who owned one hundred acres of land could vote for Thomas Jefferson and Aaron Burr, or for President Adams and General Charles Cotesworth Pinckney. Burr was tagged with the label of Big Business. Pinckney was an aristocrat. John Adams held too tightly to old-fashioned governance. But the name of Thomas Jefferson rang with articulate ideas, such as freedom of the press, freedom of religion, trial by jury, no standing army, and State Sovereignty. Just as clearly rang his condemnation of Federalist practices. He called them centralization, stock-jobbing, speculation, plundering, office-seeking and office-holding, all monarchistic policies." These words the people could understand, and from the people came a toast, "To Thomas Jefferson, the pride of Republicans, and the terror of aristocrats."

As Marshall had his "Hail Columbia," so Jefferson was given a song.

> "Rejoice! Columbia's sons, rejoice
>   To tyrants never bend the knee,
>   But join with heart and soul and voice,
>   For Jefferson and Liberty."

By December thirtieth, 1800, it was clear that Adams and Pinckney had been defeated by a small majority, and that Burr and Jefferson each had seventy-three electoral votes, thus throwing the election into the House of Representatives; and the campaign began all over again. Federalists were bitterly split, largely because of a feud between Alexander Hamilton and John Adams. Both factions sought to use Marshall's influence. Marshall announced that he would

147

take no part in the business. He felt that the country was
in danger from both candidates, adding that if Jefferson was
elected, "no consideration could induce me to be Secretary
of State while there was a President whose political system
I believed to be at variance with my own."

If he asked Polly's opinion this time, she might have urged
him to speak out for his cousin, agreeable to any loss of office
that sent her husband home. All of their friends looked for
this to happen. She may fearfully have pushed him to withdraw altogether from Washington when the press reported
that there was talk of a tie even in the House, in which case
Congress would appoint an Executive until another election could be made, in which case again, a Richmond paper
said, "The government will be at an end."

Maryland and Pennsylvania were arming to march on
the Capitol, breathing threats that any man appointed by
Congress must be assassinated. Jefferson himself was quoted
as saying that the "middle States" would arm and "dethrone"
any "usurper" appointed by Congress. And Federalists were
answering that they were ready to repel any such force with
"ten thousand . . . swords."

Along the streets of Richmond, chatter was aquiver with
"civil war." At the foot of Capitol Square hill the armory
was enlarged and restocked to resist Congressional encroachment if it should come to a matter of war. A chain of mes-
sengers sped day and night between the citizens of Richmond and their agents in Washington.

It may have taken all of five days for the press to deliver
news from New York, and as many weeks for word of hap-
penings in Europe. But the new found passions of independence caught rumor out of the air and spread the papers
with columns of exuberant denunciation.

Fisher Ames of New England wrote, "Newspapers are
an over-match for any government. They will first overawe
and then usurp it."

Suddenly on January twentieth, 1801, in the midst of
this acrimonious battle of pens and printing presses, President Adams appointed John Marshall to the seat of Chief
Justice of the Supreme Court of the United States. Marshall,

Courtesy of The John Marshall House

THOMAS, oldest son of Polly and John Marshall, done by Fevret de St. Memin in 1807.

said President Adams, "possessed to an extraordinary degree the faculty of putting his own ideas in the minds of others," and was "in the full vigor of middle age, in the full habits of business." "I was pleased as well as surprised," says the Autobiography, "and bowed my head in silence. The nomination . . . was I believe when taken up unanimously approved" by the Senate.

Jefferson, never doubting that the presidency was in his hand, was chagrined, for he had counted on conferring this office on a Republican, and had already dangled it before his avid supporter Judge Spencer Roane of Virginia. Nor was Polly pleased at any honor which threatened to take her husband away from Richmond.

On February seventeenth, after balloting thirty-six times in six days, the House of Representatives elected Jefferson to the presidency by a small majority, with electors from South Carolina and Delaware abstaining, and others casting blanks. Aaron Burr was named Vice President. Thereafter, between President Jefferson and Vice President Burr lay enmity as cold as steel in the night, and between President and Chief Justice, scorn that would be a stone upon which the sword of government would be honed.

It is to be wondered whether, on March fourth, 1801, Polly was in Washington to witness that strange moment of history when John Marshall administered the oath of presidential office to Thomas Jefferson, at Jefferson's special request. Two cousins faced each other across an oath of loyalty to one nation, one striving for a worthy central government with suffrage limited to a knowledge of stewardship, and the other for unlimited suffrage and limited government.

Mrs. Adams was not present. She had departed for Quincy in the middle of February. President Adams was not present. He left the White House four hours before he might brush sleeves on the doorstep with the incoming President.

Nor did the Chief Justice-Secretary of State attend the inauguration ball. He sat in his boarding house writing to his friend General Pinckney that he was not hopeful of "public prosperity & happiness . . . under Democratic guidance.

The Democrats are divided into speculative theorists & absolute terrorists. With the latter I am disposed to class Mr. Jefferson."

The office of Secretary of State was at once given to James Madison. The first lawsuit under the spoils system developed, and appeared in the Supreme Court as Marbury *vs* Madison, Marbury being a disappointed Adams appointee to a minor office, and Madison being the new Secretary of State. Openly the case was looked upon as a rope upon which the administration hoped the Court might hang itself. It lay unsettled for over a year, during which gentlemen of both persuasions believed that the new Chief Justice would go down to political ruin when he handed down a decision no matter what it might be. All the while not even the companion of his thoughts could fathom Marshall's mind or guess what he intended to declare was constitutional law in the matter. The question visited the garden of their companionship like raucous jackdaws when the lark would have been most generous with joy.

What a squawking and a singing there was when Marshall set birds of every feather flying off the perch by rendering the opinion that the law upon which the Court was asked to act was unconstitutional. Therefore the Court could not act, and therefore the case must be dismissed. And how he loved Polly's laugh when he told her in those few words! It had taken eighty-five hundred words to tell the Court the same thing. But in telling them he fixed the supremacy of the Constitution over Congress, and made the Court keeper of the Constitution.

Forthrightly now the goal before Chief Justice Marshall was "a firm and solid government competent to the security of rational liberty." And to this end he labored even when his heart and mind were bleak with worry over Polly.

He voted only once again in his life. That was to oppose a second term for Jefferson.

For this collection, no letters written by J Marshall to My dearest Polly between August of 1800 and January of 1803 have been found. Nor is there anywhere a record of words spoken when Governor Monroe informed Marshall of the death of the only Monroe son. When Marshall laid his wide hand on his friend's shoulder in the mystical brotherhood of those who have stood at the closing doors of Heaven, no words were spoken.

Tucked away among Marshall papers is a clipping from a newspaper of 1802, which says: "On Saturday, May 22, at 12 o'clock Mrs. George Washington terminated her well-spent life. Just before she died she chose a white satin gown for her burial." Which goes to show how Jeffersonian the press was. There was a time when it would have said Madame Washington, or even Lady Washington.

When Marshall came to the High Bench there was only one incumbent who had been on the first Supreme Court under the Constitution. In 1789 President Washington appointed William Cushing of Massachusetts, to be Associate Justice. Cushing was noted for his fastidious dignity. He wore a great wig so pompously that little boys followed him about the streets of Philadelphia, never rude, only awed and curious. It is said that when the Justice turned and saw them, his dignity was not shaken by annoyance. He believed it was his eminence that rendered them pop-eyed and open-mouthed, and bestowed a benign smile on the lads.

The Supreme Justices rode circuit to sit with the furthest District Courts in this people's empire. It is said that Justice Cushing had a special carriage designed for these journeys. It had four stout wheels, was comfortably slung, well cushioned and carried compartments for lunch, liquid refreshments, books and a writing desk. Mrs. Cushing travelled with him, accomplishing the difficult feat of reading aloud as they jogged over stumpy roads. Cushing's patriotism veered toward aristocracy. As vice president of the Massachusetts Convention he had done much to whip enough votes into line for ratification of the Constitution.

Marshall had presided over only two sessions of the Supreme Court when Jefferson gave the signal for an assault upon the judiciary. An Act to improve the system as designed by the Judiciary Act of Congress in 1789 had been passed by a Federalist Congress in 1801, which, among other revisions, would relieve the Supreme Justices from sit-

ting in District Courts. Jefferson's assault was to begin with
a repeal of the Act of 1801. The gentlemen of House and
Senate thereupon engaged in much vituperative oratory. In
terms of human nature the conflict was between new-
formed authorities, the President's, versus the Court's power
to decide the constitutionality of laws passed by Congress.
The administration's attack was directed toward the removal
of all Justices of Federalist appointment. To hold his place
on the Bench now became in Marshall's mind the impera-
tive call of patriotism.

An Act to repeal the Judiciary Act of 1801, and to re-
strict the Supreme Court to one annual session, passed both
houses—not, however, before Jeffersonians, fearful that the
Court would declare the repeal unconstitutional, managed
to suspend the Court for over a year, and not without a
slip on the part of the Jeffersonians who overlooked Section
Twenty-five of the Act they reinstated. The flaming words
of that Section are: "The appellate jurisdiction of the Supreme Court of the United States extends to a final judgement or decree in any suit in the highest court of law or
equity of a state, where is drawn in question the validity of
a treaty, or statute of, or an authority exercised under the
United States and the decision is against their validity."

Thus it was that in January of 1803 Marshall was out
upon judicial circuit. He exhibited none of that parade of
dignity that marked Cushing's progress about the countryside. Marshall at this time generally rode horseback, with a
servant riding along to carry his portmanteau. He travelled
fifty miles a day, he says, stopping two nights between
Richmond and Raleigh, North Carolina, sometimes at a
friend's residence, and sometimes at a wayside inn. On this
trip Peter, not Robin, was his body servant, and not much
assistance. Upon arrival at Davis' Tavern, Marshall wrote to
Polly:

Rawleigh Jany 2d 1803

My dearest Polly

As I know you will feel the same pleasure in hearing from me that
I do in writing to you I sit down to tell you that I find everything

here as pleasant as I cou'd expect & that my journey has been not a disagreeable one. The weather was uncommonly mild & tho rain was continually threaten'd it did not begin to fall till I was safely hous'd. This was extremely fortunate, but with this my good fortune ended. You will laugh at my vexation when you hear the various calamities that have befallen me. In the first place when I came to review my funds, I had the mortification to discover that I had lost 15 silver dollars out of my Waist coat pocket. They had worn through the various mendings the pocket had sustained & sought their liberty in the sands of Carolina. I determin'd not to vex myself with what cou'd not be remedied & order'd Peter to take out my cloaths that I might dress for court when to my astonishment & grief after fumbling several minutes in the portmanteau, staring at vacancy, & sweating most profusely he turned to me with the doleful tidings that I had no pair of breeches. You may be sure this piece of intelligence was not very graciously receiv'd; however after a little scolding I determined to make the best of my situation & immediately set out to get a pair made. I thought I shou'd be a sans culotte only one day & that for the residue of the term I might be well enough dress'd for the appearance on the first day to be forgotten. But the greatest of evils I found, was followed by still greater. Not a taylor in town cou'd be prevailed on to work for me. They were all so busy that it was impossible to attend to my wants however pressing they might be & I have the extreme mortification to pass the whole term without that important article of dress I have mention'd. I have no alleviation for this misfortune but the hope that I shall be enabled in four or five days, to commence my journey homewards & that I shall have the pleasure of seeing you & our dear children in eight or nine days after this reaches you. In the mean time I flatter myself that you are well & happy.

Adieu my dearest Polly

I am your ever affectionate

J Marshall

Marshall's dollars seeking liberty seemed only a part of the fractiousness of the world. Six months ago news of the death of his father in far-off Kentucky had set the floor of life aslant. Now that this great rock of his youth could no longer be seen and touched, a secure foundation for the children of the nation seemed a more than ever cogent need. Strength became his aim.

There are those today who remember that in the Marshall yard stood a great oak tree, a remnant of the forest, encircled by a bench whereon it is said the Chief Justice was often seen, sitting to sort out the parts of his legal problems. It is

said that little Mary, seeing him there, would run along the
path toward him, then stop, remembering that she must not
disturb him. Gathering her skirts in her fists she would tiptoe up to settle herself beside him on the bench, glaring at
the brothers who were creeping over the grass to join her.
Then a squabble would break the silence. But Marshall,
without a word, would show that there was room for all,
making of himself a barrier between factions. Then he would
return to his cogitations, for the children were not alien to
his thoughts. Under the noisome overreaching of men, grab-
bing for each other's advantage, there was a pattern of right
and wrong, a definite line that even children could be taught
to know as justice.

In this Summer of 1803 the oldest of the Marshall sons,
Thomas, graduated from Princeton. Then the Chief Justice
took his family to Oak Hill, which, at his father's death,
came to him. Marshall now owned nearly two thousand
acres of that "upper country" which lifted forested hills to
the foot of the Blue Ridge Mountains.

When they returned to Richmond in the Fall, gossip was
saying that James Monroe had exceeded his authority
in Paris when, with Robert Livingston, he effected the purchase of vast Louisiana territories for the United States at
a bargain price. No one spoke of an experiment Monroe had
witnessed on the Seine River in which steam had propelled
a boat. All were too busily counting States who were protesting that the government had taken too much power unto
itself when it added a cumbersome area to the nation. Senator Plumer of New Hampshire was quoted as saying, "Adopt
this western world into the Union and you destroy at once
the weight and importance of the Eastern States, and compel them to establish a seperate and independent empire."
Tapping Reeves of Connecticut took a poll in his neighbourhood and reported, "All believe we must seperate, and that
this is the most favorable moment." In Boston, Marshall's
friend Fisher Ames was saying, "This country is too big for
union, too sordid for patriotism, too democratic for liberty."
Timothy Pickering wrote, "I do not believe in the practical-
ity of a long continued union."

But Polly was filled with a different kind of amazement. Could it be that with New England tottering on the verge of secession, her husband could think of sending her sweet boy, Jaquelin, to Harvard?

Chapter XIV

A Newspaper

FACTIONS NOW were no longer national purposes. They had become political parties. That Republican machine built by Jefferson's brilliant mind covered the Union as surely as Cromwell's had covered England, both motivated with man's right to his own government. Jefferson's machine was a later model, geared with a press. The newspapers accumulating on the tables and mantels of Polly's house in 1804 were balanced between the parties. There was *The Virginia Gazette*, edited by Augustine Davis, a Federalist. He was one of the earliest postmasters to lose his job under a change of parties, which rather shocked him, for the ink had hardly smeared type to quote Mr Jefferson's inaugural announcement, "We are all Republicans, all Democrats." He was so indignant when he had to print the news that his own son was given the post in his stead, that defiantly he changed the name of his paper to *The Patriot*.

With this caption, Polly placed it on top of the pile. Under it lay *The Examiner*, edited by Republican Meriwether Jones, who had employed a well-educated, drunken sot, James Thompson Callender, partisan for the nonce and for a price. He came from Scotland seeking journalistic adventure. His peregrinations between Federalism and Republicanism landed him several times in gaol for libel, whence he dated his reports.

Beneath *The Patriot* lay the *Washington Federalist*, which used to be the *Virginia Federalist*, but had moved to a more congenial atmosphere.

Then came *The Enquirer*, edited by that hot-blooded Republican Thomas Richie, but owned by his cousin, Judge Spencer Roane.

One periodical lay open and worn in a chair where the boys had dropped it. This was *Bannaker's Almanac*, compiled by a free Negro in Northern Virginia.

Polly tucked one paper under her arm and though it was Republican in sentiment, she carried it to her chair by the

157

window. This was *The Virginia Argus,* a semi-weekly, edited
by Samuel Pleasants, of whom one who remembered wrote
that he was "more expert in wielding the scissors than the
pen." It was very true that his news culled from other papers
was generally cold, but he was a Quaker, and everyone
knows that Quakers are home-minded. On his sheets familiar knowledge paraded with enough variety to be interesting and yet not exhausting.

The *Argus* ran such advertisements as: "Book, by S.
Pleasants jr. Everyman his own Doctor, or the Poor Planter's
Physician." "Book,—The Married Lady's Companion, or
Poor Man's Friend—In Four Parts—1. An Address to the
Married Lady Who is Mother to Daughters. 2. An Address
to the newly married Lady. 3. Some important hints to
the Midwife. 4. An essay on the Management and com-
mon diseases of Children. By Samuel K. Jennings."

Patent medicines such as Cordial Restorative Balsam, Eye
Salve and Aromatic Snuff were advertised, and something in
large print described as "The Pile of Volta, consisting of
300 plates . . . erected by Dr. Trent of this city, for the purpose of administering the new and surprising influence
called Galvanism, in palsies, rheumatism, blindness, deaf-
ness, etc, etc, etc."

Well, Polly was neither blind nor deaf. She did not have
palsy or rheumatism. At least none of her doctors had so
named her ailments. She might come under et cetera, for
she had tried everything else.

Polly could read whose slaves had run away, what merchant was setting out for Europe and would be happy, for
a commission, to attend to business for any gentleman who
had matters abroad. She could read whose plantation was
for sale. James Monroe was offering his farm in Albemarle
County, also his Kentucky lands, 20,000 acres on which
iron and coal had been found. "Cash, good bonds, or liqui-
dated accounts of Col Monroe's would be acceptable as payments." Had he not sold those military warrants yet? Well,
it was hard to understand gentlemen and money. They always had none, but they were always spending. It was said
of Colonel Monroe that he was his brother's keeper, going

further into debt for him. It was also being said that he had purchased a low mountain that truly sat at the feet of his idol on Monticello, and that he had ordered a small "cabban castle" built upon it so situated that a doorway framed a daily vision of the seat of the "Llama of the Mountain," as Polly heard her husband call his cousin Jefferson.

Here was a notice that the clergy of Richmond were raising a fund for a new school. More French schools were offering their select form of education. Mr. Dandridge was opening another of the numerous country academies. Side by side with such culture were notices of the dates of the Scottsville Races, the Broad Rock Jockey Club and the Fairfield Races, with their purses of £ 100, £ 400 and more.

Discreetly Polly's eyes slid over the words, "Sports of the Pit," but somehow she got the idea that at Sussex on the 2nd of May next, a main of twenty-one Cocks would be fought for One Thousand Dollars!

She read that subscriptions were being taken by Mr. Pleasants for a life of George Washington which was soon to appear. Her husband was still hoping to keep it secret that he was the author.

She read that Robert Gamble & Son were receiving by ship *Fame* from Europe an assortment of general merchandise, "which they were disposed to sell for cash, country produce, or to punctual customers on the usual terms for credit."

She lingered, remembering awhile, over the notice: "Died at Bath in England on February 7th last—William Bingham Esq. of Philadelphia."

The Theatre, Polly knew, distributed its own handbills with such titles as, "The Actor in Distress, in which Mr. Hopkins will endeavor to explain, 'What a man is like.'" This performance had been "For the benefit of Mrs. Hopkins." Box seats cost 4s 6d; in the Pit 3s. Marshall's early Account Book indicated that he never attended the plays alone. One item appears to have been a theatre party for Colonel Monroe. So ardently did Marshall enjoy the plays that, after his death, a new theatre was built and given his name. So Polly knew when she saw that subscriptions were asked for a new playhouse now that his hand would come generously from his pocket. When she saw that a lottery for an "academy" was authorized by the Legislature, she knew that her handsome mirror frame would be fringed with tickets. He would also answer the request for funds for sufferers from a fire in Norfolk. He would subscribe to the Bank of Virginia, and, through Mr. Gamble, to the Richmond and Columbia Turnpike Company.

In detail *The Argus* spread an account of proceedings in Congress. A reader might doze off in the monotony of questions and answers as easily as if she had been present in the audience. And here was John Randolph, present in letters to the paper, as usual protesting, delaying and obstructing.

On March third, Polly read about the celebration of George Washington's birthday in the city of Washington. The report was clipped from a Washington letter. The affair began at four o'clock in the afternoon, very aristocratically, with a dinner provided by Mr. Stelle at his tavern. The Judges of the Supreme Court were there, with the Federal members of both Houses of Congress, and gentlemen of Washington, George Town and Alexandria.

It was all very orderly, with pre-arranged toasts. The first: "The Day which cherishes affection for the memory of Washington,—our Country inherits his services,—the World his example." Seventeen cannon saluted this sentiment.

Other toasts were to "The People of the United States," "The Friends of the People, not their Flatterers," "The Legislature & Executive Authorities with Constitutional powers, not more powerful than the Constitution," "The Judiciary, —as free from persecution as from patronage," and "To the true Seamen of the United States. Protection at Sea & Relief on shore: but not to fugitives who assume the character & abuse it." Will people never forget the Jonathan Robbins affair? she wondered.

Following these prepared sentiments, said *The Argus,* there were extempore toasts, to "Pickering, Religion and Morality, essential supports of a free Government," "Marshall—That rare patriotism which prefers public interests to public favor," "Chase—The man who dares be honest in the worst of times," "Stedman—Oppressed humanity relieved by exports not imports."

"The day," concluded the Washington correspondent, "was enjoyed by all, in harmony & cheerfulness," and ended with a grand ball. Editorially, *The Argus* looked down its Quaker nose with scorn at this celebration, claiming that the Federalists were using the memory of Washington as a political instrument, and calling shame on a party, "who in a sinking state, could take such liberties with the name of a man who belongs to the nation." There had been only a desultory celebration of this birthday in Richmond.

In the next issue, however, Polly read about what she had seen and heard with throbbing head on March fourth, an all-day, all-city jubilation in which the Republicans celebrated the anniversary of their accession to the Presidency and to control of both Houses of Congress. This affair began in the morning "with cannon discharged from Capitol Hill," followed by "an Oration by the school teacher, James Ogilvie," who narrated historic events "in a style unusually nervous, candid and eloquent."

Between four and five o'clock there was a "very elegant dinner" at Bell Tavern, "attended by Governor Page, Chancellor Wythe, Judge Nelson, Dr. W. Foushee, Maj. Wm. Duval and others." The band from Mrs. West's played throughout the afternoon. "The greatest hilarity and harmony prevailed." The first toast was, "The 4th of March, The day on which the will of people prevailed against the intrigues of party and schemes of ambition." Three cheers and three guns followed this, to which Polly added a genteel, "Pooh!"

The second toast was to "The people of the United States. May they never require Federal guardianship to save them from their worst enemies— themselves." Five guns and music followed this.

"Thomas Jefferson" brought on five guns and three cheers.

Then was given, "Congress, guardians of peace, and national economy." Cheers.

"The judiciary, as free from patronage as from persecution!" A few cheers.

Polly caught a snatch of a letter from a Hanover County Freeholder, saying that this was "a time of refinement and purification in politics." She shook her head, thinking everyone was bent on washing everyone else's face.

Another letter to the editor remarks, "If what a writer of eminence has said be true viz: 'that a merry nation must be a happy one,' the American people must be the happiest on earth. . . . The Federalists have laughed incessantly for some years. Mr. Jefferson's *Philosophy* has been the butt of the joke, yes, the President of the United States is obliged to bear the degrading epithet of a *philosopher*. . . . No honest republican, who possesses the least risible propensity, can look upon this foolish ill timed mirth of the federal wits, without feeling himself an inclination to laugh at them." To Polly, a Federalist laugh was the treasure of her life.

Throughout the spring *The Argus* was advertising "A Scheme of Lottery for the benefit of William & Mary College." Eight thousand tickets at ten dollars each were for sale at S. Pleasants's Book Store in Richmond. By a series of tickets the amount was to be increased to $125,000. Throughout the summer the drawing was postponed from date to date, until Polly lost interest, though she was sure that her husband must have bought an extravagant number of tickets. He served several years on the Board of Trustees of William and Mary. He had a kind of sentiment for the College, though he sent Tom without question to Princeton.

The Argus dated July 18 was late reaching Polly at Oak Hill, and the news clipped by Mr. Pleasants from a New York paper was older still, July 11, 1804, but was very sharp. "This morning," went the clipping, "a duel took place between Aaron Burr and Gen. Hamilton, in which the latter fell, and I have just now heard (half past 12 o'clock) is dead." Then the Quaker Republican goes so far as to clip from the *Philadelphia Gazette*, "The greatest man in America has this morning fallen in a duel!"

Dear Heaven! The Marshalls will be angry. Of course

several of them are duellists, and they always hit their mark, but their mark is never a vital spot.

The next issue of *The Argus* gave a story, with all details, of the duel. General Hamilton had fired into the air. The Vice President had aimed to kill. Polly dropped the paper and quickly got to her feet. She knew Marshall in his high joys, and in his deep grief. She had never seen him angry. She must attend him closely when he returned from Frederick.

Mr. Pleasants's scissors were sharp for horrors this Summer. In August Polly read about the riot of Negroes in San Domingo, and the cruel murder of twenty-five hundred white men, women and children. A little later she read, "The outrages practiced in our harbours by British armed ships are so numerous that we find it difficult to record them with the facility with which they are committed."

But then she read that the first volume of a *Life of George Washington* would be on the book stalls on September first.

What *The Argus* for 1804 did not tell was that in January the Chief Justice had been elected to membership in the American Academy of Arts and Science, and that at thirty-eight Polly was still pretty in that pale fine look of Amblers, and that she still wore the becoming Philadelphia bonnets showing a few gray hairs in the curls escaping across her forehead. She would never sit for a portrait, though next to General Washington her husband was the most painted gentleman of her acquaintance. Already there were numerous portraits of him. It was a matter for lifted eyebrows if a lady in the Court End of Town went unpainted. Since Tom could not allow this, he did a miniature-like portrait of her, and an unknown artist copied it in larger size. Whoever the artist was, he was familiar with Polly, for the face in profile is half sad, half smiling and altogether knowing.

Chapter XV

The Court on Trial

Richmond Sept 27th 1805

My dearest Polly

I reached this place yesterday & din'd at your Mama's. I found her not so well as I had hoped. . . . [cut] continues to ride out, & is I believe recovered from a billious attack. Your sister Carrington is better & your other sisters are well. In your own family I believe there is nothing amiss.

At the Oaks you will have received fifty dollars which Mr. Morgan promised to deliver to you. I totally forgot to pay my brother Charles for John's expense. His schooling I believe is five dollars. I do not know what else may be due for him.

At my plantation I was very much vexed. Things are there very badly conducted.

I am my dearest Polly
Your ever affectionate
J Marshall

In the year 1805 Marshall had been vexed by more matters than bad management of his farm. To begin with, the Supreme Court of the United States was put on trial, not only for its life, but for the independence of justice in the nation, and in January it was necessary for the Chief Justice to leave Polly in the perils of childbirth at the age of thirty-nine, and repair to the capital ahead of the opening of the Supreme Court.

When President Jefferson was not able to rid the Bench of Federalists by the Act of Repeal of 1802, his party, through State Legislatures and Congress, hung the threat of impeachment over the heads of the judiciary. That ax had fallen on seven Federal District Court Judges in two years. Now the Republicans reached up and put a finger on the highest court in the land. Associate Justice Samuel Chase had been a strong patriot in the Continental Congresses, had signed the Declaration of Independence, and had been Chief Justice of Maryland until 1796 when President Washington appointed him to the Supreme Court of the United States. Now arraigned by the House of Representatives be-

165

fore the Senate sitting as a court of impeachment, Chase
was charged with arrogance, sarcasm to counsel, suppression of testimony, and pre-judicated decisions.

For a whole year the public mind had been flooded with
denunciatory pamphlets, painting a picture of Samuel Chase
as a tyrant in judge's robes, scornful of lawyers at the bar,
indifferent to the rights of republicans on trial, causing sar-
donic laughter at the expense of counsel in court. He had
bowed to the Attorney General in a sarcastic manner, had
presumed to address Attorney Hay, as "Young gentleman,"
ordering him to sit down. He had called William Wirt
"Young man," when everyone knew that Wirt was thirty-
nine years old and a widower. Senator John Quincy Adams
wrote that to condemn Chase *"nothings* were accumulated,
with the hope of making *something* by their multitude."

The Chief Justice, who happened to be in court when
some of these things had occurred, was called to testify
against his associate like any ordinary witness. Well did
Marshall know that it was not intended that he be an ordinary witness. His testimony was sought not to convict Chase,
but to lay a trap wherein the judiciary would destroy itself.
Not only the judiciary was at stake, but the whole system
of administration set up by the Constitution. In this trial it
would be proven whether among Anglo-Saxons there could
be a durable form of republican government. The whole fab-
rication of the great mind of James Madison seemed to
quiver like Polly's hands. "Are you sure you are right?" she
would have asked. Who was sure? The Chief Justice, who
never vaunted himself, wondered where lay the foundations
of the universe. In the Book of Job it is written that a man
is strengthened when he stands before the Just Judge even
though that Judge frowns upon him. Would there be a just
judge at the head of the Senate sitting as a court of impeachment? The man who was to sit in that high place was Vice
President Aaron Burr, himself under indictment for murder.

Early in January Randolph of Roanoke, as prosecutor for
the House, had presented the charges against Chase. Poor
"Jackie Randall" had deserted the study of law under Ed-

mund Randolph because he could not agree with the books. Sadly his indictment showed that loss. It was a hodgepodge of fancy oratory, a feeble aping of his idol, Jefferson. But since that presentation, a month had passed. Randolph had fallen into a temper with Jefferson. And independence had turned his silver into fire. What conflagration would he set off on the witness stand? Unless this trial before the Senate pleased the people the States would retreat into that Sovereignty they kept ever ready. It was the Union who stood before the bar, and if it was condemned, anarchy and confusion would roll like a thunder storm over the country.

On February fourth, the "grand inquest of the nation," as the Sergeant-at-Arms announced it, opened before a large audience, for whom the most comfortable arrangements had been made, even the erection of an extra gallery for sightseers. To Vice President Aaron Burr, as presiding officer of the Senate, fell the charge of preparing the chamber for the trial. The political machine which was pressing this indictment was to grind him out of office in four weeks time. Actor that he was, he planned his exit to be from the center of a colorful stage, observed by a fashionable audience. A half-circle of chairs draped in crimson cloth was set for the Senator-judges. For the Senate tiers of seats covered in hunters' green rose on either side of a space before the court. Blue draped stalls for the Representatives, faced the bench. And in the open space between these stood the counsel table and witness stand.

Comfortable armed chairs were provided for the Cabinet, but if members of the Supreme Court should have their curiosity or anxiety piqued to watch this performance they must squeeze into any vacant place. However there were eighty-two cases on their docket, and two of the justices, Bushrod Washington and the Chief Justice, were preoccupied in writing a fourth volume of the *Life of George Washington*. The Court record shows few absences from sessions beside that of Samuel Chase. Seldom did the audience have to move over to make room for one of the gentlemen whose sacred honor hung in the balance held by the dapper actor at the center of the stage.

Aaron Burr was small, suave and lonely, with only one real friend in that bizarre room, Luther Martin, the lion of the American Bar. Above him hung portraits of the French King and Queen, whose heads had been removed by The People. Above the minds of those learned in the law hung the trials of Warren Hastings in England. For seven years that statesman had been the scapegoat of British party politics. The House of Commons and the House of Lords had been dressed in gold and crimson for his trials. His audience had been as fashionable and more heartless than these in the Senate Chamber. Hastings had been charged by the lower House, acquitted by the upper Chamber, and the people were never satisfied.

Aaron Burr was conducting this inquest according to British custom. The accused was lame and ill. He asked for a chair when he was called to stand before the court. But English rule held that a criminal must stand during trial. It took a murmur of pity from a counsellor to cause Burr to relent and allow Chase to be seated. So autocratic and formal was Burr's manner throughout this affair that a newspaper remarked that his conduct was as rigorous as the devil and as impartial as an angel.

There was, however, a temporary rift in Burr's imperial manner, driven there by gentlemen who possessed strong conviction of personal importance. One day, he ordered the Senate to stay in after the session. He had something to say to them. Then he scolded them, like any schoolmaster, for lack of respect to his person. They had walked between him and counsel when a witness was on the stand. And they had so far forgotten themselves as to eat in court. One Senator admitted to biting an apple, off and on, another to consuming a cookie when he felt faint. One and another felt the crumbs in his pocket and smiled, until finally in disgust a Senator suggested that Master Burr needed a switch. So they all went home to dinner which they ate in open appetite.

"Jack Randall" lit his firecrackers when he opened testimony by praising the manner in court of the Chief Justice, proving by comparison the iniquity of Marshall's associate, Justice Chase. Randolph clung to this line of argument all through the inquest. It was whispered that this was a thrust at Jefferson, and political suicide for Randolph. It was small comfort for Marshall. On those tiers of seats sat twenty-five of Jefferson's party men, and only nine of the old guard Federalists. Chase had openly accused those Jeffersonians of planning, not a democracy, but "mobocracy, the worst of all popular governments."

Just as openly the Republicans were saying that they intended to replace all Federalist Justices with Republicans. This was no trial for a broken law. This was a test of the spoils system. If Chase was impeached, the whole Court would go. Its seats would be filled with progressives too obsessed with rights, too unconcerned with balanced responsibility, too careless of the honor of national contracts. Then truly the glitter of popularity would blind the eyes of justice.

When Marshall told Polly about the trial he must have told her that when he stood up between the accused Justice and the guns of the Republican faction, he felt as he did that night at the foot of Stony Point forty years ago, when tiers of British cannon were trained upon his position in the marshes. As Robin would say, he had the "innard tremblin's," and his voice just would not come out from behind the battery of his throat. When he did make himself answer the court's questions he told them that the conduct of Justice Chase as well as that of the lawyers, on the occasions being described, were "indecorous," but that no point of law had been transgressed.

In all, Aaron Burr allowed fifty-two witnesses to testify, and most of that testimony was true, but trivial. On February thirteenth, Aaron Burr interrupted witnesses to announce that Thomas Jefferson had been re-elected to the office of President of these United States, and that he himself would be superseded by George Clinton of New York. The Court record shows only Chase absent from this day's session, he being too ill to leave his lodging.

On February twenty-seventh, Marshall dispatched the

manuscript of a fourth volume of the *Life of George Washington* to a publisher in Philadelphia, apologizing for poor spelling and punctuation, which in the pressure of his affairs it had been "absolutely impossible" to correct.

On March first, the Senate acquitted Samuel Chase of all charges preferred by the House of Representatives. The American public conscience felt that its house had been cleaned.

On March second, Aaron Burr bade farewell to the Senate in a speech which drew tears from those austere gentlemen, but not from the Chief Justice. He was busy that day handing down a decision concerning the Supreme Court's appellate jurisdiction over a ruling of the Court of the District of Columbia. The High Court, he said, would use only such powers as were expressly delegated to it by law.

On March fourth, secure in his office now, the Chief Justice administered the oath of presidential office to his cousin for the second time. Between them now lay nothing but scorn.

Two days later Marshall was on his way to Richmond, where his tenth child, Edward Carrington Marshall, was waiting to be baptized by Parson Buchanan in the parlour of the Marshall mansion. Edward had been born on January thirteenth. From the beginning he was a healthy little boy, merry and alert. Polly laughed at his chuckle; for it was a direct inheritance from the Chief Justice of the United States. To the accompaniment of this gaiety, Marshall told Polly about the trial of Justice Chase before the murderer of Alexander Hamilton. When he told of "Jack Randall's" fireworks all three of them laughed. Did Mr. Randolph run and hide after the acquittal? Not at all. He galloped, with his silver spurs pricking nothing but the floors of the Capitol, toward the House of Representatives, where in a frenzy he offered a bill to amend the Constitution so that the Senate as well as the judiciary would be put under the reckless will of the people. But, though Marshall did not believe as did Jefferson, that all men are endowed with a sense of governance, he did find most of the gentlemen of Congress high-minded and talented. They had brushed aside Randolph's amendment. Marshall loved them for so often upholding the right. Polly knew that affection was mutual.

With the pretty vision of his wife and son in his eyes he went out to his office to write a publisher that he was about to go to work on the fifth volume of his *Life of George Washington*.

In September, after their usual tour of Virginia Springs, Marshall left Polly at Oak Hill. With her he left Mary, ten years old, James, five, and baby Edward. With him he took seven-year-old John to be placed in school with the children of Charles Marshall in Warrenton. Charles, the twin brother of William Marshall, was a noble character and an able jurist, practicing law all of his life on Fairfax lands. Though paralyzed, he argued his case before the court with vigor. John never forgot the sight of his uncle in a chair being carried into court by two strong slaves. He never forgot that his uncle would not allow any one to speak of "slaves." They were "our people." Martin, son of Charles, was one month younger than little John.

Charles Marshall died a few weeks after John joined his household. Thereafter Martin lived much of the time in Polly's house.

"In your own family," writes Marshall from Richmond on September twenty-seventh, "I believe nothing is amiss." That family was himself, Tom, who was beginning a law practice and writing his thesis for a Master of Arts degree, and Jaquelin getting ready to leave for Harvard. Polly's mother became very nervous when any one mentioned politics, especially when the subject was the problem of settling the people of colour. She made her own little brown maid get down and look under the bed every night before she would mount the steps and sink into a feather mattress.

In January Mrs. Ambler was frequently rendered nervous, for this cogent problem was before the Virginia Assembly. She heard that the Legislature had instructed the State's Representatives in Congress to urge the government to secure a portion of the newly acquired Louisiana Territory for free, and yet to be manumitted, Negroes. More and more wills were freeing slaves, some with provision for their living, but others turning them out to a mere chance of survial.

It had long been known that Chancellor Wythe's will was written to set his servants free, with a sum of money to provide for their living. That will was probated during the Summer. For in June the Chancelor was poisoned by his nephew who tried to destroy the will. William Wirt was counsel for defense in the trial of the nephew for murder. There was no reasonable doubt that the defendant was guilty. But the only eyewitnesses were two slaves in the kitchen. One of those had died of the same poisoned coffee, and testimony by the other, a cook, could not by law be admitted because she was a slave. This was an easy and conspicuous case for a young lawyer to win. Wirt accepted it because in 1802 he had married again, and now was ambitious to build a career to support his growing family. He was never happy to remember his defense.

In this Summer Tom Marshall won his Master of Arts degree from Princeton, and Harvard conferred the honorary degree of Doctor of Laws upon the Chief Justice. Of greater cause for rejoicing, however, was the filing of the deed in Fauquier County Court House to over one hundred and sixty thousand acres of Fairfax lands in the name of the Marshall syndicate. They paid in all fourteen thousand pounds English money for this estate. In the division of the land a year later, to the Chief Justice fell the Leeds Manor tract; to Rawleigh Colston, forty thousand acres of the far reaches of the grant along the Potomac River. To James Markham Marshall went the Shenandoah Valley acres with Goons Creek Manor. He had not waited for this deed. He had separately purchased many acres of Fairfax lands in the Shenandoah Valley.

Marshall counted on the profits from his biography of Washington to pay for his part in the Marshall syndicate. He was vastly disappointed. In three years he turned out five volumes from quill written manuscript. After the first volume reached the reading public, sales fell off, for the biography turned out to be a laborious recall of the history of Virginia from the landing at Jamestown, with eyewitness accounts of the major battles of the Revolution. Washington was left only so much personality as the bare bones of a name. But Polly found the bindings, calf with gold tooling, very handsome. They would make good table books.

Thomas Jefferson was prematurely certain that this work was a denunciation of himself and his policies. Before ever a volume appeared on the book stalls he began collecting ana to refute it. He planned, it is said, to spend Winter evenings perusing the biography of the Father of His Country and the Federalist party. It is also said that he read part of one chapter and fell asleep. Some years before this Marshall had purchased Mr. Jefferson's *Notes on Virginia;* then with suppressed amusement put it on the top shelf of Polly's handsome bookcase; for she was quite shocked to find so brilliant a writer setting forth that the earth was formed by time and elements, so contrary to the Book of Genesis.

To Polly's way of thinking Mr. Jefferson had a strange aversion to all established custom and belief. Why, a few months after his first inauguration, he had even refused to appoint days of prayer and fasting when he received the Baptist Address upon the matter. And the ladies of the Court End of Town simply could not believe it when they were told of the removal of all protocol and ceremony in White House affairs under President Jefferson.

Did he think, asked the ladies, that his personal charm could compensate for the pomp of empire? Polly, too, asked this of her mother as they strolled through the garden. Rebecca Burwell Ambler was now as daintily wrinkled as the flower of Queen Anne's Lace. On August fifth she died, and the long funeral procession of Amblers and Marshalls, Fishers, Randolphs, Tuckers, Nicholases, even Roanes wound ploddingly down the lane beside Capitol Square, up Main Street hill to St. John's Church which Parson Buchanan opened for the last earthly affair of the aristocratic old lady. Poor little Polly could not hear angelic voices welcoming her mother. She could only weep for an empty place. For her comfort J Marshall ordered a mourning ring, a ruby encircled with rubies.

Chapter XVI

The Burr Trial

IN THE YEAR 1807 government-in-evolution which had put
the Court on trial, now arraigned justice itself, and thereby brought on Polly's second serious breakdown; for the
trials of Aaron Burr for conspiracy dropped social and political Richmond into a hornets' nest of emotions with every
stinging barb aimed at her husband, while the public danger
from gossip and politics so engrossed him that she felt as
pushed aside as those figurines hidden by his papers on the
mantelpiece, and her mother was no longer across the field
to comfort her.

In this year the population of Richmond was over five
thousand. Fine dwellings now covered its hills. Busy mills
and full warehouses along its river front were interspaced
with handsome homes. This was a beautiful city set among
forest trees, with neighbourhoods separated by rugged streets
and deep ravines where wild flowers grew around springs of
pure water.

Richmond society was nearing its prime in a warmhearted,
unselfconscious culture. Artists, musicians and writers had
wandered to this friendly capital city, and then settled
among appreciative neighbours. French, Irish and Spanish
families lent a special lilt to the drawing rooms. German
Jews contributed deep-hued philosophy to conversation.
There were as many native poets and poetesses as there were
blossoms on the new Magnolia trees. This was a decorous
society, given to dinner parties, debating in rhyme, music
circles and ladies' autograph books. Every home had a calf-
bound library of classics in Latin and Greek, of political and
moral philosophy, histories, science and sermons. Nor did
these volumes rest unused on the shelves. They embellished
Richmond conversation. It was more gracious to say, "Stude
quam semper victurus, vive quam cras moriturus," than,
"Study forever, live today." It was kinder to say, "Caelum
non animum mutant qui trans mare currunt," than, "You
might as well have stayed at home." For ladies' reading there

was a circulating library replete with the latest English novels.

In spite of admiring Mr. Jefferson very much Richmonders were happily class-conscious. First families were many and large. They knew their place and were pleased to keep it, admonishing young people to "marry the one whose chimney you can see." This was Polly's society, but after this year, though her husband's star grew ever brighter there, she never again moved in its circles.

Chaos began for Polly when suddenly her candles wagged their flames violently as Marshall threw open the street door and entered like a gust of March wind. He had returned from Washington sooner than she expected him. She must have made him laugh by exclaiming, "Why, General Marshall, what a noise you make!" This night there must be laughter, for on the next day he must take up the business of the Burr trial, an affair which he says was "the most unpleasant case ever to be brought before a judge in this and perhaps any other country." Through all the confusion, malefactions, accusations and condemnation from the press, and even from counsel before him, he knew that he must safeguard the Constitutional right of every man to be held innocent until he is proven guilty, a doctrine as new as the stone tablets that Moses threw at the feet of the Golden Calf. He must uphold the privilege of habeas corpus, and maintain independence of the judiciary from executive or congressional control, while he knew that the hand of politics was most threateningly reaching for control.

Strange and mysterious had been the peregrinations of Aaron Burr after he departed from office of Vice President in March of 1805. That he was openly dissatisfied with the administration everyone knew. That he spoke openly and sympathetically of a division of the western States from the Union no one ever denied. That he encouraged war with the horrid Spaniard who was encroaching upon the lands along the Mississippi River, no one held to be anything but what was already in the hearts of the settlers there. Burr was reckless, bitter and hard, and full of charm; dangerous qualities along the frontier. He travelled about in the Spain-beset countryside making friends and enemies. Soon rumors of a plot to dismember the Union drifted back to the east, sent out some say by a Spanish spy who was paid to ruin this man whose evident influence was building defiance of both Spain and the United States.

Profligate gossip fed the newspapers across the country, conjectures and suspicions contradicting one another. Some who read were amused, and others perplexed, until in January of 1807 President Jefferson sent a special message to Congress stating that a "voluminous mass . . . of letters" to which was added "a mixture of rumors, conjectures, and suspicions concerning a general design to sever the States beyond the Allegheny Mountains from the Union, and to attack Mexico" had placed Aaron Burr's "guilt beyond question."

The President thereupon assigned General of the Army Wilkinson to capture the traitor and to destroy his property. Under orders from Wilkinson a company of soldiers moved into the Mississippi wilderness and took Burr, divesting him of all personal property, even removing from him every article of clothing that might denote a gentleman. His supposed accomplices were also arrested and dispatched overseas to Baltimore. Two of these, Dr. Eric Bollmann and Samuel Swartout, appealed to the Supreme Court, thereby giving that tribunal the opportunity to uphold the right of habeas corpus. Burr and Harmon Blennerhasset were remanded to the Fourth District Court which would be held in Richmond, a District covering the area of the supposed crime. It was the custom for the Chief Justice to sit with this court. Thus it was that Marshall hurried home.

Tonight the Marshall home must have extra candles in high sconces. Peter and Joseph must smile their kindest as they pass Madeira to neighbours who drop in when they hear of the arrival of the Chief Justice. Tonight a great soul must lay in a store of good feeling against the long weeks when it will be hard to find. Polly must preside in her shy, sweet manner.

The neighbours informed Marshall of Burr's arrival in Richmond flanked by a close military guard who appeared more respectable than the ex-Vice President. A bedraggled object he had been made to appear, with a ragged hat pulled over his face, and a dirty torn shirt hanging down over homespun breeches the color of the swamps the party had traversed on the way from the far south. It was said that the prisoner had not been allowed to change his clothing during the whole journey, even for sleep. Burr was now in the town gaol under military guard. It was said that the gaol was a filthy place infected with vermin. Polly heard still more about Burr's clothes next day, which was a day on which the month of March took its exit like a lion, and garments that could keep a man warm in Mississippi, would leave him shivering in Richmond.

Marshall lost no time in writing an order for Burr's release from military guard to civil custody, with transfer to a retired room in the Eagle Tavern, where he would be questioned by the Chief Justice and State's Attorney George Hay. The contrast between smartly uniformed soldiery and prisoner was not more striking than the spectacle of well-dressed gentlemen conducting a ragged statesman through the taproom of the town's most popular tavern. Sitting with his morning toddy in hand, Mr. Robert Taylor of Richmond watched them pass to an inner chamber, and, he says, though he hated Burr because of the death of Alexander Hamilton, the sad sight made his heart quiver. When he overheard Burr, charmingly regretful, tell the Chief Justice that he could not raise five thousand dollars bail since the government had divested him of all property, Mr. Taylor was moved to break in upon the inquest and offer to sign the bond. Then Colonel Gamble (of the dogmatic wife) rose from the bar and asked to be allowed to share the surety. It is said that Burr smiled so engagingly as he thanked these gentlemen that Mr. Taylor went further, asking if there was anything else in which he could accommodate the prisoner. Burr pointed to his ragged attire. It ended with Mr. Taylor advancing the Colonel one thousand dollars, which bought among other luxuries, the finest black silk suit the town tailors could supply.

Society turned out in such numbers to see Burr arraigned in the District Court on April first that the trial was moved from the small courtroom on the ground floor of the Capitol to the hall of the House of Delegates. There Colonel Burr appeared fashionably clad, with his powdered hair tied in a queue. His movements and manners were those of high society, and Richmond accepted him as one of her own. When his bail was raised to ten thousand dollars, Mr. Taylor and Colonel Gamble had no trouble in finding three more gentlemen to share the larger bond. Thus for seven weeks Aaron Burr had the freedom of the town. During that season when Virginia towns bedeck themselves in lilac bloom, and doors and windows stand open to air like French wine, and mint beds waft fragrance as inviting as the tinkle of ice, Aaron Burr became the toast of Polly's society.

That society was divided in sentiment between believing Burr a persecuted innocent, and wondering whether he was. All however agreed that he was a most engaging dinner companion. He was invited everywhere, except to the Marshalls'. He returned hospitality with dinners at his lodgings. It is not of record that he was so presumptuous as to invite the Chief Justice. It is of record that Marshall's friend, Burr's counsel John Wickham, invited the Chief Justice to dinner one afternoon when Burr was also a guest. To this day, controversy turns the question about. Did the Chief Justice know that the defendant would sit at the same table? Some say that he did know, and that Polly advised him not to go, but that he was loth to be critical of his friend by withdrawing his acceptance. Others say that he did not know that Burr was also invited. All concur, however, that Marshall did not converse with Burr, and left the party as the company rose from the table. Judge Tucker, a very pleasant gentleman, but not given to a Marshall point of view, says the Chief Justice did not know, and that he regretted attending the dinner. Nowhere is it found that Marshall resented being put into a compromising position by Mr. Wickham.

But press and gossip made much of the affair, which demanded that Polly use the utmost restraint when she visited in the Court End of Town. Members of her circle both read and wrote the papers which were saying that Burr was guilty and the Chief Justice prejudiced. They said that if Burr were acquitted it would be a disparagement of the Administration, and "that awful tribunal, the People, will try Marshall." She even heard gentlemen across the room declaring that the government wanted to see Burr convicted whether he was guilty or not. Polly was so small and retiring that people would sometimes forget that she was within hearing.

Especially would veterans of the Revolution raise their voices around the punch table as they recalled the English doctrine of constructive treason which dangled a noose over the heads of patriots while they wrote the Declaration of Independence. They would recount the horrors that transpired when English courts convicted suspected traitors by inference and association, and ordered them dragged by their feet through the streets of London to the gallows, where crowds watched noses and ears of the condemned being severed before execution. Jefferson was one of those who had stood under the danger, and he now declared unequivocally that of Burr's guilt there could be no doubt. Then the old fury against traitors would rise, so that the gentlemen found themselves arguing in circles. Polly, hearing in circles, suffered wrinkles in her own thinking.

The streets through which she rode became more and more crowded. Foreigners touring the new country put the Virginia capital on their route. So curious had the western world become concerning a trial for treason that involved the ex-Vice President of a nation dedicating itself to individual liberty, that by the middle of May taverns and homes were overflowing with guests. The Amicable Society was hard put to find beds for tourists, news reporters, writers, curiosity seekers, even artists. Fevret de St. Memin came to Richmond with his physiognotrace, and left many a profile portrait to hang in Richmond parlours. There is one of the Chief Justice still on the wall of Polly's house, done in that moment of stern triumph in Washington when he was up-

Courtesy of The Valentine Museum

CHIEF JUSTICE MARSHALL at the time of the trials of Aaron Burr. Done by Fevret de St. Memin in Washington in the early Spring, 1807.

holding the rule of habeas corpus for Dr. Bollmann and Samuel Swartout.

Nor were only the literate drawn to Richmond, hoping to see the downfall of a Federalist Bench. Covered wagons rumbled into town, drawing aside into the ravines between handsome residences, or going down the hill to drop their shafts on the valley floor. Out of them tumbled families who had travelled the long roads from the back country, from beyond the mountains, from Carolina farms, from Maryland, even from the hotheaded settlements of the frontier where Burr had mysteriously operated. Under these wagons for weeks the plain people lived, disputing, fighting and laughing. All of them were condemning Burr before a word of defense had been heard, remembering only the President's message that Burr was guilty beyond doubt. Jefferson was the idol of the illiterate as well as of gentlemen. An English visitor to Virginia about this time spoke of Jefferson as "the master of the Americans."

As time drew near for the court to impanel a grand jury, the first of a company of one hundred and forty witnesses brought to town by the prosecution, began to arrive. Among them were friends of the Marshalls. The Federalist Benjamin Stoddert, Secretary of the Navy during that pleasant winter in Philadelphia when James Keith Marshall had been born, and Commodores Stephen Decatur and Thomas Truxton, gentlemen irked with the Administration at the moment, were called to testify for the prosecution. They all moved politely in circles where the suspected traitor was guest of honor. Not so politely a young giant from the southwest, Andrew Jackson, stood on tavern steps, haranguing crowds, ready to do battle for Aaron Burr if opportunity should offer. He looked so dangerous that opportunity held its tongue when he denounced some of the town's favorites, Jefferson, Hamilton and Monroe, three points of the political compass. After a week or two of talking rashly and listening astutely in Richmond, Andrew Jackson wrote to a friend, "I am more convinced than ever that treason was never intended by Burr . . . I am sorry to say this thing . . . has assumed the shape

of a political persecution." And he clenched his red fists
and shook his tawny head.

More decorously Washington Irving, from Father Knick-
erbocker's New York, came to offer his services to the accused. His blithe spirit, nurtured on *Pilgrim's Progress* and
Dutch legends, could relish a conflict between fey rumor
and plodding law. He would have been a good candlelight
companion for the native of Fairfax forests. He would have
likened Polly's spirit to shimmering dew drops touched by
sun and breeze at the same moment.

When Polly rode about town she heard strangers along
the street being informed that there went the wife of Judge
Marshall, and she could see that some of them shrugged
their shoulders, and some turned to watch the carriage until
it was lost in the shadows of huge trees. The crowds through
which she passed became more and more rowdy. General
Eaton, hero of Tripoli, had been summoned to testify for the
prosecution. He was always on the streets, decked out in
Turkish finery, strutting from barroom to barroom, noisily
complaining that Richmond was a "sarcastic town" because
it did not wine and dine him as it had when he returned
from Barbary States as conquering hero.

General Wilkinson, the Government's chief witness, also
muttered about social neglect. John Randolph said that
Wilkinson was "a mammoth of iniquity" and "from the bark
to the very core a villain." More moderate gentlemen were
saying, "Wilkinson is not an accurate correct man." His testimony designed to convict Burr very nearly brought about
his own indictment. The General wrote to Jefferson, "To
my astonishment I found the Traitor vindicated & myself
condemned by a Mass of Wealth, Character influence &
Talents."

Then the story got around town that big, ruddy Samuel
Swartout was seen on the streets and in taverns with a grin
on his face. He had shoved General Wilkinson off the sidewalk. When the spluttering officer threatened retaliation,
and the New Yorker gleefully presented his big fists, the
General of the Army beat an ignominious retreat. After that

incident, whenever either of these men appeared on the streets there was disorder. Polly sometimes suspected that Peter turned her carriage to pass near these excitements.

When on May twenty-first the District Court must impanel a grand jury, every man called admitted conviction of Burr's guilt as well as of his charm. Finally since a jury must be established, those of "good conscience" though "of strong prepossession" were chosen. It was plain to every man that this jury was composed of the élite of Virginia. Fretfully the people accused the Chief Justice of prejudice when John Randolph of Roanoke was chosen to be foreman, until it was brought forward that of the sixteen jurymen, fourteen were Republicans and only two Federalists. Then too it was shown that several jurymen were earnest friends of the President, while the others were kin to Polly, or the Chief Justice, or Jefferson, or to all three. All were members of those friendly groups who gathered in Polly's parlour.

Standing on the great lock of the door to the hall of the House of Delegates, a stranger noticed something else. Young Winfield Scott from southside Virginia wrote home, "Marshall was the master spirit of the scene. It was the President who directed the prosecution." Still another reported that the Chief Justice "was occupied in hearing testimony intended not for use against Burr, but against himself."

What the Chief Justice saw was that every testimony of a witness, every argument by counsel, every protest of the defense and every demand by the prosecution was a mallet in the hands of political factions to shatter American justice. It is no wonder that he let pass some of those gay, tender moments that were the strength of Polly's poise.

Those who could get into the Hall heard, and those who crowded the Capitol Square were told Marshall's instructions to the jury on opening the inquest. "Juries, gentlemen, as well as judges," he declared, "should be superior to every temptation which hope, fear or compassion may suggest; who will allow no influence to balance their love of justice; who will follow no guide but the laws of their country . . . With a jealousy peculiar to themselves the American people have withdrawn the subject [of treason] from their

legislatures, and have declared in their Constitution that
treason against the United States shall consist only in levying war against them, or in adhering to their enemies, giving
aid and comfort." Burr was accused of levying war. The
Chief Justice pointed at the danger of inflicting punishment
in moments of public anger and gossip. "It is therefore," he
said, "more safe as well as more consonant to the principles
of our Constitution, that the crime of treason shall not extend by construction to doubtful cases." The overt act must
be proven. The court must be logical, not philosophical.
Thus the question before the grand jury was, Is Burr in-
dictable for treason in levying war against these United
States, or for high misdemeanor in preparing a war against
Spain? The Government, declared Burr's fashionable counsel, must establish in strict legal order that there had been
an overt act, and that Burr was personally concerned in it.
The law of treason had to do with an act, not a generally
evil disposition. The Chief Justice warned that gossiping
holiday crowd that the charge of treason "is the most atro-
cious offense which can be committed against the political
body, so it is the charge which is most capable of being employed as the instrument of those malignant and vindictive
passions which may rage in the bosoms of contending parties
struggling for power."

Fashionable indeed was Burr's counsel. There was John
Wickham, at the top of the Virginia bar, handsome, polished
and wealthy, with manners, the spectators said, more like
New York than Virginia. For all that he was an aristocrat,
he had an ingenious way of catching the thoughts of the
lowly in that mixed audience. They liked to see a gentleman
use his fine education on the common man. When he ridi-
culed the prosecuting attorney, as he delighted to do, they
laughed gruffly, though they were supposed to stand with
the Government. They liked to watch Mr. Wickham take
a legal volume out of the hands of the prosecution, flip a
few pages, then with a lofty "Pooh!", throw it on the table.
The audience was not sure then who had won a point, but
there was a breath of triumph in the air.

With the defense was Colonel Edmund Randolph, possessing one of the town's finest mansions, and holding no less a place in the bar of his State than Mr. Wickham. Of him in court it was said that he "spoke slowly, smilingly, and in a musical voice with selected phraseology, a gentle and polished manner," and though he was a pillar upon which the languishing Episcopal Church in Virginia rested, "the storehouse of his words seems to be in his head, not his heart." This must have struck Polly as significant, since she knew that Mr. Randolph had according to fashion been a deist until converted by his "straightlaced wife."

With Burr's counsel also was clever Benjamin Botts, the youngest lawyer on the case. He was keen-minded and polished, knowing when to let his temper fly to win a point. Then there was Jack Baker, walking on crutches to and from the court, merry fellow, given to witty and coarse anecdoting, but neither an orator nor a good lawyer. To these gentlemen of the defense Luther Martin shortly attached himself, volunteering to stand for his friend.

At once the President informed the prosecuting attorney that Martin was "an unprincipled & imputant Federalist Bulldog." Martin was indeed uncouth, generally drunk, and strangely beloved by his fellow barristers. One of the flying rumors had it that Burr's daughter, Mrs. Alston, was the love of Martin's life. She and her husband, Governor Alston of South Carolina, and their son came to Richmond soon after Martin's arrival. When the beautiful little boy, daintily dressed, appeared between his suave grandfather and the boorish attorney, many hearts were touched, but not Jefferson's. Before long he urged Attorney Hay to proceed to have Martin indicted for treasonable collusion.

District Attorney George Hay lived down the Ninth Street hill from Polly's house. Though his mind was a branch of Jefferson's thinking, she could not help feeling sorry for him. His wife had recently died. He was the plodding son of an influential tavern keeper in Williamsburg. Associated with him for the government was elderly Lieutenant Governor Alexander MacRea, a dour sarcastic Scotsman. Polly could have felt sorry for him too, for he was ever a foil for Marshall's humor. With the prosecution also was Wil-

liam Wirt, now married to an acquaintance of Polly's, a
daughter of strong-minded Mrs. Gamble. It was said of him
that he was "a handsome, fortunate, brilliant, high-minded
man," with thick golden hair, clear blue eyes and a fine
voice. To these qualities he added an enthusiastic use of
mythological allusion. It is said that he always opened his
argument with an ingratiating smile and bow to the audience.

So obviously did all of these lawyers speak continually to
the spectators rather than to the Bench or the jury, that the
Chief Justice was moved to warn them against "any attempt
to prejudice the public judgement and to try any person . . .
by artificially excited public opinion instead of by law and
evidence, a practice not less dangerous than it is criminal."

All of these lawyers were Marshall's friends. All of them
gathered for a while as usual in his dining room, or, as the
days grew hotter, on his porches. Here their voices would
rise with the vehemence of their jokes or opinions. Polly
heard her husband and Judge Tucker pounding their opposing convictions into the table, sharp thumps as to the right
of the States beyond the mountains to secede from the
Union. She must have wrung her hands until she heard the
debate burst into laughter, and, peeping through the window, saw the two judges now pounding each other's shoulder
affectionately. Such sudden change of emotion shook Polly,
especially in hot weather.

This was the hottest, dryest summer Polly had ever
known. In the steaming press she must read accusation
mixed with insinuation that if Burr should be acquitted the
Chief Justice must be impeached. The papers quoted old
speeches of William Giles urging Congress to amend the
Constitution to exclude the Supreme Court from jurisdiction
in criminal cases. Everyone was setting the trial up as a contest for power between the President and the Chief Justice,
which would have been all right for Polly if J Marshall's
smile had not given way to lines of worry around his fine
eyes.

She would have felt better if she had heard that "gentlemen of the profession who witnessed the trial, who saw the

effective dignity with which the judge presided over the
court, who heard him read those opinions, so elaborate and
right . . . regarded it as the finest display of judical recti-
tude which they ever beheld." Another who watched the
Chief Justice in this trial wrote that though he "is inferior
to Edmund Randolph in voice and manner . . . for talent he
substitutes genius, and instead of talking *about* his subject,
he talks *upon* it. He possesses neither the energy of expression nor the sublimity of imagination of Innes, but he is
superior to every other orator at the Bar of Virginia in close-
ness of argument, in his most surprising talent of placing
his case in that point of view best suited to the purpose he
aims at, throwing a blaze of light upon it, and of keeping
the attention of his hearers fixed upon the object to which
he originally directed it. He speaks like a man of plain common sense, while he delights and informs the most acute."
Very little was said of Judge Cyrus Griffen, the local magi-
strate sitting with Marshall. He was old, and often ill this
Summer.

On one of the hottest days of all, Luther Martin dared to
blow the trumpets of Judgement Day at Thomas Jefferson.
"Is this Jefferson a kind of sovereign?" he roared. "He is
no more than a servant of the people . . . The President has
undertaken to prejudice my client by declaring that of his
guilt there can be no doubt. He has assumed to himself the
knowledge of the Supreme Being himself, and pretended to
search the heart of my highly respected friend. He has proclaimed him a traitor . . . He has let slip the dogs of war,
the hell hounds of persecution, to hunt down my friend."
This blast was called forth by Burr's request that President
Jefferson be subpoenaed to bring to court that "voluminous
mass, chiefly in the form of letters" which was the evidence
upon which he had declared that Burr's guilt was fixed beyond doubt. Then gentlemen of the counsel on each side
accused those of the other side of "converting this judicial
inquiry into a political question." Mildly the Chief Justice
rebuked them. "Gentlemen on both sides," he said, "had
acted improperly in style and in spirit. They had all been to
blame in endeavoring to excite prejudice, and had accused

each other of doing what they themselves had done." Then Marshall's smile faded entirely. One of the spectators in the courtroom remarked that Marshall's black eyes were the finest ever seen except Colonel Burr's, and that when the eyes of these two men dwelt upon each other it was as if a curtain had been drawn across sunlight, leaving only a dark question hanging between them.

Slowly the inquiry moved forward, and Polly could sense a change. Men began to wonder at the Chief Justice whose reputation for fearless honesty was well known. Now at every turn of procedure he seemed to hesitate. At times he kept the court waiting while he silently scrutinized counsel or witness. Frequently he adjourned court until next day so that he might take under consideration some motion or protest. Both sides were irritated by the length of argument he permitted. He was accused of vacillating, of allowing irrelevant testimony. He was accused of trying to save the life of the man who had killed Alexander Hamilton who was the friend of the Chief Justice. Counsel for both sides found Marshall irresolute. Now the Richmond press became so unfriendly that reading it Polly's heart felt like the biscuit block when the cook beat dough.

June twenty-second was especially a day of tension throughout the town, tension and a dry, hot breeze, for this day the case was handed to the grand jury. Though the Chief Justice's instructions were directed more toward high misdemeanor than treason, Burr and his accomplice, Harmon Blennerhasset, "being moved and seduced by the devil," were indicted for treason in levying war on these United States, and for misdemeanor in setting on foot an armed expedition against Spanish territory when the United States were officially at peace with Spain.

As William Marshall, Clerk of the Court, read the indictments it is said that the brilliant eyes of prisoner and judge gazed solemnly at each other, Burr's cold, composed and furtive; Marshall's very sad.

Then was Burr again sent to the common gaol. But as this was admittedly an unhealthy place, Marshall ordered the front room of Luther Martin's lodgings across the street from the Capitol Square, barred and guarded for the prisoner's quarters under personal supervision of his counsel, which again brought down the press upon the character of the judge. Finally Attorney Hay persuaded the Executive Council of the State of Virginia to offer rooms on the top floor of the new penitentiary, a hostelry which Thomas Jefferson had designed after the Parisian prison used by Bourbon kings. It is said that the gaoler received Burr as obsequiously as an innkeeper would welcome a spendthrift patron.

When night closed down on this perplexing day, Polly may have asked the weary gentleman taking off his shoes by the light of her candle, "Is Colonel Burr guilty?" and gotten only another question, "Guilty of what?" She could try again. "Is he a traitor?" "What is a traitor?"

Pooh! Out went the candle. "I will ask Judge Washington in the morning." Then she would hear him laugh and pull on his shoes again. She would hear his feet going down the stairs, and out along the path to his office. From the window, she could watch candlelight flare up in the office until the shadow of his shoulders humped over his desk would appear as solid and safe as the cliff that had lifted the Town of her childhood. She was glad that she had made him laugh.

Long through the night he wrote. It was well known that Marshall did not consider himself the whole Court. Now he needed to test his legal judgement by that of his associates. The line was very fine between what Burr was accused of doing, and what advocates of secession were constantly demanding. How would the Supreme Court act if such men as Fisher Ames were arraigned before it? Or the Clintons of New York? Or Judge Tucker?

On the next day type in the printing shops must have become pied indeed, for the press had suddenly to empty its trays of the Burr trial and fill them with with an entirely different crisis. The *Norfolk Gazette and Public Ledger* was first with the story. On June twenty-fourth it reported "a most unexampled outrage, in the perpetration of which the blood of our countrymen has been shed by the hand of violence, and the honour of our nation insulted beyond possibility of further forbearance." The British warship *Leopard* had fired on the United States frigate *Chesapeake* within Virginia waters. Three crewmen of the *Chesapeake* including Commodore Barron were wounded, and four American-born sailors were taken prisoners by the British. The ship was so badly injured that with difficulty it put back to Hampton Roads.

A day or two later the same paper reported that President Jefferson had met this information with "action more pacifick than had been expected, when measured with the extent of the outrage." Not so the young gentlemen of Virginia. They flocked to the armories, making the Fourth of July celebration a month long. Mr. Wirt, assistant to the prosecution, left off "toiling to achieve those solid attainments, [in his case, committing to memory passages from classical mythology] which alone make brilliancy of utterance endurable in a courtroom." He decided to yield his wife back to her father, and march with the militia to relieve the citizens of Norfolk. Off they went with an "elegant stand of color, and a most delightfully animating band," all very gay and exciting if it had not been for the ladies at every window, weeping.

Then to Polly's surprise the papers began to quote her husband with respect. They spoke of his long past speech before Congress concerning the Jonathan Robbins case, calling it a decision. Was not the affair of the *Leopard* also a case for the judiciary rather than the army? the press asked.

In the interval between the indictment and the trial which was to open on August third, Marshall had time to pack Polly and the children off to Oak Hill. She went forlornly, feeling crowded out by the rowdy crowds on her streets, by crying children and barking dogs in the nearby ravine, by the distinguished gentlemen forever asking at her door for the Chief Justice, but most of all by his long silent deliberations. She thought that he would no more miss her than he would the mantel figurines she had packed into her portmanteau.

Marshall too was lonely, for even his friends were beginning to doubt the righteousness of his conduct, while Burr in his lofty dungeon was still the lion of society. In three rooms swept by breezes from the fair valley of the James,

Burr was entertaining Richmond society, not upon gaoler's bread and soup, but upon the viands of the town's best kitchens, which the ladies, especially Mrs. Gamble, spread upon his prison board.

When the trial opened, though Wirt was suffering from a collapse of martial ire brought on by the chilling attitude of Government toward his belligerency, his store of mythology was not diminished. His fancy allusions to Venus and Calypso provided bright spots for a sombre Bench, when days seemed to have been drawn out of a furnace. Marshall's silk robe was as dark and merciless as the false testimony of General Wilkinson, whose perfidy became so plain that he was not able to walk the street without being insulted.

Day after day Marshall must say there could be no treason without the deed. The prosecution had charged an overt act. Forty-eight witnesses testified for the Government. From the beginning it appeared that they knew nothing of an act committed by the defendant, only expressions of treason. Over and over Marshall must say, "No evidence certainly has a bearing unless the overt act be proved." Press and public cried, "Suppression of testimony!" Late his candle burned in his office while he wrote and thought, and bowed his head as if his mind was reaching for the Source of Wisdom.

Tom, tarrying in Richmond for experience in law, or the militia, or more likely to be near his father in this ordeal, would watch that light until the hour was exhaustingly late. Then he would go to stand in the open door of the office, just to stand in silent affection. When the Chief Justice would not look up or turn, Tom would go to sit on the circular bench under the oak tree, waiting for the candle to gut itself out. In the Summer dawn the Chief Justice would smile to find him dozing there and silently settle beside him. Leaning against the great trunk, shoulders touching, father and son would rest until the sun laid another hot day at their feet, and the fragrance of coffee and frying bacon called them to prepare for the fray again.

After breakfast they would walk together as far as the

Capitol Square where in the shadow of Mr. Jefferson's Roman temple cows were tethered to small colored boys, who lay on the grass ruminating upon nothing more consequential than, "How Mr. Grasshopper feel if he get ett by Miss Cow." The usual jovial welcome was absent from the polite greetings along the way, and with a heavy heart Tom watched until his father was out of sight in the deep entrance to the ground floor of the Capitol.

On August thirty-first, after argument had exhausted the matter, Marshall read his decision for three long hot hours, "an opinion," he stated, "which is to over rule all former precedents, and to establish a principle never before recognized, . . . in every point of view in which it can be contemplated . . . of infinite moment to the people of this country and their government. . . . The present indictment charges the prisoner with levying war against the United States, and alleges an overt act of levying war. That overt act must be proved, according to the mandates of the Constitution and of the act of Congress, by two witnesses. It is not proved by a single witness."

Then the Chief Justice mentioned the "impatience" and suspicions of gentlemen of the counsel on both sides concerning the deliberations of the court, and the threats of impeachment. He paused a moment in his reading, to let his dark eyes dwell on the perspiring spectators, many of whom he loved, many of whom were ascribing to him conduct that had deviated from the line of duty and law. That dry voice with its softening inflections reached every ear in the hall as he continued, "That this court dares not usurp power is most true. That this court dares not shrink from its duty is not less true. No man is desirous of placing himself in a disagreeable situation. No man is desirous of becoming the peculiar subject of calumny. No man, might he let the bitter cup pass from him without self-reproach, would drain it to the bottom. But if he had no choice in the case, if there be no alternative presented to him but a dereliction of duty or the opprobium of those who are denominated the world, he merits the contempt as well as the indignation of his countrymen, who can hesitate which to embrace. . . . The jury . . . will find a verdict of guilty or not guilty as their own consciences may direct."

In twenty-five minutes the jury, under Colonel Edward Carrington as foreman, brought in a verdict that "Aaron Burr is not proved to be guilty under this indictment by any evidence submitted to us. We therefore find him not guilty."

This did not suit Burr or his counsel. Martin called it, "Much Ado About Nothing," and demanded a change of language. Colonel Carrington thought that might be arranged, but one single juryman refused to accommodate the defense. The Chief Justice therefore directed that the words of the jury remain, but on the record it must be entered simply, "Not guilty." Still under indictment for misdemeanor Burr was allowed bail in the amount of five thousand dollars, which the same five gentlemen signed, and Burr went out of court to a city that was ready to make merry.

That evening the porches of Richmond homes were as gay as the beds of Zinnia blooms in the gardens about them. Punch and juleps vied with the weather to make faces red and spirits airy. But William Wirt went home to the high pitched mansion of his positive mother-in-law, and Alexander MacRea to his residence cater-cornered across the street from the Marshall house where he could watch the Chief Justice walk alone through the picket gate to his office.

In the trial for misdemeanor which followed a week later, fifty witnesses were examined, none of them giving evidence of anything except a plan by Burr to settle lands which he had purchased beyond the mountains.

Shortly there was a verdict of "Not guilty" in the charge of misdemeanor. But the Government was not through with the court. It pressed for Burr and Blennerhasset to be committed for misdemeanor in the Ohio courts. On October twentieth Marshall did this, and allowed Burr indefinite bail to appear there. Burr was so indignant at this turn of affairs that it was said that at the moment of parting he was rude to Marshall; which could hardly have bothered Marshall since he had loved Alexander Hamilton.

Thus Marshall had won the victory for which he strove, but he had no smile for his triumph. To his friend Judge

Peters of Philadelphia he wrote that he had found nothing
amusing in the whole affair. "It was deplorably serious & I
could not give the subject a different aspect by treating it
in any other manner which was in my power. I might perhaps have made it less serious to myself by obeying the public will instead of the public law & throwing a little more
of the sombre upon others."

This done Marshall says that he "galloped off to the Blue
Ridge" through a countryside that was turning crimson and
gold. Fairfax lands were rejoicing that another harvest had
been accomplished. But Polly could only see that her husband looked older. When at midday he had been too long
out of her sight she would look for him out under the trees
he loved so well. There she would find him asleep on the
ground with yellow leaves all around him. Could it be? Silver Heels tired?

Chapter XVII

A Most Attractive Household

THE CHIEF JUSTICE had only a brief respite in the Blue Ridge Mountains before he must set off for the Fall term of the Circuit Court in North Carolina. When Polly had unpacked the children at home in Richmond, with shaking hands she replaced the fragile figurines which her husband had never missed. She was still trying to keep her poise in a society that seemed to have no voice except that of newspapers. "The whole stock of national indignation and contempt" was poured on her husband's name. Impostor, they called him, ridiculous, incompetent. Even the Norfolk papers were publishing a lampoon.

AWFUL ! ! !

The public are hereby notified, that four "choice spirits" are this afternoon at three o'clock, to be *Marshalled* for execution by the hangman on *Gallows Hill,* in consequence of the sentence pronounced against them by the unanimous voice of every honest man in the community. The respective crimes for which they suffer, are thus stated on the record:

1. Chief Justice M   , for repeating his XYZ-tricks; which are said to have been much aggravated by his felonious capers in open court under plea of *irrelevancy.*

2. His quid-majesty, charged with the trifling crime of wishing to divide the Union and farm Baron Bastrop's Grant.

3. *Blunderhasset the Chemist and Fidler,* convicted of conspiring to destroy the tone of the publick Fiddle.

4. And *last*—but not 'least in crime,' *Lawyer* Brandy Bottle—for a false, scandalous, malicious Prophecy, that "before six months, Aaron Burr would divide the Union."

N.B. The execution of accomplices is postponed to a future day.

When Polly heard that President Jefferson's usual Message to Congress went out of its way to urge the House of Representatives to impeach the Chief Justice, dark shadows gathered in the corners of her mind. When word came that a well-ordered crowd of citizens in Baltimore had put on a public show of hanging her husband in effigy, her defenses went down. She became so distressingly ill that Common

Council ordered the town bells silenced for her comfort, and the night watchman dropped his cry to a murmur as he passed her house.

She lay on her bed with her face in the pillow, or sat in a chair with her hand over her eyes, murmuring, "I can't find God." No one could reach her mind with the reassurance that, though the people of the streets had sought to dishonor her husband, their elected Representatives in Congress had ignored the President's order to impeach him.

After a few black months, either Polly or the great soul beside her did find God, for her lantern began to flicker, and then to glow again. "Not a moment passed," Marshall says, "in which I did not consider her as a blessing from which the chief happiness of my life was derived."

Somewhere there must be letters from J Marshall to My dearest Polly written during the next ten years; for Polly slowly recovered, and took her place as mistress of her household. The Fishers remember that pretty Ann Fisher ran over every day from the Ambler mansion to perform the duties of housekeeper for Polly, whom she called "Aunt Marshall." It is remembered, also, that during this period the Marshalls' household was spoken of as one of the most attractive in Virginia.

Returning health in 1809 brought a softer pleasure to Polly's smile, and a deeper violet to her eyes. Around her were all of her children. There was Tom, twenty-five years old, trying to climb the broad path of his father's career in the law, though he lacked even a small measure of his father's vigorous health. There is a St. Memin physiognograph of Tom, done at Princeton, which hangs in Polly's house. It shows a beautiful young face, with Marshall features and Polly's sensitive expression.

Jaquelin was home from medical school, wondering restlessly if he should not have chosen the ministry as a profession. Mary, at fourteen, resembled her father in appearance and joyousness. She had his rich coloring and dark eyes, but, partly in one of the local French schools, and partly by aping Mammy Venus's native rhythm, she had learned to move more gracefully than her forest-loving father. She was the idol of three little brothers, John, ten, James, nine, and Edward, only four and still in dresses. She was also the idol of her cousins, Edwin, Julianna and Jaquelin Harvie from across the street.

The Ambler mansion had not died with the passing of its first mistress. Polly's sister Ann, now Mrs. George Fisher, lived there with a lively family. A block away lived Eliza, now Mrs. Edward Carrington. So extensive and well-planted were the grounds of Colonel Carrington's estate that it was spoken of as a "town plantation." Nearby, too, lived the Calls with daughters too young for the courting parlour, more compatible with Mary and her young brothers. All of these cousins enjoyed extempore welcome at each other's dinner tables.

Not only did children come and go at Polly's table, Marshall nieces and nephews came from Kentucky and the upper country frequently for prolonged visits in her house. So many were the staying guests that about 1809 the Chief Justice added a first floor room, with pleasant windows and a new fashioned small coal fireplace. The brick office that he built at this time had an upper story to accommodate visiting gentlemen.

In Polly's parlour with intaglio cupids on the mantelpiece, much courting took place, and a few weddings. The room was large enough for several couples to converse in the privacy of too much noise to be overheard. Here came Mary and Susanna Colston from Honeywood, which Rawleigh Colston had built on the upper Potomac Fairfax lands. In October 1809, Susanna was married to Benjamin Watkins Leigh, who had come over from Petersburg to court her in this parlour. She was a lovely girl, but as frail as Polly. A few years later she went to France for her health, and died on the way home. To Polly's house came Mary and Lucy Brooke, daughters of Judith Marshall, for spells of stability between wanderings to and from Kentucky. Eliza, daughter of William Marshall, often joined her cousins for days in the sociability of the Marshall house. With her came her brother William, who was known as a gay young man about town. Such were the charms of the female cousins that the Marshall house became a rendezvous for the leading young gentlemen of the city and nearby counties.

No one knew how many places to set at the dinner table. The honor of the family's hospitality lay heavily upon Joseph, the butler. At two every afternoon he could be seen, dressed in a brass-buttoned blue coat and yellow knee-breeches, pausing at the parlour door, and then disappearing. Always he seemed to be soundlessly chewing words. Finally at three o'clock he would stand in the doorway and announce, "Ladies, hizzoner de Chief Justice is done retired to his charmber to preparr for dinner."

In the parlour his voice was as soft as warm chocolate. A moment later at the back door when he yelled orders to the cook in the outside kitchen, he sounded like a timber saw in action. But softly again he spoke at the parlour door, "Gentmun, suh, dinner will be sarved in harf an hour. Hizzoner will be glad to have you remain. Covers is been sot for you all. If you carn't remain, please let the ladies retire to preparr for dinner."

The company who gathered a "harf hour" later at the table would be laughing and decorous, shy in the glow of new-found affinities. There were always toasts to drink in fine Madeira. Once when shining eyes and flushed cheeks betrayed the newly affianced, the Chief Justice looked down the long table until his eyes rested on Polly's throat where, glinting in candlelight, hung a gold locket, a symbol of some tenderness between them which time still keeps secret. With a quick smile, he caught Polly's eye and raised his glass, saying, "To all our sweethearts!" Then his eyes with a question must have turned toward Mary. Both would laugh as she said, "I'd rather have one of Mr. Harrison's horses, Pa."

In the Winter season after dinner, the company, leaving the intaglio cupids glimmering in the firelight, would repair to the New Theatre in Academy Square at Twelfth and Broad Streets. To the playhouse was but a short walk downhill, under stars shining through skeleton trees. Two and two, the company strolled, followed by Polly on Marshall's arm, and Mary with a large flock of young cousins.

In January of 1809, the cousins who came from Kentucky brought the story of Senator Humphrey Marshall duelling at dawn with impetuous young Henry Clay. Clay carried a scar for the rest of his life, but, unscathed, and opinions unchanged, Senator Marshall put his pistol back in the box, and went about his business of law, politics and history writing. He was six feet two inches tall, with the remarkable Marshall eyes, a grand looking middle-aged gentleman. It is said that though he was the Federalist most hated by Kentucky Republicans, he always carried the suffrage when he sought it.

He always carried his pistols too. His grandchildren say that Governor Scott of Kentucky, a Republican, once offered a free pardon in advance to anyone who would rid the earth of Humphrey Marshall. Immediately an ambitious young politician volunteered, seeing in this a chance to win the profitable gratitude of his party. The projected murder was well advertized. A large crowd gathered on the streets of Lexington on the day appointed. Senator Marshall, unconcerned, rode amiably into town, bent upon personal business. Suddenly from the crowd rushed the young politician, brandishing a pistol, calling upon men to watch him kill the Senator. Humphrey reined his horse, calmly asking the young man, "Have you come to assassinate me?"

"No," answered the quailing youth, pulling a second pistol from a holster. "I have brought a pistol for you too." Gravely the Senator accepted the weapon, and with a sudden movement used it to knock the would-be murderer's pistol flying among the spectators. Then he ordered the boy to mount a horse and ride ahead of him all day as he slowly went about town attending to the business that had brought him to Lexington. It is said that Governor Scott, who had suffered defeat at the hands of General Tarleton, declared that Humphrey Marshall had delivered him his worst humiliation since the Battle of Monmouth.

In this year of 1809 Marshall saw social life in Washington revive under the charming Madame Dolly Madison. Again there were high prerogative ladies and gentlemen of the Government, and delightful executive ceremony. For in March the Chief Justice administered the oath of presidential office to James Madison, who, though slight in stature, was at all times stately. There was gaiety in the air, but the foundations of the nation seemed ever to be quaking with threats of wars and tumults, and there was not yet a worthy Capitol building. The construction of such an edifice was still a confusion of jumbled contracts and architectural dreams.

The Government called Benjamin Latrobe to Washington to bring order out of the drawings and bungled construction until there was at least a wing for executive offices. With him came Mrs. Latrobe, with eyes avid to see and quill ready to record what went on in capital society in spite of muddy streets leading from one affair to another. "Mrs. Madison," she says, "has a profusion of elegant things. Among these affairs a cambric dress at $130, only a wrapper." Mrs. Latrobe went from White House musical drawing rooms to State Department dinners and dancing parties in which she found the feet and dresses of those who did not dance trod upon by those who did. Always at these affairs she heard the band play "Hail Columbia."

Always the Chief Justice was glad to adjourn court, leave this society and ride back to Richmond, to Polly and his children, and the Quoit Club, sometimes called the Barbecue Club, an exclusive membership of thirty-six gentlemen, with two parsons, the Governor of the State and the Chief Justice of these United States as honorary members. There was one other honorary member, Jasper Crouch, the mulatto cook, who, says one who remembered, "officiated at all public dinners; he acquired the gout in the congenial occupation, and also the rotundity of an alderman, and fell a victim to the good things of life."

The Club met every Saturday "during the genial season, at Buchanan's Spring, under oaks of original growth with no other shelter than the shade they afforded, and an open shed to protect the dinner table. Quoits was the game, and toddy, punch and mint julep the beverages to wash down a plain, substantial dinner without wines or dessert." Good things were served at these plain dinners, such as "steaming juicy mutton chops and deviled ham." Often at the head of the tables sat the Chief Justice, and always at the foot, a parson. The grounds upon which the Club played belonged to the worldly wise brother of Parson Buchanan.

On September nineteenth of 1809, Marshall's mother, Mary Keith Marshall, died at the home of her son Thomas near Lexington, Kentucky. The epitaph upon her gravestone, legible sixty years ago, was: "Useful, not ornamental. Good, not great," her last command to those fourteen sons and daughters who stood on the perilous brink of prosperity and power.

It was one of Polly's wonders that any one character could be both so hilarious and so solemn as her husband. William Wirt says that at this time Marshall looked middle-aged, with a swarthy complexion and "a faithful expression of great good humor and hilarity." His black eyes possessed an "irradiating spirit, which proclaims the imperial powers of the mind that sits enthroned within."

"This extraordinary man," continues Wirt, "without the aid of fancy, without the advantage of person, voice, attitude, gesture, or any of the armaments of oratory, deserves to be considered as one of the most eloquent men in the world; if eloquence may be said to consist in the power of seizing the attention with irresistible force, and never permitting it to elude the grasp until the hearer has received the conviction which the speaker intends . . . His voice is dry and hard; his attitude in his most effective orations, was often extremely awkward, as it was not unusual for him to stand with his left foot in advance, while all his gestures proceeded from his right arm . . . a perpendicular swing of it from the elevation of his head to the bar, behind which he was accustomed to stand . . . He possesses one original and almost supernatural faculty . . . of developing a subject by a single glance of his mind, and detecting at once the very point on which every controversy depends . . . the lightning of Heaven is not more rapid than his astonishing penetration."

Francis Walker Gilmer, disciple of Jefferson and Wirt, likened the Chief Justice to a great bird which flounders awhile on the earth and then suddenly takes off in majestic flight. Be that as it may, Polly was content for him to be an eagle in court robes if only she could persuade him to be more careful of his appearance in the Court End of Town. There instead of wings he wore shoes too often tied with a leather thong where a buckle should have been. She would have preferred crested feathers to the old hat he wore when he set off for a meeting of the Amicable Society at Mr. Wickham's. But, half smiling, she remembered that he probably would forget and leave the hat somewhere along the evening's way. She frowned at the faded sack coat he persisted in wearing when he had such a neat blue one hanging in the wardrobe. She planned to stay awake one night until he was asleep, and then to remove the offending garment and hide it. He would fumble around for it, she knew, when he dressed for one of those pre-dawn walks he loved.

Morning and evening he was off for walks, just walking, not going anywhere, but always ending up somewhere full of human nature and good stories. Many a morning he followed the lane that dropped to Shockoe Valley which lay veiled in mist beginning to turn golden. Under the gold he could see a row of farm carts with smoking lanterns hung on their tilted shafts, and beyond them the vague shadow of a shed, from which came the noises of tethered horses and mules trying out their feet after the long night.

Beside the carts in summer stood pyramids of vegetables between baskets of eggs and crates of barnyard fowl, while strings of fish and sora hung from wagon hoops. At the edge of the Creek, crocks of butter shared the cooling waters with melons and the feet of small colored children. In winter there were piles of lightwood faggots, bundles of dried herbs and sassafras root, strings of red peppers, hams, slabs of bacon and crocks of lard, nuts and dried fruits, and great clumps of silver-berried shrubs, all aglow in the light of small fires. After Christmas, softened skins hung from the wagon hoops, antlered deer, beaver, fox, and now and then the rough pelt of a bear.

But the Chief Justice was concerned with the farm people who had slept, Winter or Summer, in their carts. Some of

them were white overseers of plantations. Some were free-
holding small farmers. Many were colored slaves with their
own and their master's produce to sell. A few were free
Negroes from small gardens. All of them would be heating
strange pieces of pork on small braziers, to pack between
slabs of cold cornpone for breakfast. Liquid concoctions,
too, would be steaming with a woodsey aroma. All of these
people knew the simple man who walked among them while
daylight slipped over the Valley. They called him "General
Marshall," and were delighted whenever he spoke to them
by name.

When he climbed the hill homeward, he would have a full
basket on his arm, or, since he often forgot his basket, bulging pockets, and fowls hanging from his elbows, while his
hands grasped the tops of heavy cloth bags. Not everybody,
however, knew that this homey figure had any eminence.
Strangers often thought him a clodhopping farmer. One
young gentleman, a recent arrival in town endeavoring to
set up a fashionable residence, bought a buxom turkey in
market, and daintily looked around for a porter. Seeing a
sturdy yokel lavishly laden, the rich young man ordered
"my man" to carry the turkey to a house that he would show
him. The Chief Justice, suppressing a smile in those brilliant black eyes, added the turkey to his own provisions, and
at a respectful distance followed his employer. When they
came to a gate not far from Marshall's own, he handed the
turkey over to its owner and pocketed the coin flipped in
his direction. All of fifty cents it was. But a bystander ruined
Marshall's game by bursting into laughter, and asking the
rich young man if he knew that the Chief Justice of the
United States had been toting for him? The shocked gentleman shed his pride and his turkey, and ran after the Chief
Justice with abject apology.

"Oh," said his honor, "we were going the same way."
That warm smile sealed another friendship. But Marshall
declined to return the fifty cents.

Marshall's evening walks were westward, to watch the
departing sun sign a gilt-edged note for another day. Then,
with windows and stars beginning to twinkle along the way,

he would hurry toward the home that held the beacon of his life. When he came within sight of these windows he would see the shadow of a fashionable cap pass across one and then another. He knew that Polly would be looking for him. His step took on an eager spring.

On October nineteenth, 1809, Polly crossed one of life's new thresholds. She acquired a daughter-in-law. At Weyanoke on the James River, when the hunter's moon was riding high, and the woods rang with the music of horn and hounds, and gentlemen with red cheeks and red noses gathered in plantation mansions to make merry because the season had fulfilled their hopes, then Tom Marshall took lovely Margaret Lewis as his bride. For a wedding present the Chief Justice gave them Oak Hill, for it was plain that Tom's health needed mountain air, and that his avocation was farming, not practice of law.

To welcome the young couple to Fauquier County there was a galaxy of cousins, Amblers, Marshalls, Smiths, Keiths, et cetera. There also was an ancestral ghost. Back in the days of the Scottish rebellions, James Keith, born about 1700 in Scotland, was ready to graduate from the divinity school of Aberdeen Cathedral at the age of seventeen. Then it was discovered by the English authorities that he had been acting as liaison between the Scottish underground and Stuart exiles in Europe. He was forced to escape at once on any ship ready to put to sea.

It has been said of British divinity schools of that day that they produced either atheists or angels. James Keith and his best friend stood at that dividing line when they must part. Pausing together on a darkened Scottish dock, they exchanged last confidences, and whispered doubts. Across the widening strip of water they promised each other that whichever one died first and saw mystery uncovered, would return to inform the survivor of the truth of Christianity or its fallacy. Then the ship sailed for Virginia.

James Keith was confident angel when he landed in the Dominion and found a sorry lack of clergymen. In spite of his Jacobite record, he dared to return to England for ordination by the Bishop of London. Upon arriving again in

Virginia he was elected by the vestry of Curles Parish to minister to that shrine of the Randolphs. There he picked his bride, Mary Isham Randolph, daughter of Thomas Mann Randolph of Tuckahoe. She was first cousin to Jane Randolph of Dungerness who became the mother of Thomas Jefferson.

In 1730 the Keiths came to Fairfax lands in Prince William County, to Hamilton Parish, which reached from the tide line to the western slopes of the Blue Ridge Mountains. There until his death in 1751, James Keith served a sprawling string of wooden chapels-of-ease and one brick church, connected only by glades of a virgin forest. Shortly before he died those who attended him saw a strange figure beside his chair. No word did the shade speak, but an expression of gladness lit the dying minister's face. Ever since, in the Blue Ridge mansions of Keith descendants, if a young person flaunts unbelief, a hand is seen to touch his shoulder.

The Reverend James Keith was the father of Mary Randolph Keith who married Thomas Marshall in the ironworker's cottage near Germantown. When she died, the mourning ring ordered by the Chief Justice was an amethyst engraved with the Keith arms and the words, "Veritas vincit." Polly often held this to the light wondering if there had been stained glass in Aberdeen Cathedral as glowing as this jewel. She had never seen colored windows in a Virginia church. In fact, at this time Virginia churches were fortunate if there was any glass at all in the windows. The Court End of Town still had no Episcopal church, but in the year 1810 subscriptions were being solicited for the erection of one on Shockoe Hill.

While citizens were busy with this matter, Colonel Edward Carrington died, and St. John's Church was again opened for a funeral. It was his desire to be buried there, whether or not there was a new church nearer his home. When Patrick Henry had cast his challenge of death or liberty to the convention gathered there, Edward Carrington heard it as he stood on the grass beside a window. In the shocked silence that followed the burning words, Carrington bent down and struck the earth, saying, "Here would I be

buried." So there beside the window of the frame church,
Eliza stood, watching yellow leaves fall into a grave, while
Parson Buchanan's Scotch voice, rich with wisdom, read,
"Death is swallowed up in victory."

Afterwards, Eliza tried to adopt her five-year-old nephew,
Edward Carrington Marshall. But he would have nothing
of it. Occasionally he stayed at her house long enough to
eat all her cookies and play with all her toys. But he was a
Marshall, and to his father's house he would return. So
Eliza, like bereft aristocrats of old England, became a votive
of church and charity. She held weekly prayer meetings in
her handsome parlour, taught Sunday School classes, and
was often seen entering the cabins of destitute free Negroes
with baskets of food and clothing. She occupied her lonely
hours writing a novel, and continuing the family chronicle.

Her friend, Mrs. William Wirt, was also in mourning.
This Fall her father Colonel Gamble had been killed in a
shocking accident. It was his habit to read the paper as he
rode horseback down the hill to his counting house on the
bank of the canal. One day as he passed a warehouse, someone threw a buffalo skin from an upper window. The horse
shied, throwing Colonel Gamble against the wall. He was
carried unconscious to his home, where he died three days
later.

About this time Marshall seems to have decided to subject Mary to the ennobling influence of his sister Elizabeth,
Mrs. Rawleigh Colston. He and Polly journeyed with their
daughter to Honeywood and left her to be taught with several cousins by a tutor in the house. Mary bewailed her fate.
She never did like those teasing Colston boys. Edward now
was a young widower and the very likeness of a gloomy day.
Mary, having been told all her life of Aunt Colston's goodness, was scared of her. And Uncle Colston, well, Uncle
Colston was so sharp at counting that he would have made a
good banker.

Mary had endured only four months of school when she
wrote the following letter which suggests that her freehanded method of spelling may be one reason she was not
a favorite of Mr. Le Roy, the tutor.

Honey Wood Feb 1st 1811

I fear my dear mother will be fatigued to death with my lettres, but I cannot let Cousin Edward go as near Richmond as Alexandria without giving him a lettre to some of my Richmond friends, and as I am sure my dear mother cares more for my lettres than any other person I determined to trouble her with another, though I have not received an answer to my two last. I hope you will find it convenient to send for me in April, I cannot help hoping for the best, indeed I frequently put myself in mind of the old proverb of living in hope if I die in dispaire. I said the other day, I hope I may get home in April, and Aunt ask'd me how I could think of such a thing for it was impossible for me [to] get home for no person was going down that way I told her I hoped you would send for me, she said you may as well think of that no more, for your mother will not take the trouble to send for you. I could not help crying to think I should not get there. I hope to finish French before April, but the roads will not be passable until then. I intend to write you a French letter the first time I write an exercise without a fault which I hope will be soon. The other day while we were setting at breakfast. Uncle saw three letters of my writing on the mantle piece he ask'd whose they were and I told him, he said that there had been letters enough written and received by one person in this family to keep a man, and that very well too for a winter. I thought it was at me, however I said nothing, but I could scarcely restrain my tears, after a short silence he said he should take care to have all the letters of his family seperated from the rest and keep an account of the postage to see how much came to at the end of the year. I could not kepp my seat to save my life. I got up and ran up stairs. I got up all my letters that came by the post and found that the postage amounted to 95 cents, and I intend to keep a regular account of my postage and give it with the money to uncle the day I leave this place, indeed I am not much affraid of not being able to pay, or indeed that I shall be in debt for the postage of my letters, for Aunt has got every cent of the money you gave me when you went away except the dollar and quater you gave me for Rose and James. I think if I was absolutely in want of anything which thank gracious I am not I would not ask Uncle Colston for a cent, thank gracious my father is not like him, he does not grudge every half cent that he is obliged to spend. I wished very much to get some muslin for a cap for sister and a half handkerchief for you but Aunt had no money she said the last time she went to Martinsburg and I will not ask her to get it for me again, indeed I hope to be at home time enough to work the cap for sister, and the handkerchief are not so fashionable as some that I think you will like better. I am very anxious to receive an answer to my last letter for until I do I shall expect to go home in April. I hope to receive it sunday, I shall be almost affraid to open it, The letter my brother wrote the first of November be so directed by Hagerstown, it was published in two papers and would have carried to the general post office in a day or two. Mr. Le Roy has given one great encouragement to day he says I improve every day. He has been very angry twice and he went in to Uncle each time, the first time was on saturday, we were conjugating the verbs Rawleigh had a knife in his hand with which he was playing. Mr. Le Roy told him to put it down he did so but took it up again almost immediately, and it made Mr Le Roy so angry that he went in the house immediately, the second time Tom, Tom Marshall and myself were talking he told us to tend to our exercise we all turned and began to write, in a short time the two boys turned and began to talk. Mr. L. R. was very angry and threatened to go in the house, Tom M told him to go then for he did not care and that made him very angry and he went directly to Uncle. It is late, Susan is not very well, and has been calling to me to come to bed for the last half hour. Adieu my dearest mother, My fervent pray is that you may enjoy good health and find convenient to send in April for your

M. M.

P.S.

Ah my dearest mother you know not how I wish to return to Richmond. I cannot help crying to save my live. Cousin Edward says it will be impossible for Jaquelin to come for me, April is so busy a month, indeed my dear mother I do not think I shall be able [to] live a twelve month from Richmond, is it not cruel of Cousin Edward to take from me my only hope ah my god how little feeling he must have to take from me my only hope my life, he does not know what it is to be absent from with a desire to see ones parents for he has so little feeling himself that I do not believe he wished his parents at all. My letter is written very badly but I wrote it at night the p.s. is worse though it is written by day light but I have cried until I have given myself so violent a head ach that I can with difficulty tell one letter from another. I know you will say I am wrong but indeed, indeed my dearest mother I cannot express my feelings. They are too strong for all my endeavours, ah who is it that has any feeling that would not feel as I do. Cousin Edward appeared to me to take delight telling me it would be impossible for me to go home until the fall and when he found I was ready to cry he broke out in a loud laugh. Uncle says he does not think you love me enough to go to the trouble and expense to send for me. Adieu once more my dearest mother. I am your affectionate daughter. Mary M.

CHAPTER XVIII

The New Church

THE THEATRE in Richmond was closing a fine season on December twenty-sixth, 1811, with a program by Mr. Placide's Company. It was as usual a double feature. The title event was *The Father or Family Feuds, to be followed by A Comic Song* by Mr. West. The second feature was *Raymond and Agnes, or The Bleeding Nun,* with Mr. West and Mrs. Placide.

This was a high light of Richmond's social life. Many dinner parties preceded the play. It is not of record that Polly attended one of them, but a young lady says she saw Judge Marshall at Mr. John Gamble's dinner. She says he was "tall, handsome and plainly dressed, with his hands clasped behind him as he conversed with Mr. Henry Lee." She adds that "Judge Marshall was not a graceful man in society. He was abrupt and nervous in his movements and could not hand a lady a chair except most awkwardly with both hands, or a cup of tea without spilling it."

After the parties all the fashionables of the city, young and old, went down the hill to Academy Square. The Christmas star dropped its light unnoticed in the glow of new lamps before the handsome residences. The Chief Justice did not go to this performance. He returned to sit with Polly in the brief respite when Christmas visitors were out of the house. It may be that Margaret, Tom's wife, sat with them, for Tom went on to the play with a cousin from Wythe.

As the hands of the French clock marked the hour of eleven, and confidences were being sealed with good night kisses, out on the street the watchman's "Oyez" suddenly became a scream. Night-blackened windowpanes began to glimmer, then to glow with horrid red. When the sash was thrown up, the family crowding at the window saw a great ball of flame beyond the nearer house tops. It seemed to burst from a spot a little past Twelfth Street, a little down Broad. It could only be the playhouse. Polly put her face in her hands praying. She and Margaret murmured the same

209

name, "Tom." Hatless and coatless men rushed past the window, calling for General Marshall. But he had already gone ahead of them. Polly looked for Mammy Venus, and for Robin, and for one and another of the servants; for there was a gallery for people of color, and they were enthusiastic theatregoers.

Smoke and bedlam and flashing firelight, with a sense of helplessness, overwhelmed Polly. She could only cling to Margaret, not knowing whether her sorrow was for herself or for Margaret, until someone, no one could remember who, rushed through the house calling that Tom was all right and down there fighting the fire with his father.

In half an hour the theatre building was a smoking ruin. One third of the audience were either unidentifiable corpses, or were dying in nearby residences. All night the heavy odor of smoke hung in the Marshall house, as women, white and colored, gathered balms, tore bandages, and made coffee for the stunned and grimy men and women who passed by the opened doors and windows, or came in to tell Polly and Margaret what valiant work their men were doing. It was not until morning that Polly heard that Tom's companion had jumped from a window and broken his neck.

By daybreak the Common Council had met to form committees to go from house to house through the town, making a tally of all citizens and visitors known to have gone to the theatre the night before. It was discovered that hardly a home was untouched by the tragedy. There were seventy known dead and countless injured. The leading lady in *The Nun* was dead. The new Governor of Virginia, William Smith, had perished trying to find his small son who had already been rescued. That young Attorney Botts who had shone at the Burr trial, with his wife and niece were dead. The son of Judge Pendleton and the son of Major Gibbons of Stony Point fame were dead. Of those who had played through the Marshall house as children, Mary's cousins, Edwin and Julianna Harvie were victims. Fifty white women and eighteen men were among the known dead. There had been only one exit for them. The gallery for servants had been crowded, but only four perished, due, it is said, to outside stairs reserved for their use. A gigantic Negro man named Gilbert belonging to Mrs. Mayo, shared with young Dr. McCaw the honor of saving the greatest number of lives. These two stood under a window catching women and men as they jumped with clothes and hair aflame. Both of these men carried scars of the fire all the rest of their lives.

Darkness came swiftly to the stricken city that afternoon. In a candle lit hall William Marshall reported to the Common Council that he had talked with the bereaved families, and whereas the remains of those unfortunate persons who had perished in the conflagration could "not with convenience be removed from the spot on which they were found, and some of them so far consumed as to fall to ashes, . . . it would be more satisfactory to their relations that they should be interred on the spot where they perished, and that the site of the theatre should be consecrated as the sacred deposit of their bones and ashes."

The Common Council at once resolved that all citizens be asked to wear crepe on their arms for a month, that the two parsons be requested to preach funeral sermons on the next Wednesday, which day would be set apart as a Day of Prayer and Humiliation, that Chief Justice Marshall be appointed to head a committee to receive funds from all citizens and strangers who might be inclined to contribute, and to make arrangements for a suitable monument to be raised over the ashes of the victims of this tragedy.

On Sunday while the city was still bathed in tears, there was an elaborate funeral procession for a Mrs. Patterson and Julianna Harvie, whose coffins were a symbol of all the lost. Governors from nearby States attended in honor of Virginia's executive whose ashes lay on the field of disaster.

The whole nation grieved for the city. Congressmen and Senators wore crepe. Newspapers published numerous odes and elegies, and tributes to the young, the beautiful, the influential, and the brave who were lost to the nation. Finally a flock of sermons winged across the big cities, solemnly proclaiming the mournful dispensation of Providence upon Richmond for the sin of attending theatrical performances.

The Association For Building A Church on Shockoe Hill
at once approached the Committee For A Suitable Monument, inviting them to join their organization. Together
they would erect a monumental Church. This met with no
protest. The Common Council purchased the whole of Academy Square as the town's official contribution. The architect, Robert Mills of Charleston, South Carolina, was immediately retained. On August first, 1812, the cornerstone
was laid.

In March of 1812, the Right Reverend James Madison,
president of the College of William and Mary, died. Following his death there was a convention of Virginians who
loved church service according to the Book of Common
Prayer, called by the two surviving members of the Standing
Committee of the Episcopal Church in the State. These two
members had attended the national Episcopal Convention in
New Haven, and heard "the imputation thrown out couched
in the following mortifying words: 'The Church in Virginia
is, from various causes, so depressed, that there is danger of
her total ruin, unless great exertions, favored by the blessings
of Providence, are employed to raise her.' "

In May, fourteen clergymen and fourteen laymen, one
half of them from the city of Richmond, met in the State
Capitol in an abortive effort to name a bishop of Virginia.
A year later as the monument began to assume the appearance of a church, built of stone, octagonal in form with large
triple windows in each of the panels and smaller clerestory
windows, with a dome and deep columned porch, another
Episcopal Convention was called in the Capitol. Delegates
from Monumental Church were the Honorable John Marshall and Dr. McClurg. This Convention called the rector
of the new church, the Reverend Mr. Richard Channing
Moore of the Philadelphia churches that Polly found so
beautiful.

Then this Convention took another step. They voted for
a Bishop. When the ballots were counted, Mr. Moore was
found to be elected by all save one vote. That one was for
the Reverend Mr. Buchanan. In the Fall these Episcopalians
set out for Philadelphia to attend the consecration of the Vir-

Courtesy of Frederick W. Franck

FAUQUIER WHITE SULPHUR SPRINGS showing cottages of Monroe and Marshall side by side between the fountain and the inn. By Ed. Byers.

ginia bishop. There they heard Bishop Hobart of New York say: "The night of adversity has passed and the morning . . . of a long and splendid day is dawning on the Church in Virginia. I think I see a pledge of this manifested by laymen of the highest influence and talents, and by a few zealous clergy. They have combined, and they resolve under God that the Church in Virginia shall not perish."

On April thirteenth, after due notice in the newspapers, the pews of Monumental Church were auctioned to the highest bidders, and the deeds to them deposited in the office of the Hustings Court. The Chief Justice bid in pew number twenty-three, which was fifth from the chancel on the left as one goes up the aisle. Just in front of this pew William Marshall bought number twenty-five. Attorney George Hay bid in his selection. So did Drs. McClurg and Foushee, and the Brockenboroughs and the Haxalls, Pages, Warrells, Curries, and Williams aplenty. There were Messrs. James Brown senior and junior. There were Fishers, Calls, Nortons, Pleasants, Wickhams, Harvies. In fact a visiting clergyman wrote home: "The congregation of Monumental Church comprehended probably the largest amount of intelligence and refinement, and a greater proportion of men distinguished for talent and influence, than any congregation in the Union."

Ten pews were bought in by the trustees for notable visitors. A portion of the gallery was set aside for strangers, and a pew for people of color, though in large numbers they were already attending the First Baptist Church a few yards down the hill. Over thirty thousand dollars was realized from the sale of pews, which added to the memorial fund, rendered the church out of debt by midsummer, when it was dedicated. Parson Buchanan conducted the service, with the Reverend Mr. Wilmer of Alexandria preaching. Then Parson Buchanan returned to the ancient church on Richmond Hill. Citizens whom he had so charmingly comforted in the State Capitol voted to pay him a salary of two hundred dollars a year.

On November fifteenth, 1814, Bishop Moore consecrated Monumental Church as a place of worship and a perpetual memorial of man's immortality in the hand of God. The capital of Virginia became a citadel of the Book of Common Prayer.

Chapter XIX

"Old Cushing Is Dead!"

WHILE THE EPISCOPAL CHURCH in Virginia was breaking from the tomb, many things were happening in the nation at large. The French were still sinking American ships on the high seas. The English were still violating the flag of the United States. President Madison was threatening to declare war on Great Britain too precipitously for Federalists, not quite fiercely enough for Republicans, and now, to Secretary of State Monroe's disgust, not blinking an eye at the French. Vice President Clinton was for peace and patience with both nations.

The Supreme Court had convened in Washington as usual on the second Monday in February in the year 1810, and as usual, Justices had left their wives at home, a custom instituted when capital boarding houses were jovial and comfortless. Washington in this year, in spite of Mrs. Madison's brilliant entertaining, was not even as handsome as Richmond town had been when Polly first saw it. The President's palace was tight against the weather, but half painted, half furnished. A mile down a muddy road stood the scaffolded walls of the state building, surrounded by rough shacks where the necessities of executive life were supplied, a print shop, an oyster house, a washerwoman, a shoemaker, grocer and tailor. Along the road between them stood numerous crude boarding houses. At the best of these brandy, candles, whiskey and wood were provided along with bed and meals for ten dollars a week. Notice, please, there was bed, not room, for that price. A room held as many beds as space allowed.

More than two thousand persons waited on by more than six hundred Negro slaves sojourned in Washington when Court and Congress were in session. So uncomfortable were living conditions for members of the Government that it was proposed to Congress to move the capital to Baltimore. That failing of support, it was suggested that a cheaper house be

215

found for the President, and the Congressmen move into the palace. Nor did this meet with the approval of the majority of the people's representatives, who continued to grumble and talk about the city that was to be.

The Supreme Court Justices made arrangements to lodge as far as possible in one house with a common "study," a fireplace, and a dining room. Before that study fire, and around that dinner table, for five or six weeks each winter, unprecedented issues of constitutional government were drawn through seven dedicated minds sharing knowledge, experience and wisdom in level-eyed appreciation of one another.

As Professor A. L. Goodhart, Master of University College of Oxford, says, the framers of the Constitution "showed skill in what they included, and genius in what they omitted, . . . and left it to Marshall and his Court to fill these gaps by necessary implications and to give such words as 'commerce' and 'contract' the specific national meaning which best served the philosophy of the Constitution as they understood it." In 1810 the Court gave the word "contract" specific national meaning in the case popularly known as the Yazoo Land Claims in Georgia.

Joseph Story of Massachusetts, thirty years old, as counsellor for New England claimants in this case, argued before Marshall for the first time in Court, and for the last time publicly. Hereafter their differences were to be turned and turned about before the friendly hearth of the study.

Joseph Story had grown up near Boston in a large family of brothers and sisters who were noted for beauty and intelligence. Their superior social position was not shaken when their wealthy and aristocratic circle of friends looked askance at the Storys' enthusiasm for Jeffersonian policies. The young barrister, completely at ease in any well-bred company, did not hesitate to seek, in his well-mannered way, the companionship of the Justices of the Supreme Court in Washington. He was so impressed with their dignified good fellowship, and so charmed by their personalities, that he arranged to have dinner in their dining room as often as possible.

At Marshall's table there were four Federalists, and three Justices who had been appointed by Jefferson. The Federalists in addition to the Chief Justice were William Cushing of Massachusetts, who had administered the oath of presidential office for Washington's second term, suffering old Samuel Chase, and Bushrod Washington. Story wrote home that Washington had no visible sign of greatness, only a gentle simplicity and frankness, one eye, and a habit of using a profusion of snuff.

Story found that Justice Washington used snuff even when sitting upon the Bench. One day when the Court was absorbed in listening to Henry Clay plead a case, Washington opened his snuff box. But before he could enjoy it, Clay stepped over and helped himself to a pinch. After a good sniff, Clay remarked to the surprised Justice, "Ah, I see you use Scotch," and then resumed his peroration. This was only one of the high tribunal's laughs.

Jefferson's appointees on the Bench were Todd, Livingston and Johnson. Thomas Todd of Kentucky, though he came from the frontier, always appeared trimly clad in fine quality smallclothes, with carefully powdered hair. He had a genteel manner of kindness and assurance. Story was to say of Justice Todd, "He never gave up to party what he thought belonged to the country." Brockholst Livingston of New York was generally soft-spoken, but Story was to find that he was the firebrand of the Bench. When partisan ire was aroused, his words became the whiplash of conscious superiority, while Jeffersonian democracy left no mark on his baronial manners. William Johnson of South Carolina gave Story a moment of mild condescension. Here was a good-natured alderman, Story thought, imbued with a strong sense of State Sovereignty. These men were supposed to belong to Story's faction.

He was supposed to find the Chief Justice an aristocratical moneycrat. But before long he wrote his wife: "I love his laugh. It is too hearty for an intriguer, and his good temper and unwearied patience on the Bench and in the study." Of Marshall in Court he wrote: " Enter but the hall and you saw him listening with a quiet, easy dignity to the discussions at the Bar; silent, serious, searching; with a keenness of thought which sophistry could not mislead, or error confuse, or ingenuity delude; with a benignity of aspect which invited the modest to move on with confidence; with a conscious firmness of purpose which repressed arrogance, and overawed declamation. You heard him pronounce the opinion of the Court in a low, but modulated voice, unfolding in luminous order every topic of argument, trying its strength, and measuring its values, until you felt yourself in the presence of the very oracle of the law."

The Justices, in turn, seemed to be impressed by Story. It was said of him that he had merry eyes and a gleeful voice, and that he was "remarkable for the fulness and fluency of his conversation. It poured from his mind . . . sparkling and exhaustless. Language was a wide open sluice through which every feeling and thought rushed forth."

One afternoon at the dinner hour the Chief Justice watched the attractive young talker for a while, then got up and, with great hand outstretched, walked up to Story, saying, "Young man, you are mine." Story descendents disclaim this tale, averring that he was no man's man, which in a way was true, for he says, "I was of course a supporter of Mr. Jefferson and Mr. Madison, . . . but . . . kept an independent judgement."

It was not long before Story found that though Jefferson and Madison had a fund of political wisdom, Marshall had a treasure of amusing anecdotes, and Story considered it a man's duty to laugh at least four hours a day. Marshall and Story laughed their way into each other's hearts. Story exclaimed, "I am in love with his character, positively in love." And Marshall says that this friendship "was one of the choicest treasures of my life."

In September of this year, 1810, Jefferson from his mountain top wrote to President Madison: "I observe old Cushing is dead. . . . The event is a fortunate one, and so timed as to be a Godsend to me. I am sure its importance to the nation will be felt, and the occasion employed to complete the great operation they have so long been executing, by the appointment of a decided Republican . . . Who will it be?"

From September all through the brittle Winter and then the steaming Summer of 1811, Madison and Jefferson put their heads together to answer that question. Jefferson warned the President, "It will be difficult enough to find a character of firmness enough to preserve his independence on the same bench with Marshall." He wrote other things of Marshall, bitter things which the recording angel probably sketched but lightly on his book, knowing they would be erased when these two patriots saw no more through politics darkly, but as history sees them.

The new Justice must be a New Englander. Joseph Story came to Madison's mind. Jefferson demurred. Story was too young, and besides Jefferson suspected him of being at heart "unquestionably a tory." But Madison could not forget the splendid mind and undaunted independence of the young barrister with the polished and vivacious manner. When Alexander Wolcott's appointment was rejected by the Senate, and John Quincy Adams declined the seat, President Madison forthwith appointed Joseph Story to be Associate Justice on the Supreme Court of the United States, for which office he was unanimously confirmed by the Senate.

In June of this year, while Jefferson and Madison were debating this appointment, Justice Chase, full of pains and troubles, died, leaving another vacancy to be filled by the Republican President. With slight ado Madison named Gabriel Duvall of Maryland in time for him to be confirmed by the same Senate that seated Story. Thus two new Justices came to the Bench in February of 1812.

The Chief Justice was not present to welcome them. Fresh from the horrors of the theatre fire, he was travelling to Washington the last of January in the public stage when the vehicle overturned with such a sudden jerk that his collarbone was painfully broken, and he had to stop over at the house of a friend. It was two weeks before he was able to resume his journey. When he did arrive at the lodgings of the Justices he found that the case before the Court was Fairfax Devisee *vs* Hunter's Lessee. As usual when Fairfax titles were the issue, Marshall retired from the Bench. Hence, when he did appear in his usual high place in the middle of February, Joseph Story had already "risen above the sphere of party; and with the ermine of office put on the sacred robe of the Constitution and the law," as Justice Todd said of him.

Story settled into the high judicial family as one who belonged. Within a few days he wrote his wife: "My brethren are very interesting men with whom I live in the most frank and unaffected intimacy. Indeed we are all united as one, with a mutual esteem which makes even the labors of jurisprudence light . . . We moot every question as we proceed, and my familiar confreres at our lodgings often come to a quick decision . . . I begin to feel the weight of depression . . . wearing away, and a calm but ambitious self possession succeeding in its place."

Marshall's humor was the outspoken delight of his brethren. Their frequent greeting was, "Did you hear the Chief's latest quip?" His good stories were the pride of the dinner table. Someone told that on a brief visit to Philadelphia during the Winter, Marshall had dropped into a gentlemen's club where the members were entertaining themselves with impromptu verse making. One would call a word and demand a poem upon it. "Paradox" was suddenly assigned the Chief Justice. For a minute Marshall gazed absently through a doorway where he could see at the bar several gentlemen he recognized as Kentuckians. Then he solemnly recited:

> In the bluegrass regions of Kentucky
> A paradox was born
> The corn was full of kernels
> And the colonels full of corn.

In spite of the fact that the best Madeira served in Washington was labeled *The Supreme Court,* Story could write to his wife that the Justices in their masculine existence were very sober. They maintained a rule never to indulge in alcoholic beverages during the Court session—except when inclement weather made it medicinally advisable. "But it sometimes happens," he admitted, "that the Chief Justice will say to me when the cloth is lifted, 'Brother Story, step to the window and see if it does not look like rain.' And if I tell him that the sun is shining brightly, Judge Marshall will sometimes reply, 'All the better, for our jurisdiction extends over so large a territory that the doctrine of chances makes it certain that it must be raining somewhere!' " Thereupon a bowl of Madeira with a dash of brandy would be set upon the table.

Nor did the Chief Justice, when he was home in Virginia, require total abstinence of his co-workers on his Henrico County farm, where, he says, he spent many hours in "laborious relaxation." Often he was seen of a morning riding out of town with a bag of seed across the back of his saddle and a jug of rum hung on the pommel. One day as he passed among the market people, he laughingly showed them that he had lost the cork, but was not dismayed, for his thumb exactly fit the mouth of the jug. The farmers smiled, but were more interested in the bag of seed, for the Chief Justice was so notably clever a planter that he was president of the Agriculture Society of Virginia. The rum was to reward brisk workers.

Returning from Chickahominy on June first, 1812, Marshall found a letter from Secretary of State Monroe with information that President Madison had declared war on Great Britain. Marshall had opposed this declaration. Nor was it popular with the people at large. A few day after the declaration there was a riot in a Washington theatre because the band refused to play patriotic airs. With difficulty the manager of the place quelled the disturbance, and compelled the band to play "Hail Columbia." In retaliation the musicians played that aristocratic tune, and played it, and played it, without variation until the patrons went home earlier than usual.

Nor did society acknowledge a state of war. Though American troops were taking a severe beating along the Canadian border, White House drawing rooms continued as usual. Receptions and teas were as frequent and gossipy as ever. State Legislatures were only passingly interested in this war. They were preoccupied with local business and local independence. State banks were too busy getting the best of National banks to bother with defense financing.

But the citizens of Richmond had seen British gunboats on the James River several times in the last twenty-five years, and promptly moved to reopen that small armory at the foot of Capitol Square, which had been built as a measure of State Sovereignty. There the Chief Justice, who was still General Marshall to Virginians, drilled a vigilance guard. Tom Marshall took the stump throughout the surrounding counties to raise recruits for the militia, but with little success. This, said the lowlanders, was a war for the people beyond the Alleghenies.

The Virginia State Legislature, however, had an eye on those Alleghenies and the rich lands beyond them. The lawmakers took a long look at the Erie Canal project, and at the increasing facility with which steamboats were navigating New York waters. Thereupon they ordered the appointment of a Commission to View Certain Rivers Within The Commonwealth of Virginia to discover an available route, whereby the Virginia seaboard might be connected with the valleys of the Mississippi and Ohio Rivers. To his delight the Chief Justice was chosen to lead this exploration. He was a hale fifty-nine years old, and had viewed many a secret valley of this wilderness between Virginia and Kentucky, listening to the voice of power in many a nameless torrent.

Leaving Polly and the children at Oak Hill with Tom's Margaret, he shed his uniform, donned the leather breeches and fringed coat of frontiersmen, and set out for Lynchburg where he joined seven other hardy gentlemen from Virginia and Kentucky. On September twelfth, "supposing the Autumn to be the season which afforded the fairest prospects," they boarded a flatboat with Negro men to pole it, and began to "take levels by sections" up the western reaches of Jackson's River, New River, Kanawha and Gauley Rivers, and several creeks running into these streams.

Polly, sitting with Margaret by early pine knot fires, would worry, wondering whether the General thought of his weakened collarbone when he tried to change seats on the flatboat, which she felt sure would be careening between rocks. Well it might have been, for the Commissioners' report told of "a vast volume of water" rushing between "enormous rocks" and "perpendicular cliffs" which were "awful" and at times "discouraging." She would shake off her anxiety, remembering that he would be happy on any adventure that took him into the wilderness to encounter his favorite antagonist, a tumultuous stream, and to observe his favorite majesty, a trackless sky above rampant earth. She may have received a letter from J Marshall dispatched at the place where the river crossed the road to the White Sulphur Springs. If so, it has not been found for this collection. And he was back at Oak Hill when the persimmons were ripe.

The Commission's View delivered in the next year advised the Virginia Legislature that a route was possible and would be expensive, and that the expense must be weighed with the opportunity of binding more closely the union of these States with "a central channel of communication," a measure of great importance in war, and in peace a highway to progress.

When Marshall brought his family home to Richmond in this Fall of 1812, Polly found oil lamps on the mantels of her parlour and library. She was not sure she liked such glaring light. Candlelight made people's eyes shine. She loved to look at a candle flame. It somehow passed through her eyes to warm her shivering soul.

As Winter came on, Tom Marshall must have been often in Richmond on the business of recruiting militia, for the war had skirted the mountains and moved southward along the seaboard. British warships were in the Chesapeake Bay. The United States Ship *Constellation*, with guns ready, stood alert in the Norfolk Navy Yard.

In March amid the increasing show of war, the Chief Justice administered the oath of presidential office to James Madison for the second time. Good soldier Colonel Monroe was still Secretary of State. There was a false sense of optimism at large, for the American navy, child of the Federalist party, was winning victories. But then in June the British slipped around ships and soldiers at Norfolk and took the town of Hampton.

Across garden fences in Richmond and around tea tables, ladies gossiped of "most disgraceful barbarities" practiced by the enemy on the people of Hampton. They accused the British of "unspeakable violation of the rules of civilized warfare." Suddenly while the ladies chatted, the bell in Capitol Square began a violent ringing, not solemnly tolling, but catching the pace of the newly uniformed youth racing toward the armory. Then from the Square came the boom of a cannon, Once! Twice! Three times! The invasion signal!

Teacups were dropped into their saucers. Tables were overturned and ignored. Gentlemen rummaged in closets and brought out firearms. Every able-bodied man, musket in hand, rushed to the Square crying, "Where are they?"

"There was nothing wanting but composure," says William Wirt, who was both councilman and militiaman that day. Someone said that the British were at West Point, only thirty miles from the city. Fair time there would be for the ladies to escape to the upper country. The militia ran home again to see that valuable furniture, books and silver were packed into wagons to accompany the families to inland plantations. Mr. Wirt says that the ladies took so long to dress for escape that panic was dispelled before any of them were ready.

Polly, however, did leave for Oak Hill with seventeen-year-old Mary, fourteen-year-old John, twelve-year-old James and seven-year-old Edward. There she remained with Margaret and her little John. Tom and Jaquelin were left in Richmond with the militia.

The Chief Justice too was in Richmond, serving on a Vigilance Committee appointed by the City Council to "organize and carry into immediate operation such defensive measures as they think best for the general defense of the city." He was also on the committee chosen by his fellow citizens to confer with Governor James Barbour on such matters as stacking arms and storing ammunition in the armory, and to see that all uniforms were unpacked, and new ones designed and manufactured. Dr. Foushee was also on this committee.

When he and Marshall fell into step on the way to the Governor's office, it is to be wondered whether they argued powers of government or discussed Polly's latest ailment. Somewhere along the way Marshall lost faith in the efficacy of the medical profession. But gentlemen who differed about theories and policies stood shoulder to shoulder when the Governor told this committee that a British Manifesto had been released warning Americans that the British fleet now sailed with orders to "destroy and lay waste such towns and districts along the coast as may be found available."

Those who were too young to have witnessed the depredations of an English armed force now and then relaxed their warlike stance, and took leave. One of these mounted his horse and rode off in the direction of Fauquier County. From the doorway of Oak Hill he could be seen at quite a distance down the road, if anyone had been looking for him. When Jaquelin Harvie was too far away for other eyes to see, Mary Marshall recognized him. Then she would tie her dark curls back with a velvet riband as black as her eyes, and borrow her mother's shell earrings, which hung so becomingly against the fine line of her neck. She was too honest to be coy, too warm hearted to be hesitant. When Jaquelin Harvie dismounted at the door of Oak Hill she would be there to welcome him.

Since his brother and sister had perished in the theatre fire, Mary, their childhood playmate, had painted his past with comfort and his future with happy plans. They were married at Oak Hill on September eighteenth, 1813.

Soon after the wedding, a traveller along the road from the upper valley stopped long enough to tell Polly that Edmund Randolph had died within the last few days while on a visit in Winchester. When evening soothed the noisome day, and she sat alone before the fire, Polly held her thin fingers before her eyes a few moments, remembering Edmund Randolph. He was indeed a Christian gentleman, strong in his own opinions. There was a time when General Washington had doubted Colonel Randolph's patriotism. But who could follow the shifting needle of loyalties on the compass of the people's will? There was a time when Colonel Randolph sought to vindicate his conduct by attacking that of the General, but it was said that he had later expressed a desire to live long enough to record his sincere opinion of the virtues and merits of the Father of his Country. Colonel Randolph believed in the separateness of each State, while Polly's husband was forever trying to unite them, a concoction as unnatural as peaches and oysters in one pie. The States could not even recognize a common enemy.

The Supreme Court was hard pressed upholding non-intercourse statutes, and establishing the laws covering trade with the enemy. "Voyages loaded with infamy" the Court called this commerce. Desperately General Marshall was drilling militia at the foot of Capitol Square. Desperately Tom was urging volunteers. Desperately the Secretary of State was calling for conscription, which was vociferously resisted, especially by old Cushing's friends, the New England Federalists, who again cried, "Secede!" It was then that the *Columbian Centinel* named the conflict "Mr. Madison's War."

Polly and the children remained at Oak Hill during this disorderly Winter while the British threatened from every side. Nearby several executive families took refuge on those handsome estates derived from the Fairfax grants. Many executive families, however, ignored Colonel Monroe's warning and remained in the defenseless capital city. Carelessly Washington society played on. Horse races were drawing crowds who should have been building fortresses. Money flowed easily in wagers, while it lay so scarcely in the nation's Treasury that Secretary Monroe had to personally guarantee payment of War Department drafts.

In August of 1814 there was such a sudden rush of refugees to the upper country that Polly must have had a moment of remembering her flight before a British army years ago. There had been pride mixed with her fear when she had a sweetheart in the field. Now with a son in the line of battle, she had only indignation for an administration which jeopardized young manhood.

The refugees told her of the sack of Washington, of the gallant defense by militia and a few regular soldiers under

Colonel James Monroe who had gone out with them to meet the enemy. They described the terror on the streets as British soldiers ignited tar barrels on the wharves, made bonfires of books and furniture from the House of Representatives, burned the President's palace, private residences, the arsenal, the Navy Yard, and finally the Potomac Bridge. Yes, the Madisons had escaped, but only at the last minute. Polly was trembling, and smothering her cry of "Tom."

But the British had passed through Washington on the way to Baltimore, where they were repulsed and forced to take to their ships. So Polly set out for her mansion in Richmond when the hickory trees were pure gold in the Fairfax forests, and the smoke from chimneys of Fairfax devisees rose straight up into a brilliant November sky. It all seemed so rich and so warm and so good. When she saw Marshall riding out from Fredericksburg to meet her, all the universe was bound in safety.

In December, word that the Treaty of Ghent had been wrung from Britain reached Polly simultaneously with news of General Jackson's victory over the British at New Orleans. As a rule Polly was dubious when peace was declared. Too often a treaty was the subject of angry conversation when gentlemen foregathered. Now everyone was glad, and the country had a new hero, General Andrew Jackson. She remembered him when crowds tarried on the streets of Richmond to hear him defend Aaron Burr.

A sense of good will sifted through gentlemen's talk like that star dropping its light through the Christmas night of 1814, undimmed by the ghost of old Cushing hovering near, solicitous about that serenity. For at the next session of the Supreme Court, 1815, his successor, who had been chosen to make the Court forget the ancient sentiments of the staunch Federalist, read such a mandate as might have come from Cushing's own quill. The high Court of the State of Virginia, with Judge Roane as its head, was ordered to reverse itself.

In 1809 David Hunter had renewed the suit of Hunter *vs* Fairfax Devisee in the Virginia Court of Appeals where

Judges Roane and Fleming, suffering a change of mind, demolished the Fairfax title which they had upheld on April twenty-fourth, 1794, in the same court. James Markham Marshall was now the Fairfax Devisee, and executor of Denny Martin Fairfax's will as it pertained to Virginia property. No demurrer was made by the Virginia court when the cause was appealed to the Supreme Court of the United States in 1811. Due to illness of the majority of Justices, the Court did not sit in that year. Therefore it was in Story's first session, 1812, that the case was argued. Implications of such national scope clung to the issue that the Court took decision under advisement for a year. When the Court convened in 1813 both Justice Washington and the Chief Justice, being too closely interested, retired from the Bench. Justice Todd was ill. Therefore when, on March fifteenth, Judge Story rendered the Supreme Court's reversal of the Virginia court, Justices Duvall, Livingston and Story concurred while Justice Johnson dissented.

The opinion of that majority was that since Virginia had taken no steps to acquire legal possession of the disputed land before the Treaty of Peace, she could not do so afterwards. Thus, it declared, the Hunter patent "issued improvidently and passed no title whatever." To uphold the State of Virginia's grant, said the Court, "would be selling suits and controversies throughout the whole country." Hence a mandate of the Supreme Court was directed to the Judges of the Virginia Court of Appeals to enter judgement for the Fairfax Devisee.

Down in Hanover County on one of the handsomest plantations of that handsome county, Judge Spencer Roane, president of the Virginia Court of Appeals and friend of Jefferson, read that opinion and then called on members of the Virginia Bar to give it long and serious consideration. This done, he set about purchasing a lot in Richmond near the Marshalls.

Feeling, which had been high, said the press, subsided, but not before Polly heard that Judge Roane had spoken of her husband as a "deplorable idiot." Many a time she had heard him called "ambitious office-seeker," "moneycrat,"

"Englishman," but never "deplorable idiot." This must have put Polly in high dudgeon. She must have called for her carriage and ordered Peter to drive, not around the Court End of Town, but down past the shops on Main Street, hoping to pass Mrs. Roane's carriage along that way. If so she would tell Peter to go more slowly over the rough street, and she would bow to Mrs. Roane, not spitefully, nor coldly, but with a smile of kindly condescension. Then Polly would come home and instead of going up to her room, would join the young company in the parlour. She would lift her glass to watch the jewels glow in the best Madeira in town, the best Madeira for the best family of the best Justice the Court had ever had, nor did she suppose there would ever be another so superior gentleman at the head of the American judiciary. She went to sleep that night wondering how it happened that all of a sudden life seemed to be aglow and she was neither shaken nor faint.

Two years later Judge Roane had built himself a mansion on that lot near the Marshalls, some say more handsome than Polly's. It faced the street that the Chief Justice must traverse visiting friends and family. Polly wondered whether Mrs. Roane ran to the window to watch him pass. She wondered if Mrs. Roane would see how the children ran up to join General Marshall. He never went far alone. Always someone fell into step beside him to enjoy his company, and his face would light up with welcome for young and old. Judge Roane's face, thought Polly, was comical. He seemed forever to be peering over some wall and laughing at what he saw.

William Marshall died in this summer. Any break in the Marshall family circle was a heart-wrench. Polly wondered if other families loved each other with such strong and pure devotion as the Marshalls. Polly had dearly loved her mother —and Eliza and sister Lucy. She loved Sister Carrington and Sister Fisher too, but they were so genteely healthy and useful. Polly's children loved each other with that Marshall rush of affection that overran each cup of personality until they were all engulfed in one joyous stream of life.

In December of 1815 Judge Roane called the Virginia Bar into the Virginia Court of Appeals to answer the mandate of the Supreme Court of the United States, which action was in fact a trial of a State's right to decide for itself the constitutionality of Section 25 of the Judiciary Act of 1781, "The appellate jurisdiction of the Supreme Court of the United States extends to a final judgement or decree in any suit in the highest court of law or equity of a State, where is drawn in question the validity of a treaty, or statute of, or an authority exercised under the United States and the decision is against their validity." The Reporter of the Virginia Court says, "The question whether this mandate should be obeyed excited all that attention from Bench and Bar which its great importance truly merited."

During the trial, Judge Cabell said, "This Court should decline to obey;" Judge Brooke, "Obedience ought to be refused;" and Judge Fleming, that it was "inexpedient for this Court to obey." Judge Roane in summing up the opinions said, "This Court is both at liberty and bound to follow its own convictions." Then he delivered a dissertation on States' Rights, and rendered a decision that under sound construction of the Constitution, appellate powers of the Supreme Court of the United States did not extend to the Virginia Court of Appeals, and therefore obedience to its mandate was refused. Judge Roane ordered the Shenandoah court to disregard the order of the Supreme Court.

All of this with Christmas coming on! With so many spicy viands cooking in Richmond kitchens that the city smelled like one big plum pudding; with so much courting going on in Polly's parlour that she was embarrassed to hang the large clump of silver and green mistletoe that Oby had brought in from Chickahominy. She placed it, instead, in a French china bowl in the middle of the table; then, remembering that Mrs. Bingham had served more decorations than food at her dinner parties, Polly called for Joseph and made sure that there was turkey as well as ham and venison cooking, and plenty of potatoes and winter cabbage, with wine jelly as well as plum pudding, cakes and nuts with raisins. Then the mistletoe seemed to beckon her, and when she reached toward it her pale hand among the leaves looked like the ghost of all tender things.

James Markham Marshall may have watched her, for he was still in Richmond preparing the writ of error with his lawyers by which he was to take his case to the Supreme Court of the United States. Never inclined to be sentimental, he felt superior to all tenderness at the moment, for he and Charles Lee had evolved a new name for the same old cause. The case would be taken into the high Court as Martin Heir at Law of Fairfax *vs* Hunter's Devisee. General Philip Martin was now the Fairfax heir.

When the case came before the Supreme Court, as usual Marshall retired. Virginia's St. George Tucker and Massachusetts's Samuel Dexter stood together to defend the supreme power of the State of Virginia. So deeply did the issues go into the roots of free but honorable government, that at times the emotions of a lawyer would break through his cool legal argument, until one wondered which side he was pressing. Samuel Dexter was impelled to exclaim, "The taper of judicial discord may become the torch of civil war, and though the breath of a Judge can extinguish the first, the wisdom of statesmen may not extinguish the latter." He regretted that Virginia, whose cause he was arguing, denied the "complete and exclusive domination of the National Government over the whole surface of the judicial power granted by the people to the Government."

On March twentieth, 1816, old Cushing's successor again read the Court's opinion, this time unanimous. "The danger," read Story, "is much greater of anarchy in the parts than in the head. . . . It is an historic fact that the Supreme Court of the United States have from time to time sustained this appellate jurisdiction in a great variety of cases brought from the tribunals of many of the most important states in the Union, and that no state tribunal has ever breathed a judicial doubt on the subject, or declined to obey the mandate of the Supreme Court until the present occasion . . . It is the opinion of the whole Court that the judgement of the District Court in Winchester, be, and the same is hereby affirmed."

After the decision was read Justice Johnson of South Carolina asked that his reasons for concurring be put upon the record. "It will be observed," he said, "in this case that the Court disavows all intention to decide on the right to issue compulsory process to the State Courts; thus leaving us, in my opinion, where the Constitution and laws place us—supreme over persons and cases as far as our judicial powers extend, but not asserting any compulsory control over the state tribunals. . . . I view this question as one of the most momentous importance; as one which may affect in its consequences the permanence of the American union. It represents an instance of collision between the judicial powers of the Union and one of the greatest states of the Union. . . . There is one claim which we can with confidence assert in our own name upon those tribunals—the profound, uniform and unaffected respect which this court has always exhibited for state decisions, give us strong pretentions to judicial comity . . . In this court every state of the Union is represented, we are constituted by the voice of the Union, and when decisions take place which nothing but a spirit to give ground and to harmonize can reconcile, ours is the superior claim upon the comity of the state tribunals. It is the nature of the human mind to press a favorite hypothesis too far, but magnanimity will always be ready to sacrifice the pride of opinion to the public welfare."

James Markham Marshall's lovely Hester did not live to enjoy the Court's assurance of her ownership to the rolling hills beside the Shenandoah. She died on April eighteenth, 1816, shortly after the news reached Happy Creek, the French chateau her husband had built on Fairfax land.

Thus the Fairfax title rested for a while, and old Cushing, who believed that power and property should lie in the same hands, must have shaken the last of earth from his sandals, and settled down to enjoy Eternity.

Chapter XX

The Era of Good Feeling

IN THE AUTUMN OF 1816 James Monroe was elected President of these United States with one electoral ballot dissenting, and that withheld so that history would record only George Washington unanimously elected. The *Columbian Centinel,* who had named "Mr. Madison's War," was shortly and prematurely to call President Monroe's administration "The Era of Good Feeling."

For the Marshall household the sobriquet was appropriate. Both Polly and the family had become resigned to her partial invalidism. To her extreme nervousness was added an ailment which seems to have been a form of anemia, causing spells of severe weakness. At the age of fifty-one she had assumed the privileges of an old lady, while the Chief Justice at sixty-two was as eager for life as ever.

The Marshall household was as delightfully sociable as ever, and just as often full of visiting nieces and nephews. So Polly frequently withdrew to her room, which provided repose within earshot of happiness. Jaquelin was home, still a bachelor at twenty-nine. John and James, Harvard students, were there for holidays, and Edward had a gang of twelve-year-olds running in and out of the house, always remembering for half a minute to hush each other when they heard Polly's footsteps. Mary and her children were as often at the Marshall house as at home on the next block.

Though this was known in the city as a happy home, as night lowered fears crept out of the corners of Polly's mind, and she often became so terrified that Marshall left the company to lead her to her room. There in the peace of familiar things and his affection, she became quiet, while he sat all evening within sound of merriment downstairs. And contentedly, he says, he spent his evenings alone with Polly. "She had a fine taste," he says, "for belles lettres reading, which was aciduously applied in the selection of pieces she admired. This quality, by improving her talents for conversation, contributed not inconsiderably to make her a most desirable com-

233

panion. It beguiled many of those winter evenings during which her protracted ill health and her feeble nervous system confined us constantly to each other."

On fair Sundays, and always on Communion Sundays, Polly, hanging on Marshall's arm, walked down Broad Street to Monumental Church, with the younger members of the household trooping ahead or dallying behind. She was so slight of frame that, the congregation says, he carried her up the stone steps, pausing to respond to the many friends who greeted them. The congregation says they liked to watch the Marshall clan, led by the smiling Chief Justice and the tiny sweet-faced lady in a fashionable bonnet march down the aisle to the boxed-in pew behind his brother William's pew, now occupied by William's widow and two young boys, one at the wriggling age, the other oppressed with the sophistication of sixteen. This was a stepson of the widow, but the oldest man in the family, so he was always the last to enter and draw the pew door shut behind him. The congregation says they delighted to watch how the Chief Justice, when he knelt in prayer, would turn around and face the back of the pew, opening the door to make room for his long legs. Then they say that, when Communion Sunday came, three times a year, the Chief Justice would open the door and beckon his family to pass him, on the way up to the Rail, while he humbly remained in his place, never being too sure that he did sufficiently repent him of his sins, or that any man should accept that ineffable gift of God in the sacrifice of His Son for the failures of combative life. Above his family at the Rail hung the laws that must be written on the hearts of all Christian rulers if they were to administer justice and maintain virtue in the government.

The Winter of 1817 was as bitterly cold as that of 1779, which had frozen the town of York. When sleet-sheathed branches crackled against the Marshall mansion in Richmond, Polly must have recalled the frost-bitten soldiers guarding her father's rented doorway. Then she may have worried about John in the chill climate of Harvard. And then she would have thought of the free colored people living in shacks where their only legitimate possession would be firewood. Then it is certain that she sent Dick and Moses to them with many a basket of food. It is certain, too, that the servants would have proceeded on the errands stepping high in imitation of Robin, balancing baskets on their heads as he did his feathered hat, and delivered the charity with a lordly manner of condescension.

Returning, they would always go by the post office. The latter part of February they brought their mistress this letter:

Washington Feb. 14th 1817

My dearest Polly

Since my being in this place I have been more in company than I wish & more than is consistent with the mass of business we have to go through. I have been invited to dine with the President with our own secretaries & with the minister of France & tomorrow I dine with the British minister. I have been very much pleased with the French minister & with his lady. She is among the most simple & domestic women I ever saw. Speaks of the comfortable habits of our country with great approbation & with regret of the increasing luxury of those who possess but moderate fortunes. In the midst of these gay circles my mind is carried to my own fireside & to my beloved wife. I conjecture where you are sitting & who is with you to cheer your solitary moments. I am most anxious to know how you do but no body is kind enough to gratify my wishes. Mr. Wirt I understand came yesterday & I looked eagerly for a letter today—but no letter came. I still retain some hope of receiving one tomorrow when I shall certainly see him.

Our weather continues intensely cold & I am more the grieved at it because I am sure it must prevent your riding out. You must not fail when you go to Chiccahominy on the 21st to carry out blankets enough to keep you comfortable. I am very desirous of hearing what is doing there but as no body is good enough to let me know how you do & what is passing at home I could not expect to hear what is passing at the farm.

I am my dearest Polly
your ever affectionate
J Marshall

Feb. 15th

I have kept my letter open till to day in the hope that Mr. Wirt would bring me a letter. I have the extreme mortification to find that he has brought none.

If Polly had sent a letter to Marshall by Mr. Wirt, it would probably have been lost in a shuffle of foolscap since

Mr. Wirt was carrying about the manuscript of a biography of Patrick Henry of which he was the exuberant author. He passed around the privilege of reading his manuscript as if it were a tray of finest oysters and he requesting suggestions for seasoning. One batch of chapters, says Mr. Wirt, had just been returned by "several old gentlemen," who were Judge Roane, Judge Tucker and the "honorable Thomas of Monticello." When as custom demanded, he paid his respects to the Justices in their lodgings, he exhibited his opus, and reported that some of the old "gentlemen" had criticized his description of Henry offering those famous resolutions against the Stamp Act to the House of Burgesses. They had inferred that Wirt gave the tale too much decoration. Wirt replied that his authority was Edmund Randolph's manuscript *History of Virginia,* and that his own description wore "but Quaker drapery compared with the account he [Randolph] gives of the affair."

Wirt had another iron in the fire. He let drop that gentlemen who had read his *Patrick Henry* now pressed him to write a biography of the Chief Justice. That could not have been Judge Roane who made the suggestion. Or could it? Marshall may have had his suspicions, for it is said that with a gleeful smile he exclaimed, "I hope to God they will let me alone till I am dead."

Prodigal public sentiment returned to the Father of His Country, and Polly fled the noise of repentant citizens celebrating Washington's birthday. Bells rang. Cannon boomed. Whites and blacks, men, women and children made a great disorder in honor of the man who was notable for unbending dignity. She took refuge at Marshall's farm, Chickahominy, a word the Chief Justice could never spell twice in the same system. When Polly arrived there she paused on the stoop before the farmhouse door to study the row of whitewashed cabins, each with its pennant of smoke flying from a squat chimney, each with its chicken yard and pig sty, with colored children swathed in strips of blanket, running from the kitchen house followed by a Negress smoking a corncob pipe of the farm's tobacco. Polly recalled that George Primrose, son of the Vicar of Wakefield, had said, "Monarchies are for poor people. Commonwealths for the rich."

February of 1817 was the last month in which the Madisons' social reign radiated in splendor from the rented Tayloe house. There the Chief Justice was a dinner guest with the de Neuvilles. At this time a wise hostess entertained French and British ambassadors separately. Thus it was another afternoon when the Chief Justice dined at the Madisons' with Sir Charles Bagot.

That Marshall was "much in company" was true of all Washington when the Court was sitting. A newspaper of that day says, "The arrival of the Judges, counsellors, parties, etc. connected with the high Court creates a great stir in the Metropolis. There are tea and dinner parties daily." And a visitor to the capital wrote: "The truth is that at Washington society is the business of life." Charles Ingersoll coming from sedate Philadelphia wrote: "Fie upon them for dining out so constantly! But how can they help it under this raging star. . . . It seems to me that dinner giving system has encreased very much since I first knew this watering place . . . where amusement is a business, a need, to which almost everybody is given up from 5 o'clock till bedtime. All the secretaries give dinners and balls frequently. . . . The Court and the Bar dine together with the President. In my opinion a Judge should never dine out in term time except Saturday and Sunday if then. In England, I am told, they hardly ever do, and I fancy the pillars of Westminster Hall would marvel much if they could see the Supreme Court of the United States begin a days session, aye, after robing and taking their places, by receiving from the marshal their cards of invitation and taking up pen and paper to answer them before the list of cases is called for hearing."

William Wirt's business in Washington at this time was his second case before the Supreme Court. He says that to be called before the high tribunal made him "feel young again, and touches nerves which have been asleep ever since 1807 (the era of the Burr trial) . . . to take by the beard the first champions of the nation." His case was an appeal from a North Carolina court judgement concerning a prize taken at sea, the question being whether the captured ship and cargo were neutral or hostile. Wirt says he was bound to contend they were British as against the contention that they were Russian. He was dismayed that the issue of fact must be decided upon "a hundred dull, deranged ship documents" which were almost impossible of clothing with his classical ornamentation. Even so, he managed to produce "a powerful and splendid effusion, grand, tender, picturesque, and pathetic . . . lofty and touching." For four hours he impressed the Justices and held fifteen or twenty ladies in the audience silent until dinner time. Afterwards when he received compliments on his oration, he would ask whether those who praised him came from New England; for, he said, "what is common animation in Virginia would be thought poetic frenzy by Easterners."

On March first, 1817, the Chief Justice was seen to smile when he read a note handed him by a messenger, and that bright roguish expression was reflected a moment in the eyes of his brethren of the Bench as they wondered what good story they would be told at dinner. There was really nothing comical about the note. It was addressed to "Honorable John Marshall Chief Justice of the United States," and read:

Washington March 1st 1817

Sir

I propose to take the oath which the constitution proscribes to the President of the United States, before he enters on the execution of his office, on tuesday next, at 12 oclock, in the chamber of the House of Representatives; and have to request, that you will have the goodness, to meet me there for the purpose of administering it.

I have the honor to be with the greatest respect Sir
Your most obt servant.
Jas. Monroe

There was a cold peremptory tone to friend James' request. Even Jefferson had invited Marshall to perform this rite with more friendly deference. It may be that Monroe had forgotten that there was no rule binding an incoming President to be sworn into office by the Chief Justice, who might or might not be his friend.

Whatever the cause of Monroe's chill manner, he was not allowed an inauguration in the chamber of the House of Representatives. Speaker of the House Henry Clay, who cherished a coldness toward Monroe, put so many difficulties in the way of the customary use of that chamber for such an occasion that a committee in charge of arrangements hastily called on the architect, Benjamin Latrobe, to supervise the erection of a Greek portico out of doors in front of the Capitol. The committee trusted that Divine Being, whom Americans had a way of claiming as a Fellow Citizen, to send propitious weather. And He did. Winter broke suddenly. Monroe's Era of Good Feeling came in on a lamb-like day, warm and softly stirring.

This was a gala inauguration. It has been estimated that between five and eight thousand persons thronged the streets around the portico. On the outskirts of the official area carriages so blocked the thoroughfare that occupants left them, and proceeded afoot heedless of the mud that clogged all routes to the Capitol. The incoming executives were escorted on horseback by a cavalcade of officeholders, grandees from various States, for to be an officeholder, a gentleman must be a landowner, and freeholders were still predominantly gentry.

The Chief Justice's smile seemed lit by the radiance of the weather as he watched Monroe and Madison walk down the platform together, for he had a warm affection for both of them, and at times a conviction that he was wiser than either of them. Madison withdrew so quietly and quickly that even Marshall did not notice his absence until the ceremonies were over; for Marshall's attention was fixed on his playmate grown so great. Across the oath of office these two gazed into each other's eyes with a challenge that was suddenly merry and friendly.

Then the audience standing in the sunshine, heard the new President say that with all its troubles this "mild, parental system of government" had made the individual citizens happy and the nation prosperous, and that the States still "enjoyed their seperate spheres." After the inaugural address the President and Mrs. Monroe, their daughters and son-in-law, received the citizenry in their rented house. In the evening the irrespressible American taste for pomp indulged itself in a Grand Ball at Davis' Hotel.

Count Serurier wrote: "Mr. Monroe is not a brilliant man, and no one expects to find a great captain in him: But he served through the War of Independence with much bravery under the orders and by the side of Washington. He is a man of great good sense, of the most austere honor, the purest patriotism and the most universally admitted integrity. He is loved and respected by all parties."

Not until New Year's Day of 1818 did a President of the United States again entertain in the palace. Then the press reported: "The President's House, for the first time since its re-aerification, was thrown open for the general reception of visitors. It was thronged from 12 to 3 o'clock by an unusually large concourse of ladies and gentlemen, among whom were to be found the Senators, Representatives, Heads of Departments, Foreign Ministers, and many of our distinguished citizens, residents, and strangers."

Marshall was not among those guests. He was in Richmond where high society was cosily conversing before fashionable small coal fires, entertaining with music in parlours bristling with holly and mistletoe, discussing Maria Sedgewick's latest novel. All this he must leave the last week in January when liming should begin on his farms and fields made ready for ploughing. As the States grew more fractious his interest in the land seemed to grow more compelling. Thus when he foregathered with his brethren of the Bench in the Washington boarding house study, methods of farming vied with judicial opinions for the largest share of conversation. The Justices would hardly have decided whether it increased a crop to roll the land before planting, when they must comb or powder their hair, bundle up in great coats, call their coaches and join the full swing of capital society.

The President's house was again the center of that society, but with a condition that touched Marshall's understanding. The lady of the house had spells of illness. Polly who knew the Monroes intimately could see her husband at his laughing, happy ease in their company. Wistfully she admired

Elizabeth Kortright Monroe. Her graciousness made her a perfect helpmeet for a public gentleman. When Mrs. Monroe was ill she looked pale and romantic, while Polly in her spells fluttered and shook, and, yes, sometimes cried out. Mrs. Monroe was like an angel molded in glass. The fashionable world thought her a perfect First Lady, but through the glass always Polly would see tears for a little dead son.

Polly had known the small Monroe daughters before their sojourn in French finishing schools where they had been on intimate terms with crowned heads. To Polly's way of thinking the present system in Europe of crowning and uncrowning heads did nothing but confuse society. The eldest of the Monroe daughters, upon her return to Virginia, had married the son of a tavern keeper, widower George Hay. Of course Mr. Hay was United States Attorney General for Virginia, appointed to the office through Jeffersonian politics. To Mrs. Hay, Polly heard, were delegated the duties of hostess when her mother was too ill to appear, and Mrs. Hay was not fond of Jeffersonian democracy. She was haughty and visibly discontented with Washington society, causing a crisis in foreign and domestic diplomacy by refusing to call on ladies of Government and embassies. This kept Secretary of State John Quincy Adams busy soothing feminine pride in five languages.

The President, too, was put to it to keep peace at state dinners with such a rebel as hostess, so he fell upon the custom of inviting gentlemen only to these affairs. Once a week he entertained thirty or forty of these in "a very laborious way . . . in a vast cold hall," where dinner was served in "French style a little Americanized." Gentlemen as they arrived seated themselves in the drawing room, maintaining a solemn mien until they were summoned to the dining room. How solemn was Marshall as he told this to Polly?

Even in the dining room amid an array of liveried servants, handsome victuals were consumed in silence, except upon that occasion when the French minister angered the English minister with an insulting grimace. Across the table swords clashed. The President's chair crashed as with a clatter he raised his own weapon and separated his guests.

Sharply he ordered their respective carriages, and sent them home. Then silence again as the meal was resumed, until coffee was served, a little Frenchified, in the parlour. This night the guests were home by nine o'clock, bursting with conversation about the matter.

Dinners given by the Secretary of State were quite gay. Once a week Mr. Adams entertained brilliantly at a sumptuous board. Every two weeks Mrs. Adams gave a grand ball, for which the French legation, arriving in gilded coaches with footmen in gilded livery, put on a gaudy show that outshone all embassies. The social functions of Secretary of War, John C. Calhoun of South Carolina, were too gracious and easy to admit of such a fancy performance. In fact it was told Polly that the Calhouns were the most generous and amiable host and hostess in the capital. It was also said that Mr. Calhoun was the most agreeable member of the Cabinet. He was however a smouldering brand under the Era of Good Feeling.

Sitting alone by her bedroom window, half listening to the sounds of happy life downstairs, Polly watched a streak of Winter sunlight creep across the sill. This bit of brightness had travelled to the corner and was fast fading when Jaquelin, the unwilling doctor, cautiously opened her door, and seeing her in quiet spirits, entered with a letter in his hand. It was good medicine for her. She opened it and read:

Washington Feby 16th 1818

My dearest Polly

Yesterday I received Jaquelin's letter of the 12th informing me that your health was at present much the same as when I left Richmond but that you had just recovered from a cold. The weather has been so very cold as to fill me with apprehensions for you. Indeed my dearest Polly as we grow older we suffer more from the cold & ought to use more precautions against it. Your fears of being too warm push you into the other extreem & you expose yourself to more cold than is consistent with your health or safety. Let me entreat you to be more careful in this particular.

I am as usual in good health for an old man & very busily employed. No resolution is taken respecting the time of our rising but I conjecture it will be about the middle of March. Farewell

my dearest Polly. That you may be happy is the fervent prayer of
your affectionate
J Marshall

Polly was still squinting at this as if her eyes would
squeeze the last drop of affection from the words, when Jaquelin showed her that there was another letter on the page.
It began:

My Dear Son

I have received your letter of the 12th & thank you for the
information it contains. I do not wish the overseer to attempt
ploughing when the ground is unfit for it, but I am anxious to
know what he is doing. I gave him explicit instructions to prepare
a great deal of plaister & I wish to know whether he has observed
them. I also directed him to avail himself of the first hard weather to draw in the stalks & hay that was in low grounds intended for the farm pen. I am anxious to know how the grubbing & cutting advances & where the people are now at work, also whether this
dry windy weather has enabled him to burn any of the places which
I directed. It will perhaps be well to direct him to write me an account of everything & give you the letter.

I do not wish the packages you mention to be sent by post. Should
a private conveyance offer, send them. If that indorsed Thos. P.
Devereux can come free from postage send it—not otherwise.

I do not recollect how my account stands in the Bank & therefore send you a note to indorse & negotiate & pay Mr. Cocke for
his corn. 20 barrels would amount to 90$. I have advanced him 30$
consequently you are to pay him 60$. What is James doing? I hope
he has engaged in a course of reading. I am your affectionate father
J Marshall

Marshall had been one of the first in Richmond to subscribe to the Bank of the United States, adding to his holdings through the years. When it became evident that a case
involving the constitutionality of national banks would
come before the Supreme Court, he sold his investment,
while Judge Roane's son was purchasing four thousand nine
hundred dollars of the stock. William Roane was a healthy
looking young man, Polly thought, watching him swing past
her house without so much as a glance across her fence.

On Marshall's return to Richmond, Polly was downstairs
looking for him. She waited until the hubbub of welcomes
had died down, and there was no one else around to hear,

then she confided a rumor to him, which he must promise
not to mention, and never to look knowing when the prin-
cipals were around. The "doctor," Jaquelin, was obviously
courting a pretty neighbour, Elizabeth Steptoe Clarkson.

Early in April, as Marshall walked out to admire the
dawn, he found his son-in-law, Colonel Jaquelin Harvie,
tramping a groove into the sidewalk before his house. Marshall would slip his arm into the younger man's, and together
they would march to and fro, until the house door would be
thrown open and Mammy Venus call them in to see the
newest grandchild, Mary's daughter Ellen.

Thus was Marshall's joyous life branching out in new
families. Thus was Polly's fluttering anxiety spreading
abroad. On New Year's Day, 1819, "the doctor" and Elizabeth Clarkson were married, and went to live on their wedding gift of Fairfax lands in Fauquier County. On March
twenty-ninth, 1819, Fielding Lewis Marshall, fourth child
of Margaret and Tom Marshall, was born; and on the next
New Year's Day, Jaquelin's daughter was born, and named
Mary Ambler. On the third day of the following February,
Polly's son John, who had been born while his father was
in France, married Elizabeth Alexander of Baltimore. She
was eighteen years old and he twenty-two, old enough maybe, but on the other hand, so young!

Shortly the Marshalls found this young lady to be full
of human wisdom. Agnes, seventeen year old daughter of
Robin Spurlock, became so troublesome in Polly's household, so wilful and feckless, so quick to hear "sperrits" and
so slow to hear the housekeeper's orders, that Marshall,
rather than sell her out of the State as so many owners did
with unruly slaves, gave her to Elizabeth Alexander Marshall, who had shown a kindly skill in training difficult Negroes. Thus Agnes Spurlock lived a long time nursing Marshall babies in Fauquier County

John built Mt. Blanc on his rolling Fairfax acres. There
he lived as a statesman, several times representing his
county in the Virginia House of Delegates. It is said that he
was a handsome, gay hearted gentleman, always well-to-do
and popular. Polly loved him especially. He loved his father.

Courtesy Va. State Chamber of Commerce

OAK HILL IN FAUQUIER COUNTY. Original house to right, built by Colonel Thomas Marshall, 1773. Larger house built by Thomas, son of the Chief Justice, about 1820.

There are two letters from J Marshall to My dearest Polly in the year 1823. One in April was written from General Blackwell's plantation in Fauquier County where the Chief Justice had stopped overnight on his way to visit Jaquelin, the doctor, at Prospect Hill. The Blackwells had resided longer in this county than the Marshalls. General Blackwell was a veteran of the Continental Army, and carried political weight for Tom.

Warrenton Apl 11th 1823

My dearest Polly

I am thus far on my way to the Doctors & I purpose proceeding on my journey after dinner. I have had a comfortable travel of it—though I found the road about Elk run excessively bad. There has been a vast deal of rain on this side of Richmond all the way; a good deal more I think than we had. I did not find Mr. Skinker at home, in consequence of which I came last night to General Blackwells. I found my old friend quite well but almost blind, which he ascribes to reading by candlelight. Tom was at Genl Blackwells in the course of the day a few hours before me on his electioneering business. From what I can learn the election will be close & is very doubtful, more doubtful than I had supposed it to be from what I heard in Richmond. Tom will lose some Federal votes who had en-[ga]ged themselves before his being known as a candidate.

I have just returned from Mr. Bells but did not find him at home. I have requested him to bring his papers to court.

I must repeat my request that you will ride regularly & market liberally.

Farewell my dearest Polly
Your ever affectionate
J Marshall

Tom's electioneering was not successful in 1823. He had represented Fauquier County in the Virginia Assembly in 1814 and 1817, but in 1823 his anti-slavery sentiments were too outspoken and the question of emancipation too perplexed for his platform to be popular. However by 1827 an anti-slavery faction under his leadership was strong enough to return him to the House of Delegates. Again in 1830 his name is on the roll of Delegates and remained there until his death in 1835. In all of his service he declared that the institution of Negro slavery "is ruinous to the whites, retards improvements, roots out an industrious population—banishes the yeomanry of the country—deprives the spinner, the weaver, the smith, the shoemaker, the carpenter of employment and support. The evils admit of no remedy, and are increasing and will continue to increase until the whole country will be inundated by one black wave covering its whole extent, with a few white faces here and there floating on the surface."

In October Marshall was sitting with the District Court in Norfolk. From there he wrote Polly.

Norfolk Oct 25th 1823

My dearest Polly

I have the mortification to tell you that it will not be in my power to come up till tuesday. The case will not be finished till saturday.

I had a very pleasant sail down the river and got into Norfolk about eight. I board in a very agreeable house & am treated by the gentlemen of the town with a degree of kindness & attention & attention which exceeds even what I had expected. Yet I am much disappointed at not being able to return as soon as I had hoped.

I am my dearest Polly your ever affectionate
J Marshall

The Chief Justice could hardly have been wasting his time travelling by sail. He must have been aboard the steamship *Powhatan* which ran from Richmond to Norfolk by day on Wednesdays and Saturdays, and from Norfolk to Richmond over night Mondays and Thursdays. The fare for adults was nine dollars, half price for children and servants. If the case was finished on Saturday, Marshall would have Sunday and until four o'clock Monday to enjoy the friendliness of Norfolk, a town where he was always honored.

Did it give Polly a smile to read that he was mortified to be delayed in returning to her hearthside? The first thing he did every spring on his return from the Supreme Court session in Washington was to set out for the upper country.

A clergyman visiting Fauquier White Sulphur Springs found the Chief Justice occupying his usual cottage there, and wrote of him: "I had seen him before on the Bench at Washington. . . . He was not very graceful. He had never trained his knee to fawning, but he was polite . . . for at out meals he uniformly stood till the last of our little group had come and then waited till the writer had said grace."

Still another remembered that this resort had no rings for the game of quoits, and that he had seen the Chief Justice "emerge from a thicket which bordered a neighbouring brook; carrying as large a pile of . . . flat stones as he could hold between his right arm and his chin; he stepped briskly up to the company and threw down his load among them, exclaiming, 'There! Here are quoits enough for us all.' "

CHAPTER XXI

The Colonization Society

THERE WERE SINGING BOATMEN on the James River in
the Era of Good Feeling. Their song was:

> I'm gwine down ter town,
> I'm gwine down ter town,
> I'm gwine down ter Richmond town
> To cyar my baccer down.

Their cadence was the jog of mules on the tow path of the
James River & Kanawha Canal, pulling bateaux laden with
tobacco grown on plantations up the river. Some of the
singers were free Negroes bringing their own product to
markets; others came at the behest of owners.

There were singing carpenters at work on new mansions
for Richmond citizens. Their song was a colored preacher's
sermon set to the count of their labor:

> King Jesus a-hammerin',
> King Jesus a-sawerin'.

There were bricklayers with balanced hods on their heads,
mounting ladders in a procession, stepping and swaying to
the rhythm of

> I'll be free, when I see
> Dem pearly gates,

never stumbling as long as they worked in antiphonal company.

This mysterious, laughing, alien people sang their work,
their religion, their fears; and though their dance lyrics
were wild and weird, their lullabys were the essence of tender protection. Their sojourn among Richmond citizens was
the source of a rare kind of patience, affection and caution,
emotions which shook Polly with sudden change.

For like their music that swung high and low the colored
population was marked with contrast. There were such good
members, and such bad ones, such cheery and lazy people,
such sullen and dangerous ones. Their humor was so loud

249

and unrestrained; their suffering so deep and silent. Their philosophy was the cushion of Polly's domestic crises, their loyalty the watchman at her door. The danger that lurked among them was the terror that stalked her nights. Though they practiced bowing deference to members of the white race over twelve years old, Polly knew they were not an humble people.

In 1823 the population of Richmond was about one third persons of color, and of that fraction about two thirds were the earthly possession of white families. The presence in Virginia of both bond and free had long been a problem of beneficence and order, but "because of the delicacy of the question," says the historian of the situation, in legislative halls this was discussed in secret. Nor was it discussed openly in Polly's parlour, for gentlemen were given to sudden strong language when describing the perils involved.

Well Polly knew that for upwards of forty years gradual emancipation of all slaves had been the hope and purpose of the best families of the upper Southern States. But how to accomplish it safely and justly remained an urgent question. "We have the wolf by the ears," said cousin Jefferson, "and it is as dangerous to let go as to hold on." Ex-President Madison spoke of the institution of slavery as "that great calamity which has so long afflicted our country and filled so many with dispair." Silver voiced Randolph of Roanoke, who had written a will freeing three hundred slaves, shook his long finger at fellow planters and calculated that Negro slavery would die a natural death due to such labor consuming all profits.

There were times when Tom Marshall, keeping his mother company, would rise from his chair and close all doors. Then, with more confidence in her interest than concern for her nerves, tramp from window to window rehearsing vehemently his arguments for abolition of slavery. Polly never quite listened as he talked, for her attention would veer to visions of starving colored children and feeble old Negroes set adrift in freedom. She could not say whether or not Tom was right. There were clergymen and knowing gentlemen, even pious ladies, who were saying that the institution of African slavery in American homes was the means whereby more heathen were converted every year than could be reached by missionaries in a century. Clergymen who preached to colored congregations said that they eagerly accepted a knowledge of Jesus as Lord and Lover of their souls. Therein lay the strangeness of these people. They seemed so of the earth earthy, and yet the very air about them was crowded with souls. All creatures had souls, all moving elements. Wind and water spoke to them. A cloud could give a command that would circumvent an overseer's order. That Mystical Spirit who was and is and evermore shall be readily became their awe-filled delight.

Sometimes Polly's confusions were deepened by the contrast of her father's religion of shalt and shalt not with Mammy Venus's and Robin's, "All God's chillun gwine to Hebben."

A number of gentlemen who passed through Polly's parlour, among them her cousin, Colonel John Ambler, had at one time and another, purchased land beyond the Alleghenies upon which to settle their colored people in gradual emancipation, each family supplied with tools, land, and a year's supply of necessities. In a year most of these colonists were back in familiar neighborhoods. There was nowhere else for them to go. New States promptly passed laws forbidding them entrance. Those Southerners who would abolish slavery in gradual resettlement were again thwarted.

While Tom Marshall was campaigning for this method of emancipation, elder citizens were deeply worried about the free colored population, which in Virginia had increased from less than three thousand at the close of the Revolution to nearly forty thousand in 1823, an increase vastly beyond means of livelihood.

Under the British King manumission had been a restricted process, but in 1783 the Virginia State Legislature hastened this process by an Act permitting owners to free slaves by deed of will or writ of manumission. Many wills were so written, most of them making provision for one generation of males or devising trust funds for the females to the second or third generation. This bounty always gave out, and always poverty stalked the free Negro. It was not in his nature to be provident, nor was it his nature to be law abiding.

Some few free colored persons made comfortable livings as musicians, bricklayers and carpenters. Free mid-wives and wet nurses commanded good wages. Here and there a smithy, baker or drayman maintained independent business in good civic standing. They were magical farmers, but in the Era of Good Feeling less than two hundred free Negroes owned property in Virginia, a condition duplicated in all the farming States. Far the greater number of the free colored population everywhere were destitute, a drifting, shiftless, dangerous element in any community.

Three times between 1800 and 1817 the Legislature of Virginia had petitioned the President and Congress to procure territory for colonization of these people on their own farms; with desultory response from the federal government. After the third of these memorials, as James Monroe was about to take Presidential office, a meeting of the foremost gentlemen in Washington at the time was called by the Reverend Mr. Robert Finley of New Jersey and Elisha Caldwell, clerk of the Supreme Court, to discuss "this delicate and important topic which may emphatically be said to come home to the business and bosom of every man."

This meeting had taken place at Brown's Hotel on December twenty-first, 1816, and so important did Marshall hold the matter that he came on from Richmond to be present. Senator Henry Clay of Kentucky had presided, with John Randolph of Roanoke as self-appointed whip and Daniel Webster of Massachusetts powerfully holding the steeds of argument to the road.

"If," Senator Clay had said, "we were to invoke the greatest blessing on earth, which Heaven in its mercy could now bestow on this nation, it would be the separation of the two most numerous races of its population and their comfortable establishment in distinct and different countries."

That the source from which these people had come would be the rock to which they could most happily return soon became the vision above the conference, and the discussion moved forward to evolve a method whereby free Negroes in America could with their own consent be returned to their native land on the west coast of Africa as an independent democratic nation.

Thus, adopting a plan devised by the Reverend Mr. Finley, these gentlemen organized the American Society for Colonization of Free People of Colour in the United States on the Coast of Africa. Justice Bushrod Washington was elected president. Vice presidents were Senator Henry Clay, William Crawford of Georgia, Andrew Jackson of Tennessee, and two Virginians, John Tyler and Bishop Meade. The Reverend Ralph Randolph Gurley of Washington was acting secretary. From various States a Board of Managers was appointed, gentlemen "who ranked among the most distinguished for talents, virtue and patriotism in the Union."

A constitution was adopted which bound the Society to function as a private charity supported by gifts from a voluntary membership. The declared purposes were "to remove to the African coast with their own consent such of the coloured population of the United States as are now free, or may be emancipated either by the laws of the several States or the humanity of individuals," and this to do by "all gentlemanly and Christian means."

An early statement of the Society explained: "We all perceive and bewail the existence of an intermediate class, occupying the middle ground between freedom and slavery without possessing the unrestricted enjoyment of the former, or the careless security of the latter condition. Despised and suspected by the white man, and envied by the slave, the free negro wanders an out cast in the very midst of society."

Looking always toward gradual abolition of slavery, members agreed that no force of arms or law could terminate the slave traffic until it was cut off at the source of supply which was the African kings. An Annual Report of the Society says, "As an eloquent son of Virginia once said, 'Hannibal must be conquered in Africa.' It is by planting colonies at the most prominent points and enlightening the natives that the trade is to be abolished."

Therefore the Society assumed the duty to "prove by actual experiment, that a colony of civilized blacks may be established on the southern coast of Africa; that a suitable and healthy situation may be found and procured by purchase from the natives . . . that colonists in abundance and of a proper character may be found . . . that a regular and extensive commerce between this country and that to be established . . . must increase . . . with the consequent discouragement of the slave trade in that quarter; and that the colony may very soon be placed in a condition to govern and protect itself, and not only to provide for its own wants by the products of its agricultural industry, but to have a large surplus for commerce with this country and Europe," thus rendering these people "respectable members of the social compact, ornaments to service and the arts, or chosen vessels for the propagation of the word of life."

Though funds were readily underwritten for the dispatch of missionaries to explore the practicability of securing lands on the south western coast of Africa, prosecution of the Society's purpose was beset with obstacles. Since President Monroe was declaring a doctrine of no colonization on the American continent, he could hardly lend the facilities of the government's foreign office to negotiating an African colony, until by time-consuming explanation he could be convinced that the Society was pursuing private beneficence, not American expansion. And then agents who finally went to purchase land found native kings flatly and fiercely averse to cessation of the slave trade. The first land chosen turned out to be disease ridden, the first shipload of colonists victims of the ferocity of neighbouring tribes.

But the gentlemanly and Christian effort persisted, until in the last year of the Era of Good Feeling, 1823, a colony protected by forts had been systematically seated, with a capital village of two hundred substantial huts and a mayor hiring his servants. Acreage had been opened and allotted to free American Negro farmers. Two churches and five schools were functioning. All children over five years old could read. Under pressure from the Society, Congress had made slave carrying at sea an act of piracy punishable with death. English and American cruisers were so assiduously patrolling the African coast against slavers that all European flags had disappeared from the traffic except that of the king of Spain, who explained that his trade "originated in motives of humanity intended to avoid the greater evils growing out of the barbarous state of the African continent."

In repatriating Negroes learned in the American system of farming and neighbourliness, the Society believed that it was engaged in "illuminating that benighted region with the light of liberty, and science, and the benign influence of religion."

Then often in October of 1823, when Polly stepped out on her porch to welcome the cooling air, she would see a short fat Welshman, Mr. William Fitzwhylsonn, opening the gate to her husband's office. The bond between the plump little gentleman and the tall thin Chief Justice was a simple matter. Mr. Fitzwhylsonn was one of the town's best booksellers and a veteran of the Revolution, but of the enemy army. As chief drummer for Lord Cornwallis he had rolled parley from the top of a rampart below York Town when the British were ready to acknowledge defeat. Polly wondered whether the Welshman had settled among his captors in order to teach them "the English tongue grammatically," as he now advertised, or because he was intrigued by the many music circles he found active in the Colony. He certainly was an enthusiastic member of all such circles in Richmond, besides conducting a popular school. But Polly did not like him. He was a solemn jokester, capping her husband's stories with a twist that threw the laugh back upon the Chief Justice. This Polly considered presumptuous, and turned away indignantly when Marshall joined in the laughter, making himself even more ridiculous by hugging the bookseller. Now falling yellow leaves too, seemed bent on applauding the Welshman, rushing to pat him on the back before he disappeared in the door of his best customer.

However in this October, Mr. Fitzwhylsonn had not come to sell books. He had come to borrow a great heart and a weighty name. The Colonization Society was running into strange opposition. "In the minds of some," say the minutes of the Society, "are prejudices and uncertainties." This might be due "to a lack of understanding of the pure and non-political spirit of the enterprise, a want of more diffused knowledge rather than any material hostility to its principles. . . The doubtful require time for information; the timid await the issue of experiment; and even those prompt and generous spirits whose delight it is to take the lead in every laudable adventure will sometimes pause to contemplate at leisure those very purposes they are most solicitous to effect." Therefore it seemed of the first magnitude of importance that there be more local participation in this "great object of social solicitude." Thus Mr. Fitzwhylsonn was calling on the foremost gentlemen of Richmond and Manchester, those twin cities linked by Mr. Mayo's toll bridge across the James River.

That the Chief Justice came forward with his name, his time and his money to strengthen this work at a time when his friends were suspicious of its nature is attested in the Society's final tribute to Marshall in 1835.

On November eleventh, 1823, so well had Mr. Fitzwhylsonn pleaded the need for Colonization, that a large concourse of citizens in the hall of the House of Delegates formed the Richmond-Manchester Society Auxiliary to the American Society for Colonization of Free People of Colour of the United States on the Coast of Africa. The Chief Justice was elected president, Governor James Pleasants vice president, Mr Fitzwhylsonn and eleven other gentlemen appointed to act as a Board of Managers. Leading business men of the two cities were delegated to go out into the wards and explain to white and colored that the true purposes of this chapter were "by private charity permanently to promote the happiness and prosperity of our country . . . in a voluntary act of service . . . to afford such of the free people of colour in our country as may consent to emigrate the means of transporting them to Africa, and there to provide for their comfort for a reasonable period, and until by their own industry they can make the necessary provision for themselves."

Many would be the advantages to the free Negroes. They would be independent in the land of their forefathers, among

their own people, dictating their own laws, owning their
land, conducting their own industries and commerce. They
would have civil and political rights which the policy of
our nation denies them here. Their nation would be a worthy fellow in the compact of nations.

Many would be the benefits to the United States. For
one hundred and fifty miles of seacoast the nefarious slave
trade would be eradicated. A country rich in gold, ivory and
rare plants would enchance our trade, and the products of
our manufactories would find an open market. Gradual
emancipation would be voluntarily accomplished peacefully
as slave owners found this an opportunity to relieve their
sensibilities and their fortunes without throwing the danger
of hardship upon their colored people.

For awhile in Richmond, applicants for the voyage were
so numerous, say the minutes of the Society, "that there was
much perplexity in making selections." Shortly agents from
Haiti took advantage of this enthusiasm, attempting to lure
labor to that island. The gentlemen of the town studied these
offers, then went out into the wards to persuade the Negroes
that Haiti was not a happy chance for them. There they
would not be independent citizens. They would be exploited
labor in a strange land into whose law and religion they
could not fit.

Polly found herself urging Eliza to dispense this caution
with victuals and clothing when, well protected, she visited
the destitute shanties in the town's wooded ravines.

In the first month the Richmond and Manchester Society
sent five hundred dollars to the parent Society. In the first
year, by its individual effort, the auxiliary sent out two ships
with one hundred and eighty colonists, equipped for a year
at a cost of four thousand dollars.

Four thousands dollars, and the difference in the city
could hardly be noticed! At heart Polly was glad. The General's people went cheerily about the outbuildings behind
her mansion. She could stand on her porch and listen to the
rhythmic chant of coal hucksters along the street, smiling
when the song was broken by sudden bursts of laughter.
She could call out to admonish little boys who threw

things at fat washerwomen who with basket on head were swaying their way from big house to cabin.

Four thousands dollars! Why Polly would not take that sum for Mammy Venus alone, nor for the troublesome children of Robin. She had heard gentlemen in the North called generous for giving the Society one hundred dollars. But look! When a Southerner released a servant he gave many times such value. Open-handed, her friends were giving their money and their people, a warmhearted, happy way of life. Cousin John Ambler was impoverishing himself and his many heirs by selecting whole families of his people for repatriation, making much of escorting them to the port to see them happily aboard.

Each embarkation from Norfolk or City Point on the James River was a State ceremony with the Chief Justice and other dignitaries present. Those were no slavers chartered to carry the voyagers home. They were regular merchantmen, advertising comfortable quarters for the colonists. And while they were loading, white families crowded around colored families on the dock. Youngsters, white and colored, reached across to smack the sides of the restive vessel that was taking favorite people from each other.

These were poignant events, with last minute changes of minds, last minute messages, dark and white hands clinging until the last minute. Then when sobbing and keening seemed about to overcome the company the Reverend Mr. Gurley would begin to pray, using words that threw a simple bridge of faith across the seas. When all were quiet he preached to them, admonishing the colonists to preserve a spirit of unity and Christian love, to resolve to suffer, yea, to die, rather than create disorder, for disorder would be ruinous. He endeavored to inspire them with a sense of homecoming to their ancestral lands, and to take pride in the chance to be a perpetual light in a dark continent. Then free men of color raised their right hands and took an oath of loyalty to the colony's constitution, while bandannaed women swayed together humming weirdly, and children of both races stood silent in wide-eyed awe. As the great ship moved out with the tide, from deck and wharf rose familiar hymns, swung high and low in that mystical rhythm which was a gift from the jungles of Africa to the fields and streets of America.

Chief Justice Marshall was president of the independent Virginia Society for Colonization when it was formed in 1827, serving in this office until his death, contributing to its treasury, urging and explaining its functions as the tide of division threatened confusion.

His own will devised emancipation for Robin "if he should chuse to conform to the laws on the subject, requiring that he leave the State, or if permission can be obtained for his continuing to reside in it." If Robin should choose to go to Liberia he was to have one hundred dollars; if not, fifty. If Robin should choose not to accept freedom, he was to select as his owner one of the Marshall sons or daughter. In which case he was to be held in trust, and treated as "a faithful and meritorious servant," and be provided with a woman to wait on him in his old age.

Mammy Venus and Agnes Spurlock lived the rest of their long lives nursing Marshall grandchildren, refusing to emancipate their white folks.

Chapter XXII

The Steamboat Case

In 1824, as usual, Polly took refuge at the farm from the soul-shaking noise that issued the Twenty-second day of February in and out of Richmond. The day fell on Sunday, but she was in no sabbath mood as she was handed into the carriage by her son-in-law. She was torn between apprehension and reprehension. She had been stopped on her way down the steps from the Ninth Street door by a friend who informed her that on Thursday evening last, as the Chief Justice was returning from the President's drawing room, his foot slipped on the bottom step of his carriage, giving him a bad fall, from which he suffered a dislocated shoulder and bruised head. A surgeon had been called. The bones had been reset and the head bandaged, but it was said that the Chief Justice would be confined to his lodgings for several days.

The news had come through to Richmond quickly, for now with a steamboat from Washington to Fredericksburg, travel time was cut in half. The steamboat made six miles an hour while still the post stage barely made four. Moses drove Polly's horses at a brisk clip, even risking a few bumps over frozen ruts, for all the family were concerned when Polly worried, and now the servant knew she would be stringing the news through and through her mind until it would scorch like a garland of red peppers.

And so she was! General Marshall should not have fallen on that carriage step. He might have hurt himself badly. Maybe he had. Maybe they were not telling her all. His foot had slipped after leaving the President's drawing room. Not that broad, strong, forest-treading foot! Colonel Monroe's drawing rooms, she had heard, were as stiff as his dinners. The stiffer the company, the stiffer the punch! He should have known better. This had happened before. Or, then, maybe there was ice on the step. Robin had been careless about cleaning the carriage. But how terribly painful the resetting must have been. And how his poor dear head

261

must ache. Had his hair been properly brushed for the evening? He was too stubborn, or too happy, to remember his position when he went in society. And he was so clumsy. Dear Heaven, what a peculiar gentleman he was!

It was the end of the week when Polly, back in her mansion, received two letters speeded on their way by the new mode of transportation. One was from the Chief Justice, and the other was from her son Tom, who seems to have been able to get to his father in Washington shortly after the accident, which had occurred on a Thursday, and to return by steamboat as far as Fredericksburg, then taking horse to arrive at Westover Plantation by Tuesday evening. This was unbelievable speed.

Polly opened her husband's letter first.

Washington Feby 23d 1824

My dearest Polly

I was made extremely uneasy today by being informed that you had heard of my fall before my letter reached you and had supposed me to be hurt much worse than I was in reality. I had hoped that my letter would be the first communication you would receive on the subject.

I have been disappointed in being kept longer from court than I expected. Old men I find do not get over sprains and hurts quite as quickly as young ones. Although I feel no pain when perfectly still, yet I cannot get up and move about without difficulty, & cannot put on my coat. Of course I cannot go to court. I believe confidently however that I shall go the beginning of next week. Altho I do not get well as immediately as I expected myself the doctors say I mend a great deal faster than they expected. Everything is certainly in the best possible train. The swelling has gone entirely down, and I have not the slightest appearance of fever.

I have been treated with a degree of kindness and attention which is very flattering. All my friends have called to see me. The President himself has visited me and has expressed his wish to serve me in any manner that may be in his power. I have however in reserve a still higher compliment which would very much surprize you and all others who know me. All the ladies of the secretaries have called on me, some more than once, and have brought me more jelly than I can eat, and have offered me a great many good things. I thank them but stick to my barley broth.

Not withstanding these attentions I have a plenty of time on my hands in the night as well as in the day. How do you think I beguile it? I am almost tempted to leave you to guess till I write again. But as I suppose you will have rather more curiosity in my absence than you usually show to hear my stories when I am present, I will tell you without waiting to be asked. You must know then that I begin with the Ball at York, and with the dinner on the fish at your house the next day; I then retrace my visit to York, our splendid assembly at the Palace in Williamsburg, my visit to Richmond where I acted Pa for a fortnight, my return that ensueing Fall and the very welcome reception you gave me on your arrival from Dover. Our little tiffs & makings up, my feelings while Major Dick was courting you, my trip to the cottage, the lock of hair, my visit again to Richmond the ensueing fall, and all the thousand indescribable but deeply affecting instances of your affection or coldness which constituted for a time the happiness or misery of my life and will always be recollected with a degree of interest which can never be lost while recollection remains.

Thus is it that I find amusement for those hours which I pass without company or books.

Farewell my dearest Polly. I beg you believe that tho confined I am free from pain & shall soon be free from confinement

Yours ever
J Marshall

Polly knew that President Monroe would go at once to see Marshall. Seated before the fire in the judicial study, each man would lay aside his office. She wished she might be there to hear them tell each other, "You are all wrong," while all the time one could feel the affection flowing between them, like the motes in this flood of sunshine falling about her chair. She was still smiling as she read again that she was expected to be surprised to know that ladies had paid him flattering attentions. He was not himself surprised. And that mention of barley broth. Verily she believed that a bad shoulder would no more restrain his appetite than the presence of his enemies. And his cup of welcome would always run over for a pretty lady.

And now, who would the ladies be? Of the Cabinet wives, Polly knew personally only Catherine, wife of Attorney General William Wirt and daughter of strong-minded Mrs. Gamble of Richmond. The Wirts had ten children, all living. Polly put out her hand, running her fingers across and across the ladder of sunbeams as if she were climbing it to Heaven. Catherine was a genuine, lovable, pretty person, said to be the least intelligent of a brilliant family, and sentimental. She was writing a book, Polly recalled, on the symbolism of flowers. Also Polly recalled that the Chief Justice often remarked that of all the places in Washington to spend an evening the Wirt household was one of the most delightful. He did not slip on the carriage step after a visit to the Wirts.

Then there would be Mrs. Calhoun of the fanciful name, Floride. When the Chief Justice spoke of Secretary of War, Mr. John C. Calhoun, his eyes twinkled merrily for a moment, then became grave, for he believed Mr. Calhoun to be a dangerous politician—but such a proud patriot, so fiery and high-minded, so brave and generous, with such flashes of remonstrance. Mr. Calhoun and his wife had the same bewitching beauty. She was one of those half French Charlestonians, aristocratic, wealthy, it was said, and charming. Polly suddenly decided that Mrs. Calhoun's jelly was soupy.

But now Mrs. Southard would be different. She lived among the Quakers of New Jersey. Though she may have a dozen servants, her finger would be on every turn of the domestic wheel. She probably offered the "other good things."

The Secretary of the Treasury was Mr. William Crawford, born a Virginian, and now from Georgia. He was probably also born an Episcopalian, though now a Baptist. But Polly had been taught to be charitable to those beyond the Episcopal pale. Her husband, she knew, drew no lines among the churches. The Church was the Court Room, and God was the Law, and God and His angels the Bench. All congregations were equal in His sight, and in his sight. Mr. Crawford was said to have bad health, so Mrs. Crawford's jelly would be rich and firm. It is to be hoped that Mr. Crawford and Colonel Monroe never met in the sickroom. It would have been hard for the General to have to act as peacemaker if his head ached.

Peacemaker! Polly raised her head in the sunlight, and her laugh was almost a girlish giggle. J Marshall recollected "with interest" that occasion when John Ambler had tried to act as peacemaker. She slid the locket to and fro on the chain around her neck, remembering that her face had been hidden in her arm when John Ambler cut a curl from her head right here—no, here. Had she forgotten? Well, she had been weeping, for she had just rejected the Captain again, and as usual he had mounted his horse and departed. John Ambler had sent the tress anonymously to Captain Marshall, intending to lure him back to The Cottage. Interest, fiddlesticks! It was weeks before Captain Marshall presented himself again at her father's door!

Polly's cheeks were quite pink as she opened her son's letter. Tom was like his father, only a softened likeness, not so demonstrative in affection, but always smoothing the way, pushing back the crowd, hushing the noise. She read his letter.

Westover Feby 28th 1824

My dear Mother,

I had a more pleasant ride on Tuesday than I anticipated, and reached this place about 6 O'clock. It was a happy circumstance that I concluded to come down on that day, for I found my little Nancy very much indisposed. The same cause makes it necessary for us to postpone our return to Weyanoke; for although she is better thank God, yet she is not well enough to be taken out.

I promise myself the pleasure of hearing by this evening's mail that my father has so far recovered the effects of his false step as to attend in Court. I have done a little in the way of transcribing for him, but not much. To day I have been playing chess with Mr. Taylor of Norfolk, who came up yesterday in the steam boat.

You may tell Agnes, when she comes to see you that her mama, and the children with the exception of little Nanny, are well; and that I hope she will be very attentive to her studies, and observe carefully the injunctions of her friends.

With the hope that I shall hear that your health was not interrupted by the fatigues and exposure of your trip to Chickahominy I remain, my dear mother, your affectionate son.

Thos. Marshall

Tom's daughter Agnes, eleven years old, was in one of the numerous girls' schools in Richmond. Sick little Nancy was six months old. Polly counted on her fingers. Several of Tom's children had died at birth, but there were still five little Marshalls at Oak Hill, John, Agnes, Mary, Fielding Lewis, and little Ann, called Nancy. Polly was eventually to count two more children for Tom: Margaret and Thomas who became a Colonel in the Confederate Army, giving his life for State sovereignty.

Newspapers in the North were also watching the mail for word that the Chief Justice had so far recovered as to take his place in Court. They were saying that his accident was a double misfortune. Such important cases were before the Supreme Court that his absence was a serious matter. The disposition of one of these, popularly called the "Steamboat Case," was being urgently awaited all over the country. The papers were saying there had never been an issue before the Court that had excited more widespread interest, or deeper concern. On the record this case was called Gibbons *vs* Ogden, and had to do with the monopoly of steamboat business exercised by Messrs. Fulton and Livingston.

With the first puff of smoke from Robert Fulton's stacks, monopoly of river routes grasped the nation's waterways, pouring royalties into Fulton's pockets. Under this monopoly States granted exclusive franchise, again setting up tariff barriers against each other, and refusing to honor navigation licenses issued by the United States Government. As steam traffic spread to all the eastern waterways and threaded the Mississippi River system, States multiplied their separate navigation laws, thus damming the flow of commerce.

An Act of New York State Legislature in 1808 granted to Robert Fulton and Robert Livingston the exclusive right, for the duration of thirty years, to "navigate" all boats moved by fire or steam on all waters within the State of New York. Under this monopoly Aaron Ogden operated such boats between New Jersey and New York. Then Thomas Gibbons appeared on this run with two steamboats licensed by the United States to operate on "coastal waters."

Ogden applied to the New York court for a restraining order to Gibbons and got it readily, for that court held that the State law was not in collision with the Constitution since the Constitutional clause said, "Congress shall have power to regulate *commerce* with foreign nations and among the several states and with Indian tribes." Nowhere in the clause did the word *navigation* occur. Gibbons retained Daniel Webster and William Wirt, and appealed to the Supreme Court.

The Chief Justice was still on his seat at the center of the Bench on February fourth when argument opened. He was feeling hale and hearty, but his Brother Story was stiff and bruised. So was one of the chief litigants, Aaron Ogden. These two gentlemen travelled from New York on the same stage, which was a springless vehicle with backless cross seats, and only a canopy for shelter in case of rain. Just after leaving Baltimore, either a driver of a wagon going their way became too exuberant, or his horses too gay, for the wagon sideswiped the stage, turning it over. When Justice Story and Mr. Ogden scrambled out they found themselves without serious injury, but regretted that they had not taken the steamboat.

When, in an "excessively crowded court-room," Marshall nibbed his quill, pushed up his sleeve and nodded to council to begin, Daniel Webster rose, glanced courteously at the row of Justices in their massive robes, then fixed his sombre eyes on the Chief Justice, and in a voice that was called "bewitching," expounded the menace of monopolies to the Court.

He says that he "never experienced more intellectual pleasure than in arguing that novel question to a great man who could appreciate it, and take it in; and he did take it in as a baby takes in its mother's milk."

Rivers and bays, so went Webster's argument, are often boundary lines between States, and it was all too obvious that if States made separate laws governing those waterways, embarrassment would necessarily happen to general intercourse of the whole community. Such events, he continued, were creating a most unpleasant state of things. By New York law no one could navigate her waters without a special license under pain of forfeiture of the vessel. Under Connecticut law any such licensed vessel is forbidden to enter her waters. New Jersey established an Act of Retortion under which any party of New York restraining a vessel from the ancient shores of New Jersey entering New York waters would be liable for treble the cost of damages.

"If there were no power," exclaimed Daniel Webster, "in the general government to control this extreme belligerent legislation of the States, the powers of the government are essentially deficient in a most important . . . particular." He pointed out that the sorry state of trade and commerce had been the greatest cause of the Revolution; but that the framers of the Constitution had been obsessed to improve and benefit trade and commerce; that indeed the Virginia resolutions, which were the immediate cause of a meeting to frame a constitution, put forth as their main object the power of Congress to regulate trade not only with foreign nations, but urgently between States. The newspaper, *The Washington Republic,* says, "It was one of the most powerful arguments we remember to have heard."

Counsel for Ogden replied that five times since 1790 New York legislatures had passed exclusive navigation laws and no court or Federal authority had questioned one of them until now, nor had challenged the difference between "navigation" and "commerce" as considered in those acts.

Then William Wirt arose, and in that happy and friendly manner of his, told the Court their duty. "Here," he said, "are three States on the eve of war. It is the high province of this Court to interpose its benign and mediatorial influence."

Day after day crowds filled the courtroom for the hearings, listening intently even when one counsel's argument lasted two whole days. Press correspondents sat with pens poised to put yea or nay to dispatches to be rushed north, south, east or west. Everywhere anxiety was on edge for the high court's answer. Then the Chief Justice slipped on the step of his carriage, and had to remain all bandaged in his lodgings.

To those lodgings came not only the ladies of the government, but also Congressmen, Senators and members of the Cabinet. Their talk like a strong current tossed up the flotsam and jetsam of a flood of theories and policies as a government cut its way from a wilderness to the wide plains of industry and productive wealth. Some men were riding the current toward new things. Others like stalwart oaks would hold their ground until it was washed out from under them.

John Randolph of Roanoke could hardly be called an oak, so frail was he in appearance. Men likened him to a galloping ghost with a voice of music forever crying, "Resist! Resist!"

Often he came to Marshall's room reporting with alarm the iniquitous measures before the House of Representatives such as those ordering the Federal government to engage in improvements of roads and waterways within the States in a plan to link them in common systems of communications. Randolph's speech of protest in the House was repeated to the Chief Justice. "Look well," Randolph had admonished the legislators, "to the collossal power with which you are now arming the government. . . . Should this bill pass . . . then we who belong to that unfortunate portion of this confederacy which is south of Mason and Dixon line . . . must resort to the measures which we first opposed to British aggressions . . . to maintain that independence which . . . is every day sliding from under our feet. . . . Sir . . . We shall keep on the windward side of treason—but we must combine to resist, and that effectively." It was all, said Randolph, "a coalition of knavery and fanaticism."

Marshall might have laughed heartily at Randolph's dramatics except for that aching shoulder. He could only smile as he replied that for his part he considered internal improvements to be the nation's most pressing concern, that, "and our coloured population."

Randolph would agree to the latter concern, which would remind him of South Carolinian John Calhoun. Then he would tell Marshall that Henry Clay and John Calhoun both had an eye on the presidency, and that he, Randolph, had his eye on Henry Clay. The Chief Justice would merely continue to smile. Randolph well knew that Marshall would not involve his office in politics. But Randolph also knew that Marshall had a warm affection for Henry Clay.

When dinner time approached, and the other Justices returned to the lodgings, callers would take their leave. Through the long evening hours the brethren of the Supreme Bench would report the day's hearings to the Chief. Argument and rebuttal would be aired and discussed while the Judges, it may be, nibbled on the ladies' jellies and other good things.

It may be that the Chief Justice had in hand notes which Tom had transcribed from the report of the case called The Brig Wilson *vs* the United States, tried in the District Court holden at Richmond in May 1820. His eye may have lingered on that phrase of his decision which used the word "navigation." The Brig had endeavored to land a shipload of Africans at Norfolk in contravention of a law of Virginia which prohibited the importation of slaves. There was no question of the effectiveness of that law. The issue was whether the vessel was subject to seizure by the *Federal* government. Marshall held that it was. The commerce clause covered slave trade, and an Act of Congress protected this State law, but, "Every power," declared the Court then, "that pertains to navigation [is] rightfully exercised by Congress."

By March second, the Supreme Justices had come to a unanimous decision concerning the Steamboat Case. It was written, some say, by Joseph Story. Webster says, however, that it was taken word for word from his argument before the Court. For the momentous reading of the decision the Chief Justice ventured out of doors for the first time since his accident, and took his place on the high Bench.

The newspaper says, "His return to his elevated and important station is welcomed by every member of the Bench and Bar, and the whole community. The Court-room was thronged at an early hour." That throng stirred with pleasure, as Marshall entered the hall. When the doorkeeper endeavored to adjust the heavy black robe over the injured collarbone he probably got much advice from ladies of Secretaries sitting nearby in the audience; for the new courtroom in the basement of the Capitol had no robing room. The Justices were of necessity robed in full view of visitors. But when all were draped, the dignity of the Court settled upon them, and solemnly they marched along the carpeted aisle to a platform raised three feet above the floor of the "triangular semicircular" chamber to take their place on a long seat that was verily the Supreme Bench.

The bar stood until the Chief Justice had taken his seat,

then they subsided in cushioned armchairs on rollers. Between them and the platform stood a handsome table holding two brown pitchers of water and a few glasses. When Marshall began to read the Court's opinion his voice was so feeble that spectators left their seats to push between that table and the dais, and stand in unbroken silence while he read for forty-five minutes.

Marshall must have smiled when he read, "Judges must exercise in the examination of the subject, that understanding which Providence has bestowed upon them, with that independence which the people of the United States expect from this department of the government." Beyond doubt this sentence was Story's own, for it was a picture of his mind, God, independence and justice, a trinity of youthful faith in human nature.

The decree found null and void the New York law withholding use of her waterways from vessels licensed by the United States. Justice Johnson of South Carolina felt that the opinion was not written in sufficiently strong terms. Therefore he asked that he might file his opinion separately, for he held that "if there was any one object over-riding every other in the adoption of the Constitution, it was to keep the commercial intercourse among the States free from all invidious and partial restraints."

A few days later the New York *Evening Post* called the decision "One of the most powerful efforts of the human mind that has ever been displayed from the bench of any court. Many passages indicated a profoundness and a forecast in relation to the destinies of our confederacy peculiar to the great man who acted as the organ of the court. The steamboat grant is at an end."

It seemed for a while that Monroe and Marshall might occasionally see eye to eye in affairs of the nation, until with a mighty burst of oratory and indignation the bill for using United States Bank profits for internal improvements (provided the States concerned desired those works) came up in Congress. When the bill finally passed, Monroe vetoed it as being inimical to State independence. Marshall believed in coordinated internal improvements.

As Marshall travelled home on a steamboat, he must have thought much about that veto, for the company on board, who were gentlemen of government and finance, were talking of overland travel with steam propelled engines. Internal improvements would be more and more vital to the State's progress.

As the vessel entered Norfolk harbor, threading its way between ships with sails and boats with smoking stacks, Marshall may have wondered if Polly would be expecting him. He had written her two days before he left Washington. But his quill ever seemed dull when he longed to light all her candles with his love.

Washington March 23d

My dearest Polly

The time now approaches when I shall again see my beloved wife whom I hope to meet in tolerable health and spirits. I shall reach Richmond in the steam boat which comes up on friday night but suppose I shall not be at home till saturday morning. I imagine the boat will not be up before nine oclock at night in which case I shall remain in it all night. If I do not come up till it is too late to come home I wish you would direct Oby to come down to Rockets very early in order to carry home my portmanteau.

I have not the use of my arm sufficiently to put it into the sleeve of my coat, but I am entirely free from pain. I was very much surprised at the arrival of John and Elizabeth last tuesday evening. They came by this place in their way to Baltimore, in consequence of the Baltimore boat being stopped for repairs. They proceeded on wednesday in the stage & on thursday John returned on his way to Fauquier. All was well.

I am just called in to conference. Heaven bless you my dearest Polly

I am your ever affectionate
J Marshall

Occasionally steamboats on the James River collided. Once it was the *Patrick Henry* and the *Thomas Jefferson* who punched each other in the bow. The two captains afterwards were as irreconcilable as their ship's names might suggest, using language that could have been borrowed from hotheaded patriots.

Chapter XXIII

Master Of The Human Heart

Polly went to Oak Hill this summer, but there she could find little peace. Even with the new house and the old one holding hands through an arcade, the place was overrun with children, guests, county farmers and politicians, for Tom was increasingly a public servant, and Oak Hill a center of county politics. The only peace for Polly was out under the old trees on the lawn. Even there she would be followed by one or another of the household, running out to see whether she was nervous.

Certainly she was nervous. But could not they see that what she needed was to look up into those great boughs so everlastingly sure of re-creation? If they would only leave her alone out under his trees her spirit could soar into that green assurance, as her fears so often were lifted and enfolded in his sturdy tenderness.

Marshall brought her home earlier than usual, so that she was in Richmond when that festive young gentleman, William, son of William Marshall, died of a gay life. A few weeks later Polly's physician, Dr. Foushee, died, and Mary's daughter Susan was born without his familiar ministrations.

Walking home slowly one Sunday afternoon from a visit to the new baby, Polly and her maid stepped aside to let a parade of Sunday School children pass. They were marching in sharp military form, for at their head was the smiling Chief Justice of the United States. He was an expert in "footwork," he said, having practiced it in the army for six years.

To the children of Richmond he was General when they wanted to parade, and Judge when arbitration was in order. As he walked along the streets it often happened that a child ran up to catch his hand, and share an exciting bit of information: "Johnny can kick a stone farrer than Janie can." And sometimes, holding two small boys arms length apart, the Chief Justice held court there on the sunny sidewalk, the issue being, "Aint my mother's nose reddern his mother's

273

nose?" The Chief Justice would then hand down a decision
in cross-my-heart-and-hope-to-die secrecy.

In November there was an affair in Richmond conducted
by those whom the press called "Virginia's fairest daughters."
The government and the military were supposed to be in
charge, but when General Lafayette returned on a visit to
Virginia the ladies took command of hospitality. They descended on the Eagle Tavern. Dispensing with Mr. Tavern
Keeper, they turned an army of servants to sweeping what
had been swept, scrubbing what had been scrubbed, and
pushing favorite chairs out of sight. Mrs. Eliza Carrington
arrived with a white satin embroidered bedspread to replace
Mrs. Tavern Keeper's best, already laid on the bed for the
guest. Eliza explained that the spread had cost two hundred
and fifty dollars, so Mrs. Keeper felt better. There were
balls and receptions and dinners and teas to be arranged,
but first there was a wily provision to be made. The ladies
ordered gloves made with a portrait of Lafayette on the back
of the hand, thus to cause the Marquis to kiss his own image.

Then on a russet autumn day the Chief Justice and Mary
set out for York Town, where a welcoming committee was
to board the steamboat *Virginia* and proceed down the river
to meet the steamboat *Petersburg* with Lafayette and his son,
George Washington Lafayette, on board.

It was funny, Mary thought, to hear her father and Colonel Monroe and other gentlemen who had fought with Lafayette calling him Marquis, and never General. And there
was no deference in their tone of voice. It was as if old
soldiers were calling each other by a nickname; and he,
replying to addresses of welcome, used the term, "We Americans."

Polly was the center of excitement, suppressed out of consideration for her nerves, to be sure, but nonetheless prick-
ling. Sister Carrington and Sister Fisher accompanied by
step-nieces from the Call household, were constantly tipping
in to display the latest finery purchased for the grand ball.
They would whisper, squeal with admiration of each other,
and suddenly with finger on lip gather up their baubles and
depart, shaking their heads.

Polly felt like a withered leaf in the midst of a fresh bouquet until the day Mary came in a blue mull dress embroidered in garden flowers. She wanted her mother to decide whether it was fine enough for the ball. Polly gazed and gazed at her daughter. Her desolation dissolved, and she exclaimed softly, "You are beautiful!" Then the tiny mother was gathered into her daughter's arms, while Mary spoke tender grateful words that only Polly understood.

It was well that Polly had sleepless nights during this festive week, for these would be the only hours Marshall would be free to tell her of the events of Lafayette's visit, of the gaiety and heartbreaks of reunion, of the handsome ladies and compliments flitting about, of the good food and warming drink. Heartily he laughed as he told her of being the day-long companion of ardent Republicans within the confines of a steamboat deck, while the band played the Federalist tune, "Hail Columbia." It was a pity that Spencer Roane had departed this pleasant earth before this merry mingling of enemies. He might have observed that plump veteran of Cornwallis' army, William Fitzwhylsonn, solemnly beating a drum while gazing at the Marquis with so knowing a look that it might almost have been said to be a wink. He might have heard the Marquis' French amazement when he recognized the drummer upon the ramparts at the surrender of the British army. And there too was Colonel Huger who had been a friend of Dr. Bollmann who had been a friend of Aaron Burr. Beside him stood Benjamin Watkins Leigh, now married to Judge Wickham's daughter; and of course the company brought up that old story of Mr. Leigh winning Miss Wickham by writing a poem, not to her charms, but ridiculing Marshall for dining at the Wickham house with Aaron Burr. John Wickham had seen the poem and was so amused by it that he invited the poet to call; and when Leigh arrived in the Wickham parlour there was Miss Julia Wickham very beautiful in a very fetching dress. Then Polly went to sleep with a laugh to pillow her nerves.

She could barely endure the day of the grand ball, but she was downstairs earlier than usual next morning to catch the gossip her sisters would bring, whispering. Eliza, when she arrived, could hardly untie her bonnet strings so eager was she to talk, and for the life of her she could not remember to keep her voice low. Had she danced? Indeed, yes. She had been attended most of the evening by the Marquis— that is on one side. Mr. Calhoun was on the other side. She had the honor of a kiss. The Marquis seemed to feel that the ladies were bestowing decoration for valor when they allowed themselves to be kissed. And he had a way of making each lady think that she was the sole benefactress.

Was Floride Calhoun there? And was she very beautiful? Yes, but not as beautiful as Mr. Calhoun. Indeed Eliza believed Mr. Calhoun was thought to be the most handsome and fascinating of all gentlemen present, a perfect Southerner, so romantical! Richmond ladies now have enough finery to last for years. We really ought to have grand balls more frequently. But hush! Eliza must run. This is the day for the Bible Class to meet in her house. And did Sister Marshall know that the Marquis had been made an honorary member of the Virginia Bible Society?

This was a gay week and a hearty one. Everywhere the Chief Justice was as honored as the Frenchman. He presided at the Masonic dinner, and was selected by his fellow citizens to make several addresses. He was given the seat of second honor at public and private dinners. He made all of these occasions sparkle with good stories of war and politics. The Chief Justice says that Polly would not always listen when he tried to repeat these stories to her. But she did warm her spirit in his joy; and when he was off again to another gathering, she would cuddle her hand in her mother's paisley shawl and try to sleep until he came in.

Polly saw the Marquis at morning service in Monumental Church. The choir in the loft behind the congregation had never sung more triumphantly than on that day. Organ and building seemed to become one musical instrument, softly resounding and echoing. Polly's frame was not shaken by this enchanting harmony. The town was full of harmony, and music was the feature of many an affair. Miss Eliza Lambeth sang so beautifully and so frequently that the Chief Justice was inspired to write in her autograph album:

Courtesy of Miss Douthat

"Mammy"

Drawing of Agnes, unruly daughter of Robin Spurlock, by Catherine
Douthat, youngest of the great-grandchildren to be rocked by her.

From The Chameleon to The Mocking Bird.

Where learnt you the notes of that soul-melting measure?
  Sweet mimic, who taught you to carol that song?
From Eliza 'twas caught, whom e'en birds hear with pleasure
  As brightly she trips the green meadow along.
O breathe them again while with rapture I listen,
  Every beat of my heart is responsive to thee;
And my eyes to behold thee with ecstacy glisten,
  With thy gray breast reclined on that high poplar tree.

It was not the sweet liquid note of the blackbird,
  Nor was it the partridge's whistle so clear,
Nor was it the soft sounding lay of the bluebird,
  With these, sly deceiver, you've cheated my ear.
Nor was it the call that deceived the young redbreast,
  Nor sweetest of all, the shy woodlark in air;
But the song, little ministrel, of her that can sing best
  The sounds that have so often delighted my ear.

Then come, airy warbler, live near to my dwelling
  And in circles around move thy bright glossy wing,
Keep my heart then forever with ecstacy swelling,
  O cheat me thus sweetly whenever you sing.

Did Marshall really think of himself as a chameleon? Was
it that the door of his heart opened to so many beautiful
things? In a letter to John Randolph of Roanoke he speaks
of himself as a centipede who always had one foot on the
ground, and of "Jack Randle" as a horse who cleared at one
leap both fence and ditch.

Lafayette's visit slipped so happily into Christmas preparations that Polly thought her husband had forgotten the
restlessness of the gentlemen of Congress until the year
turned shivering into January of 1825. The day before he
left for the Court session, he stood with his back to her fire,
coattails carefully held aside, and such a smile on his face
that Polly was silent, waiting for his amusing thought to
emerge. Then he told her that the Congress seemed to have
changed its collective sentiment about the odiousness of his
character. He had heard that Senator Talbot from Kentucky
had spoken of him with flattering attention, calling him the
"wise, *mild* and guiding influence of this solemn tribunal,"
meaning the Supreme Court. Mild, mind you! And Senator
Talbot went further. He spoke of Marshall's "purity" and

"correctness" of judgement being "impartially dispensed."
Then Marshall dropped his coattails to raise his arm in that
familiar gesture to emphasize that these pleasant remarks had
been made during a debate on the floor of the House over a
bill designed to limit the jurisdiction of the Supreme Court.

These debates were still in progress when Marshall arrived
in Washington to open Court. Lafayette was still the guest
of the nation in the capital. President Monroe was quite
cheerful in spite of an incident that might have given a less
noble man moments of resentment. In January the Congress,
without a quiver, presented Lafayette with two hundred
thousand dollars and a township of land, while Monroe's
just claim upon the nation's treasury for thirty thousand dollars was persistently ignored. Marshall, however, says nothing of these things when he writes his first letter home
in this session. His mind is still warm with happiness.

Washington Feby 8th 1825
My dearest Polly

I reached this place yesterday & payed our accustomed visit to
the President whom I found in good health & looking quite cheerful. I am now sitting by a good fire in an excellent room, the same I
occupied last year, scribbling to my beloved wife. Neither Judge
Johnson nor Story has arrived, and our brother Todd I am told is so
very unwell that we have reason to fear we shall never see him again.
Story too has been sick, but is on the way and we look for him
to day.

I have never found the roads so good before in the winter
season. I reached Alexandria on saturday evening before five, and
have never before got in by daylight, seldom earlier than nine, and
once or twice as late as eleven. I rejoiced that I had not taken the
steamboat.

I have seldom gone counter to your advice without repenting it,
but as I came on friday & saturday, hugging myself up in my warm.
cloak, I could not help congratulating myself on the comfort I
enjoyed compared to the suffering I should have felt had I come
without it.

I rode from Hanover court house to Fredericksburg with a Mrs.
Stone, formerly Miss Booth, a niece of Mrs. Dandridge. She told me
that the first ball at which she had ever been was in Richmond when
she accompanied her aunt in Mrs. Ambler's coach, and that both
you and myself were in the same carriage, then unmarried. She said
she had never seen me since, and that when I got into the stage she

remembered the evening and all she saw as perfectly as if it had been yesterday.

I dined on sunday with my aunt Keith. She was at first very much affected, but became cheerful in a few minutes. I was visited on saturday night by my nephew William Marshall, son of my brother Lewis, who is studing divinity at the Theological school in Alexandria. He is a very promising and a remarkably fine looking young man. He dined at my aunt Keith's on sunday, & I was very much pleased with him.

I cannot help hoping that Mr. Picket has been able to fill the icehouse on friday & saturday. If those two days have passed away without accomplishing the object I fear all the [chance] is over & that we must look elsewhere unless he should fill it with a cargoe [torn] worth. He spoke of this bef [torn]

Farewell my d [torn]

Catching chance weather was the Tidewater Virginia farmer's way of life, and to fill an icehouse from local ponds was gambling with some sprite of the atmosphere. Rarely did the plantation owner win sufficiently to rescind his regular order for ice from Kennebec River in Maine. Sailing vessels brought that New England product into the James River, where it was unloaded at Rockett's a wharf at the foot of Richmond Hill. From there it was carted to counties as far away as the Piedmont. City dwellers were supplied with that luxury from small commercial "ice houses" on Richmond's hills.

William Marshall, son of Dr. Louis Marshall of Kentucky, was "studying divinity" at the new Theological Seminary near Alexandria, Virginia. In 1779, when the "professorship of divinity" was abolished at the College of William and Mary because it was part of the Establishment of the Church of England, deism flowed into the vacuum. This philosophy that religion is not a revelation, but rather a product of the human intellect, pervaded even the Board of Visitors for a time. Various efforts were made over a period of forty years to establish a new professorship of divinity at the College. Despairing of that in 1823, the rector of St. Paul's Episcopal Church in Alexandria, the Reverend William H. Wilmer, collected a small body of students in his house, calling them the Virginia Theological Seminary, which became the first Episcopal Seminary in the republic.

In Marshall's own mind there was a wide distance between instinctive belief in a God of unspeakable majesty and the cold written word of theology. In the wilderness of his youth, he had gone to church with his father, and read variants of religious philosophy, some in stumbling translations. In his juvenile view there was a shelf for the things of the mind, and a forest and family for things of the heart. Then he had come out of the wilderness into an army full of young men of an age most susceptible to infidelity. Deism was the fashion, and Marshall took it under consideration, while he continued to practice life from the hand of God.

After the return of the Episcopal Church to Virginia in 1812, Bishop Meade had a brief moment of concern because the Chief Justice would not come to the Communion Table. One summer week he joined Marshall travelling between Richmond and Frederick County. Passing a country church, the Bishop was moved to put some questions of faith to his fellow traveller. The Bishop continued the trip in sweet content. For Marshall had told him that every night he got down on his knees and said the prayers his mother had taught him, which were "Our Father Who art in Heaven" and "Now I Lay Me Down to Sleep, I Pray Thee, Lord, My Soul to Keep." Every night down on his knees, in wayside inns crowded with strangers, in lodgings with Justices of the Supreme Court of the United States, beside Polly's bed, "I Pray Thee, Lord, My Soul to Keep"—every night!

Before Marshall again wrote to Polly he had heard that another Kentucky Senator, Richard M. Johnson, had risen in the Congress to move for a new law curtailing the independence of the Supreme Court. He, too, had poured a little balm on the wound he would make. He prefaced his motion with the words: "Our nation has been blessed with a most distinguished Supreme Court . . . eminent for moral worth, intellectual vigor, extensive acquirements, and profound judicial experience and knowledge. . . . Against the Federal judiciary, I have not the least malignant emotion." But the enormous powers of the Court must be restrained.

It was well that some gentlemen disclaimed malignant emotions in this piping session of Congress. The longest and hardest fought campaign for presidential office was nearing an end. For a second time a presidential election was to be thrown into the House of Representatives. The candidates were Henry Clay, though born in Virginia now representing the west; William Crawford, a paralytic, supported by Virginia and North Carolina; fiery Andrew Jackson, standing for the far South; and John Quincy Adams for New York and New England. There was much tapping of shoulders among the gentlemen of the House, with low-voiced suggestions that "voters depend on you" for this one or that.

Jackson held the majority of electoral votes, but not enough to elect him. Adams was his strongest opponent. When Clay let it be known that he favored Adams, George Kremer, a Jackson man and Representative from Pennsylvania, published an anonymous letter in the *Columbia Observer* accusing Clay of bargaining with Adams to give his support in return for the office of Secretary of State. Clay at once challenged the writer to make himself known and settle the matter in a duel. Kremer avoided the duel, and extricated himself from Congressional censure by pleading freedom of speech and press. Clay did, however, eventually fight a duel over this issue, but it was with Randolph of Roanoke, when that fiery statesman spoke of Clay's adherence to Adams as "the coalition of Blifil and Black George—the combination of the Puritan with the blackleg." Adams was elected in the House on the first ballot. John C. Calhoun was elected Vice President, and Clay became Secretary of State.

Polly knew the story of Clay and Kremer by the time she received the following letter:

Washington Feb. 27th 1825

My dearest Polly

I have been feasted within a few days by two letters from Richmond, the one from our nephew George & the other from our son. They both afford me the pleasure of hearing from you. I am happy that the 22d had passed off with so little inconvenience to you.

Both these letters give me a piece of intelligence which surprises me very much. Our nephew Edward Colston has I am told overcome all his prejudice against the Richmond ladies, and is about to carry one of them to Honey wood. He has at least this consolation—she is young enough for him.

Tell Mr. Cole that last night the taylors boy brought home my new suit of black. I have not yet tried it on, but take it for granted it will fit me. You know I always expect the best. I have his piece of cloth and shall bring it with me. Tell him also that Kremer is coming out as I am told with a most scurrilous piece of abuse against Mr. Clay. This was to be expected. Kremer will probably keep himself up by it in the district [Kentucky] whatever may be thought of him elsewhere.

I received a letter today from your cousin Mrs Walker thanking me for my check & telling me she had received a subscription raised by Mr. Tucker among the members of Congress which would enable her to subsist for some time. She says nothing about the office concerning which she had written to me [torn] made to me [torn] suggestion of the [torn] occasion.

I have [torn] your cousin Ro [torn] choly and ful [torn] money waited on [torn] her tomorrow.

Farewe [torn]
I am y [torn]

Edward Colston, bane of Mary's winter at Honeywood, had been married before, to his cousin Jane Marshall, whom he had courted in Polly's parlour. She had died a few months after the marriage. For eleven years Edward had remained a fractious widower, living alone in Washington or Richmond when he represented his district in Congress or in the Virginia Assembly. On May fifth of 1825, at the age of thirty-nine, he married Sarah Jane Brockenborough of Richmond, aged twenty, and took her to Honeywood in Berkeley County which was still part of the State of Virginia. Here Edward Colston had been born, and here he died, a Federalist by birth and training. He did not live to see Honeywood devastated by Federal soldiers in a war fought to defend Virginia's sovereignty.

The Chief Justice had reason to remark upon the softness of the fabric of his new suit of black, for it had been made in America, in New England where the weaving mills were putting cloth factories forward in the country's growing industry. Writing on March ninth, 1825, Marshall tells more of the new suit: "I administered the oath to the President in the presence of an immense concourse of people, in my suit of domestic manufacture. He too was dressed in the same manner, though his cloth was made at a different establishment. The cloth is very fine and smooth."

This was the seventh time that Marshall administered the oath of Presidential office. In 1789 the first President delegated the task of designing a fit inaugural ceremony to Edmund Randolph, who chose the Chancellor of the State of New York, Robert Livingston, to administer the oath of office. For Washington's second inauguration old Cushing solemnly swore the Father of his Country. John Adams was inaugurated by Chief Justice Ellsworth, and Thomas Jefferson invited his cousin Marshall to perform the rite. Twice his insatiable enemy had said the noble words after Marshall. Twice Madison, in great dignity, took the oath from him. And twice James Monroe had stood before his friend and sworn to honor the Constitution and, whatever his words might have been, at heart vowing to preserve to the people their sovereign States. Now, as stiff as a Pilgrim's staff, John Quincy Adams promised to uphold the Constitution and keep the country on a tightrope between tyranny of the people and tyranny of government. A thankless task it proved to be.

From his farm in Quincy, Massachusetts, the second President of the United States wrote to his son, fifth President, advising him not to be too much disturbed by the appearance of disunion in the country. "Prophesies of division have been familiar in my ears for six and thirty years," he wrote, which would put that period of unrest right back to the ratification of the Constitution.

When John Randolph of Roanoke filed letters written to him by Marshall, he labeled the bundle, "That great master of the human heart."

CHAPTER XXIV

"My Old Wife"

THESE ARE THE YEARS in which Marshall spoke of Polly as "my old wife," not a reminder of girlish charms, but a quiet voice when the world's was harsh, a hand to clasp when the rooms of life became empty, fulfillment when the future looked bleak. These are the years of the Marshall family longest remembered in Richmond. Ancient citizens spoke of Polly as a sweet faced, pitiful invalid who appeared in society only at church on Communion Sunday. They remembered Marshall as one of Richmond's best loved citizens, a tall old gentleman with a quick smile and a friendly hand for everyone. It was said of him that though people often disagreed with his policies, "his placidity, moderation and calmness, his benevolent heart and his serene and often joyous temper, made him a cherished companion."

These are the years of Polly's life longest remembered by the grandchildren. They remembered her as the thinnest little old lady they ever saw, who was often ill; and that it was the law that they must whisper and tiptoe in her presence; and that girl babies were given her name as if it bestowed a blessing. The grandchildren remembered that Polly had a housekeeper, Mrs. Frances Martyr, who wore spectacles so blurred from inspecting steaming pots on the new range in the kitchen that they thought she had no eyes until the day they found her wiping her glasses on her apron. Then they saw that behind them lived gentle brown eyes that smiled without wrinkles. The children were convinced that she had no feet, for her shoes never appeared beyond the bulging circle of her long skirts. They suspected that she rolled about house and out-buildings on hidden wheels, so swift and smooth was her progress. They loved to watch kittens of dust run before her when she walked through a room.

All of the grandchildren spent a part of each holiday at Polly's house. They would run up the steps to the door on Ninth Street, and when it was opened by the Chief Justice

285

and he threw up his hands as if in great surprise, exclaiming, "Darling little love!" why, then it would seem to each child that bright, sweet light flowed about him, and the earth under his feet became his sure possession.

They remembered peeping into the dining room when a lawyers' dinner was in progress, remembered the laughter, the jewel glow of raised wine glasses, the bowing and smiling servants; and then the pompous manner of Joseph and Robin when they turned and shooed the children away.

The grandchildren remembered old soldiers of the Revolution always at one door or another of the house and the office. These ancients never came as beggars, they came as comrades. They did not come to tell their needs, but often and often they went away to sleep better at night, knowing that a home or a name had been saved. Never did the gift that passed from the General's hand seem charity. It was simply a matter of comrades travelling hand in hand.

Down in the valley there was a carriage shop patronized by the Chief Justice. Here, he often found the son of the owner, sitting in a corner, lost in a book. One day the Chief Justice asked about the book, and, gently probing the boy's interests, discovered a would-be medical student. One thing led to another between the boy and the Chief Justice, and when Dr. James Beale graduated from Pennsylvania Medical School, he frankly and gratefully admitted that the "old Chief" had given him his profession.

When Edward Carrington Marshall went to Harvard, though he called himself "a merely literary man," he had come into the full inheritance of his father's joyous sociability. Harvard at heart was a religious institution, but by the time the Marshall boys matriculated it had accumulated a tradition of student independence. Within its handsome gates stood a Tree of Liberty, so named because it was the meeting place of insurgent students. There stood a Freedom Tree, too, which frequently sheltered riotous learning. Food was the usual cause of rebellion. Students had no choice of boarding houses. They were required to live in College Halls and eat in College Commons. For a long time wine was served with every meal, even breakfast. But in Edward's day only cider was put on the tables, and that in quart-size pewter cups which passed from mouth to mouth. On one occasion the young gentlemen became so incensed that one of them had to be "rusticated" for hitting a professor over the head with a potato (the allowance was two potatoes a day per student).

There were other causes for insurrection, such as compulsory attendance at Morning and Evening Prayer. A youth could endure prayer with grace, but the long dissertations by theological students left the mind open to temptation. Meditation under the drone of pious learning produced "pull crackers" attached to the lid of the Bible so that the next service opened with explosion; while holes drilled in chapel candles filled with gunpower caused the lesson to end without Amen.

In Edward's second year at Harvard the student body, imbued with every man's inalienable right to the pursuit of happiness, had become so disorderly that a committee of seven from the Board of Overseers had been appointed to reform discipline in the College. Justice Joseph Story was chairman of this committee. It is well that deliberations were held behind closed doors, for the chairman's sense of humor could not have been restrained when some of the monitors gave testimony.

Edward wrote his mother about the reforms recommended by the committee. Henceforth a college officer would visit every student's room every evening. Reports would be sent to parents quarterly. The student would be required to take notes at lectures and to pass annual examinations. Edward must have told Polly that a new "scheme of discipline" had been adopted in the following steps: "caution, warning, solemn admonition, official notice to parents, rustication and expulsion." But henceforth a student might lodge and board out in the town of Cambridge, provided a monitor looked in upon him once a day.

The recommendation which most upset the student body was that which called for classification according to proficiency, and division into sections for recitation. Edward says that these rules were peaceably established. But he was wrong. Within a year it was found that peace lay only in rescinding them. The student body was absorbed in reading and inwardly digesting the recommendations when Edward wrote a second letter to Polly:

Cambridge. Nov 8th. 1825

My dear Mother

I gave you in my last an account of the change in our college government. All have submitted so quietly, that nothing of interest has turned up. Probably no life is so uninteresting to others as that of a merely literary man. An indolent collegian especially has nothing to say for himself, but to complain of the dull uniformity of his life. I am daily resolving to do better, but cannot become diligent. My whole history can be summed up to you in a few words. I am very hearty, with perhaps too many amusements, and by no means so studious as my beloved mother would wish me. I gave you in my last an account of my studies, which are Electricity, Astronomy, and Moral philosophy. To give you a just idea of my situation, it will be necessary to inform you of my various companions, and you may feel some interest in knowing them. Besides my chum and Turner, I most frequently meet with Bonaparte, Cheves, Mr. Bruce & Birchett. The four last are young men of decided talents & acquirements. Birchett is a nephew of Uncle Taylor's, and promises himself some distinction. He is well read, smart, and possesses an ardour of temperament which will often make him eloquent at the bar. He is very friendly to me and I love him very much. Mr. Bruce is another virginian & law student. He is a hopeful son of Mr. Bruce, a very rich merchant in Halifax county. I have told you before of the strong resemblance that my acquaintance bears to his uncle the Emperor Napoleon. He is not distinguished as a scholar, but is thought to have a strong mind, and is remarkable for what is termed common sense. He will make a fine business lawyer. Cheves is the son of the famous Langdon Cheves. He is also designed for the bar. He has some celebrity for talents, & probably has more genious than any that I have described. He possesses a fine imagination, and is nick-named among us the "philosopher," from his fondness for fanciful theorizing. I have quite a large circle of acquaintances, but am most intimate with these gentlemen. We have a large table, confined to Southerners, and what are called gentlemen Yankees.

I look forward with great anxiety to the time of my graduating and returning to my dear parents. That time is now not quite ten months off. I hope you have as fine weather as we have, nothing

can surpass the exquisite mildness & cleaness of the atmosphere that
we have had here generally this fall.

Give my love to Father & Sister

I am my dear mother your

affectionate son

Edward C Marshall

This was a fashionable and affluent set Edward had
joined. And he must have taken up with them early in his
college career—in fact he had hardly been in Cambridge
long enough to matriculate, in the summer of 1823, when
his father was repaying Joseph Story for a loan to Edward,
explaining that he had thought he had given the young man
at least enough money to last until college opened. Jerome
Bonaparte was a rich young commoner with a regal ambition
and not much heart. Cheves of South Carolina was also a
wealthy youth, son of the famous Langdon Cheves who had
saved the Bank of the United States and then gone on to
Congress and Cabinet. The son Cheves had forsaken practical finance for theorizing, and felt himself superior in that
line, for everyone knew his father had been the first man to
speak publicly of a separate Southern Confederacy. James
Coles Bruce, scion of one of Virginia's earliest First Families,
was second to none in wealth. When he married and set up
housekeeping in Halifax County, Virginia, there were silver
pitchers and basins in the bedrooms. Birchett, nephew of
Uncle Taylor, was purely family affection. He may have had
pockets full of cash—most of the Marshall clan did. But the
Taylors were rich in Marshall affection. Judge George Keith
Talliaferro Taylor had married Marshall's sister Jane, much
against Marshall's judgement, for Judge Taylor was ten
years older than Jane, Marshall having been eleven years
the senior of his own bride.

Edward took time from his studies to run down to Quincy
to visit his father's old friend John Adams. That must have
been a cozy visit before a roaring fire, for Edward says the
old New Englander declared that his proudest deed had
been his gift of John Marshall to the United States.

This visit must have been about the time news got abroad
that Boston had conferred its highest honor upon the Chief

Justice whose opinions found so little approbation among his fellow Virginians. He was elected to membership in the Bunker Hill Association. How gaily he must have gone into a quick step caper before Polly!

Shortly after that merry moment the Chief Justice heard that back in the wintry month of February his brother, Alexander Keith Marshall, outstanding lawyer and staunch Federalist, had died in Kentucky. Then too came news of the death of General Charles Cotesworth Pinckney, and across another empty place in life Marshall reached for Polly's hand.

In December of 1825 Congress met in a strangely changed mood. These gentlemen in top hats still wished to censure the Supreme Court, but mildly and with compliments. William Wirt, still Attorney General, wrote, "The importance of that court in the administration of the Federal Government begins to be generally understood and acknowledged. The local irritations at some of their decisions in particular quarters (as in Virginia and Kentucky for instance) are greatly overbalanced by the general approbation with which those same decisions have been received throughout the Union. . . . It is now seen on every hand that the functions to be performed by the Supreme Court are among the most difficult and perilous to be performed under the Constitution."

Daniel Webster offered a bill in Congress to increase the number of the Supreme Justices to ten, and to require that a decision be the opinion of a two-thirds majority of the Court. This was tabled by both Houses, but not before Senators had surprised even themselves with statements of faith in the Court. Senator Rowan of Kentucky began a speech with a diatribe upon the "encroachments" of the Court, and ended by commending the "unsuspected integrity" of its members. Others pointed with dread to the vast power of the Court, then spoke of its being safe in the hands of Justices whose talents were of the highest order and whose integrity was spotless. Especially did Marshall receive this kind of praise. Senator Van Buren complained that a "kind of idolatry for the Supreme Court" had grown rampant, then heard himself speaking of the talents and "spotless integrity" of the incumbent Justices, adding, "That uncommon man who now presides over the Court . . . is in all human probability, the ablest judge now sitting upon any judicial bench in the world."

How smiling the brethren of the high Bench must have been around the dinner table these afternoons! Smiling, not to say laughing—just a twinkle of victory in an arduous struggle, just a bond of manly affection. "The harmony of the bench," wrote the Chief Justice, "will, I hope never be disturbed. We have external & political enemies enough to preserve internal peace."

Thus the session of the Supreme Court in the winter of 1826 was a happy one. The first letter from J Marshall to Polly shows this cheerfulness.

Washington Feby 5th 1826

My dearest Polly

I am now in an excellent room with a good fire and am a day sooner than usual in Washington. My usual practice has been to remain a day in Alexandria, but I came on this morning from a desire to end my journey while the weather is good. Mr. Washington and Mr Duval are here, and we expect our brothers Story and Thompson to day. Judge Johnson unfortunate took the course by way of Norfolk & cannot, in consequence of it, be here til wednesday or thursday. Mr. Todd is unable to perform the journey.

The roads were not quite so good as they were last winter, but we found them better than usual. We arrived in Alexandria at seven. I have not called on my aunt Keith for which I am truely sorry, but I could not call without giving up the stage, and as I am under the persecution of the Influenza I was desirous of getting as soon as I conveniently could to the end of my journey.

Tell Mr. Harvie I entirely forgot his overshoes & did not think of them till I was out of town. The weather however continued so moderate that I did not feel the want of them, & I think it extremely probable that, had I brought them, I should not have carried them back to Richmond. I dare not trust myself with anything which can be lost.

Tomorrow we shall open court & wait on the President; but serious business will not commence till tuesday. Farewell my dearest Polly I am your ever affectionate

J Marshall

A week later the Chief Justice is still cheerful, though feeling his age. He dearly loved Tom at all times, but his affection glowed with pride whenever it seemed that this oldest son needed his assistance. So many people depended on him, Marshall says, that he could not always supply their need as quickly as their necessity demanded. He seems to have had under consideration a recent request from Tom for a loan. It is to be wondered whether Polly had already sent $200 to Tom, for she had her own fortune. To her inheritance of the Jacqueline estate had been recently added another legacy. Parson Buchanan, whose poverty-stricken years had been eased as a member of the Ambler household, died in 1822, leaving the fortune that his worldly-wise brother had bequeathed him to be divided between the Ambler sisters. It seems that as Polly grew more ailing, she became emotional when she sat at her desk facing a clean page upon which she must write "My dearest—." What? Captain? General? Judge? She never thought of writing, "Light of my lantern of life." Most of her letters ended as a blank page. But she could sign her name with ease on a check.

Washington, Feb 12th 26

My dearest Polly

I am settled down in my old habits as regularly as if I were still on the right side of seventy. I get up as early as ever, take my walks of three miles by seven, think of you, & then set down to business. I have had a pretty severe attack of the influenza, & the cough & confusion in my head still continue, though the soar throat has left me, & the inflamation of the stomach has entirely subsided. If you had no other reason to know how old I am you would be reminded of it by my dwelling thus on a trifling indisposition. Our brother Story just arrived today while we were at dinner. He was stopped a week at Phil by the influenza which he has had pretty nearly as bad as myself. It only indured me to push forward & not stay a day as usual in Alexa in order to visit my old & good aunt (Mrs. Keith)

I have not heard a word from Fauquier since leaving Richmond, but expect soon to receive a letter from Tom as I have written to him to inform him that you will advance the 200$ he wants;—or rather that I read your wishes so plainly that I had determined to furnish them myself.

I have received three invitations for evening parties this week. See how gay Washington is & how much miss Jones has lost by her journey to Richmond. If you were here and would go with me I am not sure that my influenza or court business would keep me so constantly within doors, but as it is I do not feast my eyes with gazing at the numerous belles who flock to this place during the winters. If Lucy Fisher could persuade _____ to become a candidate for congress & persuade the people to elect him, she might come & have a charming time of it. Farewell my dearest Polly, however I may jest about trifles I am always sincere & earnest when I say that I am most affectionately your

J Marshall

Polly's nineteen-year-old niece, Lucy Fisher, was currently being courted by a young scientist, Dr. Daniel Norborne Norton of Richmond. She married him shortly, but never persuaded him into politics.

Even the mildest of the Winter did not make the Chief Justice forget his ailment. On the twelfth of March he still was hampered by the disease, though not enough to keep him from attending entertainments. He went to the theatre, not only for the play, but for the joy of seeing people. One evening as the Chief Justice came down the aisle on the arm of Judge Story the audience rose to their feet and applauded the old aristocrat, who beamed happily, seeing in the gesture not honor, but a response to his own affection for them.

William Wirt says of Marshall at this time: "I verily believe there is not a spark of vanity in his composition—unless it be that venial and hospitable nature which induces him to pride himself on giving to his friends the best glass of Madeira in Virginia."

These are the ephemeral things of history, and Marshall knew it. He wrote to his friend Joseph Pickering, "Those who follow us will know very little of the real transactions of our day, and have a very untrue impression respecting men & things."

And then he wrote to Polly:

Washington March 12th 1826

My dearest Polly

John passed through the city a day or two past & altho I did not see him I had the pleasure of hearing from Mr. Washington who saw him as he was about to get into the stage that you were as well as usual. I was particularly glad to hear this as I could not help fearing that the uncommon warmth of the season had relaxed your system so as to distress your feelings. I hope you ride constantly as exercise will I think be of great advantage to you.

I enjoy my usual health. I am not sure that I have any remnant of the influenza, though I sometimes think that it has not entirely left me. I was in a very great crowd the other evening at Mrs. Adams' drawing room, but I see very few persons there whom I know & fewer still in whom I take any interest. A person as old as I am feels that his home is his place of most comfort, and his old wife the companion in the world in whose society he is most happy.

I dined yesterday with Mr. Randolph. He is absorbed in the party politics of the day & seems as much engaged in them as he was twenty-five years past. It is very different with me. I long to leave this busy bustling scene & to return to the tranquility of my family & farm. Farewell my dearest Polly. That Heaven may bless you is the unceasing prayer of your ever affectionate
                                           J Marshall

Marshall did not go alone to the drawing rooms of Washington. It was said that often the guests would see Judge Story bringing in "the tall majestic, bright eyed old man, old by years, by the lines in his composed face and by his service to his country;" and the people crowded around him. With them always, adding to the repartee that sparkled in his company, was John Randolph of Roanoke, coughing and proclaiming his bad health, the very picture of a reed shaken in a wind before which it refused to bow. But there was always a jest passing between the Chief Justice and the unbending States Rights champion.

The Attorney General William Wirt would be in that crowd too. He says, "I am a great favorite with the Chief as he certainly is with me. . . . I do not believe he has an atom of gall in his whole composition on any subject other than that of politics. . . . Politics apart there is not a better natured man on this earth than the old Chief—and a more powerful mind was never sent on this earth."

When Marshall returned to Richmond in the mild Spring weather of late March he bought Jane Austen's novels to read to Polly in the evenings. "Her flights," he says of Miss Austen's muse, "are not lofty. She does not soar on eagle's wings, but she is pleasing, interesting, equable, and yet amusing."

There were burdens on Marshall's heart in this Spring of

1826. Both his dearly loved friend and his implacable enemy were old and in financial straits. Monroe's claim against the United States government was being investigated item by item in Congress as if it was a milliner's bill. The sentiment of citizens of Richmond was so aroused that a testimonial dinner was arranged for him at the Eagle Tavern, with the Chief Justice presiding in all his warm affection for his life-long friend. For Thomas Jefferson's relief the Virginia Legislature had allowed a public lottery to be prepared "for the benefit of the venerable Mr. Jefferson." But independently in many cities of the Union, private committees were formed to raise subscriptions, "not over 5$ each," to relieve the ancient statesman. In Richmond on July ninth, a resolve to raise such a fund was "unanimously adopted by the large and respectable meeting of citizens held at the Capitol." This was an informal committee with one and then another gentleman in the chair. It is said that the Chief Justice presided at such a meeting when word was brought that the master of Monticello had died on the fourth instant. Two days later news reached Richmond that on the same day in Quincy, Massachusetts, John Adams had died. Rumor readily took up the tale that each of these statesmen with his last breath had thanked Heaven that he left the other still wrestling with aristocracy on this earth.

Then the Chief Justice was named to a committee requested to prepare a joint memorial service befitting these two who had so deeply distrusted each other's vision of democracy, until in old age they were able to clasp hands over a world they were unable to rearrange. William Wirt of the facile tongue complained that he had been assigned an irksome task when he was asked to do such diverse justice in one encomium.

In 1827 the sessions of the Supreme Court were lengthened in order to accommodate business which was yearly increasing. The Court now convened on the second Monday in January. Marshall was punctual in arriving at the capital, but he was depressed. He wrote to Joseph Pickering, "I find myself almost alone in the world. With the exception of Judge Peters yourself and Mr. Wolcott I can hardly find any person who was conspicuous on the great theatre of our country when I first began to mix in public affairs. Things are very much changed as well as men."

Another presidential campaign was starting a noisy and scurrilous race. Supporters of secession, nullification and of Federal power all claimed the Constitution as their peculiar fortress. Now Andrew Jackson and Henry Clay stood for the West, John Quincy Adams for the North and John C. Calhoun for the South.

In 1828 the Chief Justice found paved streets in Washington. He also found Winnebago Indians wandering about the town, beginning to know what it meant to be Americans endowed with individual liberty. They were having a good time running after white ladies on the streets. To restrain them was a touchy diplomatic matter.

The Court sitting later than usual this year gave the weather a chance to sprinkle sparkles on the waters of Bay and river, and to tint the shore line with hazy green. So the Chief Justice chose to travel home by steamboat *Potomac*. As the vessel drew into the dock at Rocketts, in the early morning light Richmond gleamed upon her hills. Above the town sat the Capitol building, withdrawing her sovereign skirts from Federal dust. Out from Capitol Square ran streets, with brick sidewalks dallying before handsome residences. Church steeples were beginning to rise above trees like stamens of a full blown city.

How sweet it all looked to Marshall as he rode up the hill from the dock! How sweet Polly's mansion as he turned into Marshall Street! How sweet her face at the window! In the next moment she stood at the top of the porch steps with welcome like pale flowers opening in her outstretched hands.

A day or two later he wrote to Joseph Story: "I had a pleasant sail through a smooth sea to Norfolk & thence to Richmond. I have seen scarcely any person out of my own family since my return, but, if I may credit appearances, there is rather a more stormy and disturbed atmosphere on land than I could have supposed possible. I am however on the wing for my friends in the upper country, where I shall find near and dear friends occupied more with their farms than with politics."

Unhappily along the way, however, he heard that the *Richmond Whig & Advertiser* was quoting a dispatch from a Baltimore paper which purported to quote the Chief Justice as saying, "I have not voted for twenty years; but I shall consider it a solemn duty I owe my country to go to the polls and vote at the next presidential election, for should Jackson be elected, I shall look upon the government as virtually dissolved."

Marshall at once wrote the editor that he had always thought it right for him, holding the office he did, to abstain from public declarations on elections. He had, he said, in private stated that if he should vote in this election, he believed it would be for the President because of a strong sense he felt of injustice done Mr. Adams and Mr. Clay in public charges of corruption.

To Justice Story, Marshall wrote that he had refuted the report, "not because I have any objection to its being known that my private judgement is in favor of the re-election of Mr. Adams but because I have great objection to being represented in the character of a furious partisan. Intemperate language does not become my age or office, and is foreign to my disposition."

It seems that the Chief Justice made some such remark to a "nephew" who inadvertently let it get to the press, who stretched it to fit public interest. The nephew also wrote a denial of the story as reported, but the press had gone on to other matters, and dropped this one as it stood.

Could this have been "our nephew William," son of Dr. Louis Marshall, who studied divinity at the Seminary in Alexandria? He was now living in Baltimore, encumbered with a wife and two infants, bored with preaching and trying teaching. Shortly after that dinner with Marshall at Aunt Keith's, William had married pretty Ann Lee of Alexandria, daughter of Light-Horse Harry Lee, and sister of a young officer in the United States Army, Robert E. Lee. This William Marshall was never in sympathy with State Sovereignty.

Disturbed and provoked over the whole incident, though he was, Marshall's spirits rose with the road as it climbed to the upper country. No longer could he travel by horseback, even when a servant accompanied him on another horse to carry his desk and portmanteau. Now he travelled in a two-wheeled, one horse gig, or sulky, often picking up a friend going his way. This was the season of promise on the farms. Fields of wheat and barley lay lush and green. Lambs and colts were in the meadows, and all the farmers were busily counting chickens before they hatched. Happily he visited the circle of his sons' plantations, advising them on farming, finance and child-raising. Gayly he disseminated the rich wisdom of his life to grandchildren, always to the clink of a coin passing from his pocket to theirs.

Over-production was always the farmer's problem. The Chief Justice constituted himself marketing agent for his sons, buying in the over-plus. At Oak Hill he found Tom's children in the throes of whooping cough. Tom was absorbed in contriving a large roller to give "corn fields the degree of compactness requisite for a wheat crop." He was doing a good amount of business selling young horses foaled and broken in his fields. Marshall purchased a fine animal to be delivered to Richmond in the early Fall.

By May first, the Chief Justice was so refreshed that he blew in at Polly's door like a mountain breeze.

All through the Summer he still could laugh, though he says the "rancorous malignity" of the political campaign was more than a gentleman could stand. Sometimes the neighbours saw Polly sitting beside him on the bench under the thinking tree. Chester Harding who was making portraits and busts of him found a deeper sweetness in Marshall's smile.

In September Tom wrote his father that he was delighted with the operation of his roller, that a drought caught the fields of grain which had waved so lush and green in April, causing a flurry of rising prices and speculation, and that he was so busy seeding that he had not found an opportunity to send down either the horse purchased by his father, or one for Aunt Carrington.

Thus when the Chief Justice attended Hanover Court this month, he drove a friendly old mare from his town stable. When he returned he had a story to tell Polly, but he would not divulge it until her curiosity had been properly stirred. Smiling broadly, he made no haste. He removed his topcoat and folded it before throwing it over a chair. He took the time to inspect his hat for traces of dust. Slowly he arranged his long whip (cut from a tree along the way) in the hall closet. He began to ask about the servants, when Polly cut him short with: "You might as well tell me what is amusing you!"

Then his hearty laugh burst forth. With it still rumbling through his words he told her that he had taken a short cut home through a woods road, which was just a matter of ruts between saplings, but beginning to glow with yellow leaves and goldenrod. As the old mare jogged along, Marshall was thinking too little about the stumpy road, and too much about politics. He did not know what the mare had on her mind, but both of them were surprised when the gig jerked to a sudden stop. A tree had projected itself in the way of a shaft, breaking it in two. Chagrined, the Chief Justice got down from the gig to search in vain for a leather thong to mend the shaft. He was in a sad dilemma. He stood there disgusted with himself, with the tree, his mare and General Jackson for making life so difficult.

Presently he heard a whistle beyond the bend in the road, such a whistle as colored people use to scare off haunts; and sure enough, through the shadows came an old Negro. When "good-days" had been exchanged, Marshall asked the man if he could help him.

"Yassuh," came the answer, "I kin fix dat in no time short effen you got a knife."

The Chief Justice produced a knife, and sure enough, in no time short the Negro had cut a withe from a sapling, made a splint and bound up the shaft strongly.

Putting a piece of money in the gnarled hand, Marshall said, "Henry, how come you did so well what puzzled me so long?"

"Dat de way 'tis," replied Henry. "Some folks jest natchel-
ly got more sense dan t'others."

Again Marshall left Polly in this Autumn of 1828. He
was appointed by the State Legislature to serve as delegate
to a convention in Charlottesville, whose duty it was to
devise a system of internal improvements to be under State
control. There was, however, talk, when Randolph of Roanoke was not within earshot, of asking for a Congressional
appropriation to develop the harbor at Richmond as a port
for seagoing vessels. Also, steam railroads were beginning
to thrust through the countryside. A Norfolk paper was
soon to comment: "The Locomotive has one contrivance of
a peculiar character. It carries a brass whistle, which is
blown by the steam, whenever any animals may come upon
the tracks, or a cross roads is passed. No words can describe
the shrill, wild and unearthly sound produced by this arrangement. In going through the woods the noise is peculiar-
ly startling, and it can be heard for miles."

At Charlottesville, as everywhere else in the State, the
presidential campaign set the atmosphere a-prickle. Marshall wrote to Story, "The spirit of party is more bitter than
I could have supposed possible."

But the parties were giving themselves new labels. Numbers of old Federalists were calling themselves Jackson's
Men. Other Federalists were aligning themselves with Republicans and changing their name to National Republicans.
The election of Jackson would overthrow the Jeffersonian
party succession as Jefferson had overthrown the Federalist,
and who could say whether the foundation of a nation
would endure lacking either of these?

Tucked among the papers found at Leeds Manor was the
following item in J Marshall's handwriting:

Lines written for a lady's album

Written, on the request of a lady that I would inscribe my name
in her book of Autographs; but withheld, in the apprehension that
it might be thought light and unbecoming the gravity of seventy-
three

In early youth, when life was young
   And spirits light and gay,
When music breathed from every tongue
   And every month was May;

When buoyant hope in colours bright
   Her vivid pictures drew,
When every object gave delight
   And every scene was new;

My heart with ready homage bowed
   At lovely woman's shrine,
And every wish that she avowed
   Became a wish of mine.

Now age with hoary frost congeals
   Gay fancy's flowing stream,
And the unwelcome truth reveals
   That life is but a dream;

Yet still with homage true I bow
   At woman's sacred shrine,
And if she will a wish avow
   That wish must still be mine.

My old wife! My youth grown rich and tender with years!

Chapter XXV

A New Day

THESE WERE THE DAYS of the rise of the American System, which now is called Capitalism. The Jeffersonian dream of a nation of rural progress was fading out behind Henry Clay's vision of national power derived from industrial wealth. In December of 1828 it became known that John Quincy Adams, the unionist, had lost the presidency to Andrew Jackson, the individualist.

As the first of January drew near, Marshall prepared with many misgivings to leave Polly for the Court session in Washington. His misgivings were for her failing health and for the future of the nation. Polly was more than ever distressed by noise, especially at night. She was more fearful of the corners of her room and the shadows under her bed. Talk of dissolution of the Union seemed to encircle her with dark faces. If she fell asleep in her chair, she would awaken with a feeble cry, and tremble until the miracle of her husband's smile quieted her, and she could laugh a little old-lady chuckle with a glint of apology in her eyes. Of the nation Marshall says: "The union is thus far continued by miracles. I fear they cannot continue longer."

All of January there were only four justices sitting on cases before the Supreme Court. Judges Duvall of Maryland and Thompson of New York were ill, and Judge Johnson of South Carolina was delayed on his way to Washington, nursing injuries suffered when the stage in which he was travelling turned over on a bad stretch of road. Newly appointed Associate Justice McLean of Kentucky, Justices Washington of Virginia and Story of Massachusetts and the Chief Justice gathered at the dinner table to discuss a case which seemed to cause no great public sensation, and soon arrived at a unanimous decision fixing the human status of slaves in indemnity claims. The case of Boyce *vs* Anderson had been brought on from the Kentucky Circuit Court to the Supreme Court. An owner of four slaves who had been drowned in a Mississippi River packet accident sued the

303

Steamship Company for loss of property. The Chief Justice read the Court's opinion: "In the nature of his character a slave resembles a passenger, and not a package." Therefore the owner could not collect damages.

This was only a straw in a heavy docket. A note of relief opens the following letter from Marshall to Polly:

Washington Feb 1st 1829

My dearest Polly

Our sick Judges have at length arrived and we are as busy as ever we will be. I do not walk as far as I formerly did but I still keep up the practice of walking in the morning. We dined on friday last with the President, and I sat between Mrs. Adams and the lady of a member of Congress whom I found quite agreeable as well as handsome. Mrs. Adams was as cheerful as if she was to continue in the great house for the ensuing four years. The President also is in good health and spirits. I percieve no difference in consequence of the turn the late election has taken.

General Jackson is expected in the city within a fortnight, and is to put up in this house. I shall of course wait on him. It is said he feels the loss of Mrs. Jackson very seriously. It would be strange if he did not. A man who at his age loses a good wife loses a friend whose place cannot be supplied.

I dine tomorrow with the British minister and the next day again with the President. I have never before dined twice with the President during the same session of the court. That on friday was an official dinner. The invitation for tuesday is not for all the other Judges and I consider it as a personal civility.

Tell Mr. Call all the secretaries are sick and Mr. Clay among them. He took cold by attending the colonization society and has been indisposed ever since. The town it is said was never so full as at present. The expectation is that it will overflow on the 3rd of March. The whole world it is said will be here. This however will present no temptation to you to come. I wish I could leave it all and come to you. How much more delightful it would be to me to sit by your side than to witness all the pomp and parade of the inauguration.

I hear very little from Richmond but I adhere to my old rule of believing that every body dear to me, and especially the one dearest to me is well.

Tell Mr Harvie I am greatly obliged by his letter.

Farewell my dearest Polly with the most ardent wish for your happiness

I am your ever affectionate
J Marshall

"The town was never so full," writes Marshall. It was never more excited. Daniel Webster wrote to a friend in Massachusetts: "Gen. J will be here abt. 15th Feb. Nobody knows what he will do when he does come. My opinion is that when he comes he will bring a breeze with him. Which way it will blow, I cannot tell. . . . My fear is stronger than my hope."

That master of the human heart forgot politics for a moment of sympathy for Jackson, whose wife had died during preparations to move from Tennessee to Washington. Shortly after this letter Marshall heard that Margaret of Oak Hill, Tom's wife, had died. She had been thirty-seven years old, younger than Polly when her last child was born. Margaret left seven children, one three years old. The Chief Justice could not leave Washington for the burial in the old graveyard at Oak Hill.

Nor could he leave a week later to attend the wedding of his youngest child, Edward Carrington Marshall, and Rebecca Peyton in Richmond on February twelfth. He gave them the usual wedding present of a generous tract of Fairfax lands. "Carrington," this farm was called.

Anxiously and sadly Marshall wrote to Polly:

Washington Feb 19th 1829

My dearest Polly

I send you inclosed a letter to Mr. Payne which I wish sent to him as soon as convenient. I hope it may reach you in time to go out on sunday. I imagine Oby has carried out the clover seed which was in the cellar, and perhaps what Mr Harvie was to have purchased from Mr. Lewis for me.

The day after writing my last I received a letter from my son James containing the painful intelligence that you were not quite so well as usual. I shall be very uneasy till I hear again from you. Do my dearest Polly let me hear from you through someone of those who will be willing to write for you. I will flatter myself that your indisposition is merely temporary and that it has passed away. Yet I cannot be easy till my hopes are cofirmed.

I wrote a day or two past to our son and have made a feeble attempt to console him.

I have received a letter from our son Jaquelin informing me that he has a very fine son and that Eliza is as well as could be expected. His son is named after himself. His daughters he says are

a little indisposed in consequence of confinement during the excessive bad weather they have had.

Farewell my dearest Polly, that Heaven may bless and preserve
you is the unceasing prayer

of your

J Marshall

The Chief Justice is less able to throw off his family anx-
ieties this year. He writes Polly again, too heavy hearted to
mention the whirlpool of events that surround him:

Washington Feb 28th 1829

My dearest Polly

I have looked eagerly through this week for a letter from some
one of our friends giving me some information respecting you but
have been disappointed. In spite of my firm resolution always to hope
for the best, I cannot suppress my uneasiness about you. Your general health is so delicate, your spirits so liable to depression that I
cannot control my uneasiness. I was never more closely occupied
than I have been since my arrival at this place, yet my mind wanders to that dear fire side at which is seated what is most dear to me
on earth. I believe I mentioned in my last that I had received a letter
from Edward, and that he thinks himself very happy, & yet amidst
all his happiness he thinks of and grieves for his brother. I received
a few days past a long letter from our son. It is serious and very
religious. His heavy loss has given his mind a still stronger impulse
in that direction than it had previously received. He says that he is
very much occupied with his children and I hope that will gradually
restore him to happiness. He retains John with him and superin-
tends his education.

Farewell my dearest wife. That Heaven may protect and bless
you is the constant prayer of your ever affectionate

J Marshall

John, son of bereft Thomas, was eighteen years old, the
very age at which Polly had tearfully packed John's father
off to Princeton College—the age at which a mother knows
her apron strings are cut, and a father knows that henceforth a manly shoulder touches his.

On March fourth, 1829, came that inauguration day in
which the wheel of history turned from the old aristocratic
form of representative government, and brought on the
manners of democracy. High society withdrew from White
House functions. Now The People traipsed through the
fine rooms of the executive mansion, until it was never again

called a Palace. It became just a House. Justice Story wrote that on the day of Jackson's inauguration the White House was "visited by an immense crowd of all sorts of people, from the highest and most polished down to the most vulgar and gross in the nation."

A lady of distinction who saw that crowd wrote: "The halls were filled with a disorderly rabble of negroes, boys, women and children, scrambling for the refreshments designed for the drawing rooms! the people forcing their way into the saloons, mingling with the foreigners and citizens surrounding the President. . . . It was the Peoples day, the Peoples President, and the People would rule."

After administering the oath of office to the President, the Chief Justice retired from the crowd. Next day he wrote Polly:

Washington March 5 [1829]

My dearest Polly

We had yesterday a most busy and crowded day. People have flocked to Washington from every quarter of the United States. When the oath was administered to the President the computation is that 12 or 15000 people were present—a great number of them ladies. A great ball was given at night to celebrate the election. I of course did not attend it. The affliction of our son would have been sufficient to restrain me had I even felt a desire to go.

. . . I am told by several that I am held up as a candidate for the convention. I have no desire to be in the convention and do not mean to be a candidate. I should not trouble you with this did I not apprehend that the idea of my wishing to be in the convention might prevent some of my friends who are themselves desirous of being in it from becoming candidates. I therefore wish you to give this information to Mr Harvie. . . .

Farewell my dearest Polly. Your happiness is always nearest the heart of your

J Marshall

The convention that Marshall would avoid was being called in Richmond to consider amending the old State Constitution which had been written in 1778 before Virginia had entirely outgrown royalty. Conservative citizens felt that the fifty-year-old document was well adapted to the public welfare. But the Jeffersonians found it too restrictive of suf-

frage, too lenient toward privilege. Marshall was one of
those opposed to a change, and he resisted being drawn into
the strife he knew such a convention would be. However,
on his return to Richmond later on in March, he wrote to
Joseph Story: "I have acted like a girl addressed by a gentleman she does not positively dislike, but is unwilling to
marry. She is sure to yield to the advice and persuasion of
her friends. . . . there will be a good deal of division & heat in
the Convention . . . I can no longer debate." He adds that he
has agreed to let his name be put forward as a candidate.

As the Sage says, "The joy of life is the other side of the
strength of life," and Marshall's strong spirit never lost its
wings. He was still the life of the party every other Saturday when he joined gentlemen in shirtsleeves under the
trees at Buchanan's Spring to play quoits. His ring was the
largest in the game. His laugh resounded when he won, and
his smile twinkled when he argued a close point. Now the
company most often chose to place him at the head of the
table, where he told his stories, and laughed at the quips of
statesmen, bankers and clergymen around him. Now his
name was most often sought to give prestige to committees
and enterprises.

His lawyer dinners were still the most fashionable masculine event in the city. Grandchildren still tipped through
the house all day. But at night the house must be quiet if
Polly was to sleep. Then the lamp-lit rooms were peopled
with memories. Only Polly, the housekeeper and Marshall
lived after dark in those beautiful paneled chambers. When
Summer came and windows must be opened day and night,
it was impossible to shut out the noises of a small city where
dogs could bay at the moon or the passing night watchman.
Then Marshall had to write a letter to Mr. Rawlings, a
neighbour:

July 28th, 1829

Dear Sir

The distressed I might say distracted situation of my wife at
length forces me very reluctantly to make a direct application to
you and to state to you her real situation. The incessant barking of
your dog has scarcely left her a night of quiet since the beginning

DELEGATES

1	James Monroe	Loudoun
2	James Madison	Orange
3	William B. Giles	Amelia
4	John Roane	Essex
5	Mark Alexander	Mecklenburg
6	John Y. Mason	Southampton
7	Richard Logan	Halifax
8	John S. Barbour	Culpeper
9	Charles F. Mercer	Loudoun
10	William H. Fitzhugh	Fairfax
11	Philip C. Pendleton	Berkeley
12	Archibald Stuart, Jr.	Patrick
13	John P. Mathews	Wythe
14	Adam See	Randolph
15	Philip Doddridge	Brooke
16	Littleton Tazewell	Norfolk
17	Chapman Johnson	Augusta
18	Richard N. Venable	Prince Edward
19	Philip P. Barbour	Orange
20	John Marshall	Richmond
21	James M. Garnett	Essex
22	Lewis Summers	Kanawha
23	William Goode	Chesterfield
24	Fleming B. Miller	Botetourt
25	Thomas Massie, Jr.	Nelson
26	John McCrea	Fauquier
27	Elisha Boyd	Berkeley
28	William F. Gordon	Albemarle
29	Samuel Branch (succeeded Col. Mennis)	Buckingham
30	John Coalter (succeeded John Talliaferro)	Stafford
31	Benj. W. S. Cabell	Pittsylvania
32	Samuel Clayton	Campbell
33	Richard Morris	Hanover
34	John Randolph	Charlotte
35	Benj. Watkins Leigh	Chesterfield
36	James Trezvant	Southampton
37	John Urquhart	Southampton
38	Augustine Claiborne	Greensville
39	William K. Perrin	Gloucester
40	John Scott	Fauquier
41	Eugenius M. Wilson	Monongalia
42	Andrew McMillan	Lee
43	William Byars	Washington
44	Robert Stannard	Spotsylvania
45	Abel Upshur	Northampton
46	Samuel Taylor	Chesterfield
47	John Laidley	Campbell
48	Lucas P. Thompson	Amherst
49	Gordon Cloyd	Montgomery
50	William McCoy	Pendleton
51	William Naylor	Hampshire
52	John Tyler	Charles City
53	Peachy Harrison	Rockingham
54	Walter Holliday (succeeded David Watson)	Spotsylvania
55	Alfred H. Powell	Frederick
56	Thomas R. Joynes	Accomac
57	Hierome L. Opie (succeeded James M. Mason)	Frederick
58	William Campbell	Bedford
59	John Clopton	New Kent
60	John W. Jones	Chesterfield
61	George Loyall	Norfolk
62	Hugh B. Grigsby	Norfolk
63	William Leigh	Halifax
64	Joseph Prentiss	Nansemond
65	William Donaldson	Hampshire
66	William Smith	Greenbriar
67	Augustine Neale	Richmond
68	George C. Dromgoole	Brunswick
69	William P. Taylor	Caroline
70	John B. George	Tazewell
71	William H. Broadnax	Dinwiddie
72	James Saunders	Campbell
73	Edwin C. Duncan	Harrison
74	Thomas Griggs, Jr.	Jefferson
75	Henry Chapman	Montgomery
76	William Oglesby	Grayson
77	Richard H. Henderson	Loudoun
78	John R. Cooke	Frederick
79	Andrew Bierne	Monroe
80	Alexander Campbell	Brooke
81	Charles S. Morgan	Monongalia
82	William Anderson	Shenandoah
83	Samuel Coffman	Shenandoah
84	Jacob Williamson	Rockingham
85	John Baxter	Pocahontas
86	John W. Green	Culpeper
87	Briscoe G. Baldwin	Augusta
88	George Townes	Pittsylvania
89	Joseph Martin	Henry
90	Thomas N. Bailey	Accomac
91	Philip N. Nicholas	Richmond
92	Samuel McD. Moore	Rockbridge
93	James Pleasants	Goochland
94	Fleming Bates	Northumberland
95	Alexander F. Rose	Stafford
96	Edward Campbell	Washington

NON-DELEGATES

97	Rt. Rev. R. C. Moore, Bishop of the Episcopal Diocese of Virginia
98	John Hampton Pleasants, editor, *Richmond Whig*
99	Thomas Ritchie, Sr., editor *Richmond Enquirer*
100	Mr. Briggs, Clerk of the Commonwealth
101	Mr. Stansbury, official stenographer from Washington, D. C.

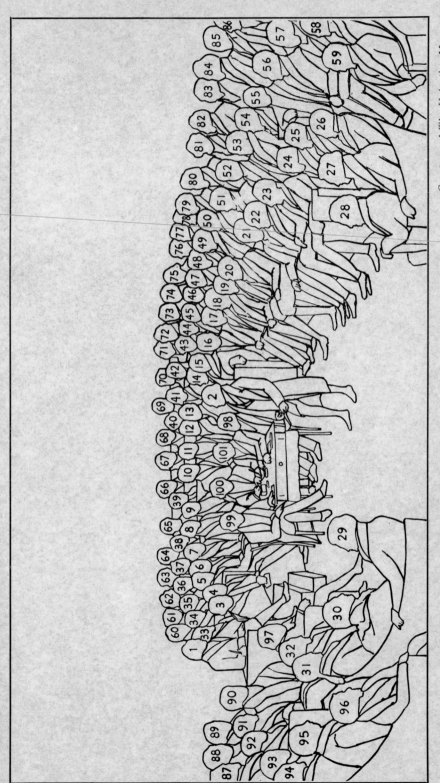

George Catlin's key to "The Last Meeting of the Giants."

Courtesy of The Valentine Museum

Courtesy of the Virginia Historical Society

GROUP PORTRAIT OF THE VIRGINIA CONSTITUTION CONVENTION, October, 1829. Entitled by the artist, George Catlin, "The Last Meeting of the Giants."

of summer. During this spell of hot weather she has been kept almost perpetually awake. Last night she could not sleep two hours. Her situation is deplorable, and if this state of things continues she cannot live.

Rather than ask what it may be disagreeable to you to do, I would without hesitation abandon my house, and have proposed it to her; but our little place in the country affords her only a confined and hot chamber in which she thinks she cannot live. She therefore insists on my communicating her situation directly to you in the hope that when it is known the cause may not be continued. It is most painful to me that any thing in the circumstances of my family should interfere in the slightest degree with the inclination of a neighbour, and I have refrained as long as possible from applying to you on this irksome subject.

Very respectfully
Your obedt.
J Marshall

We should take refuge among our friends in the upper country, but my wife cannot travel, and cannot sleep in the house with a family.

Marshall thought a long time before writing this letter. In this wide open small city a barking dog was considered a rightful and efficient protection of life and property.

All the hot season the citizens of the State were searching for delegates, one from each senatorial district, to revise the State Constitution. This was no convulsive political campaign. This was Virginia's last purely aristocratic act. With statesman-like dignity freeholders went about selecting Virginia's finest. Precinct limits were ignored. Ninety-six gentlemen were chosen because they were considered by the greatest number of voters to be the wise, the good and the experienced.

On Sunday October fourth, mellow air drifted through the open windows of the Marshall parlour, where Polly, delicately sitting in an arm chair, watched three elderly gentlemen lifting glasses of amber wine in a silent toast to each other. This was the climax of their public lives. James Madison, John Marshall and James Monroe had led the nation thus far. And now they were delegated by their State to act as beacons of wisdom and knowledge in a Convention which they knew would be stormy. Polly knew that for all their affection for each other, there was a diversity in their wisdom that would require much compromise if they were to bring about safe progress for the State they all loved.

Polly shook the blue paisley shawl from her shoulder and reached her open hands as if trying to catch the breeze, then clasped them tightly in her lap to keep them from fluttering like late butterflies, while she studied the three gentlemen.

Colonel Monroe looked older than either of the others, although he was the youngest, being seventy-one. He was infirm and sad. His wife was ill at his estate in Loudoun County. The estate was mortgaged beyond the limits even of friendship. Mr. Madison was the oldest, seventy-nine. His wife was still fascinating. It was said of the Madisons that they were an example of elegant and lovely old age. Counting on her fingers Polly came to the conclusion that Marshall was seventy-four, and that every year had added to his greatness, and to the beauty of his smile. She no longer bothered about his clothes. Now he turned and smiled at her, which rendered her so content that she almost decided to take a few winks of sleep, but quickly changed her mind. Calling for Mrs. Martyr, she took the housekeeper's arm and asked to be excused from the company.

Monday, October fifth, was such a shining, high blue-skied day that people were saying that a generous angel must have picked it especially for Virginia's Convention. Poplar trees had spread their leaves like a yellow carpet to be kicked about by the feet of "a large concourse of intelligent people from various parts of the union. Young men came on horseback from Kentucky, Tennessee and other Southern States. Statesmen of mature years and experienced ministers of foreign powers who wished to see men whose names had become historical, educated men of every profession and class came, many of them with their families, to behold the gathering and to listen to the discussions."

It was so mild a day that Polly could stand on her porch to watch the people walking toward the Capitol Square, by twos, or threes, or in larger groups, all shedding their opinions as recklessly as the trees had scattered their leaves. From crushed foliage came the fragrance of Autumn's wine,

and from the voices a vibrant sense of the future. She
reached her hand toward the passers-by in a gesture of farewell. Tom, standing beside her, caught the hand, laughing
gently. He always understood his mother's quaint heart-
throbs. After the day was over he would give her a full
account of the proceedings in the Capitol, for this Convention was of so much importance to his motherless children
that he attended the meetings until he was finally appointed
to be delegate from Fauquier.

He could tell Polly that the Chief Justice, ex-President
Madison and ex-President Monroe had led the delegates
into the hall, while an audience that packed the gallery
stood until these gentlemen were seated. Then Mr. Madison
called the meeting to order, and without delay nominated
Colonel Monroe to be president of the Convention. The
Chief Justice seconded the nomination, and without a dissenting vote Colonel Monroe was elected.

"Aren't you glad Colonel Monroe was so honored?"

"Well, but of course your father accomplished that."

"Ah, no. Virginians love Colonel Monroe."

"No matter. What happened next?"

"Then Mr. Madison and Father led Colonel Monroe to
the chair."

"Was Mr. Randolph of Roanoke there?"

John Randolph of Roanoke was very much there, wearing
black for mourning, with crepe tied on his hat and his
sleeve. "I go in mourning," he said, "for the old Constitution." He looked more like a ghost than ever, but his voice
was still like silver bells. This was the first State office he had
ever held, though his County had sent him to Congress and
Senate again and again.

Daily the story was brought to Polly by Tom, by the
older grandchildren who roamed everywhere through their
grandfather's house, and by the Chief Justice in the early
night after his dinner guests had gone. The housekeeper
was busy with Marshall's dinners in honor of distinguished
visitors to Richmond. Once of record, and probably several
times, John Randolph, John Wickham, James Monroe and
James Madison met at the table, with Senators, ex-gover-

nors, visitors from abroad; while Peter and Joseph, and it may be, Robin, smiled as they urged the guests to have more oysters, or sora, or new sweet potatoes from the Chickahominy farm.

The guests would be saying that some citizens were complaining that seven judges and so many lawyers as delegates would overbalance the decisions of the Convention. But it was remembered that Edmund Burke had warned George III that the greater part of the Americans educated themselves in the law.

Monroe was so infirm at this time that often his place as president was filled by Philip P. Barbour, until eventually Barbour was appointed permanent chairman. Madison's voice, never strong, was now so feeble that he did his debating in conversation with a few delegates at a time. Marshall's voice was sure, strong and courteous when he rose to uphold proven old laws, and to offer compromise with conflicting innovations.

Of Marshall at this Convention it was said: "Whenever he spoke, which was seldom, and only for a short time, he attracted great attention . . . his appearance was revolutionary and patriarchal. Tall in a surtout of blue, with a face of genius and an eye of fire, his mind possessed a rare faculty of condensation; he distilled an argument down to the essence."

It is said that Governor Giles came into the hall every day wearing a crutch and held it as he spoke "words like honey pouring from an eastern rock." Such words were needed; for Randolph fought every step of revision. His bitter sarcasm cut sharply into discussions, often causing a jeering laugh. He seemed to know, it was said, some weakness of every man, and uncovered it with ridicule. "Every man," he exclaimed, "thinks himself a constitution-maker, a George Mason." Not one department of the State's government, he complained, was to be "left untouched by the spirit of innovation," he "would not call it reform."

The delegates sat around a long table, all except Randolph. He sat apart, gazing sadly over the heads of the members, at a large map of Virginia. When he got the floor, which he did frequently, he said, "As long as I have had any fixed opinions I have been in the habit of considering the Constitution of Virginia under which I have lived for more than half a century, with all its faults and failings, and with all the objections which practical men, not theorists and visionary speculators, have urged or can urge against it, as the very best Constitution, not for Japan; not for China; not for New England; or for old England; but for this our ancient Commonwealth of Virginia."

It is said that the Convention "became a sectional and geographical struggle for power" between the eastern conservatives and the western radicals. Bitterly they denounced each other. It is interesting to note that Monroe voted most often with the westerners and against Madison and Marshall, as it had always been since that long passed day in Philadelphia on which Madison largely wrote the United States' Constitution, and Monroe refused to sign it.

The issues that engaged the Convention were the extension of suffrage, election by the people of officers of the government which were now appointed by the Legislature or the Governor, reform of the County Court system which was in fact a monopoly of the privileged, and readjustment of the basis of representation in the legislature. This last issue bid fair to tear the State apart. The slave-owning tobacco and cotton planters of the Tidewater strove to maintain the "combination of persons and property" basis, which counted one-third of their slaves as part of the population. The westerners who owned comparatively few slaves demanded representation based upon the white population only, and the same in all areas of the State.

Another item of sharp contention was an age limit to be set for a seat in the Senate. There had been no such requirement when Randolph had gone to Congress at the age of twenty-seven. Now the innovators would say how old a man must be to hold office. He rose in indignation at the suggestion that a gentleman had not reached the age of statesmanship until he became thirty years old.

It is said that at this time Randolph's devotion for the old Chief Justice "amounted almost to idolatry." Randolph's

sarcasm became so bitter that men began to hesitate to engage him in public debate. But when Marshall spoke, Randolph's rebuttal was tempered with courtesy.

When argument on the basis of representation built up
to an impasse, Marshall spoke for compromise, suggesting
"an exact compound of both schemes" which would count
the whole white population, not just freeholders, and three-
tenths of the colored, bond or free. He hailed the first sign of
willingness to adjust differences "with as much joy as the
inhabitant of the polar regions hails the reappearance of the
sun after his long absence of six long tedious months. Can
these appearances prove falacious? Is it a meteor we have
seen and mistaken for that splendid luminary which dis-
penses light and gladness throughout creation? It must be
so if we cannot meet on middle ground. If we cannot meet
on the line which divides us equally, then take the hand
of friendship and MAKE an equal compromise."

Delegates and spectators knew that the old statesman had
gone far toward middle ground when he relinquished freehold suffrage. But, he said, "Give me a constitution which
shall be received by the people, a constitution in which I
can consider their different interests to be duly represented,
and I will take it, though it may not be that which I would
most approve."

"Sir," answered Randolph, "I am not a prophet or a seer,
but I will venture to predict that your New Constitution, if
it shall be adopted—does not last twenty years. . . . If it
were a proper subject for betting, and I was a sporting
character, I believe I would take ten against. . . . Sir, how
often must I repeat that change is not reform. . . . I have
no favor for this Constitution. I shall vote against its adoption, and I shall advise all the people of my district to set
their faces—aye—and their shoulders against it. . . . Numbers," moaned the silvery voice, "and numbers alone are
to regulate all things in political society. . . . We have
capitulated to King Numbers."

Shortly after Christmas the Convention moved from the
Capitol to the Baptist Church which stood a few yards down
the hill from Monumental Church. Spectators had be-

come so numerous that it was feared the gallery of the Hall
of the House of Delegates could not safely hold the weight
of the crowd. James Madison and the two Marshalls were
often seen walking down the hill together. Tom Marshall
became delegate from Fauquier early in January.

On January fourteenth, the new Constitution, enrolled
on parchment of the largest size, was brought into the Convention and presented to the Chair, Philip Barbour, ready
for his signature. But John Randolph was not through with
it. He at once arose and said it was as plain as any proposition
in Euclid—Sir, it is plainer—that only to the freeholders
qualified to vote under the old Constitution should the new
document be submitted for ratification or rejection. Voters
had elected delegates only to consider revision of the old
one. When the ballot was taken by ayes and noes, Giles
and Benjamin Watkins Leigh stood with Randolph and
twenty-five others for the old freehold right of suffrage. The
two Marshalls and James Madison were among the sixty-
six who would at once accept extended suffrage.

Polly thought it very proper for the Reverend Mr. Croes
of the Episcopal Church to dismiss the Convention with a
prayer that members would separate with a spirit of charity
and friendly feelings.

At the last moment Randolph had put one more motion
before the Convention, a resolution praising Philip Barbour for his impartiality, dignity and distinguished ability
in facilitating the dispatch of business from the Chair. Polly
nodded her head approvingly, but wanted to know what
the company had said about Tom's father. This caused
Tom to give that laugh compounded of his mother's sweetness and his father's joy. Why, the Chief Justice and Colonel
Monroe and Mr. Madison together were the keystone upon
which the conflicting parties depended for unity. Debaters
frequently spoke of these three as patriarchs who honored
the Convention with their presence. But Tom could tell his
mother this thing: his father had compromised, but had saved
the State from unlimited manhood suffrage. For voting
there were still property qualifications, or a record of responsible housekeeping had to be shown. Still only white males

who had reached the age of twenty-one were allowed a ballot. But Randolph was not happy. He went home muttering,
"A king may make a peer. Only God can make a gentleman."

Now January was well on its way out. The Supreme
Court had sat three weeks without the Chief Justice. Marshall had to be off for Washington as soon as Robin could
be got ready to accompany him.

CHAPTER XXVI

Eighteen-Thirty

THE MARSHALL HOUSE in Richmond settled down as an old house should when life is busy elsewhere. The mansion was showing its age, for Polly could not stand the odor of new paint or the sound of a hammer. It made her nervous to see a servant washing a window. But the household brass shone. An old Negro could sit on a box all day polishing brass as contentedly as if he were polishing his way up the Golden Stairs. Polly never demurred at that labor. She often stood watching it silently, not knowing what she thought, just watching a shining road reach upward.

When in 1830 Court opened in Washington, there was another empty place in the circle of Marshall friends. Associate Justice Bushrod Washington had died on January fourth in Philadelphia, while the Virginia Convention was in session. Many great men died in Philadelphia, for the best physicians practiced there. On the Bench only Marshall was left of the old Federalist regime. Valiantly he resumed his leadership, more formal now since the Justices no longer lodged in the same house. Judges Story, Baldwin and Thompson clung to the old companionship at a table with Marshall at its head. After a few days there Marshall wrote Polly:

Washington Jan 31th 1830

My dearest Polly

Everything goes on as usual. I take my walk in the morning, work hard all day, eat a hearty dinner & sleep sound at night, and sometimes comb my head before I go to bed. While this operation is performing I always think with tenderness of my sweet barber in Richmond. It is the most delightful sentiment I have. Edward I doubt not has informed you of his fine large boy, & that Rebecca is as well as could be expected. He seems to be quite as proud as I was at the birth of our first born. Thus the world goes on.

I dined on tuesday with the President, in a very large mixed company. I sat by Mrs. Donalson, the President's niece & found her a very agreeable and lady like woman. She is I believe popular, but not so popular as Mrs. Madison was. I saw Tom Francis about a

317

week past, but I am so occupied that I believe he thought I neglected
him. I certainly saw very little of him. He has now gone to visit his
brother. Judges Johnson & Mclean do not live with us, in consequence of which we cannot carry on our business as fast as usual.
Judge Thompson is sick. The rest of us are very well. I have heard
no word respecting you since I parted from you; but hope dear hope
paints you to my imagination as in good health & happy.

I have I fear bad news from Potomac. I wrote to my tenant Mr.
Sprigg a letter which I hoped would produce my rent but his letter
brought neither money nor promise. My other tenant at Anderson's
bottoms seems to expect to bring me in debt. One of my neighbours
claims a valuable part of my land. Thus it fares with those who do
not look after their own affairs.

It is only from you my dearest Polly that I always find things better
than I had expected. Farwell my dearest your happiness is the
constant prayer of your ever

affectionate
J Marshall

Portraits of Marshall at this time show that his hair had
become gray and thin. It would not have been much of a
task for Polly to keep it smooth now. It was never Marshall's
grooming that gave him prestige. Young James A. Seddon,
who was a spectator in the Court this year, wrote of the
Chief Justice: "I saw him in the Supreme Court. . . . in the
dignity of his official robes and central position and with all
the interesting surroundings of his bretheren of the Bench,
the illustrious Bar, and of the distinguished audience of
strangers and public men. He presided in simple majesty,
with perfect ease and naturalness of manner; without a trace
of ostentation or self-consciousness of position. Amiability
and firmness blended admirably in his expression, which
alone seemed to guide and control, without need of utterance, the order and proceedings of the court."

When President Jackson reduced White House drawing-
rooms to democracy, members of the Supreme Court and
Senate became Washington society. The parlours of the
beautiful Mrs. Edward Livingston, wife of the Senator from
Louisiana, became the rendezvous of "the wise and fashionable." Justices and Senators with their wives and daughters
gathered there in the elegance that had not forgotten the

regal salons of Europe. Dinners of Secretaries, too, were handsome and decorous, and could be selective in their invitations. Marshall wrote Polly about his evening at the Van Burens':

Washington Feb. 14th 1830
My dearest Polly

I have nothing to tell you but the splendid dinner parties to which we are invited. On friday we dined with the Secretary of State who gave a dinner to a young lady from Charleston just married to a nephew of the President. I sat between her and Mrs. Livingston of Louisiana, a very fine woman indeed with whom I was very much pleased. The bride appeared to be quite happy and to be glad that she was married. We dined after six and sat at the table till after eight. When we retired to the sitting room three young Ladies who professed a great desire to be acquainted with the Judges were introduced to me, and you would have been quite surprised to see how gay spritely and gallant the wine made me. Yesterday I dined with the British minister. He always gives most excellent dinners & very superior wine, but we had no Ladies. It was some compensation for this deficiency that we sat down to table but an hour sooner than when we dined with the secretary of state. I hope very sincerely that we shall not be invited out again, as I greatly prefer remaining at home and attending to our business.

I find the influenza as prevalent here as it was in Richmond. Three of our Judges are laid up with it—not so as to prevent their going to court, but so as to prevent their going to dinner parties. Judge Duval is carried home by a relapse of his son.

I had a letter two or three days past from James. All well. Edward, he says, is the most delighted Father he ever saw. I suspect he saw one that was quite as much delighted when he looked in the glass.

I do not expect to hear from you till after the 22d. I shall be very impatient to know how you pass through the celebration of that day, and what news you collect at the farm.

Farewell my dearest wife. Your happiness is the constant prayer of your affectionate

J Marshall

Was Polly surprised that wine and three young ladies made her husband "gay spritely and gallant?" Or did she smile slightly, and then close her eyes over tears, dimly grateful that his life was still abundant?

Edward's first child was born on January seventeenth of this year, and named John Marshall. At this time James Keith

Marshall had three sons and two daughters, one named Maria Willis, and one, Mary Ambler. Eventually he had twelve children. Four of his five sons served in the army that marched to oppose military invasion of the State of Virginia. The fifth was chosen to stay at Leeds Manor to protect and feed women, children and slaves.

Polly still fled the noise of celebration on Washington's birthday. At the farm, smokeshouses were redolent of plenty. Pastures were turning green. A few lambs bounced among the ewes fenced into the house yard, and peach buds were bronzy pink. Here resurgent life brought Polly wistful silence. She returned to Richmond depressed and fatigued. When Marshall heard about it, the news had been softened by a youthful writer. He wrote Polly cheerily:

Washington Feb. 28th 1830

My dearest Polly

I was very much relieved yesterday at receiving a letter from our Grand daughter. Though she said you were indisposed, she mentioned it in such a manner as to convince me that the indisposition was slight and would yield to the sun shine we have had since. I had been a good deal alarmed at not receiving the letter a day sooner. I have been accustomed to hear from you so regularly on your return from Chiccahominy that my fears got the better of me and I became extremely uneasy. Our Grand daughters letter removed those fears. Tell her I am much obliged by it, and am much pleased also with the letter and at the neat lady like hand in which it is written. I am only sorry for one piece of intelligence she gives me—it is that her cousin John has had a relapse.

I have just received a letter from James. All well in Fauquier. He has sold his horse for $1000—a sum of money which will be quite convenient to him.

I have looked with the more pleasure at the bright sun we have been favored with for the few days past because I have believed that it would tempt you to take those rides which are necessary for your health.

Mr. Story has been laid up for a week under the hands of the Doctor; but is now up again and attending court.

Farewell my dearest Polly
I am your ever affectionate
J Marshall

There were ten Marshall granddaughters at this time,

eight of whom might have achieved a lady-like handwriting. The letter may have been written by Tom's motherless Agnes who had been often in Richmond. More probably it was from Mary's oldest daughter Mary, now fifteen years old. Marshall seems to be sure that Polly knows who it was. Also she could indentify which of the four cousins John was in bad health.

One thousands dollars for a Leeds Manor horse!

In the fresh bright hour of a March morning Marshall writes again to Polly:

Washington March 7th [1830]

My dearest Polly

I am just returned from my mornings walk of three miles and all my brethren are fast locked in sleep in their rooms. I steal a few minutes from my business which I devote to you. While thus employed, my imagination transports me to Richmond and I participate in all your little solicitudes. I picture to myself everything which passes between the time fo your coming down stairs and breakfast, and wish I could breakfast with you. I was about to say that I feared the morning was too unpromising to admit of your riding out, but I recollect that you do not ride on sunday. We have had so much bad weather that I am apprehensive you have not taken as much exercise as is necessary for health. I must exhort you a little on this subject.

I dined yesterday with my old friend Mr. Swan, and except that the dinner was not on the table till six every thing was delightful. Mr. Story remained at home. He thinks he is not well enough to dine out. I had some conversation with Mr. Mercer about our nephew William. You know he is engaged in Miss Mercers school. He has I am told given over preaching. I fancy he did not succeed well in the pulpit.

Tom Francis took his seat in the stage but a few days past for Kentucky. I thought he would have preferred staying in this country, and was a little apprehensive at one time that he intended to do so. I fear he has found more of pain than pleasure in his visit. Mr. Coleman who married our niece Lucy has been to see me. He is in Congress and is a strong Jackson man. Our nephew Tom son of Humphrey, is an equally strong Clayite and is I am told to be brought forward in opposition to Mr. Coleman at the next election. The Kentucky part of our family is I find a good deal divided in par-

ty politics and of course not very harmonious. I am sorry for it. Party
success is but a poor compensation for family feuds.

Farewell my dearest, I am
your ever affectionate
J Marshall

Richmonders had a saying: "As pious as an Ambler," and
Polly kept the Sabbath according to her father's discipline.
The horses were not hitched on Sunday, nor was a slave
made to work on Sunday except in the kitchen or the nursery. In 1830 Polly no longer attended church. It is remembered that on Sunday mornings now, after breakfast, the
Chief Justice would gather his tiny wife into the same chair
with himself, and together they would read Morning Service from the American Book of Common Prayer.

"Our nephew William" again, son of Dr. Louis Marshall
of Kentucky, is now twenty-seven. Shortly after Marshall's
talk with Mr. Mercer, William took up the study of law,
which proved to be the path that fit his feet. For he acquired
the reputation of being an able jurist, becoming Chancellor
of Baltimore and later United States District Attorney, which
office he held during the years in which his brother-in-law
was leading the Army of Northern Virginia. It is said that
his wife Ann tried to dissuade her brother from resigning
from the Federal Army. When she died, in 1864, William
made his way westward, a brokenhearted man without a
foothold on Fairfax lands.

"Nephew Tom son of Humphrey" and Marshall's sister
Mary, did defeat the Jackson man, his cousin Lucy Cole-
man's husband, for a seat in Congress in 1831. This Tom
Marshall married the most beautiful woman in Kentucky,
Eliza Price, but she was a niece of Henry Clay, who car-
ried a scar from a duel with her father-in-law.

"Tom Francis," whose name was Thomas Francis Marshall, was also a son of Dr. Louis Marshall, and like his
father had no use for Henry Clay. He had been in Washington to observe the proceedings of Congress. Being a
strong unionist, there is no wonder that he found more of
pain than pleasure in his visit. It is certain that when he and
the Chief Justice met briefly they enjoyed exclaiming over

the terrible state of the country with so many radicals in
Congress and in the administration.

John Quincy Adams talked of secession as if it were just
around the corner. Congress was passing tariff laws that so
irked the cotton-growing states that talk of secession became
louder in the South than it had been in the North. That
intriguing gentleman from South Carolina, Vice President
Calhoun, was warning the Southern States against oppres-
sion by Northern legislators, using that dangerous word,
"Nullification." The North and West now held the weight
of representation in Congress. Differences of politics were
so sharply drawn that the country seemed to be three separate parts, while at its head that proud democrat, President
Jackson, was showing the fist of personal power.

It was well that Tom Francis returned to Kentucky
when he did; for things grew worse. His State was uncon-
stitutionally printing paper money. Georgia was violating
the contract by which she had assigned territory to the Cherokee Indians. An injunction from the Chief Justice of the
Supreme Court of these United States to the State of
Georgia was answered by a resolution of the Georgia State
Legislature ordering her Governor and state officers to disregard any mandate of the Supreme Court and denouncing
the Chief Justice for a "flagrant violation of her rights."
Strange to say, the President of the United States seemed
to approve of this defiance.

To the implication by counsel that the State of Georgia
might be impelled by force to obey the edicts of the Supreme Court, the Chief Justice replied that physical force
was "questionable interposition" which was too patently "the
exercise of political power to be within the judicial department." Partisan cries of rights and wrongs were swarming
like hornets from a nest struck from a woodland tree.

On the other hand, Tom Francis might have derived some
comfort if he had stayed in Washington long enough to see
Daniel Webster rise up in court like a giant shaking off
Lilliputians, and answer a challenge of the Supreme Court's
usurpation of States' power. "So long," he said, "as the
Court maintains its talents, its integrity, and its independ-

ence, the great constitutional interests of the States are safe. If the Court should be broken down and the places on the Bench filled with ignorant men, violent partisans and desperate politicians, the strength and security will be undermined, and the very first serious convulsion that occurs will endanger the very existence of the Republic."

Tom Francis would not have believed that the high Bench could ever be filled with partisans and politicians, but his uncle knew better. Marshall was privately thinking of retirement, delaying only because he dreaded the appointment of a Republican in his place. He was longing for the tranquility of his farm, and the affection of his fellow citizens in Richmond without the stab of party dissension.

At the end of March Marshall returned to his home in Richmond where a geranium plant on Polly's window sill tempted him to pinch a leaf, and chuckle at the memory of a wide blue dress on a narrow little girl in the ballroom of the Palace in Williamsburg, and then to turn and touch the fashionable muslin cap that crowned that same blessing of his life.

Summer of 1830 crept into the Marshall garden and went untrimmed on its lush way. Trespassing morning glories trumpeted from ragged hedges. Picket gates lost their hinges and swung agape for friend and dog. For the servants, too, were old. On the bench around the great oak, the master of the estate sat in patient enjoyment of family and friends, who were irresistably drawn to join him there.

All unknown to these friends a new experience had descended upon Marshall. For the first time in his life he was suffering a nagging pain. No longer could he throw his quoit without clenching his fist afterwards. Only Polly knew of this pain. All Summer while the States fumed, she watched him managing his farm more and more from his office. She knew he was half sick when reluctantly he left for the upper country. His nephews there were having problems with the uneasy Fairfax titles.

One September evening, on his way to sit in the District Court at Frederick, he stopped at McGuire's Hotel in Winchester. Dusk was drawing a curtain across the windows of the common room where four young gentlemen lounged, grumbling about the fallacy of religion. As Marshall drew his chair up to a table, he heard one of them exclaim that Christianity was just a long established prejudice without a leg of reasonableness to stand on. One after another they demolished faith with sweeping defiance.

As Marshall listened, was there an echo of Polly, wailing in his heart, "I cannot find Him, I cannot find Him." So devout and yet so shaken! He must have smiled, for one of the young men suddenly asked, "Well, old man, what do you think of these things?"

It is said that Marshall got up from his chair as if he would leave the room, but then sat down again a little nearer the debaters, with his hands clenched on his knees. It may be that in this moment, as so often under his thinking tree, a pattern fell into place. For his hands relaxed, and as quietly as one speaks to a child, as humbly as one acknowledges the presence of God, he talked to those sophisticated gentlemen, quoting not only Holy Writ, but the religious philosophers of France, Greece, Germany and England. One of the young men afterwards said that it was as if a beam of light had slowly spread through the room, that to describe it would be to attempt to paint sunbeams. They listened, asking questions, until the innkeeper's oil gave out, and they groped their way to bed in darkness which had become a priceless gift of stars and rest. In the courtroom next day, they were at first aghast to see who had been their teacher, and then elated that such a radiant mind would judge their causes.

Chapter XXVII

"Farewell, My Dearest Polly"

THEN A STAR led Christmas Day to the Marshall house, a quiet house lit with the love of two old people. Granddaughters stepped in to touch Polly's face with cold rosy cheeks, and with laughing protest to catch their grandfather's hand as it went to his pocket. Grandsons made no protest, eagerly accepting the dollars, giving in return deep-voiced reassurance that they would be discreetly spent. Mrs. Martyr hovered around, pointing with obvious secrecy to cupboards where oranges and nuts might be hidden. And when the short day drew on its travelling robe of crimson and purple, old servants puttered in to light oil lamps, and to say good night with respectful affection. Gradually the house went to sleep.

But the Chief Justice must have been restless. For when Congress had opened in the fall, he and his associate Justices had been violently assailed in resolutions to pass laws designed to deprive the Supreme Court of its constitutional duty to review State laws which might endanger the national honor. The 1831 session of the Supreme Court would be one of the most difficult in its history. Before he left for Washington, snow was flying as softly as a touch of the Hand that was and is and evermore shall be.

Early in the session the Chief Justice, in effect upholding a State law, dismissed a land claimant's case brought on from the Kentucky court, with a statement of the High Court's attitude in this clash of powers. He said: "We have been admonished of the jealousy with which the States of the Union view the revising power intrusted by the Constitution and the laws of the United States to this tribunal. To observations of this character the answer uniformly given has been that the Judicial Department is marked out by law. We must tread the direct and narrow path prescribed for us. As this Court has never grasped at ungranted jurisdiction, so will it never, we trust, shrink from the exercise of that which is conferred upon it."

Then Marshall trudged back to his rooms through snow that was so dirty where man had trod, so beautiful on the roof tops, so wholesome on the fields of winter wheat. Changing his wet shoes, he sat down to write to Polly:

Washington Jany 30th 1831

My dearest Polly

I had the pleasure of hearing today from Colo. Lambert that you were in your usual health and that our friends in Richmond were generally well. He says you are pretty well off for snow though you have not quite so much as we have. The slays are still traversing the streets in every direction and the snow of yesterday is still on the roofs of the houses.

I believe I told you in my last that I was to dine with the minister of France on tuesday. I did so and had a very excellent dinner but rather a dull party. Neither the minister nor his lady could speak English and I could not speak French. You may conjecture how far we were from being sociable. Yesterday I dined with Mr. Van Buren the secretary of State. It was a grand dinner and the secretary was very polite, but I was rather dull through the evening. I make a poor return for these dinners. I go to them with reluctance and am bad company while there. I hope we have seen the last, but I fear we must encounter one more. With the exception of these parties my time was never passed with more uniformity. I rise early, pore over law cases, go to court and return at the same hour and pass the evening in consultation with the Judges. Visitors sometimes drop in upon us, but their visits are short and we always return them by a card.

I saw Mr. Robinson yesterday evening and had the pleasure of hearing from him that my sister Colston and family were in good health.

Farewell my dearest wife. Your health and happiness are my constant prayer. Your affectionate

J Marshall

Marshall may have been dull at some dinners, but he came home from one on February seventh in such gay spirits that he had to tell Polly about it:

Washington Feb 7th 1831

My dearest Polly

I have seen—who do you think I have seen? Guess—I am sure you will not guess the person and I will therefore tell you without keeping you longer in delightful suspense. I have seen Mrs. Sedgwick, the author of Hope Leslie. I called on her today, a compliment I pay very few ladies, and she thanked me for it. She is an agreeable, unaffected, not very handsome lady, but not the reverse, of about thirty. I was surprised, though I should not tell her so, at her remaining unmarried. I am sure she would have no objection to a respectable good tempered husband, and I heartily wish her one. I was pleased with her and shall read her new novel with the more pleasure for having seen her.

We are still bound up in snow and ice. The mail does not arrive regularly and I know nothing of what is passing in Richmond. I cling however to the hope that my friends are well, and that my dear wife especially continues in a state of undisturbed quiet and of reasonable happiness. For myself I am too busy to be unhappy. Except that I do not take my usual exercise, I pass my time as I always do in Washington. This winter is just like the last so far as respects myself, and the last was just like a dozen of its predecessors. Everybody says it is exceptionally cold and I agree that what everybody says must be true.

I suppose you have heard that we have lost our marshal. Poor Ringold is out of office, and I greatly fear that his family and himself will be distressed. He has just left us. Brother Story and myself condole with him very sincerely and he is grateful to us for our friendly regard.

Farewell my dearest Polly. That you may be happy is the constant prayer of your affectionate

J Marshall

On the back of this letter there is evidence that the Chief Justice was still plagued with lost papers. He writes a note to "My dear Son," and as the original paper was preserved with other papers of Edward Carrington Marshall, it may be presumed that he was the son Marshall addressed:

My dear Son

Mr. Storrs lent me a critique on our declaration of independence written by a gentleman in England in 1776 which he values very highly as it is curious and is the only copy in the United States. Its loss cannot be supplied, and I would not lose it for 100$—indeed not for 1000 I put it in an old candle box in the office in which I proposed to bring some books and papers with me to Washington. The morning I left Richmond it was necessary to change the box for a smaller, and in the hurry of taking out papers I left this pamphlet behind. Mr. Storrs has asked me for it and I am beyond measure mortified at not having brought it. Will you examine the papers remaining in the box for this pamphlet and write to me immediately

stating the results of the search. If you find it and meet with any
person coming to Washington with whom it may be safely trusted
I will thank you to inclose it to me. If you meet with no person I
do not want it to be trusted to the mail till the roads get better.

Your affectionate Father
J Marshall

The session over which Marshall presided after writing
this letter was one of the most colorful in the history of the
Supreme Court. It was the day of feathered hats and silk
dresses for the ladies. It was the day of skin caps and leather
breeches for Cherokee Indians, of fringed jackets and moc-
casins for frontiersmen, and for the newsmen, of long slim
broadcloth trousers and coats with lapels rolling back to
show modish stocks. These were crowded together in an
audience whose emotions were assailing the law as recklessly
as ever they had in the Burr affair, while Marshall's fixed
purpose for the judiciary was decision by law, and not by
heart.

The case before this court was The Cherokee Nation *vs*
The State of Georgia. Marshall described it thus: "This bill
is brought by the Cherokee nation, praying an injunction to
restrain the State of Georgia from the execution of certain
laws of that State which as is alleged go directly to an-
nihilate the Cherokees as a political society, and to seize
for the use of Georgia the lands of the nation which have
been assured to them by the United States in solemn treaties
repeatedly made and still in force.

"If courts were permitted to indulge their sympathies, a
case better calculated to excite them can scarcely be imagined. A people once numerous, powerful, and truly independent, found by our ancestors in the quiet and uncon-
trolled possession of an ample domain, gradually sinking
beneath our superior policy, our arts, our arms, have yielded
their lands by successive treaties, each of which contains a
solemn guarantee of the residue, until they retain no more
of their formerly extensive territory than is deemed necessary to their comfortable subsistence. To preserve this remnant, the present application is made. . . . The question is
has this court jurisdiction?"

For the Indians William Wirt argued the case with so much pathos and classical eloquence that even the Indians were seen to have tears on their coppery cheeks. Story says that he saw tears on the face of the Chief Jutice. Those tears closed the argument, for there was no rebuttal. The Governor of Georgia refused to honor the Court's subpoena.

Wirt had presented the case as a foreign nation against a State of the Union, which caused a difference of opinion between Marshall and his friend Story. On this issue Story and Thompson joined in dissenting from the majority opinion of the Court. When the Chief Justice stood up to deliver that decision it is said that his voice and manner were more than usually gentle and courteous.

The Cherokee nation, declared the decision, was not a foreign nation. "The relation of the Indians to the United States is marked by peculiar and cardinal distinctions which exist nowhere else." They were "a domestic dependent" people, acknowledging themselves "in their treaties to be under the United States," in a "state of pupilage." The case was not a matter of State laws versus national authority. This was a matter of a national contract establishing a separate people on land that the State of Georgia had suddenly coveted. The Supreme Court had no jurisdiction. But the administration had a duty to protect the terms of a national contract. Story and Thompson held that Indians in such a case must be dealt with as a foreign nation.

The Press liked this decision of the Supreme Court. A Whig paper, the *New York Daily Advertizer,* picked up the rumor that Marshall intended to retire, and remarked editorially that the country was appalled at the prospect, which would be "one of the greatest Calamities that could at this time befall the United States. In our estimation, he is, beyond question, the most important public character of which the Union can now boast. Probably much more that is interesting to the welfare of the Country may depend upon the continuance of his judicial life for some time to come, than upon that of any other individual in existence. . . . The safety of the very Union might be hazarded by the appointment of a successor. . . . The mischief which a

nullifying Chief Justice might introduce into the execution
of the laws and the administration of justice would be
boundless and in the highest degree fatal to the peace and
safety of the Union."

As the session drew to a close the justices were grumbling
about their customary lodgings. Mr. Brown, in whose house
they had boarded for so many years, had not kept up with
modern conveniences. Several of the Judges were talking
of boarding elsewhere in 1832. Marshall says that he withdrew from the discussion for he felt serious doubts that he
would be with his brethren next term. He did not choose
to permit his wishes or convenience to weigh a feather in
the permanent arrangements of the Bench, since he was "a
bird of passage whose continuance with you cannot be long."

At home in Richmond he writes some verses for a lady's
Album. Now he is willingly a "captive ear" listening to
March blasts against the crown glass panes. Now he sinks
without resistance into the big chair before the cupids on
his mantelpiece, content with "elegance refined."

> Oh think not, lady, that the truant Muse
> Comes, at my bidding, to her wonted shrine;
> Thy gentle mandate she will not refuse,
> Though oft she *frowns* disdainfully at mine.
>
> In earlier days, when Love inspired the Lay,
> And Hope gave promise of bright, sunny hours
> I hailed the spring—and chiefly thee, sweet May!
> Month of the balmy breeze and fragrant flowers.
>
> But now that Friendship claims the altered line,
> And memory sadly would retrace the past;
> Though flowers may bloom, and vernal suns may shine,
> I woo thee, Winter! with thy freezing blast.
>
> 'Tis then, that striking on the captive ear,
> The thrilling harp with sweet effect recalls
> The woodland chase—the stag's pathetic tear;
> Or warrior-march in measured cadence falls.
>
> 'Tis then that freely flows the tide of song,
> Fraught with the gay or grave—as humour reigns;
> The willing soul, in fancy swept along,
> Lives in the raptures which the poet feigns.

> Then give me winter—better far than these,
> Than harp or song—the music of the mind;
> When social converse lends its power to please,
> And thought meets thought, with elegance refined.

As April unfurled Spring over Richmond, Marshall was so evidently in pain that his friends began to urge him to see a physician. But he said that he had no confidence in doctors. For upwards of thirty years he had watched them treating Polly to no avail, while he brought her out of her spells with the conjuration of laughing affection. Now, however, he was assailed with sweat-streaming pain, with no magic for it, and he had the circuit to travel. Sometimes he was prevailed upon to take a palliative, but the pain returned two-fold, and to his orderly mind that seemed unreasonable.

When he set out in his gig for the District Court in Raleigh, North Carolina, Polly made him a cushion to ease the trip which she knew would cause him much suffering. It was sheep shearing time on the Chickahominy farm. Did Oby bring her in a sack of wool, all boiled and sunned until it was fluffy and sweet? She prepared it, he says, as if his heart was wrapped in the comforting attention.

Raleigh May 12th 1831

My dearest Polly

I reached this place yesterday evening less fatigued than I should have been had you not been so attentive as to prepare me a good cushion. Just as I was preparing to go to bed some person thundered at my door which happened to be locked. I opened it and in jumped a young lady who gave me such a smack as I have not received in many a day. She called me Unkle and expressed great satisfaction at seeing me. She had heard that I was sick and intended to resign which she had been very sorry indeed to hear. She then entered into a long desertation about her misfortunes and I was seriously apprehensive that she did not mean to leave until I should be impolite enough to fall asleep in my chair. I was however very grave and she found out that I was fatigued and took her leave with the opinion that she would call me again this evening. She will be certainly as good as her word since I will have a bank note the less after seeing her. She is my old acquaintance returned. The long cases will not come on so that you will see me the next week. I write because I know you wish to hear what for a journey I had. It has been cold enough but in other respects not disagreeable.

Your own
J Marshall

It would be interesting to discover the tragedies of the bouncing young lady who kept the Chief Justice awake. He seems to have known how to soothe whatever worries she had. By the year 1831 the Marshalls and Amblers had taken root far and wide in the South and West. At that time no Marshall had settled further north than Baltimore.

On his return to Richmond, Marshall was called upon to serve on a committee in the State capital, again to consider improvements to the Richmond harbour. Virginians were protesting that to use Federal funds in such a project would be to condone Federal interference with States Rights. Marshall could not sit long to argue the matter, for, he says, his nerves, digestion and head were seriously uncomfortable. The medicines he took made him more ill than ever. He felt completely unfit for business. He wrote Story that he was cogently tempted to resign his high office, for he found himself unequal to the effective consideration of any subject.

Doctors must have found him an exasperating patient, for he later confessed that it was his own fault that Richmond physicians had not been able to diagnose his ailment. He probably concealed his symptoms, diverting the doctors with politics, which would have been a handsome bone of contention between the Chief Justice and the Richmond medical profession.

The hot season dragged on. Marshall's suffering became such that he would move only when it was necessary. Often he was seen sitting under his thinking tree, not in the familiar attitude of meditation, but of despair and exhaustion. There the news was brought him of the death of James Monroe at the home of his daughter in New York, on July fourth. To a sufferer, bereavement takes on a shade of envy. Marshall could smile that Monroe had emulated his idol, Jefferson, even in the choice of a day to die.

Finally the Chief Justice was prevailed upon to seek medical advice from the nation's foremost surgeon, Dr. Philip Syng Physick, in Philadelphia. The latter part of September he took the painful journey, and from his boarding place wrote Polly:

Philadelphia Oct 6th 1831

My dearest Polly

Doctor Physic has employed the time since my arrival at this place in examinations and inquiries as preparatory to making up his final opinion respecting the course to be pursued. He deliberates very much, is determined to do nothing rashly, and seems anxious to be perfectly master of my case. His intelligence, his extraordinary attention, and the deep interest he takes in my welfare, as well as the feeling he shows, have acquired my perfect confidence, and give me the most exalted opinion of his skill and goodness. He seems to be idolized in Philadelphia, and I do not wonder at it.

I have just come out of his last examination, and I believe he has decided on the treatment of the disease. He has not however as yet commenced with it. I have most sanguine hopes of his being able to restore me. All that man can do I am sure he will do, and I flatter myself that his efforts will be successful. I anticipate with a pleasure which I know you will share the time when I may sit by your side by our tranquil fire & enjoy the happiness of your society without inflicting on you the pain of witnessing my suffering. But it will be a long tedious time before that period can arrive. The Doctor has not spoken definitely respecting the time, but I think I cannot be with you until the meeting of the circuit court on the 22d of Nov. if then.

I am treated with the most flattering attentions in Philadelphia. They give me pain, the more pain as the necessity of declining many of them may be ascribed to a want of sensibility. I mentioned to you the persevering earnestness with which Mr. Peters and his amiable family press me to take a room in his house. I have been equally pressed by Dr. Gillespie. All the gentlemen of the city, especially those of the bar have been most painfully solicitous to show their affectionate and respectful regards. These almost force me into movements which irritate my complaint. To day I am to receive a very flattering address from the young men of the city which will I ardently hope be the last.

I am not sure that the Governor may not require my subscription or a part of it for the [blotted] I forgot it or should have arranged it before my departure. May I trouble you to mention it to Mr. Harvie and to furnish him with any small sum that may be required.

I am not sure that some more lime and salt may not be necessary for steeping and [blotted]—ling my seed wheat. Should the overseer ask for any Oby can purchase it. The lime 2 [blotted] per barrel and the salt at the same price per sack.

Farewell my beloved wife. To hear that you are happy and in at least you usual health would be my greatest gratification.

My love to our friends

Your ever affectionate

J Marshall

The city of Philadelphia which always opened its heart to Marshall, now lifted his spirits with flattering attentions. He declined the invitation of the Bar Association for a dinner in his honor, but agreed to meet them in a body at the Court House. He also agreed to sit for a portrait by Henry Inman ordered by the Bar Association, an occupation that always gave Marshall pleasure. That the Peters family and Dr. Gillespie urged him to stay in their homes was no surprise to Polly. The Peters were staunch Federalists and eminent jurists and patriots. Polly remembered the mansion called Belmont set in a beautiful English park where three generations of Peters had lived.

Dr. Physick eventually diagnosed Marshall's ailment as stone in the bladder, and decided that an operation which he had perfected, and for which he had devised the instruments, was urgently needed. But for several years Dr. Physick had been partially retired due to his own bad health. He intended to turn the case over to his son-in-law, Dr. Jacob Randolph. Dr. Randolph wrote, "Taking all the circumstances into consideration, and knowing well this would be the last time he [Dr. Physick] would ever perform a similar operation, I felt desirous that he should finish with so distinguished an individual; and accordingly urged him to do it himself." Dr. Physick, thereupon, set October tenth as the day for an operation.

But on October twelfth, the patient was still waiting for the treatment. He employed the day in writing letters, turning occasionally from his well travelled desk to stretch his feet painfully toward the fire a male nurse kept blazing. It would be enlightening, and perhaps amusing, to call up the ghost of that nurse and find out what the conversation of a great master of the human heart was on the eve of the day that he expected would find him in the novel situation of being eased into eternity by a man trained in the process.

The lively curiosity and ready laugh of the Chief Justice, even in pain, must have provoked tales and prognostications, one upon another, until dutiful night closed down on the game.

Before he was tucked in with hot water bottles, Marshall had written at least three letters. To Polly he wrote:

My dearest Polly   Philadelphia Oct. 12th 1831

The rains of the last two or three days have confined Dr. Physick, whose health is delicate, to his house, and prevented my entering on the course he has prescribed. To day we see the sun and I hope his operations will begin. My room is now preparing and he has just left me with directions to take a tablespoonful of castor oil two hours after dinner. He encourages me with the expectation of being restored to perfect health, and my hopes are sanguine as usual. Every accomodation I can wish is afforded, and my own Landlady is extremely attentive to me. She has engaged one of the best male nurses in the city who now attends me altho he is not needed, and will do everything I can require. I still continue to receive the kindest attentions from all who see me, and have a prospect of being as comfortable as is compatible with my situation.

Cary Ambler called on me yesterday and left his card. I am sorry that I had stepped to the office of a portrait painter who is employed by the gentlemen of the bar to take my portrait. I did wrong to go out, but could not resist the desire to comply with their request. The Doctor has laid his interdict on my going out again. I have just learned this morning that Edward Ambler is in town. I am sorry that I cannot go to see him. Dr. Physick I hope will be able to place him once more on his legs.

I have just received a long and very friendly letter from my brother Story. He speaks of coming to this place on purpose to see me. Mrs. Story I am told is still much depressed.

I do not wonder that people who have time hanging on their hands are fond of boarding houses. I find this quite agreeable. If I had my Richmond barber I should I think be quite contented.

I over eat myself every day inspite of the wise resolutions I continually form. The potatoes with butter and the sickle pears are irresistable. I must of course take [torn] thing solid, and after finishing my Bucks county fowl I think I will command myself as to the farther temptations which remain but I have never succeeded. In spite of myself I take pear after pear till I am almost ashamed of the number I have eaten.

My affectionate love to our friends
yours ever
J Marshall

The letter seems to have been hastily brought to an end, probably by the appearance of the landlady announcing that ex-Governor Giles of Virginia would like to see the Chief Justice. Upon the departure of this guest Marshall wrote to James Keith Marshall a letter intended for all the Marshall brothers.

Philadelphia Oct. 12th 1831

My dear Son

Mr. Giles will give you all the information respecting my health which it is in my power to communicate, but I wish to drop a line to my sons, & as Mr. Giles goes to your house I address it to you. I have been in this place a fortnight & have gone through several thorough examinations. The symptoms were such as to indicate different complaints, & several experiments were made before the Doctor suspected that I was afflicted with stone in the bladder. He then tried the sound & found reason to believe that this was my disease. Three days after the experiment was repeated and his suspicions were confirmed. Hoofbower recommended the usual operation which was delayed first by the difficulty of procuring a proper room, for Philadelphia is crowded to overflowing, & afterwards by the rains which confined Doctor Physick to his house. The weather clears up this morning & I have seen the Doctor. A family which occupies a very convenient room resigns it to me today (being about to leave town tomorrow) & it will soon be in readiness. If the weather continues fair the operation is to be performed tomorrow. I have the most sanguine hopes of being myself again. The Doctor inspires me with perfect confidence in both his skill & attention. I have never seen a medical gentleman who watched the symptoms with such vigilance, & listened to his patient with such patience, & showed so much feeling & solicitude respecting him. I submit myself to him with a certainty that he will do all that can be done to restore me.

My accommodations are as good as they can be. I have everything that can contribute to my comfort, & am as carefully attended to as can be. I hope therefore that in a fortnight now I shall be able to let my friends know that I count upon the restoration of my former strength & comfort with reasonable assurance of not being disappointed. Tell Major Ambler that his brothers, Edward & Cary are in Philadelphia. I have not seen them but hope that the Doctor will be enabled to put Edward once more on his legs.

Present me affectionately to all the families.
I am your affectionate Father
J Marshall

This letter was addressed to Morelands, the first residence

of James Keith Marshall on Leeds Manor. Construction on the present house was not begun until 1832. The Ambler brothers mentioned were the sons of Colonel John Ambler, once of Jamestown where his second wife, Lucy Marshall, lay in the shadow of the deserted church.

It seems that Marshall's spirits rose all day as he approached the possibility of relief from pain. He wrote to Joseph Story, no longer closing the door on the future. With a certainty that he would be there, Marshall took up the problem of lodgings for the Justices the next January. He would not, he told Story, object to staying in a house "half way between the Palace and Georgetown," but feared the situation would not suit the taste of the other brethren of the Bench. He told Story that he already felt stronger every day, and was even so much encouraged that he thought Judge Baldwin's politics had improved.

Dr. Randolph left an account of the operation performed next day: "It will readily be admitted that, in consequence of Judge Marshall's advanced age, the hazard attending the operation, however skillfully performed, was considerably increased. I consider it but an act of justice, due to the memory of that great and good man, to state, that in my opinion, his recovery was in great degree owing to his extraordinary self possession, and to the calm and philosophical views he took of his case, and the various circumstances attending it.

"It fell to my lot to make the necessary preparations. In the discharge of this duty, I visited him on the morning of the day fixed on for the operation, two hours previous to that at which it was to be performed. Upon entering his room, I found him engaged in eating his breakfast. He received me with a pleasant smile upon his countenance, and said, 'Well, Doctor, you find me taking breakfast, and I assure you I have had a good one. I thought it very probable that this might be my last chance, and therefore I was determined to enjoy it and eat heartily.' I expressed the great pleasure I felt at seeing him so cheerful, and said I hoped soon all would be happily over. He replied to this that he did not feel the least anxiety or uneasiness respecting the

operation or its result. He said he had not the slightest
desire to live, laboring under the sufferings to which he
was then subjected; that he was perfectly willing to take
all the chances of an operation, and he knew there were
many against him; and that if he could be relieved by it he
was willing to live out his appointed time, but if not, would
rather die than hold existence accompanied with the pain
and misery he then endured.

"After he had finished his breakfast, I administered to
him some medicine: he then enquired at what hour the
operation would be performed. I mentioned the hour of
eleven. He said, 'Very well; do you wish me now for any
purpose, or may I lie down and go to sleep?' I was a good
deal surprised at this question, but told him that if he could
sleep it would be very desirable. He immediately placed himself upon the bed and fell into a profound sleep, and continued so until I was obliged to rouse him to undergo the
operation.

"He exhibited the same fortitude, scarcely uttering a
murmur, throughout the whole procedure, which, from the
peculiar nature of his complaint, was necessarily tedious."

Dr. Randolph further wrote, "The Doctor performed the
operation with his usual skill and dexterity. . . . The result
of the operation was a complete success."

From Massachusetts, on October twenty-ninth, Joseph
Story wrote to Judge Peters: "Pray tell the Chief Justice
how deeply everybody here has been interested in his situation. He is loved and revered here beyond all measure,
though not beyond his merits. Next to Washington he stands
the idol of all good men. And who so well deserves it? I
look upon his judicial life as good now for at least six years
longer."

On November eighth, Marshall wrote Polly a letter of
which we have only a fragment:

I have at length risen from my bed and am able to hold a pen. The
most delightful use I can make of it is to tell you that I am getting
well . . . from the painful disease with which I have been so long
affected. . . . Nothing delights me so much as to hear from my
friends and especially from you. How much was I gratified at the

Courtesy of The Valentine Museum

CHIEF JUSTICE MARSHALL, 1831, one of several by Henry Inman. Original in Virginia State Library.

line from your own hand in Mary's letter. . . . I am much obliged by your offer to lend me money. I hope I shall not need it but can not as yet speak positively as my stay has been longer and my expenses greater than I had anticipated on leaving home. Should I use any part of it, you may be assured it will be replaced on my return. But this is a subject upon which I know you feel no solicitude. . . .

God bless you my dearest Polly love to all our friends
Ever your most affectionate
J Marshall

Two days later he wrote to Joseph Story: "I have had a most tedious confinement. At length, however, I leave my bed and walk across my room. This I do with a tottering feeble step. It is, however, hourly improving and I hope next week to take the boat for Richmond in time to open my court on the 22nd. Dr. Physick has added to consummate skill the most kind and feeling attention. I shall never forget him."

Dr. Physick refused to render Marshall a bill for his services. Marshall was so touched by this kindness that before leaving Philadelphia he ordered a handsome silver wine cooler for the surgeon "as a tribute of gratitude for restored health."

In Richmond Marshall had only about two weeks to sit with Polly by the parlour fire in the afternoons, to draw the paisley shawl closer about her shoulders when the street door opened for sons, or daughter, or grandchildren. Sisters Carrington and Fisher were always in the other room whispering. And daily the gentlemen of the town came to rejoice over the recovery of the old Chief. Sometimes he would tip out of the parlour to laugh with the children in the dining room where there was always cake in a drawer of the sideboard. But back to Polly's side he would go to watch the fragile lantern of her face light up when he reappeared. That she tarried on the threshold of death was clearly evident.

On December fourteenth he left her to go out to his office and answer a letter from the Reverend Mr. Gurley, executive Secretary of the American Society for Colonization of the Free People of Colour. Mr. Gurley was requesting the Chief Justice and ex-President Madison each to write for the press a statement which would counteract misrepresentations by non-slave holding States of the true beneficent purpose of the Society. Because of prejudice, funds from voluntary gifts were very low. Marshall drew his paper forward on his desk, nibbed his quill and wrote that "the present state of my family is such as to prevent my preparing anything for publication." Then he discussed the Constitutional power of the General Government to use the funds brought the treasury from sale of lands ceded by Virginia and other States, for he believed that national funds must eventually support in part this work so important to the safety of the whole Union. State Legislatures must pass "permanent laws" to give the Society pecuniary aid. Mr. Gurley could have read weariness in every line of this answer.

Again on December nineteenth, Marshall went out to his office to write to James Markham Marshall. This was a business letter concerned with the recent discovery of a will of Denny Martin Fairfax, which again disturbed the Fairfax titles. Marshall dallies with points of law as he writes, answering a question and then asking and answering it again, as if he were fending off some thought that he could not bear to put into writing.

Then in a last paragraph, like tears that can no longer be contained, the words flow from his quill. "My poor wife lies dangerously ill and has been so for more than a fortnight. She is confined to her bed and my fears are stronger than my hopes though the doctor thinks her rather better today."

It is certain that he folded and sealed this letter before blowing out the lamp and throwing a cloak over his shoulders. When the neighbours heard the office door close, they must have gone to the windows to watch until the house door opened, and for a minute the tall humped figure stood against lamplight. Then the door closed and silently the night watchman rounded the corner swinging his lantern.

Indoors, Marshall dropped his cloak for Robin to catch. He hugged the nearest grandchild, and reminded weeping Eliza that this was not the season for tears.

Then slowly, his great hand on the banister pulling him

up each step, he went to Polly's room, to sit in lamplight by her bed as he had done so many evenings. Presently the locket hung too heavily against the pulse in her throat. She pulled at the chain until he unfastened it. Brightly she watched while he locked it around his own neck.

On Christmas Day, with her hands in his she died. Greatness knelt to pray the Lord her soul to keep.

Once more J Marshall wrote to Polly. On Christmas Day a year later, when irrepressible gaiety of grandchildren broke through the surface of his sorrow and festive candlelight glittered in the wrinkles around his eyes, he went out to his office where Robin kept a strong fire going on the hearth. Around him in that room, piled on shelves, stacked on the floor and rustling with every wind of movement near the desk waited the history of his State. As he had done so many times before, he pushed aside all this public business, reaching under it for a clean sheet of paper. Then through tears he wrote:

This day of joy & festivity to the whole Christian world is to my sad heart the anniversary of the keenest affliction which humanity can sustain. While all around is gladness my mind dwells on the silent tomb, & cherishes the remembrance of the beloved object which it contains. On the 25th of December 1831 it was the will of Heaven to take to itself the companion who had sweetened the choicest part of my life, had rendered toil a pleasure, had partaken of all my feelings & was enthroned in the inmost recesses of my heart. Never can I cease to feel the loss & to deplore it. Grief for her is too sacred ever to be profaned on this day, which shall be during my existence devoted to her memory.

On the 3rd of January 1783 I was united by the holiest bonds to the woman I adored. From the hour of our union to that of our seperation I never ceased to thank Heaven for this its best gift. Not a moment passed in which I did not consider her as a blessing from which the chief happiness of my life was derived. This never dying sentiment, originating in love, was cherished by a long & close observation of as amiable & estimable qualities as ever adorned the female bosom.

To a person which, in youth, was very attractive, to manners uncommonly pleasing, she added a fine understanding & the sweetest temper which can accompany a just & modest sense of what was due herself.

I saw her first the week she attained the age of fourteen & was greatly pleased with her. Girls then came into company much earlier than at present. As my attentions, though without any avowed purpose, nor so open nor direct as to alarm, soon became ardent & assiduous her heart received an impression which could never be effaced. Having felt no prior attachment, she became, at sixteen, a most devoted wife. All my faults, and they were too many, could never weaken this sentiment. It formed a part of her existence. Her judgement was so sound & so safe that I have often relied upon it in situations of some perplexity. I do not recall ever to have regretted the adoption of her opinion. I have sometimes regretted its rejection. From native timidity she was opposed to everything adventurous, yet few females possessed more real firmness. That timidity so influenced her manners, that I could rarely prevail on her to display in company the talents I knew her to possess. They were reserved for her husband, & her select friends. Though serious as well as gentle in her deportment, she possessed a good deal of chaste, delicate & playful wit, and, if she permitted herself to indulge this talent, told her little story with grace, & could mimic very successfully the peculiarities of the person who was the subject. She had a fine taste for belle lettre reading, which was judiciously applied in the selection of pieces which she admired. This quality by improving her talents for conversation contributed not inconsiderably, to make her a most desirable & agreeable companion. It beguiled many of those winter evenings during which her protracted ill health & her feeble nervous system, confined us entirely to each other. I can never cease to look back on them with deep interest and regret. Time has not diminished & will not diminish this interest or this regret. In all the relations of life she was a model which those to whom it was given, cannot imitate too closely. As the wife, the mother, the mistress of a family & the friend, her life furnishes an example to those who could observe it intimately which will never be forgotten. She felt deeply the distresses of others & indulged the feeling liberally on objects she believed to be meritorious.

She was educated with a profound reverence for religion which she preserved to her last moment. This sentiment among her earliest & deepest impressions, gave a color to her whole life. Hers was the religion taught by the Savior of man. Cheerful, mild, benevolent, serious, humane, intent on self improvement & the improvement of those who looked to her for precept or example. She was a firm believer in the faith inculcated by the church in which she was bred, but her soft & gentle temper was incapable of adopting the gloomy & austere dogmas which some of its professors have sought to engraft on it.

I have lost her! And with her I have lost the solace of my life! Yet she remains still the companion of my retired hours,—still occupies my inmost bosom. When I am alone and unemployed, my mind unceasingly turns to her. More than a thousand times since the 25th of December 1831, have I repeated to myself the beautiful lines written by Gen. Burgoyne under a similar affliction, substituting Mary for Anna.

> Encompassed in an angel's frame,
>   An angel's virtues lay;
> Too soon did Heaven assert its claim
>   And take its own away.
> My Mary's worth, my Mary's charms
>   Can never more return.
> What now shall fill these widowed arms?
>   Ah, me! My Mary's urn!
>   Ah, me! Ah, me! My Mary's urn ! ! !

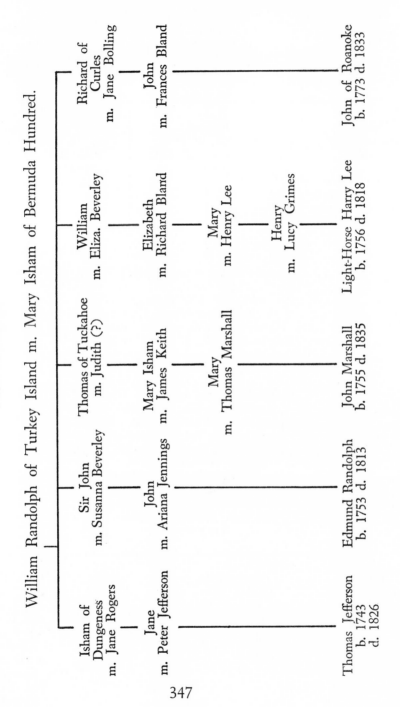

FIVE COUSINS

William Randolph of Turkey Island m. Mary Isham of Bermuda Hundred.

Isham of
Dungeness
m. Jane Rogers

Sir John
m. Susanna Beverley

Thomas of Tuckahoe
m. Judith (?)

William
m. Eliza. Beverley

Richard of
Curles
m. Jane Bolling

Jane
m. Peter Jefferson

John
m. Ariana Jennings

Mary Isham
m. James Keith

Elizabeth
m. Richard Bland

John
m. Frances Bland

Mary
m. Thomas Marshall

Mary
m. Henry Lee

Henry
m. Lucy Grimes

Thomas Jefferson
b. 1743
d. 1826

Edmund Randolph
b. 1753 d. 1813

John Marshall
b. 1755 d. 1835

Light-Horse Harry Lee
b. 1756 d. 1818

John of Roanoke
b. 1773 d. 1833

347

AMBLERS

Richard Ambler
b. Yorkshire, England, 1690, d. York Town, Virginia, 1766, m.
Elizabeth, daughter of Edward Jacqueline of Jamestown Island, 1724.

John	Edward	Jacquelin
d. without issue; inherited Jamestown estate which he left to his nephew namesake John of The Cottage	b. 1733, d. 1768, m. Mary Cary, d. 1782, at The Cottage	b. 1742, d. 1798; m. Rebecca Burwell, daughter of Nathaniel Burwell of Gloucester Cc Va.

Issue dying young

Three children dying before 1779
and
John (of The Cottage)
b. Jamestown Island, 1762,
d. Richmond, 1836, m. 1st. Frances
Armistead, 1782, d. 1787, leaving
two children, Edward and Mary Cary,
2nd, Lucy Marshall, 1791, d. 1795,
leaving one son, Thomas Marshall,
b. Jamestown Island, May 1792,
d. Fauquier Co., 1875; 3rd
Catherine Bush (Widow Norton), 1799,
whose son by her 1st marriage,
Dr. Daniel Norborne Norton,
m. two of Polly's nieces,
1st Lucy Ambler's daughter
Elizabeth Call (who had married 1st
Ann Ambler's son George Fisher),
2nd Ann Ambler's daughter
Lucy Fisher

Eliza	Mary Willis	Ann	Lucy
b. 1765, d. 1847, m. 1st William Brent. 2nd Edward Carrington	(called Polly) b. 1766, d. 1831, m. John Marshall	b. 1772, d. 1832, m. George Fisher had numerous posterity	b. 1776, d. 17 m. Daniel C: and died leav one daughte Elizabeth wh m. 1st her cou George Fishe 2nd Dr. .Nort widower of h cousin Elizabe Call Fisher

Three
children
dying before
the age of
ten

MARSHALLS

John Marshall, b. in Dublin, Ireland, a descendant of the brother of the Earl of Pembroke, signer of Magna Carta. Captain of cavalry in the army of King Charles I of England. Church of England supporter, he came to Virginia about 1650 to escape Cromwell's rule. Settled near Dumfries, an important seaport of Virginia. Fought in the Colony's Indian wars. Tombstone stood near Dumfries until 1861.

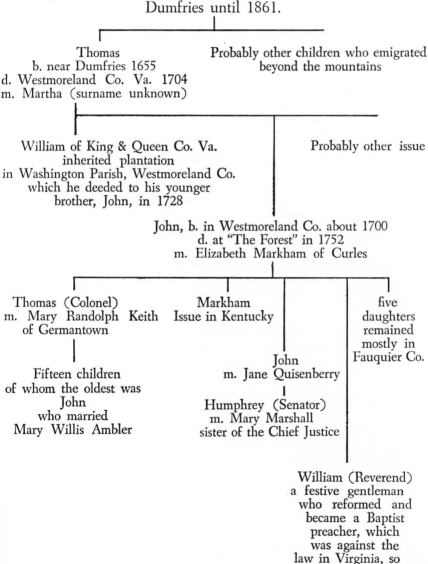

Thomas
b. near Dumfries 1655
d. Westmoreland Co. Va. 1704
m. Martha (surname unknown)

Probably other children who emigrated beyond the mountains

William of King & Queen Co. Va. inherited plantation in Washington Parish, Westmoreland Co. which he deeded to his younger brother, John, in 1728

Probably other issue

John, b. in Westmoreland Co. about 1700 d. at "The Forest" in 1752 m. Elizabeth Markham of Curles

Thomas (Colonel)
m. Mary Randolph Keith of Germantown

Fifteen children of whom the oldest was John who married Mary Willis Ambler

Markham
Issue in Kentucky

John
m. Jane Quisenberry

Humphrey (Senator)
m. Mary Marshall
sister of the Chief Justice

five daughters remained mostly in Fauquier Co.

William (Reverend) a festive gentleman who reformed and became a Baptist preacher, which was against the law in Virginia, so he moved to Kentucky

Fifteen Children of Colonel Thomas and Mary Keith Marshall

John, b. Germantown, Prince William County, Sept. 24, 1755.
d. Philadelphia, July 6, 1835.
m. Mary Willis Ambler (Polly).
Chief Justice of the United States.
Six children survived Polly. Two of these died before the Chief Justice.

Elizabeth, b. Germantown, 1758, d. Honeywood, Berkeley Co., Va. 1842.
m. at Polly's house, Rawleigh Colston, on Oct. 15, 1785.
Son Edward m. 1st, Jane, daughter of Charles Marshall. Son Thomas m. Eliza Fisher, niece of Polly. Daughter Susan m. Benjamin Watkins Leigh.
These three did their courting in Polly's parlour.

Mary, b. Germantown, 1757, d. Kentucky, 1817.
m. her cousin Humphrey Marshall (U.S. Senator) on one of his trips from Kentucky on business in the Capitol of Virginia, 1780.

Thomas (Captain) b. Germantown, 1761, d. Kentucky, 1817.
m. 1st, Susanna Adams who lived only one year. In Kentucky, m. Frances Kennon, 1790. Their daughter Eliza Colston m. Martin P. Marshall, son of Charles Marshall, after courting in Polly's parlour, 1819.

James Markham, b. Germantown, 1764, d. Happy Creek on Fairfax lands, 1848, m. Hester Morris, 1795; Lieutenant in Alexander Hamilton's regiment at battle of Yorktown. Son Robert Morris m. Lucy, daughter of Charles Marshall 1819.

Judith, b. 1766, The Hollow, m. George Brooke; daughters visited often in Polly's household.

William, b. Jan. 31, 1767, The Hollow, d. Richmond, 1815.
m. 1st, Alice Adams, had three children; 2nd, Mary Macon, had two children; 3rd, the Widow Maria Winston Price, no children. Clerk of District Court and vestryman of Monumental Church.

Charles, b. Jan. 31, 1767, The Hollow, d. Warrenton, Va., 1805, m. Lucy Pickett, 1787; left several young children, all of whom found Polly's entaglio cupids smiling upon their romances in her parlour. Martin P. m. Eliza, daughter of Capt. Thomas Marshall of Kentucky; Lucy m. Robert Morris Marshall of Fairfield on Fairfax lands; Jane m. Edward Colston and died two years later, at Honeywood.

Lucy, b. The Hollow, 1768, d. Jamestown Island, 1795, m. John Ambler, left one son Thomas Marshall. She was the only child of Col. Thomas and Mary Keith Marshall to predecease them.

Alexander Keith, b. Oak Hill, 1770, d. Kentucky, 1825; m. Mary McDowell; was Clerk of the Kentucky Court of Appeals, often in State Legislature.

Lewis, b. 1773, Oak Hill, d. Buckpond, Kentucky, 1866, m. Agatha Smith; president of Transylvania College in Kentucky, and Liberty, which became Washington College in Virginia; an M.D. but preferred the practice of education to that of medicine. Son William m. Ann Lee, sister of Robert E. Lee, General C.S.A. Changed spelling of his name to Louis.

Susan, b. 1774, Oak Hill, d. Kentucky 1858; m. Judge William McClung.

Charlotte, b. Oak Hill, 1777, d. Kentucky, 1817, m. Dr. Basil Duke.

Jane, b. Oak Hill, 1779, d. Mt. Ephraim, Fauquier Co., 1866, m. Judge George Keith Talliaferro Taylor, 1799, of Spring Garden near Petersburg. For a while after his death in 1815, she ran a girls' school in Petersburg. The Marshalls loved "Uncle Taylor," though he was considered too old for his bride, being ten years her senior. He did his courting in Polly's parlour.

Nancy, b. Oak Hill, 1781, d. Kentucky, m. Col. Joseph Hamilton Daviess who appropriated his middle name from his enthusiasm for Alexander Hamilton. He claimed that through his newspaper President Jefferson had been induced to order the arrest of Aaron Burr. Col. Daviess was killed by Indians in the battle of Tippecanoe.

Grandchildren Born Before Polly's Death

Children of Thomas and Margaret (Lewis) who were married October 19, 1809
John, b. Weyanoke, 1811
Agnes, b. Oak Hill, 1813
Fielding Lewis, b. Oak Hill, 1819
Anne, b. Oak Hill, 1823
Margaret, b. Oak Hill, 1824
Thomas (Colonel, C.S.A.) b. 1826
Then Margaret died in childbirth in February, 1829

Children of John and Elizabeth (Alexander), married February 3, 1820
John, b. 1821
Ashton, b. 1824
James Edward, b. 1830

Children of Mary (Marshall) and General Jaquelin Harvie, married September 17, 1813
Mary, b. Richmond, 1815.

Ellen, b. Richmond, 1818
Virginia, b. Richmond, 1821
Susan, b. Richmond, 1824
William, b. Richmond, 1826
Anne, b. Richmond, 1828
Emily, b. Richmond, 1830

Children of Jaquelin and Eliza (Clarkson), married January 1, 1819
Mary Ambler, b. 1821
Eliza, b. 1827
Jaquelin Ambler, b. 1829

Children of James Keith and Claudia (Burwell), married December 22, 1821
John, b. Morelands on Leeds Manor, 1822
Nathaniel, b. Morelands, 1824
James, b. Morelands, 1826
Maria Willis, b. Morelands, 1828
Mary Ambler, b. Morelands, 1830

Children of Edward and Rebecca (Peyton), married February 12, 1829
John, b. 1829
Mary, b. 1831

Children of Polly and J Marshall

Thomas, b. July 21, 1784
Daughter, b. 1786, name unknown, d. Aug. 1792
Jaquelin Ambler, b. Dec. 3, 1787
Son, b. 1789, name unknown, died young
Daughter, b. and d. in this period, name unknown
Son, b. Feb. 1792, name unknown, d. Aug. 1792
Mary, b. Sept. 17, 1795
John, b. Jan. 15, 1798
James Keith, b. Feb 13, 1800
Edward Carrington, b. Jan. 13, 1805

BASIC SOURCES

I

It is said that thirty years ago there was a "trunk full" of letters beginning "My dearest Polly," and signed "J Marshall." For this study only forty-two were found complete or in part. One was lost before Polly died. Four were found in other publications. Three original letters are in the Marshall House in Richmond, Virginia. One is owned by Mrs. Alexander Sands of Richmond, and another by Mr. Andrew Hogue of Beckley, West Virginia; there is one in the Alderman Library of the University of Virginia. Three are fragments cited in other publications.

In that handsome collection, *The Papers of John Marshall,* in the Library of the College of William and Mary in Williamsburg, Virginia, there are twenty-eight original "Dearest Polly" letters, deposited there by Marshall descendants in 1955 when the College was doing year-long honor to the bicentennial of the birth of John Marshall. This generous library has been the main field of study for this interpretation. Related papers were acquired from the Virginia State Library, the Alderman Library of the University of Virginia, the New York Public Library, Duke University Library, the Virginia Historical Society, the Library of Congress, the Valentine Museum in Richmond, Virginia, and the Headquarters of the Yorktown National Battlefield Monument Park.

Manuscripts used are:

Papers of John Marshall, College of William and Mary, consisting of several hundred original manuscripts, documents, memorabilia and photostats of original papers owned by other individuals and organizations. Included among the papers is John Marshall's "Accounts and Law Notes" (1784-1796), deposited with the College Library by Dr. H. Norton Mason.

Letters and papers of Mrs. Edward Carrington (Eliza Ambler) owned by Mrs. John Latane Lewis of Williamsburg, Virginia, with photostats of these in the Virginia Historical Society, and typed copies owned by Judge Leon Bazile of Hanover County.

The Eulogy, a memorial of Polly written by her husband. Copy of the original made at Leeds Manor about 1889 by her great-granddaughter, Claudia Hamilton Norton Mason.

II

Printed Books:

A Bibliography of John Marshall, James A Servies. (Washington, 1956).

An Autobiographical Sketch, John Marshall, written at the request of Joseph Story in 1827, James Stokes Adams. (Ann Arbor, Michigan, 1931).

Life of John Marshall, Allen Bowie Magruder. (Boston & New York, 1885).

Life of John Marshall, Henry Flanders. (Philadelphia, 1904).

Life of John Marshall, Albert J. Beveridge. 4 vols. (Boston, 1916-1919).

Life of George Washington, John Marshall. Second edition. (Philadelphia, 1832).

The Marshall Family, W. M. Paxton. (Cincinnati, 1885).

The Supreme Court in The History of The United States, Charles Warren. 2 vols. (Boston, 1937).

Richmond in Bygone Days, Being Reminiscences of an Old Citizen, Samuel Mordecai (Richmond, 1856).

Fauquier during the Proprietorship, H. C. Groome. (Richmond, 1927).

Other Material:

Notes in the handwriting of Claudia Hamilton Norton Mason, taken in conversation with granddaughters and grandsons of Chief Justice Marshall at Leeds Manor from 1880 to 1900.

The Marshall file in the Valentine Museum in Richmond, Virginia, and other papers collected by Edward Valentine between 1870 and 1920.

Richmond tradition and Marshall family memories.

The Marshall House, Richmond, Virginia, maintained by the Association for Preservation of Virginia Antiquities.

Other sources noted by chapters.

Care has been exercised to reproduce the letters with as little editing as possible.

NOTES BY CHAPTERS

CHAPTER I. POLLY. 1777-1780.

The character of Mary Willis Ambler, called Polly, was discovered in The Eulogy, in her husband's letters to her, in the papers of her sister Eliza (Mrs. Edward Carrington), and in the known sentiments of her children and grandchildren. Description of other Ambler personalities and family life, together with a reflection of the Ambler family attitude toward Thomas Jefferson was also found in the papers of Éliza Carrington. A photostat of the Letter Book of William Reynolds of York Town and a typescript study by Edward Riley entitled *Yorktown During the Revolution,* both in the Headquarters of the Battlefield National Monument Park in Yorktown, Virginia, with files of the *Virginia Gazette,* 1779-1780, in the College of William and Mary, tell the conditions in that town. The military rank and service of the Marshalls are in John Gwathmey's *Historical Register of Virginians in The Revolution* (Richmond, 1938). J Marshall himself describes the operations and condition of the Continental Army and State Militia in his *Life Of George Washington,* second edition, volume 1, chapters XVIII and XIX. The "cousins" of the Ambler girls who were in Winchester in 1777 were the children of John and Edward Smith of Shooters Hill in Gloucester County, now Middlesex. John Smith the elder had married Mary Jacqueline of Jamestown, an aunt of Jacquelin Ambler. (Three generations spelled the name Jaquelin differently: Edward Jacqueline, first generation; Jacquelin Ambler, second generation; and Jaquelin Marshall, third generation.) This John Smith lost his estate in the collapse of Speaker of the House of Burgesses John Robinson's Money Scheme shortly before the Revolution. His sons went out into the fabled Fairfax wilderness to recoup the family fortunes. A piece of a blue taffeta dress worn by Polly is still in the possession of one of her great-great-grandsons. The change in curriculum at the College of William and Mary is told in *Vital Facts of The College of William and Mary* (Williamsburg, 1955), and by Dr. G. MacLaren Brydon in *Virginia's Mother Church,* volume II (Philadelphia, 1952), pages 430-432. The political story is taken from *History of The Colony and Ancient Dominion of Virginia* by Charles Campbell. Marshall's own movements during 1779-1780 are told in his *Autobiographical Sketch,* hereafter called the *Autobiography.*

On May 18, 1780, the name of John Marshall was inscribed on the rolls of the charter chapter of Phi Beta Kappa in the College of William and Mary between those of Joseph Cabell and Bushrod Washington. Earlier the name of a youth from Essex County had been enrolled, Spencer Roane.

CHAPTER II. A NEW WORLD. 1780-1784.

We move now into *Richmond in Bygone Days, being Reminiscences of an Old Citizen,* by Samuel Mordecai (Richmond, 1856), and *A History of Richmond,* by Mary Newton Stanard (Philadelphia, 1923), assisted by diorama scenes of the development of Richmond, Valentine Museum, Richmond, Virginia. Louise Pecquet du Bellet in her *Some Eminent Virginia Families* (Lynchburg, 1907) gives a description of The Cottage in Hanover County, and tells of John Ambler's enlistment in the State Militia. For a touch of Marshall's own charm we have drawn on memories of old Richmonders who remembered those who remembered him. To the above sources must be added the Marshall family Bible records, owned by the heirs of Mrs. John Marshall, nee Claudia Marshall Stribling, of Fauquier County, great-granddaughter of Chief Justice Marshall. These give the time, place and celebrant of the marriage ceremony of John Marshall and Mary Willis Ambler. Descriptions of Virginia weddings of that day may be found in several places, but Mrs. Margaret Ritson most appropriately describes one in her *Poetical Picture of America, Being Observations Made, During a Residence of Several Years at Alexandria and Norfolk in Virginia, From The Year* 1799 to 1807, (London, 1809). The *Life Of James Monroe,* by William Penn Cresson, (Chapel Hill, 1946), and *History of Henrico Parish and Old St. John's Church,* by Lewis Burton and J. S. Moore (Richmond, 1905), contribute to this chapter. The late Ellen Harvie Smith made a study of the succession of Marshall residences in Richmond. The slave Robin eventually gave himself the surname of Spurlock with which he endowed a numerous progeny, some of whom were musically inclined, and some, says Miss Catherine Douthat, had no taste for law and order.

CHAPTER III. THE MARSHALLS ON FAIRFAX LANDS. 1659-1784.

The history of Fairfax lands, which is so large a part of Marshall family history, is taken from many sources, but chiefly from Dr. T. J. Wertenbaker's *Virginia Under The Stuarts* (Princeton, 1914); Samuel Kercheval's *History of The Valley of Virginia* (Woodstock, Virginia, 1902); *Fauquier County Under The Proprietorship,* by H. C. Groome, (Richmond, 1927); *Virginia Land Grants,* by Fairfax Harrison, imprint; *Old Prince William Landmarks,* by Fairfax Harrison, imprint; *The Supreme Court In United States History,* by Charles Warren (Boston, 1937), volume 1; Henry Wheaton's *Reports of Cases Argued and Adjudged in The Supreme Court of The United States,* 1816; and *An Oldtimer in Warrenton and Fauquier County,* a series of articles by Louise Evans in *The Fauquier County Democrat,* 1951-1955. The Foley grant is today called The Free State by its neighbours. A homespun blanket used in the rented ironworker's cottage is still in the Marshall House in Richmond. A description of Lord Fairfax's death is found in Henry Howe's *Historical Collections of Virginia* (Charleston, 1847).

Letter: from J Marshall to James Monroe, Richmond, February 14, 1784, is quoted through the courtesy of the Manuscript Division, New York Public Library (Monroe Papers).

CHAPTER IV. THE AMBLERS. 1697-1785.

Jacqueline and Ambler records are most easily found in *Some Eminent Virginia Families*, by Louise Pecquet du Bellet. Eliza Ambler Carrington tells this chapter in notes she made for a family history. She does not tell, however, that the silk and velvet coverlet begun but never finished by Mary Jacqueline, Mrs. John Smith, at Shooters Hill is still in the Marshall House in Richmond.

CHAPTER V. THE CONSTITUTION. 1785-1789.

All that "Marshall says" concerning the state of the Confederation and his estimate of James Madison is quoted from the *Autobiography*. It was Patrick Henry who in a speech before the Virginia Convention described the constitutionalists as avenging the hand of Heaven. The Massachusetts farmers whose remarks are quoted were Samuel Nason and William Widgery, speaking in the Constitutional Convention of that State, January, 1788. The story of the Constitutional Convention in Richmond, June, 1788, is taken from the biographies of John Marshall by Allen Bowie Magruder, Albert Beveridge and Henry Flanders, and from accounts by Mordecai, and Mrs. Stanard.

CHAPTER VI. THE FIRST LETTER. 1792.

The Marshall House still stands at the corner of Ninth and Marshall Streets in Richmond, in the custody of the Association for Preservation of Virginia Antiquities whose headquarters are in the house. The original deed and insurance policy hang on its walls. Marshall's Account Book for this period and Mary Wingfield Scott's *Houses of Old Richmond* (Richmond, 1941) leave us with no uncertainties about the building of Polly's mansion. Old press clippings collected by Edward Valentine and a scrap book kept by John Marshall Douthat lend color to the background of this chapter. The list of gentlemen appearing before the District Court is on page 154 of the *History Of Fredericksburg*, by Alvin Embrey (Richmond, 1937). An account of Captain Thomas Marshall's removal to Kentucky was found in *Sketches of Western Adventure, 1755 to 1794*, by John A. McClung (Dayton, 1854).

Letter: from J Marshall to The Honble. Mr. Justice Story, Richmond, June 25, 1831 is in volume XIV, second series, Massachusetts Historical Society *Proceedings*, 344-346.

CHAPTER VII. GENERAL MARSHALL. 1793-1795.

The Timothy Trittle case is reported in Warren's *Supreme Court*, volume II. What "Marshall says" is from his *Autobiogra-*

phy and his *Life Of Washington,* volume II, chapter X. There, also, is an account of the Fauchet affair. The famous observation upon the fickleness of American public sentiment was made by a British traveller, Isaac Weld, and is here taken from Beveridge, volume II, p. 117n. Washington Irving in his *Life of George Washington,* volume 7, (New York, 1857), says, "About this time a society was formed under the auspices of the French minister, and in imitation of the Jacobin clubs of Paris. It was called the Democratic Society, and soon gave rise to others throughout the Union; all taking the French side in the present questions." A few pages on, Irving remarks that "Col. Parker of Virginia wished that there was a stamp on the forehead of everyone to designate whether he was for France or England." Jefferson's letter to the Anglo-Italian lady, Maria Cosway, is quoted from Helen Duprey Bullock's *My Head and My Heart* (New York, 1945), page 142.

CHAPTER VIII. THE SECOND LETTER. 1796.

Additional sources for this chapter were *History of The Post Office to the Year 1829,* by Wesley Rich, imprint; *Memoirs of William Wirt,* by John P. Kennedy (Philadelphia, 1849); *Romantic Days in the Early Republic,* by Caroline Crawford, chapter I (Boston, 1912); *Portrait of A Colonial City, Philadelphia, 1690-1838,* by Harold Eberlein and Courtlandt Van Dyke Hubbard (Phildelphia, 1939). History of the Richmond theatre used throughout this study was found in Susanne K. Sherman's *Thomas Wade West, Theatrical Impresario 1790-1799,* and her notes for a study of the Southern Theatre from its beginning to 1812. Marshall in his *Life Of Washington,* volume II, chapters XI and XII tells the story of Monroe in Paris and of the French agent M. Adet in America.

Letters: to "My dearest Polly," Philadelphia, February 3, 1796, and from Colonel Thomas Marshall to J Marshall, Buckpond, Sept. 9, 1796 are from the College of William and Mary.

CHAPTER IX. LETTERS FROM AN ADAMS MAN. 1797.

History followed in this chapter is still as Marshall tells it in his *Washington,* volume II, chapters XI and XII. The Latrobe diary reference is taken from a typescript of the original in the Maryland Historical Society's archives. Washington's request of Marshall to use "a little judicious flattery" on Edmund Randolph is preserved in the notebook of Claudia Hamilton Norton Mason as it was told to her by her uncles, the grandsons of Chief Justice Marshall, who had seen the original letter. Also used for this chapter were *New Letters of Abigail Adams,* edited by Stewart Mitchell (Boston, 1947); *The Forgotten Patriot, Robert Morris,* by Eleanor Young (New York, 1950); *History of The American Stage* in volume 14 of

The Pageant of America series. Catherine Gamble was found in *Richmond Portraits in an Exhibition of Makers of Richmond*, by Louise Cadot Catterall (Richmond, 1949). It is difficult to discover which "Mrs. Hayward" spent the Summer of 1797 in a handsome house on the banks of the Schuylkill River. Howards were Heywards when they arrived in Virginia in the seventeenth century to become one of the "high prerogative" families of the Colony. This friend of the Marshalls may have been a member of this family. Marshall's statement of election results is taken from his *Washington*, volume II, page 421.

Letters: from Marshall to Judge Iredall, Dec. 15, 1796, is quoted through the courtesy of the Duke University Library; those to "My dearest Polly," Alexandria, June 24, 1797; Philadelphia, July 2, 1797; Philadelphia, July 5, 1797; Philadelphia, July 10, 1797; Philadelphia, July 11, 1797; postmarked July 12 [1797]; Philadelphia, July 14, 1797; Bay of the Delaware, July 20, 1797, are from originals in the College of William and Mary.

CHAPTER X. LETTERS FROM AN ENVOY EXTRAORDINARY. 1797-1798.

Beveridge in his *Life of John Marshall* uses three lengthy chapters in volume II to discuss this mission. With characteristic precision Marshall cuts the story down to a few terse comments in his *Washington*, volume II, chapter XI. Eliza Carrington still reports on Polly in her letter book.

Letters: to "My dearest Polly," Thursday Aug. 3, 1797; The Hague, Sept. 9, 1797; Paris, Nov. 27, 1797, are from originals in the College of William and Mary.

The tradition that William Tazewell of Williamsburg joined the mission was found in Wyndham Robertson's *Pocahontas, Alias Matoaka, and her Descendents* (Richmond, 1887), page 70.

CHAPTER XI. THE "UN"LUCKY LETTER. 1798-1799.

The description of the arrival at Mount Vernon of the two gentlemen is found in *A Life Of George Washington*, by James Kirke Paulding (New York, 1835), volume II, pages 191-192. George Wythe Munford in *Two Parsons* (Richmond, 1884), vividly described election day in Richmond, 1799. He, however, says that Clopton won the greatest number of votes, while the Congressional Record says that Marshall took the seat as Representative from Richmond in the House when the Sixth Congress opened in November of 1799. John Randolph of Roanoke is described and generally reported upon by Powhatan Bouldin in *Home Reminiscences of John Randolph of Roanoke* (Richmond, 1878), and *John Randolph of Roanoke, A Study in Conservative Thought*, by Russell Kirk (Chicago, 1951). The letter from Thomas Jefferson to Marshall is copied from the original in the Marshall House in

Richmond. Marshall's reply is in the National Archives, and is here copied from Beveridge, Volume II, page 347.

Letter: to "My dearest Polly," Aug. 18, 1798, is from the original in the College of William and Mary.

CHAPTER XII. CONGRESSMAN. 1799-1800.

Social life in Philadelphia is depicted in the second chapter of *Romantic Days in the Early Republic*, by Mrs. Crawford; *Social Life in the Early Republic*, by Anne Wharton (Philadelphia, 1902); in *New Letters of Abigail Adams, Portraits of a Colonial City*, and *Diary of Independence Hall*, by Harold Eberlein and Courtlandt Van Dyke Hubbard (Philadelphia, 1948). Marshall's *Washington* tells the story of the announcement of the death of Washington and the Congressional Resolutions. This account of the Gabriel uprising is found in a fragment of the depositions of witnesses in the Virginia Historical Society library, to which are added tradition of old citizens and the "Sixth Annual Report of the American Society for Colonization of Free Persons of Colour in the United States," *North American Review, XLII*, and Cresson's *Monroe*. President Adams requested Samuel Dexter of Massachusetts, at the time Secretary of War and Finance, to act in the office of Secretary of State long enough to affix the Seal to the commission of John Marshall as Chief Justice. The item from the *Norfolk Gazette and Public Ledger*, Feb. 2, 1809, is copied from a typescript among the Papers of John Marshall, College of William and Mary.

Letters: to "My dearest Polly," Aug. 8, 1800, is from the original in the College of William and Mary; that of Aug. 1, 1800, is from the original owned by Mrs. Alexander Sands of Richmond, Virginia.

CHAPTER XIII. J MARSHALL, CHIEF JUSTICE. 1800-1803.

Jefferson's campaign song is borrowed from Mrs. Bullock's *My Head and my Heart*, page 151.

Letter: to "My dearest Polly," Jan. 2, 1803, is from the original in the Marshall House, Richmond, Virginia.

CHAPTER XIV. A NEWSPAPER. 1804.

Files of the *Virginia Argus* were used in the Virginia State Library. Editors of 1804 are described by Mordecai. Mrs. Hopkins, for whose benefit Mr. Hopkins was advertising a dramatic performance, was Elizabeth Arnold, who two years later was Mrs. David Poe and became the mother of Edgar Allan Poe.

CHAPTER XV. THE COURT ON TRIAL. 1805.

Henry Adams' *John Randolph of Roanoke* in American Statesmen series, (Boston, 1894), and Bouldin's *Reminiscences* with Warren's *Supreme Court* tell this story. The ruby mourning ring is owned by Polly's great-great-grandson, Dr. Hatley Norton Mason.

Letter: to "My dearest Polly," Sept. 27, 1805, is from the original in the College of William and Mary.

CHAPTER XVI. THE BURR TRIAL. 1807.

Beveridge's *Marshall*, volume 3, Chapters VI, VII, VIII, and IX, discusses the Burr affair. The story of the trials was taken from *The Trial of Aaron Burr* by Joseph Brady, Clerk of the District Court of Eastern Virginia (New York, 1913); Kennedy's *Wirt*, Volume 1, Chapters XIII, XIV and XV; *John H. B. Latrobe and His Times*, 1804-1897, by John E. Simms, and notes taken from *William Wirt Henry* by Edward Valentine with undated press clippings in the Valentine Museum. *The Chesapeake Affair*, by John Emmerson (Portsmouth, 1954) covers that crisis with excerpts from newspapers of that day. All quotations of Marshall's opinions are cited from Brady and Beveridge. A booklet entitled *St. Memin's Portrait of Chief Justice Marshall* by Christian Klacker (New York, 1901) tells of the physiognograph.

CHAPTER XVII. A MOST ATTRACTIVE HOUSEHOLD. 1807-1811.

The lampoon from the *Norfolk Gazette and Public Ledger*, Nov. 9, 1807, is taken from a typescript among the Papers of John Marshall, College of William and Mary. Sally Marshall Hardy of Louisville, Kentucky, great-granddaughter of Chief Justice Marshall, recorded memories passed on to her by his children and grandchildren in *The Green Bag*, December, 1896. From undated press clippings preserved by Mrs. Edwin Wright of St. Davids, Pennsylvania, great-great-granddaughter of the Chief Justice, and the scrapbook of John Marshall Douthat, with items collected by Edward Valentine, comes much of this chapter. Old Richmond tradition and Paxton's *Marshall Family* also contribute to this chapter. Polly's gold locket is now owned by her great-great-granddaughter, Mrs. Kenneth Higgins of Richmond. It is not known which of the Keiths was father to the Reverend James Keith who came to Virginia. It is certain that he was of the family of Keiths who for ten generations were Earls Mareschal of Scotland. The secret of his place on the family tree perished when James contributed the autobiography, which he had written in Greek, to the Revolutionary war effort. The paper was used for wrapping bullets.

Letter: from Mary Marshall to "Dear Mother," Feb. 1, 1811, is from the original in the College of William and Mary.

CHAPTER XVIII. THE NEW CHURCH. 1811-1814.

History and Reminiscences of Monumental Church, by George Fisher (Richmond, 1880), reproducing press articles and reports of the Episcopal Conventions, definitively covers the theatre fire and the rise of the church. Also an ample file in the Valentine Museum preserves the story in contemporaneous language and sentiment. The "cousin from Winchester" is listed in newspaper rolls of victims as "Mr. A. Marshall from the western part of the State."

CHAPTER XIX. OLD CUSHING IS DEAD. 1810-1816.

The account of the meeting of Marshall with Story was told to a social gathering of lawyers in Richmond in 1901 by a Justice of the Supreme Court of Massachusetts. The lawyers ask to remain anonymous and prefer that the name of the Justice be kept secret. The account of Marshall's expedition in search of a western water route may be found in the *Annual Report* of the James River and Kanawha Company, No. 11, 1846. Warren's *Supreme Court*, Volume 1, is still the source for the Fairfax land cases together with the full report of Martin, heir at law and devisee of Fairfax *vs* Hunter's Lessee, *Wheaton's Reports*, Volume 1, 1816. Judge Roane's family history was garnered from encyclopedias of American Biography and Miss Scott's *Houses of Old Richmond*, to which is added talk about town.

A note on the Supreme Court borrowed from *Travels in The United States of America and Canada*, by John Finch (London, 1833), pages 206, 207:

"A stranger will be much gratified at Washington by viewing the Supreme Court of the United States. Its power is more extensive than any other court of judicature in the world; it decides on questions that arise between the different States. As the population of these nations increases, so much more important will its decisions become, and one wrong judgement might involve the United States in discord. The representatives and senators of the various States meet in their respective capitols; every thing reminds them of the power of their native land; the federal government is at a distance, or overlooked in the prosperity of their own. Sometimes, laws are passed which contravene the spirit of the federal government, and invade the rights of other States. Individuals who are aggrieved bring their suit before the Supreme Court. The difficulty of the task is much enhanced by the incessant care with which the Semi-Sovereignty of the States is guarded. It is considered the great bulwark of liberty. . . .

"The hall in which they meet is on the ground floor of the Capitol. It is not remarkable for its size, but is well arranged. The floor is well carpeted, and commodious settees are set apart for the spectators. . . . It is the fashion for ladies to attend the Supreme Court when any interesting cases are to be argued, and their entrée produces some sensation in the court. But the most strict order and decorum are observed, the most profound silence. In the questions which arise between the States, they send their most eminent counsellors to argue the cause, and frequently the same persons are members of Congress. They have every motive to exertion that can stimulate the human mind. Before them the highest court of judicature on the American continent—around them, the counsellors of other States, listening to every argument—the audience, consisting of Senators, representatives, and strangers—the honor and interests of their States are alike concerned; and whether the palm of eloquence shall be awarded to a citizen of Virginia or Massachusetts, of Illinois or Missouri, is a question worth contending."

CHAPTER XX. THE ERA OF GOOD FEELING. 1817-1823.

To sources now familiar is added Margaret Coit's *John C. Calhoun* (Boston, 1950).

Letters: to "My dearest Polly," Feb. 14, 1817 and Oct. 31, 1823; to Marshall from James Monroe, March 1, 1817, are from originals in the College of William and Mary. Those to "My dearest Polly," Feb. 16, 1818 and April 11, 1823, together with the letter to "Dear Son" on the reverse of Feb. 16, are from copies made by Claudia Hamilton Norton Mason at Leeds Manor in 1889. The first recollection of the Chief Justice at Fauquier White Sulphur Springs is found in the reminiscences of the Reverend Thomas Bloomer Balch in *The True Index,* a newspaper of Warrenton, Va., Saturday, August 3, 1867. The second is cited from the Southern Literary Messenger in *The Patriot,* Baltimore, Md., September 8, 1836.

CHAPTER XXI. THE COLONIZATION SOCIETY. 1817-1824.

Twenty-three times before 1772 the Virginia House of Burgesses passed laws restricting slave trade, all being disallowed by the British sovereign. In that year the Virginia Assembly petitioned his majesty to avert from the Colony "the great calamity" arising from the continuance of this "pernicious commerce" which was "a trade of great inhumanity." This too was denied. An early Act of the sovereign State of Virginia, 1782, upon motion of Thomas Jefferson prohibited further importation of Africans for sale. In 1782 Virginia facilitated manumission, and decreed that slaves brought in after this year should be free after twelve months' residence. In 1787 a retroactive Act of Legislature validated all manumission by will under the Colonial government. Acts of Virginia Legislature safeguarded rights of freedmen in 1795 and 1803. In 1806 State law required that all freed slaves leave the Commonwealth within a year. England abolished slavery in 1807. In 1788 Connecticut and Massachusetts had laws directed toward shipowners who dealt in slaves, Delaware in 1789. Pennsylvania and New York forthrightly prohibited importation and exportation in 1788 and 1789 respectively.

Thomas Marshall's activities for abolition of the institution are described in *Virginia's Attitude Toward Slavery and Secession,* by Beverly Munford (New York, 1910). Negro songs quoted in this chapter are traditional. Minutes of the Richmond-Manchester Colonization Society are in the Virginia Historical Society. The general account of the colonization movement is found in "The Sixth Annual Report of the American Society for Colonizing the Free People of Colour of The United States" 1823, published in the *North American Review*, Number XVII, and "The Seventh Annual Report, 1825" in the same magazine, number XLVI. *The Sixth Annual Report of the Board of Managers of the Colonization Society of Virginia*, 1837, published by the Southern Churchman, Richmond, gives the Virginia story.

CHAPTER XXII. THE STEAMBOAT CASE. 1824.

John Emmerson's *The Steamboat Comes to Norfolk and The Log of The First Ten Years* (Portsmouth, 1947) is used with Warren's *Supreme Court* and Wheaton's *Reports*, Volume IX. "Major Dick" mentioned in Marshall's letter to Polly was Major Richard Anderson of Kentucky, whose son, General Robert Anderson, as United States Army Colonel, held Fort Sumter, South Carolina, in 1861. In 1824 John and Elizabeth Alexander Marshall had one son, John. She was on her way to her mother's house in Baltimore where, a few weeks later, her second son was born, Ashton. Two more children were later born to this couple, James Edward and Mary Willis. James married his cousin. Mary Morris Marshall, granddaughter of James Markham Marshall; Mary Willis Marshall, who was born after Polly's death, married Fielding Douthat.

Letters: to "My dearest Polly," Feb. 23, 1824; March 23; and to "My dear Mother," Feb. 28, 1824, are from the originals in the College of William and Mary.

CHAPTER XXIII. MASTER OF THE HUMAN HEART. 1825.

Copies of the letter from J Marshall to John Randolph of Roanoke are in the Alderman Library of the University of Virginia and the Virginia State Library. Richmond and family memories, the Valentine Museum's files. Marian Harland's *Some Colonial Homesteads* and Dr. Brydon's *Mother Church* contribute to this chapter. A few sentences from a letter to Polly concerning the "domestic fabric" are quoted by Marian Harland. The poem *For A Lady's Album* is copied from Claudia Hamilton Norton Mason's notebook.

Letters: to "My dearest Polly," Feb. 8, 1825, and Feb. 27, 1825, are from the originals in the College of William and Mary.

CHAPTER XXIV. MY OLD WIFE. 1825-1828.

Harvard University, 1639-1900 Universities and their Sons series (Boston, 1900) gives light on Edward Marshall's college career. A letter in the College of William and Mary from Tom Marshall to his father, Sept. 26, 1828, tells of his experiment with a field roller. *Lines For A Lady's Album* is in the College of William and Mary. A letter from Marshall to Story, March, 1828, is quoted from Massachusetts Historical Society *Proceedings*, Volume XIV, page 344.

Letters: to "My dear Mother," Nov. 8, 1825, and to "My dearest Polly," Feb. 5, 1826 and March 12, 1826 are from originals in the College of William and Mary; that of Feb. 12, 1826, is from copy of original made by Claudia Hamilton Norton Mason at Leeds Manor in 1889.

CHAPTER XXV. A NEW DAY. 1829.

The case of Boyce *vs* Anderson, indemnity claim for drowned slaves, is found in Peter's *Reports*, Volume II. Marshall's own copy of *Proceedings And Debates of The Virginia State Convention, 1829-1830* (Richmond, 1830) was used with Hugh Blair Grigsby's *The Virginia Convention* (Richmond, 1854).

Note on the revision of the State Constitution: When the question of revising the first Virginia State Constitution was put to a referendum in the spring of 1829, there were some 16,000 votes for revision and some 11,000 against it, the western counties being for it. When a new Constitution with broadened suffrage was submitted for ratification, the western counties with two in the east, Warwick and Lancaster, rejected it. Randolph's county, Charlotte, ratified 335 to 12. The total vote stood: for ratification, 26,055; against, 15,563.

Letters: to "My dearest Polly," Feb. 1, 1829, Feb. 19, 1829, and Feb. 28, 1829, are from the originals in the College of William and Mary; March 5, 1829, is a fragment cited by Beveridge, Volume IV, page 467. Letter to "Dear Sir," (Mr. Rawlings) July 28, 1829, is from the original in the College of William and Mary.

CHAPTER XXVI. EIGHTEEN THIRTY.

Kercheval's *Valley Of Virginia* gives most of this version of the religious debate in McGuire's Hotel.

Letters: to "My dearest Polly," Jan. 31, 1830, is from Claudia Hamilton Norton Mason's notebook, those dated Feb. 14, 1830, and Feb. 28, 1830, from originals in the College of William and Mary, that dated March 7 is from the original owned by Mr. Bernard Hogue of Beckley, West Virginia.

CHAPTER XXVII. FAREWELL, MY DEAREST POLLY. 1831.

The land claimant's case brought on from the Kentucky court, Lessor of John Fisher *vs* William Cockerell, and The Cherokee Nation *vs* the State of Georgia are found in Peter's *Reports*, Volume III, 1831. "Lines for a Lady's Album" are in the College of William and Mary. The letter quoted, J Marshall to James Markham Marshall, Dec. 19, 1831 is from a typescript made by James

A. Servies of the original in Washington University, St. Louis, Missouri. All letters from J Marshall to Joseph Story were found in Massachusetts Historical Society *Proceedings,* Volume XIV, pages 344-347, second series. The Library of the College of Physicians of Philadelphia has kindly permitted us to use pages 96-99 of "A Memoir of Dr. Philip Syng Physick, 1839," written by his son-in-law, Dr. Jacob Randolph of Philadelphia. Some details of Marshall's suffering were found in "The Case of Chief Justice Marshall," *American Journal Of Medical Sciences,* Volume 9, 1831, pages 537-538. Family letters and tradition close this chapter.

Letters: to "My dearest Polly," Jan. 30, 1831, and Oct. 6, 1831, are from originals in the College of William and Mary; that of Feb. 7, 1831, with letter on reverse page to "My dear Son," is from the original in the Alderman Library of the University of Virginia, letter dated May 12, 1831 is from the original in the Marshall House, and those of Oct. 12, 1831 are from Claudia Hamilton Norton Mason's notebook. A fragment dated November 8, 1831, is cited by Beveridge, Volume IV, page 524.

LAST NOTE.

Chief Justice Marshall lived only three and a half years after the death of his wife, residing in her house, active in affairs of State and Court, giving his lawyer dinner parties and welcoming visitors with the same friendliness; but, Joseph Story says, after the day was over he often found Marshall weeping for Polly. In 1833 his health failed noticeably. His children were pressing him to retire from the Bench and return to the upper country Fairfax lands that he loved so well. He did add a wing to the house James Keith Marshall had recently built on Leeds Manor, but session by session he delayed withdrawing from the Supreme Court. To the staunch and venerable patriot the government seemed more and more given over to politicians who would render the Union a mere league of States. He would give his strength as long as it lasted to preserve the Constitution in its balance of powers. In 1835, though ill and in great pain, he presided over the Court, delivering seven of its opinions himself. On his way back to Richmond the stage in which he was travelling overturned, increasing his suffering by an injury to his back. However, three weeks later, sadly enfeebled, he travelled to Raleigh, North Carolina, for the District Court session. On his return to Richmond he supervised the transfer of the Madeira in his cellar from demijohns to casks, chartered a sailing vessel, that being the safest mode of shipping fine wines, and sent the spirits, with his books, his papers, the letters from Polly's desk, his china and glass and a few pieces of favorite furniture, to Alexandria, whence James would have them fetched by trustworthy wagoners. Then, such was his suffering that he yielded to the importunities of his family to seek medical aid from the doctors who had once saved his life. On June twelfth, accompanied by his sons, Jaquelin the doctor, young Edward and James, who had been born in that happy Winter of the Sixth Congress, he left for Philadelphia. Arriving in that city which had always shown him "flattering attention," they took rooms in Mrs. Crim's boarding-house on Walnut Street. There on the afternoon of July sixth, John Marshall died with Polly's locket still on its chain around his neck. In announcing the death of the Chief Justice, Niles's *Register*, whose opposition to Marshall had long been called acrimonious, said, "Next to Washington only did he possess the reverence and homage of the heart of the American People." In Richmond, people spoke most often of his "warm benevolence to all men."

Index

Aberdeen Cathedral, 204.
Account Book, 7, 9, 11, 20, 30, 35, 36, 41, 43, 51, 59, 62, 159.
Actors, 36.
Adams, Abigail, 47, 92, 93, 101, 132, 136, 141, 149.
Adams, James Stokes, editor, *An Autobiographical Sketch*, John Marshall, 354.
Adams, John, 88, 89, 92, 93, 94, 102, 114, 117, 118, 122, 132, 135, 138, 140, 141, 145, 147, 149, 289, 295; Minister to England 47; Vice-President 56; President 282; dies 295; describes Marshall 149.
Adams, Dr. John of Richmond, 121.
Adams, John Quincy, 166, 219, 241, 242, 281, 282, 291, 297, 303, 304, 323.
Adams, Mrs. John Quincy, 242, 294, 304.
Adams, Samuel, 88.
Adet, M., French agent, 80.
Africa 146, 253-259 passim.
African kings, refuse to abate slave trade, 253.
Agents, American, 4, 63; French, 80, 88.
Agriculture, see Farm products.
Albemarle County, 158.
Alexandria, Virginia, 71, 98, 160.
Alien and Sedition Acts, 124, 130.
Alston, Aaron Burr, 185.
Alston, Joseph, 185.
Alston, Theodosia Burr, 185.
Ambler, Ann (Mrs. George Fisher), 1, 196, 197, 229, 274, 341.
Ambler, Cary, son of Col. John, 337.
Ambler, Edward, son of Col. John, 337, 348.
Ambler, Edward, son of Richard, 15, 38, 348.
Ambler, Eliza. See Carrington, Eliza Ambler.
Ambler, family history, 35, 37, 348.

Ambler, Jacquelin, Councillor of State, 1, 2, 3, 5, 10; Treasurer of State, 18, 19, 39, 83; dies, 113, 127, 348.
Ambler, Col. John, 15, 16, 38, 59, 264, 265, 339, 348.
Ambler, Major John, son of Col. John, 338, 348.
Ambler, John, son of Richard, 38, 348.
Ambler, Lucy (Mrs. Daniel Call), 1, 229, 348.
Ambler, Mary Cary (Mrs. Edward Ambler), 15, 16, 38, 348.
Ambler, Rebecca Burwell (Belinda), 1, 7, 19, 39, 84, 113, 126, 127, 128, 165, 171, 173, 278, 348.
Ambler, Richard, marries Elizabeth Jacqueline, 38, 348.
Ambler, Thomas, son of Lucy Marshall and Col. John Ambler, 59, 348.
American Journal of Medical Sciences, 366.
America, 232, 332.
Americans, see also The People, 109, 117, 118, 135, 161, 162, 367.
Americans, in France, 112.
Americans, "money worshippers," 111.
American System, The, 303.
Ames, Fisher, 77, 126, 148, 154, 189.
Amsterdam, 95, 100, 107.
Arlington, Lord Henry of, 23.
Armistead, Frances, first wife of John Ambler, 59, 348.
Army, British, 14, 15, 17, 28, 38, 224, 225, 226, 227, 255, 275; Confederate, 266, 322; Continental, 1, 4, 9, 17, 18, 20, 94, 245, 355; French, 109, 111; United States, 282, 297.
Arnold, Gen. Benedict, invades Virginia, 14.
Arrogance on the high seas, British, 4, 45, 60. 66, 107, 138, 163,

189, 215, 223, 225, 254; Dutch, 4; French, 65, 67, 89, 107, 111, 113, 215; Spanish, 4, 107.
Association for the Preservation of Virginia Antiquities, 354, 357.
Aurora, 126.
Austen, Jane, 294.
Baker, John, 41, 78, 185.
Balch, Rev. Thomas Bloomer, 363.
Baldwin, Henry, Associate Justice Supreme Court, 317, 339.
Baltimore, 92.
Banks, 44, 222, 243; National, 59, 99.
Bank of North America, 94; of Pennsylvania, 94, 131; of United States, 94, 131, 243, 271, 289; of Virginia, 160.
Bannaker's Almanac, 157.
Barbary pirates, 141.
Barbour, James, 224.
Barbour, Phillip P., 312, 315.
Baring, Alexander, 98.
Bay of the Delaware, 102.
Bazile, Judge Leon, 353.
Beale, Dr. James, 286.
Beaumarchais, Pierre A. de Caron, 115.
Bellamy, one of the X Y Z, 113.
Beveridge, Albert J., Life of John Marshall, 354, 357, 358, 359, 361, 366.
Bible Society of Virginia, 276.
Biddle, Charles, 77.
Bignal, John, 76, 98.
Bingham, Anna Louise, 99.
Bingham, Anne Willing, 100, 101, 133, 230.
Bingham, Maria Matilda, 101.
Bingham, William, 77, 99, 101, 133, 159.
Birchett, Edward's chum, 288, 289.
Blackstone's Commentaries on Laws of England, 7.
Blackwell, General, 245.
Blair, Archibald, 128.
Blair, Rev. John D., 104.
Blennerhasset, Harmon, 177.
Bollman, Dr. Eric, 177, 275, 339.
Bonaparte, Jerome, 288, 289.
Book of Common Prayer, English,

19; American, 125, 212, 322.
Boone, Daniel, 35, 43.
Botetourt, Norborne Berkeley Baron de, 59.
Botts, Benjamin, 185, 210.
Bouldin, Powhatan, Home Reminiscences of John Randolph of Roanoke, 359.
Boyce vs Anderson, 365.
Brady, Joseph, The Trial of Aaron Burr, 361.
Brent, Senator Richard, 99.
Brent, Capt. William, marriage and death, 36, 348.
Brig Wilson vs United States, 270.
British, in York Town, 9, 67.
British Manifesto, 1813, 225.
British merchants, debts of Americans to, 3, 31, 32, 33, 76, 78, 127.
Brockenboroughs, 126, 213.
Brockenborough, Sarah Jane, 202.
Brooke, Judge Francis T., 230.
Brooke, George, 364.
Brooke, Lucy, 197.
Brooke, George, son of Judith Marshall and George Brooke, 281.
Brooke, Mary, 197.
Brown, James, of Kentucky, 213.
Brown, John, 100, 101, 102, 113, 114.
Brown's Hotel, Washington, 252.
Bruce, James Coles, 288, 289.
Brydon, G. McLaren, Virginia's Mother Church, 355, 359, 364.
Bullock, Helen Duprey, My Head and My Heart, 358, 360.
Buchanan, Rev. John, 19, 35 104, 127, 173, 201, 206, 212, 213, 292.
Buchanan's Spring, 200, 308.
Burke, Edmund, 312.
Burns, Mr., a tutor, 143.
Burr, Aaron, 88, 97, 101, 147, 149, 162, 163, 166, 169, 175, 227, 275, 330; duel, 163; trials 175-194 passim.
Burton and Moore, History of Henrico Parish and Old St. John's Church, 356.
Cabell, Joseph, 355.

Cabell, William, 18.
Cabell, Judge William H., 230.
Cabot, George, 77, 126, 134.
Caldwell, Elisha, clerk of the Supreme Court, 252.
Calhoun, Floride, 264, 276.
Calhoun, John C., 242, 264, 269, 276, 281, 296, 323.
Callendar, James Thompson, 157.
Camillus, 104.
Call, Daniel, 304, 348.
Calls, 197, 213, 274.
Campaign songs, Jefferson's, 147; Republican, 117, 118, 200, 221, 275.
Campbell, Alexander, 76, 78, 79, 82, 85.
Campbell, Charles, *History of the Colony and Ancient Dominion of Virginia*, 355.
Capitalism, 303.
Capitalists, 49.
Capitol, Virginia, 55, 311.
"Carrington," 305.
Carrington, Col. Edward, 80, 81, 84, 103, 113, 124, 193, 205, 348, 351.
Carrington, Eliza Ambler. See Ambler, Eliza, 1, 2, 36, 103, 104, 197, 206, 229, 257, 274, 275, 298, 341, 342, 348; letter book, 2, 5, 6, 8, 10, 11, 13, 14, 15, 16, 36, 113, 348, 355, 359.
Cary, Martha, marries Edward Jacqueline, 37, 348.
Cary, Col. Miles of Warwick, 37.
Catterall, Louise Cadot, *Richmond Portraits in an Exhibition of Makers of Richmond*, 359.
Charles II, King of England, 23.
Charleston holocaust, 85.
Charlotte County, 120, 365.
Charlottesville, 17, 300.
Chase, Samuel, Associate Justice Supreme Court, 86, 161, 217, 219; trial of, 165-170 passim.
Chesapeake Bay, 1, 3, 4, 92.
Cherokee Nation vs the State of Georgia, 330.
Chesapeake, The, 190.
Cheves, Langdon, 288, 289.

Cheves, son of Langdon, 288, 289.
Church, Baptist, 314.
Church, Congregational, 137.
Church, Cooling Spring Meeting House, 29.
Church, Episcopal, 19, 28, 127, 185, 205, 212, 213, 215, 315.
Church, Established of England, 6, 9, 25, 104, 279.
Church, Goose Creek, 26.
Church, Grace, York Town, 104, 127.
Church, Jamestown, 37, 38.
Church, Monumental, in Richmond, 213, 234, 276.
Church, St. Paul's, Alexandria, 279.
Church, rule for infant baptism, 122.
Clay, Henry, 199, 217, 239, 252, 269, 281, 296, 297, 303, 304.
Clergy, no salaries, 42.
Clinton, George, 47, 169, 189.
Clinton, William, 88, 189.
Clopton, John, 117, 124, 126, 129, 359.
Cobbler's Mountain, 26.
Cocke, Mr., member of a family of notable farmers, 243.
Cock fighting, 159.
Coit, Margaret, *John C. Calhoun*, 363.
Cole, Mr., 282.
Coleman, Nicholas D., 321.
Colonization of Free People of Colour in the United States on the Coast of Africa, American Society for, 249, 253, 255, 256, 304, 341, 360, 364; Richmond-Manchester Auxiliary for, 256, 257; Virginia Society for, 257, 364; Virginia Resolution for, 145; English Society for, 145.
Colston, Edward, 206, 208, 281, 282.
Colston, Elizabeth Marshall, 28, 29, 39, 84, 119, 206, 207, 328, 350.
Colston, Rawleigh, 39, 63, 83, 119, 172, 197, 206, 207.
Colston, Susanna, 197.

Colstons, 118.

Columbia Observer, 281.

Columbian Centinel, 226, 233.

"Commerce," 266.

Commerce, American, 65, 111, 216, 268, 270.

Confederation of States for a Permanent Union, articles of, 47, 357; described, 45; by Washington, 44; discarded, 94.

Confederacy, Southern, 289.

Congress, Continental, 8, 50, 165.

Congress of the Confederation of States, 5, 31, 32, 44, 45.

Congress of These United States, 77, 80, 81, 93, 95, 102, 117, 123, 124, 125, 128, 133, 136, 137, 140, 141, 149, 152, 160, 161, 170, 195, 215, 238, 252, 254, 266, 268, 269, 270, 277, 278, 280, 282, 290, 295, 300, 313, 322, 323, 327.

Congress Hall, ladies visit, 138.

Congress, Library of, 353.

Congressional Record, 135.

Connecticut, Act of Legislature, 267.

Constellation, S.S., 223.

Constitution of the United States, compact for orderly trade between Maryland and Virginia, 46; Madison advocates convention to revise Confederation, 46; the New Plan, 47, 51; Monroe's plan for commercial economy, 53; Convention in Richmond, 51--55 passim; a Constitution ratified by eleven States, 55; by Virginia conditionally, 55; and anti-slave laws, 137; and Congress and Judiciary, 150; convention in Massachusetts, 151; mentioned, 50, 104, 135, 138, 166, 170, 184, 186, 192, 216, 220, 230, 232, 266, 269, 270, 271, 283, 296, 313, 323, 324, 327, 342, 357, 359.

"Contract," 216.

Corbin, Francis, 213.

Cornwallis, General Lord, 14, 27, 255.

Cosway, Maria, 70.

Cottage, The, 15, 19, 37, 38, 59, 263, 265, 356.

Courts, American, 138, 139.

Court of Appeals, Kentucky, 327; Massachusetts, 362; New York, 266; Virginia, 18, 41, 64, 67, 80, 227, 228, 229, 230.

Court of Chancery, Richmond, 18, 67, 112.

Courts of the Commonwealth of Virginia, 17, 18, 32.

Courts, Federal District, 56, 78, 138, 151, 152, 170, 177, 179, 183, 195, 231, 245, 303 324, 333, 335, 366.

Court, Federal District, list of first Virginia applicants, 56.

Court, General of Colony, 41, 99.

Court, Hustings of Richmond, 213.

Court, Supreme, of the United States, 53, 66, 77, 79, 117, 121, 125, 150, 151, 152, 160, 165, 170, 186, 189, 215, 216, 219, 226, 227, 228, 230, 231, 232, 237, 243, 246, 266, 267, 270, 277, 278, 280, 290, 291, 295, 296, 303, 304, 317, 318, 323, 324, 327, 330, 366.

Court, Supreme, under Confederation, 44.

Court, Supreme, suspended for fourteen months, 152.

Courts of Justice, committee for, 18, 42.

Crawford, Caroline, *Romantic Days in the Early Republic,* 358, 360.

Cresson, William Penn, *Life of James Monroe,* 356, 360.

Crawford, William, 253, 264, 281.

Crim, Mrs., 94, 367.

Croes, Rev. Mr. 315.

Cromwell, 23, 24, 157.

Crouch, Jasper, 200.

Culpeper, Thomas, Lord, granted lands by Charles II, 23; becomes sole owner of Northern Neck of Virginia, 24; appoints Receivers General, 24; daughter marries,

William, Lord Fairfax, 24; Culpeper grant becomes "Fairfax lands," 24.

Curles Parish, 205.

Curries, 213.

Cushing, William, Associate Justice Supreme Court, 151, 152, 217, 226, 227, 231, 232, 362.

Dandridge, Mrs., wife of William Dandridge, 278.

Davenport, Rev. Joseph, of York Town, 104.

Davis, Augustine, 157.

Davis' Hotel, Washington, 240.

Davis' Tavern, Raleigh, North Carolina, 152.

Days of Fasting, Humiliation and Prayer, 9, 211.

Declaration of Independence, 50, 165, 180.

Deism, 280.

Democrats, 157.

Democratic Societies, 66, 117, 358.

Devereux, Thomas P., 243.

Dexter, Samuel, 77, 231, 360.

Dick, Major, (Richard Anderson), 263, 364.

Dinners, 58, 93, 116, 179, 200, 209, 230, 235, 237, 241, 276, 286, 295, 304, 308, 311, 319, 321, 328, 336, 365.

Directory, French, 109-116 passim.

Decatur, Commodore Stephen, 181.

de Gazon, Madame, French actress, 109.

Donaldson, Mrs., niece of President Jackson, 317.

Douthat, Catherine, 358.

Douthat, Fielding, 364.

Douthat, John Marshall, 357, 361.

du Bellet, Louise Pecquet, *Some Eminent Families of Virginia*, 356, 357.

Duke University, 353, 359.

Dunlop, Mr., 83.

Dunscomb, Capt. Andrew, 120.

Duvall, Gabriel, Associate Justice Supreme Court, 219, 228, 291, 303, 319.

Duvall, Maj. William, 161.

Eaton, General William, 182.

Eberlein, Harold, *Portrait of a Colonial City*, 358, 360.

Edinburgh, University of, 115.

Ellsworth, Oliver, Chief Justice United States, 283.

Embrey, Alvin, *History of Old Fredericksburg*, 357.

Emmerson, John, *The Chesapeake Affair*, 361; *The Steamboat Comes to Norfolk*, 364.

England, 2, 65, 111, 124, 141; rewards for military service, 23.

English African Society, 146.

Era of Good Feeling, 233, 239, 242, 249, 252.

Erie Canal, 22.

Eulogy, The, 343, 353, 355.

Evans, Louise, *An Old Timer in Warrenton and Fauquier County*, 356.

Eyre, Mr. 88.

Fairfax County, 36.

Fairfax, Denny Martin, assumes name and inherits lands, 27, 41, 85, 342.

Fairfax Devisee vs Hunter's Lessee, 219.

Fairfax Heir at Law vs Hunter's Devisee, 231.

Fairfax lands, 28, 33, 43, 63, 64, 82, 86, 119, 123, 171, 172, 197, 228, 232, 244, 305, 322, 356.

Fairfax lands titles, 32, 75, 85, 232, 324; upheld by House of Burgesses 25, 41; demolished by State of Virginia Confiscatory Act, 26; and Sequestration Acts, 27, 64; upheld by Supreme Court, 228, 231; Marshall Compromise, 85; Marshall title to Leeds Manor cleared by payment in full, 172.

Fairfax, Lord Robert, 27.

Fairfax, Lord Thomas, eighth Baron of Cameron, comes to Virginia, 25; grants lands, 41, 85; death of, 27, 226.

Fairfax, Lord William, seventh Baron of Cameron, 24, 25.

Farm, Chickahominy, 142, 221,

235, 236, 243, 261, 294, 298, 305, 312, 318, 320, 324, 333, 335.

Farm products, 13, 20, 25, 29, 70, 147, 298.

Fashions, 100, 131, 132, 142, 200.

Fauchet Affair, 73.

Fauquier County, 17, 19, 23, 25, 26, 30, 82, 204, 244, 245, 311.

Fauquier County Democrat, 356.

Fauquier County Court House, 172.

Fauquier White Sulphur Springs, 246, 363.

Federalist, The, 49.

Federalist Party, 47, 81, 88, 104, 117, 124, 125, 132, 137, 138, 147, 161, 162, 173, 183, 217, 223, 282, 300, 317.

Finch, John, *Travels in the United States and Canada,* 362.

Fisher, George, *History and Reminiscences of Monumental Church,* 361.

Finley, Rev. Robert, 252.

Fisher, Elizabeth Call, 348.

Fisher, Lucy, 293, 348.

Fishers, 173, 213.

Fisher vs. Cockerell, 365.

Fitzwhylsonn, William, 255, 275.

Flanders, Henry, *Life of John Marshall,* 354, 357.

Fleming, Judge William, 80, 83, 84, 228, 230.

Foley Grant, the, 356.

Foreign Ministers, British, Sir Charles Bagot (1816-1818), 237, 241; Sir Charles Vaughan (1825-1835), 304, 319; French, J. G. Hyde de Neuville (1817-1819), 235, 237, 241; Louis Barbe Charles Serurier (1830-1831), 328.

Forest, The, 25.

Foushee, Dr. William, 41, 71, 161, 213, 224, 273.

France, 60, 64, 65, 66, 88, 109, 111, 124, 128, 133, 135, 141.

Franklin, Benjamin, describes Philadelphia, 131.

Fredericksburg, Va., 2, 28, 43,

120, 123, 278.

Frederick County, 120.

Free State, The, 356.

French Government, 80, 88, 113, 115.

French Parties, in United States, 111.

French Republic, 88.

Fries, Lt. John, 135.

Fulton, Robert, 266.

Gabriel Insurrection, 144.

Gallatin, Albert, 169.

Gamble, Catherine Grattan, 96, 97, 178, 193.

Gamble, John, 209.

Gamble, Colonel Robert, 96, 97, 102, 159, 160, 178, 179, 206.

Gauley River, 222.

George III, 312.

Georgia, State of, 323, 331.

Georgetown, 160.

Gerry, Elbridge, 95, 102, 110, 114, 116.

Gibbons, Major Thomas, 210, 266.

Gibbons vs Ogden, 266.

Gibson, Patrick, 104.

Giles, William B., 118, 186, 312, 315.

Gillespie, Dr., 335.

Gilmer, Francis Walker, 201.

Goode, Samuel, 137.

Goodhart, Professor A. L., describes duties of Marshall's Court, 216.

Goons Creek Manor, 172.

Goose Creek, 26.

Grace, brig, 95, 100, 107.

Green Bag, The, 361.

Griffen, Judge Cyrus, 78, 187.

Grigsby, Hugh Blair, *The Virginia Convention,* 365.

Groome, H. C., *Fauquier During the Proprietorship,* 354, 356.

Ground Squirrel Bridge, 144.

Gurley, Rev. Ralph Randolph, 253, 258, 341, 342.

Gwathmey, John, *Historical Register of Virginians in the Revolution,* 355.

Hague, The, 108, 109.

Halifax County, 289.

Hamilton, Alexander, 28, 49, 50,

56, 69, 70, 80, 82, 93, 94, 99, 104, 147, 163, 170, 178, 181, 188, 193; killed by Burr, 162.
Hamilton Parish, 205.
Hampton, city of captured, 224.
Hanover County, 228.
Hanover Court House, 278.
Happy Creek, 232.
Harding, Chester, 298.
Hardy, Sally Marshall, 361.
Harland, Marion, *Some Colonial Homesteads*, 364.
Harrison, Benjamin, 18.
Harrison, Fairfax, *Virginia Land Grants*, 356; *Old Prince William County*, 356.
Harvard University, 155, 156, 286, 287, 364.
Harvie, Edwin, 210.
Harvie, Ellen, 244, 360.
Harvie, General Jaquelin Burwell, 225, 291, 304, 305, 307, 335, 351.
Harvie, Julianna, 210.
Harvie, Mary Marshall, 72, 76, 91, 97, 121, 142, 144, 154, 196, 198, 206, 210, 224, 225, 233, 273, 274, 275, 282, 321, 341, 351, 352, 361.
Harvie, Susan, 273.
Harvies, 313.
Hastings, Warren, 168.
Hauteval, 113.
Haxalls, 213.
Hay, George, 166, 185, 189, 213, 241.
Henrico County, 42.
Henry, Patrick, 18, 32, 43, 45, 51, 53, 55, 78, 84, 128, 205, 236, 357.
Heyward, Mrs., 92, 98, 359.
Higgins, Mrs. Kenneth, 361.
History of The American Stage, 358.
Hite vs Fairfax, 41.
Hite, Joist, 24.
Hite, Joist, successors of, 41
Hobart, Bishop John Henry, 213.
Hobe, 99.
Hogue, Bernard, 353, 365.
Holland, 108.

Hollow, The, 26, 350.
Honeywood, 197, 206, 282.
Hoofbower, Dr., 338.
Hopkins, Mr., an actor, 159.
Hopkins, Mrs., actress, mother of Edgar Allan Poe, 159.
Hopkins, John, United States Commissioner of Loans, 91, 103.
Hopkinson, Francis, 117.
Hottenguer, 113, 115.
Houdon, Jean Antoine, 115.
Howards and Heywards, (Haywards), 359.
Howe, Henry, *Historical Collections of Virginia*, 357.
Hubbard, Courtlandt Van Dyke, *Portrait of a Colonial City*, 358, 360.
Huger, Col. Francis Kinloch, 275.
Hunter, David, 64, 80, 86, 227, 228.
Hunter vs Fairfax Devisee, 79, 86, 227.
Indians, 35, 58; Cherokee, 323, 330, 331; Winnebago, 296.
Ingersoll, Charles, 237.
Innes, James, 78, 187.
Iredell, James, Associate Justice of the Supreme Court, 64, 78, 79, 87.
Irving, Washington, 182, *Life of George Washington*, 358.
James River, 18.
James River and Kanawha Canal, *Annual Report*, 362.
Jamestown, 37, 38, 172.
Jay, John, Chief Justice, Secretary of State, 66, 68 78.
Jay Treaty, 66, 68, 69, 70, 81, 104, 138; opposed by Virginia Senators, 72.
"Jack Randle," see Randolph, John of Roanoke.
Jackson, Andrew, 181, 227, 253, 281, 296, 297, 299, 300, 304, 305, 307, 317, 318, 323.
Jackson's Men, 300, 321.
Jackson, Rachel, 304.
Jackson River, 222.
Jacqueline, Edward, 37, 348.
Jacqueline, Elizabeth, marries Rich-

ard Ambler, 38, 348.

Jacqueline, Martha, 35, 38, 41.

Jacqueline, Mary, marries John Smith of Shooters Hill, 38.

Jefferson, Maria, 132.

Jefferson, Thomas, trustee for William and Mary, 6; bill for religious freedom, 9; bill for relief of slavery, 363; Amblers and, Jefferson, 354; Governor of Virginia, 10; and press, 10; signs Marshall's law license, 14; design for courts, 17, 18; in 4th Congress, 31; on British debts, 32; retains Marshall, 32; on resistance to Constitution, 47; on division of unity, 48; would reject Constitution, 52; designs Virginia Capitol, 55; Secretary of State, 56; pulls away from Washington, 65; offers to resign, 65; writes to Maria Cosway, 70; on Marshall, 71; influence on Monroe, 80; presidential candidate, 88; elected Vice President, 88; becomes head of Republican party, 88; opposes mission to France, 89; deal with Hamilton, 93; in political triangle, 94; wins the press over, 117; calls on Marshall, 118; writes carretted note, 119; grasps Virginia, 120; on press or government, 124; and "Belinda," 127; suspects Marshall, 130; his ménage in Philadelphia, 132; does not return Marshall's call, 133; at Monticello, 141; candidate second time, 147; elected President by House of Representatives, 149; invites Marshall to administer oath, 149; Burr enmity, 149; begins fight on Supreme Court, 151, 152; non partisan announcement, 157; Lama of the Mountain, 159; Randolph of Roanoke's temper with, 167; elected second term, 169; difference with Marshall's policies, 170; reads Life of Washington, 173; *Notes on Virginia*,

173; admired in Richmond, 176; message about Burr's guilt, 177; had been in danger of British law, 180; "master of Americans," 181; influences George Hay, 185; Martin blares at, 187; subpoena, 187; and Chesapeake affair, 190; urges Congress to impeach Marshall, 195; his appointees on Supreme Bench, 217; observes Old Cushing's death, 218; opposes Story, 219; manners compared with Monroe's, 238; on emancipation of slaves, 250; in list of Presidents sworn into office by Marshall, 283; in financial straits, 295; death, 295; emulated by Monroe, 334; kinship, 347.

Jennings, Samuel K., 158.

John Marshall House, See Polly's mansion.

Johnson, Senator Richard, 280.

Johnson, William, Associate Justice Supreme Court, 217, 228, 231, 271, 278, 303, 318.

Jones, Miss, 292.

Jones, Meriwether, 157.

Judiciary Act of Congress, 1789, 151; 1801, 151; repeal 1802, 165; Section 25, 152.

Kanawha River, 222.

Keith, "Aunt," wife of James Keith, 279, 292, 297.

Keith, Rev. James, 26, 90, 200, 204, 347, 361.

Keith, James, son of Rev. James, 200.

Keith, Mary Randolph. See Marshall, Mary Randolph Keith.

Kennedy, John P., *Memoirs of William Wirt*, 358, 361.

Kentucky, 158; Act of Statehood, 44; Resolution, 69, 130.

Kentucky, District of, 18, 29, 35, 43, 44, 51.

Kercheval, Samuel, *History of the Valley of Virginia*, 356.

King, Rufus, 47, 77, 103, 104, 116, 146.

Kirk, Russell, *John Randolph of*

Roanoke, A Study in Conservative Thought, 359.
Klacker, Christian, *St. Memins Portrait of Chief Justice Marshall,* 361.
Knox, General Henry, Secretary of War, 56.
Kremer, George, 281, 282.
Lafayette, George Washington, 274.
Lafayette, General Marquis de, 8, 64, 274, 275, 278.
Lambert, Col. David, 328.
Lambert, Eliza, 276.
Latrobe, Benjamin, 87, 200, 239, 358.
Latrobe, Mary Hazelhurst, 200.
Law Notes. See Account Book.
Lee, Ann, 297.
Lee, Charles, Attorney General, 79.
Lee, Gen. Henry (Light Horse Harry), 43, 63, 67, 68, 136, 209, 297, 305, 347.
Lee, Richard Henry, 18.
Lee, General Robert E., 297.
Leeds Academy, England, 39.
Leeds Manor, 86, 172, 208, 300, 320, 339, 365, 366.
Leigh, Benjamin Watkins, 197, 275, 315.
L'Enfant, Peter Charles, 94.
Leopard, S. S., 189, 190.
Le Roy, Mr., a tutor, 206.
Letters, John Marshall, to his wife, 60, 66, 76, 90, 92, 95, 96, 98, 99, 100, 102, 107, 108, 112, 121, 142, 143, 152, 162, 235, 242, 245, 262, 272, 278, 281, 282, 291, 293, 304, 305, 306, 307, 317, 319, 320, 321, 328, 329, 333, 335, 337, 340; to James Iredell, 87-8; to Thomas Jefferson, 119; to Jaquelin Marshall, 243; to James Monroe, 31; to Mr. Rawlings, 308. Thomas Jefferson to John Marshall, 118; Edward Carrington Marshall to his mother, 288; Mary Marshall to her mother, 207. Col. Thomas Marshall to

John Marshall, 83, 288. Thomas Marshall to his mother, 265.
Lewis, Mr., 305.
Lewis, Mrs. John Latane, 353.
Liberia, 259.
Livingston, Brockholst, Associate Justice Supreme Court, 217, 228.
Livingston, Senator Edward, 318.
Livingston, Louisa D'Avezac Moreau, 318.
Livingston, Robert, 154, 266.
Lyons, Judge Peter, 80.
Lousiana Territory, 171.
MacRea, Alexander, 185, 193.
Madison, Dorothy Payne (Todd), 199, 317.
Madison, James, President of William and Mary, 6. Episcopal Bishop, 212.
Madison, James, 18, 43, 46, 49, 51, 104, 150, 166, 200, 218, 219, 223, 227, 233, 235, 239, 250, 283, 309, 310, 312, 313, 315, 341; describes constitutional government, 48.
Magruder, Allen Bowie, *Life of John Marshall,* 354, 357.
Marbury vs Madison, 150.
Maritime Policy, British, 70.
Marshall, Mrs., an actress, 76.
Marshall, "a cousin from Winchester," 209, 362.
Marshall, Agnes, 265, 321, 351.
Marshall, Anne, (Nancy) daughter of Thomas, 265, 351.
Marshall, Alexander Keith, 28, 35, 290, 351, 362.
Marshall, Ashton, 363.
Marshall, Charles, 28, 64, 83, 165, 171, 351.
Marshall, Claudia Hamilton Burwell, 352.
Marshall, Claudia Marshall Stribling, 356.
Marshall, Edward Carrington, 165, 170, 197, 206, 224, 233, 286, 287, 289, 305, 306, 317, 319, 352, 367.
Marshall, Eliza, daughter of William, 197.
Marshall, Eliza Price, niece of

Henry Clay, 322.
Marshall, Elizabeth. See Colston, Elizabeth Marshall.
Marshall, Elizabeth Alexander, 244, 272, 305, 351.
Marshall, Elizabeth Steptoe Clarkson, 244, 352.
Marshall, Elizabeth Markham, 25, 349.
Marshall, Fielding Lewis, 244, 265, 351.
Marshall, Hester Morris, 50, 70, 78, 232.
Marshall, Senator Humphrey, 199, 349.
Marshall, James Keith, 137, 181, 197, 224, 233, 243, 305, 319, 339, 352, 366, 367.
Marshall, James Markham, 20, 28, 50, 64, 70, 78, 83, 86, 115, 116, 128, 172, 228, 231, 232, 342, 365.
Marshall, Jane, 28, 289, 351.
Marshall, Jaquelin, 48, 76, 83, 91, 97, 129, 143, 155, 171, 196, 208, 224, 233, 242, 243, 244, 305, 352.
Marshall, Jaquelin, son of Jaquelin, 305, 352.
Marshall, John, Chief Justice of the United States, born and learns to walk on Fairfax lands, 26; father's companionship, 29; mother's, 29; studies law, 7; in Continental Army, 1, 5; judge advocate, 18; enrolls at William and Mary, 5, 6; finds Polly, 6, 7; resigns commission, 17; walks to Philadelphia, 17; enters politics, 17; City Recorder, 42; represents Fauquier County in State Legislature, 18; on Council of State, 18; opposed by Pendleton, 18; on committee to revise Jefferson's design for courts, 18, 42; courting, 18, 19; marries, 19; practices law, 20; joins clubs, 20, 42-3; retained by Denny Martin Fairfax, 27; tries to purchase Fairfax lands, 27; begins to differ with Monroe and Jefferson, 31; retained by Jefferson, 32; first recorded appearance before Va. Court of Appeals, 41; represents Richmond in Legislature, 42; helps to write Act for Kentucky Statehood, 44; takes over Gov. Randolph's law practice, 42; organizes lottery for a Masonic Hall, 42; delegate to Constitutional Convention, 50; applies for license to practice in U. S. District Courts, 56; declines post of Attorney General for Va., 56; his policy, 59; death of two children, 60; forms syndicate to purchase Fairfax lands, 64; elected Brig. Gen. Va. Militia, 67; mission to Smithfield, 67; Jay Treaty, 69, 70, 81, 82; rift with Jefferson, 70; declines post of Attorney General, 71; delegate for Richmond in Legislature, 72; first appearance before Supreme Court, 77-8; declines post of minister to France, 82; mission to France, 89-118 passim; return to Philadelphia, 118; declines post Associate Justice, 122; visits Mt. Vernon, 123; elected to Congress, 129; Secretary of War, 140; Secretary of State, 140; Chief Justice, 149; his policy, 150; trustee of William and Mary, 162; Harvard degree, 172; files deed to Fairfax lands, 172; inherits Oak Hill, 154; marketing, 202-3; on committee for new church, 205; meets Story, 218; stage accidents, 219, 303, 366; president of Virginia Agriculture Society, 221; commission for western water route, 222; State vigilance committee, 224; Fauquier White Sulphur Springs, 246; slips on step, 261; ladies attentions, 261; Marshall's Court, 267; welcomes Lafayette, 274; powers condemned, himself praised, 277-8, 290; member Bunker Hill Society, 290; rea-

son for not voting, 297; committees for relief of Jefferson, 295; convention for State roads, harbours and water ways, 300; delegate to State Constitution Convention, 309; becomes ill, 324; an exasperating patient, 334; treated in Philadelphia, 336-7; parts with Polly, 343; writes Eulogy, 343-4; moves out of Polly's mansion, 366; dies in Philadelphia, 367.

Administers oath of Presidential office to Jefferson, 149, 170; Madison, 200, 223; Monroe, 239, 282; Adams, 282; Jackson, 306.

Described by, Eliza Ambler, 6; John Adams, 149; George Cabot, 134; Miss Gibbons, 209; Gilmer, 91, 201; New York Daily Advertizer, 331; old citizens, 17, 54, 285, 294; Peters, 340; Pickering, 126; Schmidt, 67; Seddon, 318; Sedgewick, 134, 140; Story, 217; Webster, 267; Wirt 201, 293, 294; Nile's Register, 367.

Denounced by, Jefferson, 71, 126, 195, 219; Fisher Ames, 126; Theodore Sedgewick, 126; press, 66-7, 124, 125, 126, 180, 195; Spencer Roane, 228-9.

Modes of Travel, 75, 272, 280, 298, 333.

His prayers, 29, 243, 280, 294, 306, 318, 328, 343.

His faith, 234, 280, 300, 325.

With children, 121-2, 154, 273, 285-6, 327, 341, 342.

Writes verses, 52, 220, 277, 300, 332.

Alien and Sedition Acts, 125; Constitutional Government in U.S., 54; Democrats, 149, 150; female part of society, 140; foreign policy, 125, 138; French language, 95; good government, 150; independence of judiciary, 53, 327; Jane Austin, 294; Jefferson, 32, 133, 148, 150; Maria Sedgewick, 328-29; Monroe in Paris, 80; power of the people, 53; States, united, 31, 45, 54, 303; States independent, 44; sovereignty of Virginia, 78.

Marshall, John, *Autobiographical Sketch* quoted, 6, 29, 44, 45, 55, 68, 69, 70, 81, 125, 140, 141.

Marshall, John, *Life of George Washington*, 71, 159, 163 167, 170, 171, 172, 173, 354, 355, 358, 359; quoted, 8, 59-60, 66, 68, 110.

Marshall, John, son of Chief Justice, 113, 118, 121, 142, 165, 171, 197, 233, 234, 244, 293, 320, 351, 352.

Marshall, John, son of Edward Carrington, 319, 352.

Marshall, John, son of Thomas, son of Chief Justice, 265, 306, 351.

Marshall, Judith, 28, 83, 350.

Marshall, Louis (Lewis), 28, 64, 65, 83, 116, 279, 351.

Marshall, Lucy, wife of John Ambler, 28, 35, 59, 72, 348, 350.

Marshall, Margaret Lewis, 204, 209 222, 224, 305, 351.

Marshall, Margaret, daughter of Thomas, 266, 351.

Marshall, Maria Willis, daughter of James Keith, 320, 351.

Marshall, Maria Winston Price, 234, 350.

Marshall, Martin, 171.

Marshall, Mary. See Harvie, Mary Marshall.

Marshall, Mary, 28, 364.

Marshall, Mary Ambler, daughter of James Keith, 320, 352.

Marshall, Mary Ambler, daughter of Jaquelin, 244, 352.

Marshall, Mary Morris, 364.

Marshall, Mary Randolph Keith, 5, 26, 28, 39, 40, 201, 349, 350.

Marshall, Mary Willis, daughter of John and Elizabeth Alexander, 364.

Marshall, Nancy, 28, 351.

Marshall, Polly. See Ambler, Mary Willis. Described by Eliza, 2, 89, 113; by Marshall, 7, 21, 43, 57, 60, 73, 136, 233, 355; dances with Marshall, 6; Jefferson's shadow, 9, 124; writes her name on law notes, 7, 9; arrives in New World, 11, 13; flight from British, 14, 17, 224; marriage, 19; first home, 20; in Richmond society, 20, 31; first visit to Oak Hill, 28; Tom born, 32; second home, 35; daughter born, 41; invalidism begins, 41; third home, 41; Jaquelin born, 48; gift of mirror, 49; finds politics a storm, 55; moves into her mansion, 57; child born and dies, 57; son born, 60; death of four children, 60; Mary born, 72; a good housekeeper, 73, 91; but no ballot, 74; reads the press, 66, 124, 125, 157-63, 179, 186, 190, 195, 228; John born, 113; first serious illness, 113; visits Virginia Springs, 120; in Philadelphia, 131-140 passim; James born, 137; calls on the Jeffersons, 134; Gabriel insurrection, 143-4; portrait painted, 163; Edward born, 165; irked by Richmond society, 180; retires with figurines to Oak Hill, 190; second serious illness, 195-6; grandchildren, 233, 265, 285, 320, 321, 327; her religion, 9, 104, 322, 344; her church revives, 214; decides to become an old lady, 233; a quiet life, ill again, 308-9; dies, 343.

Marshall, Rebecca Peyton, 305, 317, 352.

Marshall syndicate for Fairfax lands, 63, 115.

Marshall, Col. Thomas, 1, 3, 4, 23, 25, 26, 35, 43, 83, 119, 130, 153, 205, 349.

Marshall, Capt. Thomas, 28, 29, 35, 58, 350, 357.

Marshall, Thomas, son of Chief Justice, 32, 76, 83, 91, 97, 103, 129, 154, 163, 171, 172, 191, 196, 224, 227, 244, 245, 250, 265, 270, 273, 291, 292, 298, 305, 306, 307, 311, 315, 351, 352, 363.

Marshall, Thomas, son of Humphrey, 321.

Marshall, Thomas, son of Thomas, son of Chief Justice, 266, 357.

Marshall, Thomas Francis, 317, 321, 323.

Marshall, William, 28, 64, 83, 171, 188, 211, 213, 229, 350.

Marshall, William, son of Louis, 279, 321, 322.

Marshall, William, son of William, 197, 273.

Marshall, Mr., 97.

Martin, Luther, 168, 185, 188, 193.

Martyr, Mrs. Frances, 224, 285, 308, 310, 327.

Mason, George, 5, 44, 46, 312.

Mason, Claudia Hamilton Norton (Mrs. John K.), 353, 354, 358, 363, 364, 365, 366.

Mason, Dr. H. Norton, 353.

Massachusetts Historical Society, *Proceedings,* 357, 365, 366.

Massachusetts, 47.

Massachusetts, Justice of Supreme Court of, 355.

McCaw, Dr. James, 211.

McClung, Dr. James, 41, 71, 212, 213.

McClung, John A., *Sketches of Western Adventure,* 357.

McGuire's Hotel, Winchester, 324.

McHenry, James, Secretary of War, 140.

McKay, Robert, 24.

McLean, John, Associate Justice Supreme Court, 303, 318.

Meade, Col. 112.

Meade, Bishop William, 253, 280.

Medicines, 158.

Mercer, Charles Fenwick, 321, 322.
Merry, Mrs., Anne, 98.
Methodists, 144.
Middle Plantation, 37.
Militia, Colony, 26; County, 67; State, 16, 120, 355.
Mills, Robert, 212.
Mississippi River, 29, 222, 303.
Mitchell, Stewart, *New Letters of Abigail Adams*, 358.
Money, inflationary, 3; shortage, 4, 32, 44; specie, 10, 102; federal funding, 59, 99; State currency, 75, 158, 159, 323; farm prices, 243.
Monroe, Elizabeth Kortright, 239, 240, 241.
Monroe, James, 18, 31, 43, 45, 51, 80, 114, 144, 145, 151, 154, 158, 159, 181, 221, 223, 226, 227, 233, 239, 241, 261, 262, 264, 271, 274, 278, 283, 292, 309, 310, 311, 312, 315, 334.
Monroe, James, described by Serurier, 240.
Monticello, 70, 159.
Moore, Bishop Richard Channing, 212, 213.
Moorelands, 338.
Mordecai, Samuel, *Richmond in Bygone Days*, 354, 356, 357.
Morris, Mary White, wife of Robert Morris, 127.
Morris, Robert, 50, 70, 77, 78, 92, 93, 94, 101, 118, 137.
Morris, Gouverneur, 52.
Mt. Blanc, 244.
Mount Vernon, 90, 103, 122, 142, 143.
Mount Vernon family, 104.
Munford, Beverley, *Virginia's Attitude Toward Slavery and Secession*, 363.
Munford, George Wythe, *Two Parsons*, 359.
Murray, William Vans, 104.
Napoleon, 110, 288.
Nason, Samuel, a New England farmer, 47, 357.

National Republican Party, 300.
"Navigation," 266, 270.
Navy, British, 222; Dutch, 107; Maryland and Virginia, 46; United States, 117, 190, 254.
Negro boatmen, 222, 249.
Negro religion, 251.
Negro singing, 13, 139, 249.
Negroes, free, 144, 145, 203, 249, 250, 251, 252, 254, 255, 256, 363; Mrs. Bird, 58; Si Gilbert, 59.
Nelson, Elizabeth Burwell, wife of William Nelson, 39.
Nelson, Hon. William, 39.
Nelson, Judge William, Jr., 161.
Netherlands, Batavian Republic, 110.
New Jersey, Act of Legislature, 267.
New River, 222.
New York, 47, 55.
New York, Act of Legislature, 267.
New York Daily Advertiser, 331.
New York Evening Post, 271, 272.
New York Public Library, 353, 357.
Newspapers, Ames on, 148; Jefferson on, Webster, on, 141.
Nicholases, 173.
Nicholas, John, 118.
Niles' Register, 357.
Nimmo, Mr., 88.
Norfolk Gazette and Public Ledger, 132, 189, 360, 361.
North American Review, 364, 366.
Norton, Dr. Daniel Norborne, 293, 348.
Nortons, 213.
Nullification, of Federal decree, 67, 296, 323, 332; of French treaties, 117.
Oak Hill, 23, 26, 28, 29, 35, 43, 59, 66, 154, 162, 165, 190, 204, 222, 223, 224, 225, 265, 273, 298, 305.
Oby, overseer at Chickahominy Farm, 243, 272, 305, 333.
O'Ellers Tavern, 118, 119.
Ogden, Aaron, 266, 267, 268.

Ohio Valley, coveted by Spain, France, England, 29.
Page, John, governor of Virginia, 161.
Pages, 213.
Papers of John Marshall, 353.
Paris, 64, 65, 88, 89, 101, 104, 109, 111, 112, 115, 121.
Parliament, 168.
Patriot, The, 157, 363.
Patterson, Mrs., 211.
Paulding, James Kirke, *A Life of George Washington*, 359.
Paxton, W.M., *The Marshall Family*, 354, 361.
Payne, Mr., an advisor on agriculture, 305.
Pendleton, Judge Edmund, 18, 43, 51, 52, 210.
Pennsylvania, State arms, 148.
People, The, 53, 68, 145, 160, 306, 307.
Peters, Judge Richard, 194, 295, 335, 336, 340.
Peters, Richard, Jr., 335; *Reports of Cases argued and adjudged in the Supreme Court of the United States*, 365.
Petersburg, S.S., 274.
Phi Beta Kappa, 10, 355.
Philadelphia, 17, 46, 47, 52, 76, 77, 102, 117, 131, 133, 317, 335, 336, 338, 367.
Philadelphia Gazette, 126.
Physick, Dr. Philip Syng, 334-341 passim, 359.
Pickett, Mr., an overseer, 279.
Pickering, Joseph, 293, 295.
Pickering, Timothy, 107, 113, 114, 118, 126, 141, 160.
Pinckney, General Charles Cotesworth, 84, 88, 89, 95, 102, 108, 110, 114, 115, 116, 119, 147, 149, 290.
Placide, Mrs., an actress, 209.
Pleasants, James, 213, 256.
Pleasants, Samuel, 158, 163.
Plumer, Senator William, 154.
Polly's mansion (John Marshall House), 56, 57, 71, 73, 115, 193, 196, 198, 210, 223, 317,
327, 354, 356, 357.
Postal service, 10, 75, 84, 92, 100, 112, 113, 207, 262, 278, 329, 330.
Potomac River, 24.
Presidential Elections, first contest, 87; second contest, 137; thrown into House of Representatives, 147, 149, 281.
Press, The, 66, 67, 68, 69, 88, 95, 113, 117, 120, 124, 125, 132, 136, 142, 148, 151, 177, 180, 195, 266, 300.
Prince William County, 25, 26.
Princeton, University, 154, 172, 196.
Proceedings and Debates of the Virginia State Convention, 365.
Prospect Hill, 245.
Prosser, Henry, 144.
Puritan party in Virginia, 23.
Quakers, 78, 93, 139, 144, 158, 264.
Railroads, steam, 300.
Raleigh, N.C., 152.
Randolph, Dr. Jacob, *A Memoir on the Life and Character of Dr., Philip Syng Physick, M.D.*, 334, 359-60.
Randolph, John of Roanoke, 100, 128, 129, 134, 160, 166, 168, 169, 170, 182, 183, 250, 269, 277, 281, 283, 294, 300, 311, 312, 314, 315, 316, 347, 359, 364.
Randolph, Edmund, 41, 43, 46, 50, 73, 82, 167, 184, 185, 187, 225, 226, 236, 283, 347, 358; Governor of Virginia, 42; Attorney General United States, 56; Secretary of State, 66; votes against Jay Treaty, 71.
Randolph, Extrs., 112.
Randolph, Mary Isham, 205, 347.
Randolph, Thomas Mann, 205, 347.
Randolphs, 173.
Rawlings, Mr., 308.
Reeves, Tapping, 154.
Republic, the, 324.
Republican Party, 59, 82, 88, 117,

120, 124, 138, 147, 152, 157, 160, 183, 199, 275, 307.

Revolution, the, 70, 120, 172, 180, 255, 268, 286.

Reynolds, William of York Town, 355.

Rhode Island, 46, 55.

Rich, Wesley, *History of the Post Office to the Year 1829*, 358.

Richmond, 11, 20, 30, 36, 51, 105, 126, 143, 144, 147, 159, 224, 230, 249, 255, 256, 272, 273, 296, 308, 341, 367; described, 13, 14, 87, 91, 224, 310; Capitol Square, 13, 14, 64, 72, 224, 310; Court End of Town, 35, 42, 104, 126, 163, 173, 205; Common Council, 121, 196, 210; Common Hall, 4, 21; celebrates Jefferson's ascendency, 161; celebrates Fourth of July, 95, 190; builds armory, 125; harbour (Rocketts), 13, 279, 296, 334; ice trade, 279; market, 13, 74, 202; politics, 69, 70, 148; society, 20, 59, 97, 175; Sunday Schools, 206, 273; business district burns, 42; theatre fire, 209.

Richmond Churches, St. John's, 29, 104, 173, 205, 213, 264; Shockoe Hill, 205, 212; Monumental, 212, 314.

Richmond Clubs and Societies, Amicable Society, 180, 202, Barbecue, 121, 200, 308; Broad Rock Track, 43, 159; circulating library, 43; Formicola's Tavern Club, 43; Jockey Club, 42, 43, 51; Masonic Hall, 42; Quoit Club, 121, 202, 308; St. Tammany, 20.

Richmond Taverns, Bell, 161; Eagle, 178, 274, 295; Formicola's, 43.

Richmond and Columbia Turnpike, 160.

Richmond Enquirer, 157.

Richmond Examiner, 157.

Richmond Whig and Advertizer, 297.

Riley, Edward, *Yorktown During the Revolution*, 355.

Ringold, Tench, 329.

Ritson, Margaret, *Poetical Picture of America*, 19, 356.

Roane, Spencer, Judge of District Court, 20, 31, 56, 80, 149, 173, 227, 228, 229, 230, 236, 243, 255, 275.

Robertson, David, 51.

Robertson, Wyndham, *Pocahontas, Alias Matoaka, and Her Descendants*, 359.

Robins, Jonathan, case, 138, 190.

Robinson, John, 328.

Rochefoucauld, Duke de, 66.

Rotterdam, 109.

Rouselle, M., dancing master, 36.

Rowan, Senator John, of Kentucky, 290.

Rutherfoord, John, 129.

St. Memin, Fevret de, 180, 196, 361.

San Domingo insurrection, 163.

Sands, Mrs. Alexander, 353.

School, Miss Mercer's, 321.

Scott, Charles, Governor of Kentucky, 199.

Scott, Mary Wingfield, *Houses of Old Richmond*, 357, 362.

Scott, Winfield, 183.

Scott's novels, 125.

Scottsville Races, Powhatan County, 159.

Secession, 60, 148, 154, 283, 296.

Seddon, James A., 318.

Sedgewick, Maria, 240.

Sedgewick, Theodore, 77, 126, 134, 140.

Senate, United States, as a Court of Impeachment, 166.

Serurier, Count Louis, 240.

Servants, see also Slavery, 317, 324, 327; Agnes, 244, 259; cook bought in Gloucester, 73; Dick, 90, 91, 235; Gabriel, 144; Gilbert, 211; Jacob, 91; John, 129; Joseph, 143, 144, 177, 198, 230, 286, 312; Jubal, 129; Moses, 143, 144, 235; Old Henry, 299; Old Sam, 5, 15, 16; Peter, 125,

143, 144, 152, 177, 183, 210, 229, 312; Pharaoh, 144; Robin (Spurlock), 20, 131, 138, 139, 152, 169, 210, 244, 258, 259, 261, 286, 312, 316, 342, 343, 356; Solomon, 144; Venus, 138, 144, 210, 258, 259.
Servies, James A., *A Bibliography of John Marshall,* 354.
Shadrack, Meshack and Abednego, 113.
Shenandoah Valley, 24.
Sheppard, Mosby, 144.
Sherman, Susanne, *Thomas Wade West, Theatrical Impresario, 1790-1799,* 358.
Shorts, Mr., 84.
Sierra Leone, 146.
Silver Heels, 5, 124, 194.
Simms, John E., *John H. B. Latrobe and His Times,* 361.
Slavery, African, 253, 255; in Virginia, 9, 25, 29, 132, 141, 145, 203, 215, 236, 257, 303, 304, 313, 314, 322, 363; Congressional consideration of, 137; Virginia legislation upon, 145-6, 251, 252, 363; Marshall fixes status of on public carriers, 304.
Smith, Ellen Harvie, 356.
Smith, Mary Jacqueline of Shooters Hill, 357.
Smith, William, governor of Virginia, 210.
Smiths of Shooters Hill, 2, 355.
Society of the Cincinnati, 20.
Southard, Rebecca Harrow, 264.
Southard, Samuel Lewis, Secretary of Navy, 264.
Southern Churchman, 364.
Spain, 29, 188.
Sprigg, Mr., tenant farmer, 318.
Stannard, Mary Newton, *A History of Richmond,* 356, 357.
State Department, 80, 81, 119, 141, 146.
Steamboats, 154, 262, 278; S.S. *Patrick Henry,* 274; S.S. *Potomac,* 296; S.S. *Powhatan,* 246; S.S. *Thomas Jefferson,* 272; S.S. *Virginia,* 274.

States, sovereign, 32, 44, 45, 46, 47, 60, 64, 77, 78, 99, 126, 147, 148, 154, 167, 217, 222, 226, 231, 240, 266, 267, 268, 269, 271, 282, 294, 297, 323, 324, 327, 334, 342, 362, 363.
States, united, 45, 46, 48, 65, 154, 157, 232, 303, 322, 324, 331; Ames on, 154; Reeves on, 144; Pickering on, 154; Plumer on, 154.
Steamboat Case, see Ogden vs Gibbons.
Stedman, Mr., 161.
Steele's Tavern, Washington, 160.
Stoddert, Benjamin, Secretary of Navy, 181.
Stone, Mrs., née Boothe, 278.
Stony Point, Battle of, 169, 210.
Storrs, Mr., 329.
Story, Joseph, Associate Justice Supreme Court, 27, 60, 216, 220, 221, 228, 231, 267, 271, 278, 287, 289, 291, 292, 293, 294, 296, 297, 300, 303, 308, 311, 317, 320, 321, 334, 337, 339, 340, 359, 365, 367.
Sully, Mathew, 77.
Swan, Mr., Washington Lawyer, 321.
Swartout, Samuel, 177, 181, 182.
Talbot, Senator Isham, 277.
Talleyrand, Périgord Charles, 110, 111, 113, 114, 116.
Tammany, Chief, 20.
Tarleton, General, 199.
Taylor, Mr., of Norfolk, 265.
Taylor, Judge George Keith Talliaferro, 288, 351.
Taylor, John, of Caroline, 41.
Taylor, Robert, 178, 179.
Tazewell, William, 115, 359.
Texel River, 107.
Theatre, French, 109; Richmond, 51, 77, 159, 198, 204, 358; Philadelphia, 76, 94, 98, 358; Washington, 221, 293.
Thompson, Rev. James, 29.
Thompson, Smith, Associate Justice Supreme Court, 291, 303, 317, 318, 331.

Timothy Trititle vs Lessee of David Hunter, 64.
Toasts, 69, 119, 160, 161, 198.
Todd, Thomas, Associate Justice Supreme Court, 217, 228, 278, 291.
Trade, 3, 4.
Treaty of Peace, 32, 60, 63, 66, 78, 79, 228.
Transylvania College, 116.
Treaty of Ghent, 227.
Trent, Dr., advertizes galvanic cures, 158.
True Index, The, 363.
Truxton, Commodore Thomas, 181.
Tucker, George T., 282.
Tucker, Judge St. George, 179, 186, 189, 231.
Tuckers, 126, 173.
Turner, Edward's chum, 288.
Tyler, John, 253.
United States, 31, 44, 45, 88, 109.
Valentine, Edward, 357, 361.
Valentine Museum, 353, 354, 356.
Valley Forge, 5.
Van Buren, Martin, 290, 319; Secretary of State, 328.
Vaughn, John, 78.
Villette, Madame, 111, 113, 116.
Vauxhall of Philadelphia, 92, 93.
Virginia Argus, 158, 160.
Virginia Assembly, 43, 45, 222, 251, 252, 282.
Virginia, Commonwealth of, 10, 14, 26, 27, 88, 126, 139, 309, 363; debts of Congress to, 31; Marshall's love for, 101.
Virginia Council of State, 4, 9, 14, 120.
Virginia Federalist, 157.
Virginia Gazette, 10, 120, 355.
Virginia Historical Society, 353, 360, 364.
Virginia House of Burgesses, 25, 26, 363.
Virginia legislature, Acts of, 17, 18, 23, 24, 26, 27, 46, 49, 72, 73, 85, 145, 146, 222, 251, 252, 295, 300, 363.

Virginia Mineral Springs, 120, 141, 171, 195.
Virginia, population of in 1787, 49.
Virginia State Constitution, 307, 309, 310, 313, 314, 315, 365.
Virginia State Library, 353.
Virginia Theological Seminary, 279.
Virginia, University of, 353, 359, 364.
Virginians, 6, 87, 93, 125.
Vital Facts of the College of William and Mary, 355.
Wadsworth, Peleg, 77.
Walcot, Mr., 84.
Walker, Mrs., 98.
War Between the States, 320.
Ware vs Hylton, 78.
Warrells, 213.
Warren, Charles, *The Supreme Court in the History of the United States,* 354, 355, 356, 358, 359, 362, 364.
Warren, William, 98.
Warrenton, Va., 7.
Washington birthday celebrations, 20, 95, 117, 160, 236, 261, 319.
Washington, Bushrod, Associate Justice Supreme Court, 121, 122, 217, 228, 253, 291, 293, 303, 317, 355.
Washington City, 100, 142, 160, 215, 221, 226, 304, 305, 307; society, 200, 226, 292, 294, 306, 318, 319, 328.
Washington College, 116.
Washington family, 85, 142, 143.
Washington Federalist, 157.
Washington, George, 1, 7, 25, 38, 44, 46, 50, 55, 64, 65, 69, 70, 72, 77, 80, 81, 84, 88, 115, 117, 118, 122, 123, 124, 128, 136, 151, 165, 225, 226, 340, 367.
Washington, John, buys Culpeper lands, 24.
Washington, Martha, 39, 143, 151.
Washington Republic, 268.
"We the States," 54.

Webster, Daniel, 252, 267, 268, 290, 305, 323.
Weld, Isaac, describes Americans 68, 358.
Wertenbaker, T. J., *Virginia Under The Stuarts*, 356.
West, Anne West Bignal (Mrs. West, Jr.), 76, 98.
West Indies, 3.
West, John Wade, 76, 209.
West, Mrs. John Wade, 76, 161.
Westmoreland County, 23, 25.
Westover Plantation, 14, 262, 265.
Weyanoke, 265.
Wharton, Anne, *Social Life in the Early Republic*, 360.
Wheaton, Henry, *Reports of Cases argued and adjudged in the Supreme Court of the United States*, 356, 362, 364.
White, Bishop William, 94, 127.
Wickham, John, 78, 112, 179, 184, 202, 275, 311.
Wickham, Julia, 275.
Widgery, William, a New England farmer, 47, 357.
Wignal & Reinagle, 78, 98.
Wilkinson, General James, 177, 182.
William and Mary, College of, Marshall enrolls, 5; tuition costs, 6; library, 7, 8; other reference, 162, 279, 353, 355, 359.
Williams, 213.
Williamsburg, 5, 9, 56.
Wills, Captain, 95, 99, 108.
Wilmer, Rev. William H., 213, 276.
Wines, Madeira, 64, 177, 366, French and Spanish, 65, *The Supreme Court*, 220.
Wirt, Catherine Gamble, 206, 263.
Wirt, William, 79, 166, 172, 186, 190, 193, 201, 224, 235, 236, 237, 263, 264, 267, 268, 290, 293, 294, 295, 331.
Winchester, Va., 2, 64, 86, 118, 119.
Wolcott, Alexander, 219.
Wolcott, Oliver, 295.
Wright, Louise Mason, 361.
Wythe, George, professor of law, Chancellor, 53, 161, 172.
X.Y.Z., 113.
Yazoo Land Claims, 216.
Young, Eleanor, *The Forgotten Patriot, Robert Morris*, 358.
Yorktown National Battlefield Monument Park, 353.
York Town, described, 1, 2, 3, 4.

PACE UNIVERSITY LIBRARIES
BIRNBAUM STACKS
E302.6.M4 M3
My dearest Polly

3 5061 00361 7595

E
302.6.
M4M3

Mason
My dearest Polly

PACE UNIVERSITY LIBRARY
New York, NY   10038
Telephone 285-3332

TO THE BORROWER:

The use of this book is governed by rules established in the broad interest of the university
community. It is your responsibility to know these
rules. Please inquire at the circulation desk.